SELECTED SPEECHES *of*
DR. D. SWAMINADHAN

SELECTED SPEECHES *of*
DR. D. SWAMINADHAN

FORMER MEMBER OF
PLANNING COMMISSION,
GOVERNMENT OF INDIA

FIRST PART

With foreword by:

Dr.G.Tulasi Ram Das, Vice Chancellor,
Jawaharlal Nehru Technological University Kakinada (JNTUK)

And

Prof. K. Lal Kishore, Vice Chancellor,
Jawaharlal Nehru Technological University Anantapur (JNTUA)

EDITED BY
DR. DEVARAKONDA SWAMINADHAN

PARTRIDGE
A Penguin Random House Company

To order additional copies of this book, contact
Partridge India
000 800 10062 62
www.partridgepublishing.com/india
orders.india@partridgepublishing.com

CONTENTS

FIRST PART

HIGHER EDUCATION

TECHNICAL EDUCATION

VALUE ORIENTATIN OF EDUCATION

ENGINEERING & TECHNOLOGY

ENVIRONMENT

SCIENCE

SECOND PART

DEVELOPMENT STUDIES

ECONOMY

FINANCE

GENERAL

PLANNING

RURAL DEVELOPMENT

URBAN DEVELOPMENT

TRIBAL DEVELOPMENT

NON-GOVERNMENTAL ORGANISATIONS (NGOS)

DEDICATION

The Author takes the privilege of dedicating the First Part of his Speeches to that great son of India, the First Prime Minister and the Architect of Modern India, **Pandit Jawaharlal Nehru and the** Second Part to **Dr. B. R. Ambedkar**, the Architect of the Indian Constitution.

FOREWORD

FIRST PART

I am highly delighted to write a Foreword to the First part of the publication of Selected Speeches of Dr. Prof. D. Swaminadhan, a Former Member of Planning Commission, Government of India. The speeches are covering a wide range of disciplines encompassing issues ranging from socio-cultural development to the tools of economic development like higher education, technical education, environment, science and engineering and technology. It is heartening to note that the area of 'Value education' which is the need of the hour is also covered. I understand all his speeches are covered in Two Parts. This First Part is covering Higher and Technical Education, Value Education, Engineering & Technology, Environment and Science.

In the context of globalization, reforms in higher and technical education have been set in motion. The need for effective co-operation between Universities, Industries, R&D National Laboratories and the National Scientific and Engineering Associations and Bodies has been well recognised to bring about relevance in Higher & Technical Education and to adequately respond to the emerging challenges of globalization in terms of the need for indigenous technology development and sharing of resources. In this context the "Swaminadhan Model for University-Industry—National R&D Laboratories—Professional Bodies and Academies Interaction for Country's Economic Development", comes quite handy and contribute towards fulfilling this need.

It is always desirable that collections of speeches by eminent personalities are published for the benefit of the general public, researchers and the policy makers. The present volume of Speeches of Dr. D. Swaminadhan adds to that list of publications. Dr. D. Swaminadhan's speeches reflected, among others, his clear foresight about the dynamics of development of higher and technical education—a rare combination of conceptual clarity and pragmatic methodology.

I consider it a privilege to write a Foreword to such a valuable collection of speeches of Dr. D. Swaminadhan which I am sure would prove valuable for the academicians, researchers, administrators, social animators and policy makers.

Dr. G. Tulasi Ram Das
Vice Chancellor
Jawaharlal Nehru Technological University
Kakinada (JNTUK), Kakinada,
Andhra Pradesh, India.

FOREWORD

SECOND PART

I am highly delighted to write a Foreword to the Second Part of the publication of Selected Speeches of Dr. Prof. D. Swaminadhan, a Former member of Planning Commission, Government of India. I have gone through the text of the speeches and found them covering a wide range of disciplines encompassing issues relating to socio-cultural development and the tools of economic development. I understand all his speeches are covered in Two Parts. This First Part is covering Higher and Technical Education, Value orientation of Education, Engineering & Technology, Environment and Science. The Second Part covers the disciplines of Development Studies, Economy, Finance, Planning, Rural Development, Urban Development, Tribal Development, Non-Governmental Organisations (NGOs) and General Areas.

It is well recognised fact that urbanisation process signifies increasing contribution of urban areas to GDP and in a sense to also the aggregate socio-economic development process. At the same time deterioration in the physical environment and quality of life in the urban areas has been increasingly found. Physical and economic infrastructure has hardly kept pace with the demands of increasing population and industrial activities which are located largely in and around urban areas. This is attributable to quite a few factors of which the financial and organisational weakness of urban local bodies and absence of facilitating environment for stepping up investment in infrastructure are probably the most important ones. Dr. D. Swaminadhan's Speeches adequately reflect this aspect.

Independent India wanted to build a modern, strong, dynamic and self-reliant nation which could stand abreast with the developed countries. Pandit Jawaharlal Nehru, the architect of modern India and the first Prime Minister, embarked on the path of planned economic development. The Planning process in India thus started in early 50's. Growth, modernisation, self-reliance and social justice are the basic objectives governing Indian planning. Dr. D. Swaminadhan's Lecturers presented a clear view about India's Planning Process.

Dr. D. Swaminadhan's versatility of knowledge is worth appreicating. His speeches on Economy, Planning, Rural Development, Urban Development, Tribal Development and on General Areas have brought out valuable ideas in the treatment of the concerned subject areas.

It is always desirable that collections of speeches by eminent personalities are published for the benefit of the general public, researchers and the policy makers. The present volume of Speeches of Dr. D. Swaminadhan adds to that list of publications.

I consider it a privilege to write a Foreword to such a valuable collection of speeches of Dr. D. Swaminadhan which I am sure would prove valuable for the academicians, researchers, administrators, social animators and policy makers.

Prof. K. Lal Kishore,
Vice Chancellor,
Jawaharlal Nehru Technological University
Anantapur (JNTUA), Anantapur,
Andhra Pradesh, India.

PREFACE

I feel it a privilege to present my Speeches for publication so that they are made available for wider dissemination. These are the selected Speeches mostly delivered by me when I was a Member of Planning Commission, Government of India. The Speeches cover a wide range of topics in various disciplines. These are covered in two Parts. This First Part covers Higher Education and Technical Education, Value Education, Engineering & Technology, Environment and Science. The Second Part covers Development Studies, Economy, Finance, Planning, Rural Development, Urban Development, and General Areas. Even though these Speeches are delivered long back the subject matters are still relevant and therefore I believe that not only the general public but also the academics and researchers will find them useful.

Prof. Dr. D. Swaminadhan
Author

HIGHER EDUCATION

ADDED ROLE FOR INDIAN UNIVERSITIES

"A University stands for humanism, for tolerance, for reason, for progress, for the adventure of ideas and for the search for truth. It stands for the onward march of the human race towards ever higher objectives. If the Universities discharge their duty adequately, then it is well with the nation and the people . . . ."

—**Pandit Jawaharlal Nehru**—

The university system in India over the years has undergone changes in terms of conditions, requirements and size. In addition, waves of socio-economic and political changes have been impinging on the system. The impact of the undesirable part of such a situation has been trying to disturb the equilibrium in universities. The system has therefore, to build up inner strengths to ward off such unwanted influences in the best possible manner and live upto the expectation of Pandit Nehru. If the university system were to respond and measure up to the expectation of Nehru in the above situation, it has to lay stress on and pursue four important elements. They are: (i) Excellence (ii) Modernisation (iii) Interaction, and (iv) Self-reliance. These are all inter-related.

True pursuit of excellence in all spheres of activities of a university will help imbibing and nurturing in the university life the qualities of humanism, tolerance, reason and adventure of ideas, search for truth and thereby help leading the humanity towards even higher objectives.

Modernisation in terms of courses, facilities, evaluation methods and faculty upgradation will in turn enrich teaching, research, examination system and extension activities. Modernisation equips better the university to play its role effectively.

Interaction and inter-dependence are well recognised concepts in the present day global situation. Universities are no exception to this. They should come out of their ivory tower concept and interact with outside world viz. the society, the government, sister institutions, lower level institutions, industrial organisations etc. Through interaction, the university's excellence should be shared for national development.

Autonomy in the true sense should be the privilege of the university system so as to enable it to respond with full vigour for fulfillment of its objectives and goals. Already considerable academic autonomy relating to offering courses, evolving evaluation methods, teaching, research and extension activities is available. Since finance is one of the important factors in achieving the goal of a university, there should be ample financial freedom as well. In the present system of funding there is rigidity coupled with deficiency. The deficiency part is going to be more in the present situation of resources crunch. Financial autonomy is vital for continuation of universities as centres of excellence and need of the hour is to initiate steps for fund generation and reduce its dependence on the Government to the extent possible, thus paving the way towards self-reliance.

Momentous changes are taking place on the international scene. The end of the cold war, the transformations in Eastern Europe, the disintegration of the Soviet Union and the imminent emergence of a common market in Western Europe are events of truly historic significance. These changes will have a profound impact on both the international relations and the world economy. Simultaneously, most developing countries have embarked on bold measures of reform in restructuring their economies and opening up to forces of competition, both domestic and foreign. All these changes certainly have an impact on the Indian economy.

India is passing through a historic moment on the economic front. The Eighth Five Year Plan is launched in the backdrop of certain strengths in the economy as well as certain concerns which have surfaced over the recent years. The Government has taken new initiatives and bold decisions to reorient and restructure the economy to meet the challenges of the present economic crisis in the country.

The above scenario necessitates certain imperatives in mobilising resources for higher education. They include avoiding duplication and wastage, increasing the efficiency of the system, optimising utilisation of the resources through pooling and sharing and the need for the universities to generate resources while maintaining intact their primary task of teaching, research and extension activities. The need for fund generation by universities is in the context of both financial autonomy and resources crunch. This implies an added role to the university system. This added role brings into sharp focus the need for interaction with other agencies.

Towards interaction and inter-dependence, one of the approaches is to forge strong linkages between universities, industries and R & D organisations. This linkage will result in: (i) pooling, sharing and optimising the use of resources, (ii) development of indigenous technology appropriate to our national priorities and resources, (iii) adapting the imported technology wherever needed for preparing the industries to meet global competitiveness, (iv) enriching teaching and research in universities with the component of practical and field experience, and (v) universities and R & D laboratories getting valuable clues for research orientation. The process of interaction will not only lead to mutual benefit of the partners but also contribute to national development.

For realising effective symbiotic relationship between Universities, R & D Organisations and Industries, a Model is formulated by me (the Model is shown elsewhere in this Book). The word 'University System' in the Model meant to include also professional institutions of higher learning in Engineering, Technology, Medicine, Pharmacy, Agriculture, Management etc., and similarly the word 'Industry' may include any other related organizations and sectors of the economy.

To bring about effective interaction, there should be specific cells/units in the Universities, R & D Laboratories and Industry to act as contact points and for coordination. Such cells/units in the universities can interact with the Industry and other sectors to acquaint with their problems, to boost their confidence in the University's capabilities, to receive consultancy assignments and to coordinate with the concerned schools and departments of the University in executing the work. In the case of IITs, the idea of an Industrial Foundation is mooted. There is also a need for creation of a National Cell to promote and coordinate the linkages between the university, industry and R & D organisations. The interaction between University-Industry-R & D Laboratories will also help towards fund generation by the universities. Funds generated by universities should not be deducted from the grant given by the government. This would act as incentive for fund generation.

Universities must enter the country's industrial life and become a part of it and thereby become a partner in progress and a frontline organisation in science and technology and scientific and technological human resource development for the industry, its promoters and the entrepreneurs as well as the technological trouble shooter for industry. It should also become a conduit between industry and scientists and technology experts in various fields in the country and abroad.

The Universities / IITs and R & D Laboratories may have their own strengths and deficiencies for consultancy. Coming together, they can cover up the deficiencies of each other with their mutual strengths and forge a cohesive and strong partnership for International Consultancy.

Joint educational International Consultancy could be offered, which may include Institution building, establishment of specialised laboratory facilities, development of curricula, organising continuing education programmes like seminars and short courses, joint research projects, faculty development and technical staff training. Through industrial consultancy, we can help foster closer interaction between the educational institutions and industry in the recipient country by sending our experienced faculty and scientists and assisting them in taking up industrial consultancy assignments and extending the specialized analysis and testing facilities available at the, universities, institutes and national laboratories in India. Consultancy services could also be extended directly to industries abroad.

Greater efforts with widened scope are needed by all universities, the national laboratories and scientific institutions to help the Indian industry. The Indian industry should on its part build up more confidence in the national laboratories, institutions and universities and utilise their expertise and resources for technology innovation and development, technology transfer and adaptation, productivity improvement, consultancy etc. In turn, the requirements of industry will provide the base for R & D activities in the national laboratories and universities. Thus there is greater need for symbiotic relationship between Universities, Industry and R & D Organisations.

Some of the other ways and means of raising resources by universities for becoming self-reliant to the extent possible, for their recurring expenses are:

i. By increasing the fees to more realistic levels
ii. By permitting to charge from foreign students a reasonable tuition fees in foreign exchange

iii. By increasing the overhead charges on the outside funded sponsored project
iv. By removing mess subsidy, if any, and
v. By continuing education programmes.

Creation of a substantial endowment or corpus fund for each university could be explored. Revenue obtained from such funds can eventually be used to reduce the required support from the government for the non-plan expenditure.

The major users of the university output are the public sector' organisations and Organised large scale industrial and service sectors. Currently, the main users have very little contribution to the universities. It may be worthwhile to examine their stronger participation by asking them to contribute directly to the universities. In some of the developed countries such participation through levy of a cess on a group of industries or through endowments is common. On similar lines each university may be associated with a group of public sector / major industries who then will be required to contribute towards financing the related university departments / schools. A capital grant may be given by industry / public sector to the university corpus. For encouragement of such a grant suitable tax incentive has to be built by declaring all such contributions under personal income tax free.

Other sources by which the endowment can be built up are:

a) Alumni endowments.
b) Endowment donations from the individuals / trusts.
c) Sale of patent right, copyright, royalties on R & D development etc. Currently the revenue from these sources is almost negligible. Further, if a patent results from aproject funded by a government agency then technically the patent rights are with the government agency. In such cases the patent right may be permitted to be retained by the university.
d) Cess may be levied by the government on certain sector of industry and funds given to universities specifically to encourage activities in the areas beneficial to those sectors.
e) Donation from the international agencies and trust foundations whose aim is not in conflict with the university's objectives and/or national interests.
f) Endowment grant from other countries with an explicit commitment to train specified manpower for them.

While the measures outlined above are for the creation of a corpus fund to provide financial autonomy to universities, it is advisable that they be permitted to raise dedicated funds for specified purpose from industry/ individuals / alumni and international organisations to partly meet the developmental needs; for example

- Funds for specific buildings
- Funds for library collections
- Funds for establishment of a research centre / research facility
- Funds dedicated to specific research programmes
- Funds dedicated for scholarship, fellowship, chair, research grant etc.

Currently while universities do accept funds for scholarship, chair etc., they do not normally accept funds for other purposes. In this country as well as abroad there has been a tradition of funds being accepted by institutions for all the above purposes. Generally, donor may require the building, library collections, programmes, scholarships, chair etc., to be named after him or somebody. This may have to be acceded to.

Management of these endowment funds will require high calibre of financial management as optimization will have to be done with respect to interest, risk, capital gains and short term / long term perspectives. It will require that each university should have an independent management body for the trust / endowment to be managed by a set of professional managers and overseered by a group of public/ government / industry representatives (trustees) who will be responsible for:

a) Making sure that endowment received are in the interest of the university and the National interest.
b) Making sure that funds are invested to yield best possible return after taking into account risk, long term and short term perspectives and capital gains
c) Making sure that endowment received for development are utilized accordingly, and
d) Receiving and encouraging such endowments.

The time has come that we have to make a beginning to change the culture of Universities to gradually move towards becoming less dependent on government funding. The various measures and approaches suggested above are to be explored while taking cognizance of the differences in universities in terms of their status—State Universities, Central Universities, developed Universities, developing Universities and their local conditions. Depending upon the university's status, it has to appropriately pick up the threads for fund generation and move towards financial autonomy. Thus, the added role of universities for fund generation and to strive to move towards financial autonomy depends on their individual status and initiative. However, one cannot ignore the imperative need for becoming self-reliant in the sense of bridging the gap between fund requirement and the fund availability from the government.

ADDRESS AT THE INAUGURAL SESSION OF THE TENTH ANNUAL MANAGEMENT CONVENTION

Shri Ashok Singh, distinguished invitees, delegates, ladies and gentlemen,
I am very much delighted for having been invited as Chief Guest at the Inaugural Session of the 10th Annual Management Convention of the Bhubaneswar Management Forum. I express my thanks to Shri Ashok Singh, Secretary General of the Bhubaneswar Management Forum for the invitation. I am glad that the Bhubaneswar Management Forum is committed to the noble cause of dissemination of management education in Orissa and to spread the management culture and ethos through organising conventions and seminars and also through publication of the journal "The Management Excellence". My best wishes go with them in all their endeavours. It is a great pleasure to visit this temple city of Bhubaneshwar, replete with exquisite stone carvings which reveal and represent a land of finest craftsmanship. Nowhere is the spirit of a great nation, with its glory of rich cultural heritage and a relentless quest for human excellence, revealed in its finest forms than in Orissa. Orissa is a land of opportunity, a land of rich resources waiting for the Midas touch of managerial competence.

Management can be termed as the nexus between a resource and its development. As every resource has a value attached in terms of its relation to man, Management essentially implies human resources development. Organisation of human beings for a common activity is as old as civilization. Management seeks to integrate and channelise the activities of an organised group towards realisation of a commonly predetermined goal. Thus, it is a vehicle of social action directed at human development and growth.

The American management expert, Peter F. Drucker had once defined management as 'an economic organ of an industrial society'. However, in his essay titled 'Management's New Role', published in 1970, he further added that the traditional assumptions of management and the emerging new realities differ from one another. The traditional role of management as an economic activity of a business or an industrial enterprise is only a special case. Our society is one of pluralist organizations including economic organisations and management of them all is the central social function in our society. The new role of management is to put into action, the specific cultural heritage of a country and of a people, for its social, economic and cultural advancement. Managerial competence is fast becoming a central and basic input for all developed and developing Countries.

HUMAN RESOURCE DEVELOPMENT:

The human relations approach to management recognises man as central to the development of any organisation. This represents a quantum jump in our understanding of the dynamics of the management process. The development of human resources thus forms a key area of management. The process of human resources development consists of upgrading the conceptual abilities and technical skills of individuals through wider exposure, mutual interaction and continual training. This enhances individual contribution and results in organisational synergy. It also results in a sense of participation and belongingness among the individuals which strengthens the organisation.

Human resources development becomes a priority area of management in a developing country like India where there is a vast human resources potential. The nation's need of the hour is to enhance the quality of its human resources through an integrated and well orchestrated human resources management for national advancement and also for all round human development on an international scale in the new world order.

The Eighth Plan envisages universalisation of elementary education, eradication of illiteracy in the age group of 15 to 35 and strengthening of vocational education during the Plan period. The thrust areas in the realm of higher education are (i) an integrated approach, (ii) achievement of excellence, (iii) expansion in an equitable and cost effective manner, (iv) promotion of value education and (v) making it relevant in the context of the changing socioeconomic scenarios. Promotion of distance education is another means of providing continuing education to upgrade the skills and widen the mental perspective of our vast work force. Another important facet of our human resources development programme is to strengthen technical education in the country. During the past four decades, there has been a phenomenal expansion of technical education in India. The thrust areas for the Eighth Plan are modernisation and upgradation of infrastructural facilities, improvement of quality, industry-institution-R & D Organisations interaction and effective resource mobilisation.

DEVELOPMENT OF MANAGEMENT EDUCATION IN INDIA:

To consolidate the gains of a concerted human resources development programme, to streamline these energies into productive channels and to concretise these achievements by translating them into the economic realm, there is a need to build up an army of talented and efficient managers by encouraging and promoting management education.

Management education in India had its humble beginnings in the thirties, through inservice management training programmes organised in commercial banks and public and private sector industrial concerns. The committee appointed by the AICTE during 1951-52 had recommended the starting of Post Graduate diploma courses in Industrial Administration and Business Management on a part-time basis for sponsored junior executives. The Committee had also recommended the setting up of a Board of Management Studies. The Board was set up in the fifties and had originally recommended seven institutes for offering management courses. During the course of time, many institutions were added to the list of institutions offering management courses. Some Management institutions like XLRI, Jamshedpur are offering good management programmes.

The All India Management Association was established in 1957 as an apex national organisation for coordinating the activities of the local management associations. The Association conducted a number of programmes for the benefit of top and senior executives and had also started a two-year diploma course in Management. The Administrative Staff College of India, Hyderabad set up in 1956, is offering managerial training courses to inservice executives.

The high point in the, development of management education in India was reached with the establishment of the Indian Institutes of Management at Calcutta in 1961, at Ahmedabad in 1962 and at Bangalore in 1972. Later, the fourth Institute was established at Lucknow during the 80's. These four Institutes represent a potent force professionalizing management in India. Two review committees were appointed on the IIMs. The first one, the Nanda Committee, was appointed in 1979, which submitted its report in 1981. The other review committee, the Kurien Committee, was appointed in 1991 and its report was submitted in 1992. The Nanda Committee recommended that the objectives should include training and education of (i) Managers for public utilities and services, and (ii) Management Teachers. The Kurien Committee reaffirmed the mission of the IIMs to strengthen management in business, industry and commerce. It further recommended that the mission statement needs to be expanded to emphasise IIM's commitment to public service and public management.

The University Grants Commission is providing assistance to about 40 universities / institutes for conducting programmes in Management Studies. The IITs also decided to develop management education programmes which started during the late 70's. The thrust of the programmes is on the management of technology. A workshop of the Directors of IITs held earlier at Delhi had recommended that IIT Management Programmes should be oriented towards management of technology, diagnostic research, human resource development and the teachers of IITs should be deployed to IIMs to study management techniques, undertake collaborative researches and carry out applied research activities.

There is a need for the IIMs to network with other academic institutions such as IITs, Universities, sectoral research / training institutions to facilitate their attempts to impart managerial skills to their students. IIMs can contribute to the entrepreneurship, technology management and industrial management programmes offered by the IITs. Management content of the B.Com. and other degree programmes offered by Indian universities could be enriched through interaction with IIMs.

MANAGING THE CHANGE PROCESS:

While the task of management education is truly gigantic, the scope of management education should be sufficiently enlarged to provide and plan for managing the change process in the society. In the present age of information revolution and fast technological obsolescence, the task of maintaining a high degree of managerial competence to keep pace with the fast changing times should be the primary concern of management in India.

The 90's have witnessed momentous changes in India and the world. The winds of change have been universal and all pervading. The end of cold war, the sweeping transformations in Eastern Europe, the crumbling of the Berlin Wall, the emergence of the European common market, the emergence of an Asia-Pacific trade region are events of lasting historical significance which have a profound impact on international relations and the world economy. Most of the developing countries have embarked on bold measures in restructuring their economies.

In India too, historic changes are taking place on the economic front. The restructuring of our economy, opening up of our trade and commerce to international pressures and competitions, added emphasis on export promotion to ease our balance of payments situation etc., call for a reorientation of our management approach.

In the context of changing domestic and global economic scenario, the Planning Commission has taken the initiative to convene meetings of the IIM Directors and other experts to discuss and formulate new approaches in the management education, training and research. The discussions resulted in identifying some vital issues and areas which would contribute towards strengthening management education, research and training in the country.

The curricula of management education need to be appropriately programmed to open up new vistas of information management and to make our managerial corps resilient against the stresses and strains of the new era of information.

The Eighth Plan envisages an annual growth rate in exports of 13.6% and an incremental capital output ratio of 4.1% which required upgrading of the management skills not just to enterprises but also of government ministries, departments and agencies and other organisations providing human capital and infrastructural services like education, health, environmental management, transportation, energy, communications etc. It is, therefore, imperative that IIMs and other Schools of Management identify strategic priority sectors that are currently not properly managed and develop the needed management expertise and diffuse it effectively to them. In this exercise close collaboration will be needed between IIMs, other Schools of Management, government organisations and other priority sectors. The Planning Commission may provide an umbrella under which dialogue and cooperation between strategic priority sectors, and IIMs could be initiated.

MANAGEMENT TRAINING:

The number of managers without any formal managerial training in the country is large. Even though there is no reliable estimate available about the number of personnel with supervisory and managerial responsibilities in the country, their number must be too large. There are estimated 1 lakh managers in Central Government Public Sector Undertakings; and possibly there may be twice that number in private corporate sector. The number of managers in the governmental administration may exceed half-a-million. There are two million small scale manufacturing units headed by entrepreneur-managers. The services sector, academic institutions, NGOs, etc. too have a very large number of managers. A rough estimate is that there may be some three million managers in the country directing, coordinating and motivating a workforce of about 60 million. This managerial army of say 3 million is highly differentiated by function, level, sector, and organisation. A significant improvement in the skills, drive, efficiency, innovativeness, quality orientation, and customer service orientation of this group of our society can generate incalculable benefits for the nation. As suggested during discussions in the Planning Commission, it is vitally important that a 'research effort' is mounted during the Eighth Plan to study the size and composition of our managerial corps, understand the roles different types of managers in different organisations, industries, and sectors are required to play and the knowledge-base, skills, attitudes needed, now and in the future, to play these roles effectively. IIMs should play a role, alongwith Institute of Applied Manpower Research, various trade, industry and sectoral associations etc., in this research task. The Association of Indian Management Schools should also be involved. Here, the Planning Commission could play a catalytic role in setting the pace and direction for management education in India.

TRAINING MANAGEMENT TEACHERS:

The four IIMs together should be able to offer short and long duration training to all the management teachers in the country. Besides strengthening the teaching and research skills of the management academics, exposing them to innovative pedagogies and providing them with depth in their areas of specialisation, a part of the training should be towards institution building so that they can develop their home schools /

departments, taking advantage of some of the values and practices that have contributed to the excellence of the IIMs. IIMs should also disseminate to other management teaching / training institutions in the country, course materials, cases, research findings etc. There is also a need for effective networking among the IIMs to avoid duplication of research work and to optimise resource utilisation. Another promising area is the management institutions-industry linkage and interaction. Yet another area of prime importance is to provide extension of professional management culture and ethos through strengthening and enlarging distance learning programmes provided by open universities, Management associations, starting of many more management training programmes, both public and in-house, and the preparation of educative audio-visual and other material for mass dissemination such as through industry and sectoral bodies, AIR and Doordarshan. Management of technology and keeping pace with high speed changes in the technological realm is another major concern of management today. The age of computers has ushered in a new information revolution. The information overload on the management community is tremendous. Unless the managerial corps is retrained and reoriented to cope with the new pressures exerted by the information age, there is a possibility of frustration setting in because of the information deluge.

CONCLUSION:

Management has to take up an increasing social responsibility to enhance the quality of life and to improve human standards. Towards achieving this end, management education should focus itself on the innovative spirit inherent in it. There should be a creative continuity and perpetual conversion of ideas into the realm of action. It is my firm conviction that India, with its large scientific and technical manpower and with its endowment of rich natural resources can be successfully launched into a galvanic growth process through the catalytic stimulus provided by quality management education. I take pleasure in inaugurating the 10th Annual Management Convention of the Bhubaneswar Management Forum and wish its deliberations a success.

CONVOCATION ADDRESS AT THE 15ᵀᴴ CONVOCATION OF THE INSTITUTE OF MEDICAL SCIENCES, BANARAS HINDU UNIVERSITY

Honourable Chancellor, respected Vice-Chancellor, Director of the Institute of Medical Sciences, Graduates, ladies and gentlemen,

I am grateful for the honour of being invited to be the Chief Guest at the 15ᵗʰ Convocation of the Institute of Medical Sciences, Banaras Hindu University, Varanasi and to deliver the Convocation address. I am highly delighted to visit this great ancient temple city, Varanasi for the second time in a span of one month. During last month, I had the privilege of inaugurating the 58ᵗʰ Annual Conference of the Indian Mathematical Society held at this great University. From time immemorial, Varanasi has been a lodestar attracting scholars and pilgrims, both oriental and occidental.

The Banaras Hindu University, whose beginnings had been so tenderly nurtured by the venerated Pandit Madan Mohan Malaviya, who was, in the words of Dr. S. Radhakrishnan, selfless, loyal, gentle but not weak, determined but not aggressive and a spirit as clear as the mountain air, was a unique experiment of residential educational culture, initiated at a time when there were only five examining universities at Calcutta, Bombay, Madras, Allahabad and Lahore. It symbolises the great Indian culture and tradition. On the shores of the holy river Ganges, this University is a beacon of knowledge attracting avid learners from all over the world. Banaras, Hindu University is also playing its role in the nation's quest for the advancement of science and technology and for enriching quality of life of its people. Malaviyaji visualised that it will be a national University both in form and spirit, transcending the racial, religious, linguistic and other narrow compartmentalisations. Today the University, with its glorious past, tradition and history, is ranked among the best in the country and abroad.

I am happy to note that the Institute of Medical Sciences, which had its beginnings in the establishment of the Department of Ayurveda in 1922 and Sir Sunderlal Hospital with 100 beds in 1926, is making a mark at the national and international level, having been recognised as one of the important medical institutions of the country. It is offering specialised medical education and services in all specialities / super specialities of modern medicine and Ayurvedic medicine. The faculties are engaged in research in the frontier areas of medical sciences, relevant to the needs of the people. In addition to 23 departments and 10 super specialities in the Faculty of Medicine and 8 departments in the Faculty of Ayurveda, there is an Advanced Centre for Molecular Biology and Immunodiagnostics. It is heartening to note that the Institute caters to the health needs of more than 10 crore population of Eastern Uttar Pradesh, Bihar and adjoining Madhya Pradesh. This service component of the Institute's functioning is laudable.

Through centuries ceremonies are created to mark important moments and changes in our lives. Convocations are such important moments in the life of a University or an Institute and its graduates. Our traditions, rituals and ceremonies surely are important. They give us a sense of identity and continuity across the years and generations; they serve to remind us of the importance of events and accomplishments; they reaffirm and give dignity to important values in our cultures, values at the core of the university's reason in pursuit of courage and integrity in the search for truth, the duty of each generation to transmit the best of its knowledge and wisdom and culture to the next, and the dignity of personal and intellectual achievement. At this moment, we pause to note the passing of time and the important changes taking place in our lives and in the life of this distinguished Institute of Medical Sciences by coming together in this ceremony—teachers, students and friends to honour our academic traditions, to celebrate your academic achievement, to share our hope for the future and to reflect upon what meaning you might ascribe to these things. I know that you are leaving this Institute with a sense of gratitude. I am sure you have been well taught and you learnt well and I offer you my sincere congratulations on your conferment of degrees and honours. We pray for your happiness and for the fulfilment of the promise as individuals and as a generation.

India has a glorious tradition of medical education, even in the pre-historic era. Great Chinese travellers like Fa Hien and Hieun Tsang described the medical education teaching of those days in the University of Nalanda. India had a glorious tradition even when there was no system of medical education in any part of the world except probably Aztec civilization in Mexico and the Egyptian civilization in the middle ages. Ayurveda and Siddha systems of medicine are well known. In addition, Unani and Homeopathy are prevalent in India. All these systems are termed as indigenous system of medicine now. Allopathy system of medicine, which is termed as modern scientific system of medicine, was perhaps brought to India by the English, French, Portuguese and the others. We have to take advantage of all these systems of medicine and a proper mix of them is to be adopted in meeting the health needs of our population.

There has been considerable expansion of institutional and infrastructural facilities for health. The number of medical colleges was only 28 in 1950. About 100 medical colleges were added in these four decades and at the end of 1991, there were 128 medical colleges imparting medical education in India. The number of hospitals which was 2694 in 1951, more than quadrupled to 11,571 by the end of 1991. As against 6515 dispensaries in 1951, we had around 28000 by the end of 1991 and the number of doctors increased from 61,840 to 3,94,068 during the same period. The number of registered medical practitioners per 10,000 population was 1.7 in 1951; it increased to 4.7 in 1991. Hospital beds of all categories were 3.2 per 10,000 in 1951 and it increased to 9.6 in 1991. Apart from this, there were 7,50,000 registered Ayurvedic and Homeopathic and Siddha and other systems practitioners, besides 4,800 integrated system of medicine people during 1989. This of course, excludes quacks. If we consider the registered practitioners of the indigenous system of medicine also, then perhaps the doctor-population ratio may come down.

The eighties have witnessed growth of community based health infrastructure as a part of the 'Health for All' strategy in the country. The number of community health centres which were 217 in 1981 grew to 1925 in 1991. There was a phenomenal expansion of Primary Health Centres (PHC) and sub-centres. The number of Primary Health Centres, from a mere 725 in 1951 grew to 22,243 by the end of 1991 and Primary Health sub-centres from nil in 1951 to 1,29,999 by the end of 1991. The number of hospital beds increased almost seven fold from 1,17,178 in 1951 to 8,06,409 by 1991. As a result of this large scale expansion in health care facilities, the life expectancy at birth, which was abysmally low at 32.1 years in 1950-51, rose to 55.9 years in 1990-91.

In spite of such an impressive expansion in the health care system, there is however, shortage of nurses, pharmacists, laboratory technicians, radiographers and dental surgeons. The number of dentists in 1951 was 3290 and after 40 years we have only 11,011 dentists. Similarly, the number of nurses at the end of 1991 was 2,64,504 as against 3,94,068 doctors. The doctor: nurse ratio works out to be 1 : 0.67 in 1991 against an ideal ratio of 1 : 3. This presents a lopsided growth picture.

The Health sector has been undergoing extensive transformation globally, reflecting to a considerable degree, changes in society more generally. It has effect on planning and management of health services, on education and utilisation of health manpower and on the full range of health related research. In the field of health services, health promotion, disease prevention and related education of the public have moved from being merely desirable aspects of health care to practical and often central themes of health programmes, with attending improvements in mortality and morbidity rates in a number of countries. The need to restrain escalation of costs of health services and balance these against their effectiveness has emerged as a permanent problem in the present day world.

The National Health Policy (1983) reiterates India's commitment to attain Health for All (HFA) by 2000 A.D. Primary health care has been accepted as the main instrument for achieving this goal. Accordingly, a vast network of institutions at primary, secondary and tertiary levels has been established. Control of communicable diseases through national programmes and development of trained health manpower have received special attention. Many spectacular successes have been achieved in the area of health. Smallpox stands eradicated and plague is no longer a problem. Morbidity and mortality on account of malaria and cholera and various other diseases have declined. The crude birth rate and infant mortality rate have declined to 29.9 and 80 as compared to 37 and 129 respectively in 1971.

However, in order to achieve Health for All, we have to still go a long way. Disease, disability and deaths on account of several communicable diseases are still unacceptably high. Meanwhile, several non-communicable diseases have emerged as new public health problems. Rural health services for delivery of primary health care are still not fully operationalised. Urban health services, particularly for urban slums, require urgent attention due to changing urban morphology.

Health manpower has also changed in concept, training and utilisation. The necessity of wider coverage, health promotion, disease prevention and community participation is leading increasingly to the active involvement of community members in the health care process. In consonance with health services in some countries, community-level health workers are trained and supervised by an intermediate level of health personnel, who serve in turn as a link with the back up referral and consultative capacities of the health system. The structures and staffing of these tiers vary greatly from country to country. The roles of health professionals too change considerably particularly to include leadership and management capacities.

Health manpower development is a critical factor for the economic efficiency of the health care system and an important response mechanism for attaining the goal of 'Health For All' through primary health care. Physicians, have by and large been in generous supply where nurses continue to be in short supply in many countries. Nowhere have physicians been produced in greater numbers than in India. While the States have been more than anxious to start new medical colleges, their efforts to develop institutions for training of paramedical staff have been entirely suboptimal. This has resulted in a considerable mismatch between the requirement and availability of health personnel of different categories. Similarly, as I have indicated earlier, there is a shortage of pharmacists, laboratory technicians, radiographers, dental surgeons, etc., in the country. Yet, health manpower planning, production and management, which constitute key elements for effective implementation of health programme, have not received enough attention.

Research emphasis in the health sector has also been shifting. Basic biomedical, behavioural and clinical research is making dramatic advances. New discoveries in genetics, immunology and cellular functions, new techniques for investigating clinical processes and new observations applied to clinical and public health systems are expected to bring increased benefits to mankind. Health systems research should address the problems of health needs, coverage of population, utilisation, costs, management, measures of effectiveness and relationship to the broader aspects-of development. Health manpower research should address the levels of manpower required, attitudes required of the personnel and the training required for developing and maintaining defined competencies.

Various institutions under the Ministry of Health and Family Welfare and medical colleges have done notable work in the field of medical research.

The Indian Council of Medical Research (ICMR) is the premier institution which is responsible for carrying out biomedical and operational research in India. Notable achievements are: demonstration of improved vector control using bio-environmental techniques for control of malaria and filaria; establishment of National Cancer Registry; multi drug therapy and short course chemotherapy for leprosy and TB respectively and a national surveillance system for AIDS infection.

It is envisaged that Research and Development activities by Indian Council of Medical Research and other academic institutions will be pursued during the Eighth Plan through the following strategies:-

i) Establishment of an integrated Biomedical Research Complex to strengthen research activities and to optimise the utilisation of the available resources and facilities.

ii) Promotion of excellence by rationalising grants to promising scientists in medical colleges and strengthening of extramural centres for research under eminent scientific leadership.

iii) Establishment of a network of research units in medical colleges for Multi-centric studies.

iv) Optimal utilisation of resources through coordination and development of proper linkages with sister agencies, commercial utilisation of research findings, constant review of the status of application of research findings by user agencies, continuing interaction with State authorities to determine area specific research needs and through providing proper guidance and assistance as well as strengthening research activities under the State Councils of Medical Research.

v) Development of a Centre for Epidemiological Intelligence.

vi) Augmentation of research activities in specific priority areas viz., integrated Vector Control Programme for Malaria, Filaria and Japanese Encephalitis, integrated control of non-communicable diseases and development of vaccines for communicable Diseases as well as fertility regulation.

vii) Enhancement of Research and Development effort on Family Planning and Maternal & Child Health.

viii) Collaboration with international agencies for transfer of appropriate technology to the Indian scientists.

The global strategy for Health for All recognises primary health care as its main engine of implementation. In promoting this concept, the Universities and the Institutes of higher learning should play their role in terms of their three normal functions viz., education, research and interaction. Interaction relates to economic development as well as societal service. The challenge to education in relation to 'Health for All' is to identify the competencies and attitudes required by health personnel to function effectively in low-cost, wide-coverage health care programmes. It should help the health professionals to understand the scientific underpinnings required for solving the health problems. The merging of functional competencies and scientific approach is necessary for dealing with the extreme complexity and rapid change of the health system. With regard to health research, the universities are in a key position to adapt recent advances in biomedical, behavioural, socioeconomic and managerial technology to local situations. The scientific community has to redirect its efforts towards developing more suitable health care technology and adapting to low-cost, wide-coverage systems. Research attention should also be diverted towards developing the health services and manpower infrastructure necessary to reach entire populations. In terms of their commitment to service, the universities should develop broader view and in their approach to service should reveal their depth of understanding and commitment to 'Health For All'. As the concept of 'Health For All' is so definitely tied-up in what happens in communities and in health service settings, without ready and continuous access to field situations in which such matters can be studied, reflected upon, and different approaches tried, the university will not be able to achieve what it supposes to be committed to. These service functions, however, are to be undertaken without affecting their normal functions of teaching and research.

There are three key factors which need focussed attention if our efforts towards the country's progress are to bear fruit in an effective manner. They are: (i) population control, (ii) eradication of illiteracy, and (iii) upholding the value system. I need not elaborate on these three areas which are well known. I would like to stress the need for everybody's contribution, including you, the new graduates, who are going into the society with great hope, in tackling these problems. I am sure that you will spare no effort in making positive contributions in this regard.

I join today, along with your teachers and friends, in the hope that you, who received the degrees and became the alumni of this University and the

Institute of Medical Sciences, will practice your profession and lead your lives, respecting the dignity of your fellow beings and the bonds that tie us together as brothers and sisters of this humanity. I once again congratulate you all on this happy occasion and wish you all success in your future endeavours.

SPEECH AT UGC SPECIAL MEETING OF VICE-CHANCELLORS ON PROGRAMME OF ACTION 92

Prof. Ram Reddy, Prof. Khanna, Shri Chaturvedi, Members of the UGC, Distinguished Vice-Chancellors, Ladies and Gentlemen,

It is indeed a great privilege for me to participate in the inaugural session of the UGC Special Meeting of the Vice-Chancellors on Programme of Action 1992. The special meeting is timely and there is need for such meetings at frequent intervals to discuss and assess the progress in the implementation of Programme of Action 1992. The National Policy on Education (NPE '92) is not having any substantial change over NPE '86. However, the POA 92 has got some changes in action strategies and programmes for implementation. These programmes and strategies include the following:

1. Consolidation and expansion;
2. Development of autonomous colleges and departments;
3. Re-designing of courses;
4. Training of teachers;
5. Strengthening of research;
6. Improvements in efficiency;
7. Creation of structures for coordination at the state and national levels;
8. Mobility;
9. Finances;
10. Review and monitoring;

11. Examination reforms;
12. Management of the university system; etc.

The above programmes are to be viewed in a broader perspective as the scope and the role of higher education could transcend the boundaries of the university system.

All these issues and programmes have been discussed in the part at various meetings. I do not intend to cover all the areas again, but I would like to confine my observations on four specific issues which need added emphasis. These are:

1. NATIONAL COUNCIL FOR HIGHER EDUCATION:

There is need for expediting establishment of a national apex body for higher education namely National Council for Higher Education as envisaged in the National Policy on Education (NPE '86 and NPE '92). A fragmented approach is being pursued in higher education. At present, there is a multiplicity of agencies charged with the responsibility of framing policy and implementation programmes and overseeing the development of specified areas of higher education and research. In the interest of greater coordination and consistency in policy, sharing of facilities and developing inter disciplinary research, the envisaged National Council for Higher Education is to be established.

2. ACCREDITATION AND ASSESSMENT COUNCIL:

Higher education means had excellence, quality, relevance, equity and cost effectiveness when we are aiming at excellent, self assessment and assessment by outside agencies of the institutions of higher education is essential. It is, therefore, as envisaged in the NPE '86 and NPE '92, the establishment of an accreditation and assessment council is to be expedited.

3. IMPROVING THE QUALITY OF UNRECOGNISED SECTOR OF HIGHER EDUCATION:

There are about 15 universities and 3000 colleges which are not yet recognised by UGC for central assistance. These institutions are offering sub-standard education and producing substandard under graduates. These institutions are in the system and we cannot ignore them when we are aiming at excellence and quality in higher education. We cannot close them nor are we in a position to provide funds for their development. Still we have helped them out to improve quality to the extent possible through relaxing if necessary, the rules and regulations and allow them to participate in the quality aimed programmes of the University Grants Commission. For example, teachers of these unrecognised institutions could be allowed to participate in the academic staff colleges' programme of UGC. Similarly, teach education programmes could be telecast under the UGC countrywide class room programme. The neighbouring institutions having good facilities would also help them out through interaction. The facilities in the Technical Teacher's Training Institutes (TTTIs) would be made available to the teachers in the unrecognised engineering colleges. We have to think about other ways and means of helping improving the quality of education in these unrecognised institutions.

4. VALUE ORIENTATION OF EDUCATION:

There has been a growing concern in the country over the erosion of essential values which is reflected in the fall of moral, social, ethical and national values both in personal and public life. Within this context, the need has been felt for launching of a programme of value orientation of education. Many high-powered Commissions and Committees on Education set up so far have repeatedly been stressing the urgent need for Value Orientation of Education. The approach was, however, piecemeal and segmental and no concrete results seem to have been achieved.

Keeping this in view the Planning Commission appointed a Core Group on Value Orientation of Education under my chairmanship. The Core Group consisted of the Chairman, UGC, the Secretary, Ministry of HRD, Secretary, AIU, representatives of NCERT, Navodaya Vidyalayas and some experts in the field of value orientation of education. The Group presented a concrete plan of action relating to various sectors of educational development. Let me share with you in brief some of the recommendations of the Group relating to higher education and Association of Indian Universities. Teacher has the most important role to play in the value development. The Group is of the view that teacher's personal, professional and social life is the crucial factor in the promotion of values. The most powerful influence of his personality lies in the 'hidden curriculum' of his personality and behaviour and the silent message which his students can and do get through his thinking, discipline of mind and refinement of taste.

The Group has recommended some reforms in the selection procedure of the teachers and a well-thoughtout programme of pre-service training of the newly recruited teachers and inservice orientation programme of the existing teachers with emphasis on Value Orientation of Education through direct, indirect and integrated methods. For this purpose, models of both preservice teacher education and in-service teacher orientation have been suggested to be taken up by the Academic Staff Colleges of Universities, National Council for Educational Research and Training (N.C.E.R.T.) and Regional Colleges of Education and pace-setting training institutions even at the District level.

University Grants Commission should carry out in collaboration with the N.C.E.R.T. a comparative study of the content of B.Ed. and M.Ed. programmes and develop self-contained Foundation and Awareness Courses relating to Education in Human Values for new entrants to the teaching profession, undertake an in-depth analysis of the content of the existing Academic Staff Colleges and prepare a well-designed course of modules incorporating value education. Earlier proposals regarding the writing of books, poems, stories, plays, parables, allegories, monographs and production of cassette tapes, documentary / full feature films relating to value education with reference to higher stages of education and in the areas of general awareness, Indian culture, unity of faiths, character building, human values, national ethos, national integration, national festivals and showing these as part of the U.G.C. National T.V. Programme for universities, should be implemented speedily. These materials should also be made available to Academic Staff Colleges which will use these for Awareness and Orientation Courses. It is also necessary to organise annual seminars of the heads of Academic Staff Colleges where the operationalisation of the programme should be discussed. The U.G.C. should initiate pilot projects in selected universities and institutions to study the impact—short, medium and long-term—on the students—present and alumni as a result of this programme. Bulletins, magazines etc. should be brought out incorporating the materials, stating the progress of work and highlight success stories. U.G.C. should assist scholars in bringing out research studies in this area highlighting the success stories about pace-setting institutions. Profile of several institutions doing innovative work should be presented in Special and Annual Reports of the U.G.C.

The task for the U.G.C. is challenging. There would be need for a Resource Centre for Value Orientation of Education, with competent staff, headed by a Senior Officer. This Centre will work as Clearing House, coordinate with various agencies, formulate programmes and projects and provide feed-back to the U.G.C. in reviewing the programmes and projects. Association of Indian Universities which is committed to the development of Education in Human Values should review their strategy of promoting Value Orientation of Education, initiate in-depth studies at the field level, bring out studies and researches and widely disseminate the results of various projects through their journal "University News" and other publications. Standing Committee on Value Orientation of Education: Since the implementing agencies at the National and State levels are too many, the Core Group has suggested that for effective planning, policy making and monitoring, a National Coordination Agency needs to be established in order to develop an integrated Plan of Action. Realising that the setting up of a National Coordination Agency may take some time, the Core Group has suggested that the Planning Commission should, in view of its integrative role, set up immediately a Standing Committee with representatives from various agencies, both at the Centre and the States, to provide an overall view of several issues, programmes and projects, draw-up comprehensive plans and projects at the macro and micro levels in collaboration with several organisations, advise on policy planning, implementation and monitoring of the programmes being implemented by various agencies at all levels and also mobilise necessary resources to promote the programme at different levels. In view of the very important objectives of the proposed Standing Committee, the Core Group has recommended that a small unit with a Senior Consultant, with usual professional and administrative support, should be set up to provide necessary technical inputs to the Standing Committee.

APPROACH TO HIGHER EDUCATION DEVELOPMENT IN INDIA IN NINETIES

Your Excellency, the Governor of Tamil Nadu, learned Vice-Chancellor, distinguished invitees, Faculty Members, students and ladies and gentlemen,

I am grateful for the honour of being invited to deliver the key-note address today on the occasion of the Silver Jubilee Celebration of the well-known Madurai Kamaraj University. This occasion has given me an opportunity to visit this great temple city of Madurai and the University. I am happy that the Madurai Kamaraj University, established in 1966, and now celebrating its Silver Jubilee, has many achievements to its credit. Through centuries, ceremonies and celebrations are created to mark important moments and changes. The present Silver Jubilee Celebration is one such important moment in the life of the Madurai Kamaraj University. Such celebrations give us a sense of identity and continuity across the years and generations; they serve to remind us of the importance of events and accomplishments; they reaffirm and give dignity to important values in our culture, values at the core of the University's, reason in pursuit of courage and integrity in the search for truth. I would like to express my warm felicitations and appreciations on this memorable occasion. It is heartening to know that the Madurai Kamaraj University has made significant contribution in teaching, research and extension programmes. The university has now more than forty departments with about 350 faculty members, of whom many have won national and international awards and honours and it has 68 affiliated colleges. Excellent contributions are made in Biology, Tamil, and Mathematics and as a result the University Grants Commission granted the status of the Department of Special Assessment (D.S.A.) for these departments. The department of Economics has also been recognised for special research support by U.G.C. I am told that both Physics and Chemistry will follow suit soon. The contribution of the university in the field of distance education is also noteworthy. The university has carved a special niche for itself in the academic world.

Higher education in this country is now being put to test. In the changed environment of resources inadequacy, restructuring of the Indian economy and global changes that have taken place recently which will have their impact on the Indian situation, how could the system cope up? What should be our policies, approaches and programmes to meet the new situation? These are some of the issues bothering our academics, educational administrators and policy makers. I thought, I should venture to tread this complex area and talk to you today on some of the related issues. That is how I titled my key-note address as "Approach to Higher Education Development in India in Nineties". Let me try to do justice to the subject within the short-time available.

In a country like India with its large population, human resource development should be assigned a key role in the development strategy. The role of human resource development (HRD) in social and economic progress has been acknowledged well. Five energisers of Human Resource Development have been identified: (i) Education, (ii) Health and Nutrition, (iii) Environment, (iv) Employment, and (v) Political and economic freedom. These energisers are interlinked and thus become interdependent but education is the key for all the others.

While education in all its forms is a vital component for the development of human resources, it is mostly the higher education which contributes to the quality of life. Higher education is a powerful tool for social, political and economic change. Its significance as a source of new knowledge, research contributions and manpower generator for all sectors of economy cannot be over emphasised. Its contribution to the country's economic development is well recognised. The approach for the development of higher education during nineties has to take into account the impact of the changed economic scenario in the country and the global changes as well.

PRESENT STATUS OF HIGHER EDUCATION:

There has been a spectacular growth in the higher education system in India during the post independence era. In 1950-51, there were 27 universities and 696, colleges with an enrolment of 3.68 lakhs students and a teaching faculty of 19,047. In 1990-91 there were 177 universities (including 'deemed' universities) and 7121 colleges with a student enrolment of 44.25 lakhs and a faculty strength of 2,13,125. Assuming even a steady rate of 4.2% growth in enrolment per year, the total student enrolment at the end of 1995 will be around 60 lakhs. Another heartening feature of the development of higher education in India is the steady growth in the enrolment of women students. In 1990-91, women were 32.5% of the total enrolment. If the upward trend in the enrolment of women continues, as it is expected to do, the demand for higher education will further increase. Expenditure on education as percentage of GNP varied from 1.2 in 1950-51 to 3.9 in 1986-87. Resources inadequacy situation in the government now necessitates universities and other institutes of higher learning to resort to taking up measures for fund generation and to gradually become less dependent on government for resources.

R & D EFFORTS:

Research activity in India is undertaken by universities and institutions / units /departments which can be classified under the various sectors as— Central Government, State Government, Higher Education Sector, Public Sector Industry, private Sector—Industry, and Non-Profit Institutions / Associations.

The higher education sector undertakes research. activities mostly of basic (fundamental) and applied research through their own funds and funds from, U.G.C. as well as through projects sponsored by the major scientific departments of the Central Government.

The philosophy that once suitable scientific infrastructure is available, technology will automatically develop as a consequential result from good science, seems to be valid. A good beginning has been made in India in establishing national laboratories and other infrastructure for R & D Development in the post-independence era. Major scientific departments with their research laboratories / institutions in the Central Government are the main vanguards of research efforts being carried out in the country.

Besides there are other Central Government Ministries / Departments who have a number of research institutions under their administrative and financial control. In addition, there are in-house R & D units of public sector industries which are mostly under the administrative control of the Central Government. But a few public sector industries are either under State Governments or the joint sector of Central and State Governments. Some private sector industries have established their own in-house R & D units. The State Governments have their own research institutions which mainly comprise of agricultural universities and their research stations besides having other research institutions directly under different departments of State Governments. There are about 450 major S & T research laboratories under the government's various departments and ministries. There are also about 1075 recognised in-house R & D laboratories in public and private sector undertakings. More than 200 consultancy firms are engaged in engineering design, analysis and research.

Resources crunch situation makes it imperative on the part of the national laboratories to generate resources through relevant technology development, design and transfer to industry. Besides there should be mutual interaction and sharing of facilities between universities and the national laboratories.

CHANGED SCENARIO

Momentous changes have taken place on the international scene which will have a profound impact on both international relations and world economy. In India too historic changes have taken place on the economic front. The government has taken new initiatives and bold decisions to reorient and restructure the economy to meet the challenges of economic crisis in the country. The Eighth Five Year Plan has been launched from 1st April 1992 in the backdrop of certain strengths in the economy as well as certain concerns which have surfaced at the beginning of the Eighth Plan. During the nineties, the country is poised to become progressively more integrated into the global economy. Competition and pace of technological change are likely to intensify in almost all sectors of the economy.

IMPACT ON INDUSTRY

In the regime of new Industrial Policy and liberalisation, the Indian industry is exposed to more domestic and global competition. To meet these challenges it requires modernisation, upgradation of the competency of the work force, utilisation of modern management techniques and increased efficiency and productivity while maintaining quality. The industries, in this context, need the help of universities and other institutes of higher learning more than ever before. They should build up confidence in the Indian Universities and other institutes of higher learning and utilise their expertise instead of looking for the soft options of consultancy and technology import.

WEAKNESSES IN THE SYSTEM

The higher education system at present suffers from several weaknesses such as increase in demand, proliferation of substandard institutions, dilution in quality and standards, failure to maintain academic calendar, outdated curriculum, disparities in the quality of education, inadequate resources and lack of adequate support for research, outdated management system etc. Most of these issues have been discussed and deliberated upon at various forums and good suggestions and recommendations were made. We need to give serious thought to these deficiencies in the system and take remedial measures.

APPROACH TO HIGHER EDUCATION:

National Policy on Education (NPE) 92 and Programme of Action (POA) 92 A revised National Policy on Education was approved by Parliament in 1992 (NPE 92) and as a result a revised Programme action (POA 92) was formulated.

The higher education sector has a bearing on all dimensions a—phases of HRD. Thus the scope and the role of higher education could transcend the boundaries of university system and in this context the POA 92 on higher education should be viewed along with a holistic perspective.

Action strategies for the implementation of the NPE 92 as specified in POA 92 include the following programmes / strategies: (1) Consolidation and expansion of institutions, (2) Development of Autonomous colleges and Departments (3) Redesigning of Courses (4) Training of teachers (5) Strengthening of Research (6) Improvements in Efficiency (7) Creation of structures for coordination at the State and National levels. (8) Mobility (9) Finances and (10) Review and Monitoring.

The U.G.C. Convened a special meeting of the Vice-Chancellors on Programme of Action (POA) 92 in May 1993 to discuss and evolve a strategy for effective implementation of POA 92 in so far as it related to higher education. The discussions resulted in a fruitful outcome and they should be pursued.

EIGHTH PLAN

The Eighth Plan document suggested the following approach to higher education: The additional enrolment in higher education during the Eighth Plan is estimated to be around 10 lakhs of which nine lakhs may be at the undergraduate level. Keeping in view the present resources crunch, this expansion in higher education is to be accommodated in an equitable and cost effective manner mainly by large scale expansion of distance education system providing opportunities to larger segments of population particularly the disadvantaged groups like women and people living in backward and hilly areas and by measures for resources generation. The programme of distance education should absorb at least 50 per cent of the additional enrolment during the Eighth Five Year Plan. Open universities should also start innovative programmes of a vocational nature for meeting the learning needs of rural areas. Opening up of new conventional universities and colleges should not be encouraged. Simultaneously, involvement of voluntary agencies and private sector participation in the opening and conduct of higher education institutions should be encouraged with proper checks to ensure maintenance of standards and facilities to make higher education as far as possible self financing.

SOME FUTURE DIRECTIONS

Consultations, including brain storming sessions organised by the Planning Commission, to consider future directions for higher education have underlined the following thrust areas: (1) Integrated approach to higher education; (2) Excellence in higher education; (3) Expansion of education in an equitable and cost-effective manner, and in the process making the higher education system financially self-supporting; (4) Making higher education relevant in the context of changing socio-economic scenario; (5) Promotion of value education; (6) Strengthening of management system in the universities.

EXCELLENCE, QUALITY AND RELEVANCE

Even though there has been a spectacular expansion in the higher education system, the quality has suffered. To achieve and maintain quality, relevance and cost effectiveness in the higher education system including Engineering, Technology and Management, the universities and Institutes of higher learning should focus on four crucial aspects. They are (a) Excellence (b) Modernisation (c) Interaction and (d) Self-reliance. They are inter-related. Self-reliance should be viewed in the context of bridging the gap between fund requirement and the fund availability from the government through adopting suitable measures for fund generation by universities. The question of access and equality should also be not forgotten.

NATIONAL COUNCIL FOR HIGHER EDUCATION

At present, the higher education system, comprising of general, technical, management, medical and agricultural streams, is fragmented in terms of structures and policies. Greater cooperation among the streams should be encouraged by promoting efforts in sharing of facilities including facilities for teacher's orientation and refresher courses and development of manpower. There should be greater coherence in policy and planning. To adequately meet these requirements, the National Policy on Education had envisaged the establishment of a National Council for Higher Education (N.C.H.E.). Establishment of such a National Council will be a right move towards achieving excellence and early action is needed in this regard.

ACCREDITATION AND ASSESSMENT COUNCIL

Another mechanism towards achieving excellence and quality in higher education is to establish the National Accreditation and Assessment Council

(NAC) as envisaged in the National Policy on Education, for examining and accrediting the higher education institutions, if they fulfil certain standards set by the Council. In the case of Technical Education, there is a provision under the AICTE Act for the establishment of a National Accreditation Board. This would also add towards pursuing excellence and quality in Technical Education. There could be a tie up between the two mechanisms.

QUALITY PROGRAMMES

Apart from continuing the existing programmes of Centres of Advanced Studies (CAS), Departments of Special Assistance (DSA), Departmental Research Support (DRS), COSIST, the Inter-University Centres and the proposed Information and Library Network (INFLIBNET), new Inter-university centres should be established to provide facilities in emerging areas like Biotechnology, Atmospheric Sciences, Oceanography, Electronics and Computer Sciences etc., by the University Grants Commission.

FACULTY IMPROVEMENT PROGRAMMES:

Faculty improvement is a crucial area in the pursuit of excellence. At higher education level, the University Grants Commission has established 48 Academic Staff Colleges for teacher orientation. These colleges cover mostly the general disciplines excluding Engineering, Technology and Management. At present, there is no specific mechanism for teacher orientation at higher technical education level. About four years ago, the Jawaharlal Nehru Technological University, Hyderabad formulated a proposal for the establishment of a. National Academy of Pedagogy in Engineering, Technology and Management (NAPETAM) in the University campus, which was approved in principle by the All India Council for Technical Education (AICTE). If such a national academy is established, it would go a long way towards teacher education at higher education level in engineering, technology and management. In addition, the University Grants Commission's Academic Staff Colleges may also be encouraged to cater to the needs of the teachers in the engineering, technology and management.

Utilisation of Modern Electronic Media:

During the recent past there have been significant developments in the field of communication technology. For example, use of satellites for telecast of educational programmes and computers for learning. Harnessing of the power of such 20th century communication revolution for educational purposes is vital for quality improvement in education especially in Science and Technology. In this context the UGC's "Country wide Class Room" programme is one of the best examples. The broadcast aims to upgrade, update and enrich the quality of education. They are attempting to overcome the obsolescence of the syllabus and present the latest advances in all fields, including the newly emerging ones. Inter-relatedness of various disciplines and of developmental problems would be highlighted. Motivation, innovation, creativity and analysis are supposed to be the guiding elements in these programmes. Such laudable and innovative programmes should be encouraged and supported by all the concerned as they would help enrich the quality of education not only in Science but also in other disciplines. Academics, Scientists, Engineers and Technologists should increasingly participate in the process of preparing these TV programmes. Radio should also be utilised for selective educational programmes.—Non-broadcast mode video educational course material should also be encouraged so that each college especially those who are in the far flung areas can maintain a library of video tapes for the use of their students and teachers. The teacher education is another important component which could be taken up through the UGC countrywide class room programme.

Information and Library Network Programme:

The proposal of U.G.C. for setting up of an Information and Library Network (INFLIBNET) is another example of trying to harness the power of the communication technology revolution. It aims at establishment of a national network of libraries and information centres in Universities, Colleges, Research and Development organisations etc. This will be done with the help of a computer communication network making use of both satellite as well as terrestrial means of communication. This project, though its initial cost may look prohibitive, could be implemented in phases while taking advantage of and integrating similar existing facilities of computer networking. If such a facility materialises, the problem relating to subscribing to costly journals by all the Universities may be minimised and dissemination of library information facilitated effectively.

INTERACTION AND RESOURCES MOBILISATION

In the changed economic scenario, it is imperative that there should be effective interaction between universities / institutions of higher learning, industry and national laboratories. It will lead to sharing and optimising the available resources, help resources generation and enrich their activities. This is going to be a major thrust in higher and technical education during the Eighth Plan and beyond. A Model for University, Industry, R & D Laboratory Interaction has been formulated by me and published. To promote university, industry, R & D laboratory interaction, the Ministry of Human Resource Development is considering constituting Standing Committee at the national level under my Chairmanship.

The question of financing of higher education and related issues were discussed at the. UGC Conference of Vice-Chancellors organised at Pondicherry University during February '93. Constructive policy recommendations were made at the Conference which need all serious consideration. The University Grants Commission has appointed a High Power Committee to examine present financial situation in regard to Central Universities, deemed universities and Delhi Colleges funded by the Central Government and to make recommendations about their financial needs and systems for the future. The Committee's work is in progress.

FINANCIAL AUTONOMY

Autonomy in the true sense should be the privilege of the university system so as the enable it to respond with full vigour for fulfillment of its objectives and goals. Already considerable academic autonomy relating to offering courses, evolving evaluation methods, teaching, research and extension activities is available. Since finance is one of the important factors in achieving the goals of a university, there should be ample financial freedom as well. In the present system of funding there is rigidity coupled with deficiency. The deficiency part is going to be more in the present situation of resources crunch. Financial autonomy is vital for continuation of universities as centres of excellence and need of the hour is to initiate steps for fund generation and reduce its dependence on the government to the extent possible, thus paving the way towards self-reliance. Creation of Corpus Fund' in universities will lead to achieving this goal.

VALUE ORIENTATION OF EDUCATION

Value Orientation of Education, commended by various high-powered Commissions and Committees and endorsed in the National Development Plans, during the last four decades, has not been implemented with all seriousness, in terms of concrete educational programmes and activities. The need for launching the programme of Value Orientation of Education, has assumed great urgency. This is particularly because of the growing divisive forces, narrow parochialism, separatist tendencies, considerable fall in moral, social, ethical and national values both in personal and public life. It is recognised that development of human values through education is a task of national importance.

Realising the urgent need for implementation of this important programme, the Planning Commission, as the highest policy and planning organisation in the country, felt it very necessary to initiate action in this important area and constituted a Core Group on Value Orientation of Education under my Chairmanship. The Core Group submitted its report which contains concrete plan of action at all levels of education. It has suggested for setting up of a National Coordination Agency for Value Orientation of Education. However, keeping in view the resources crunch, it recommended for the constitution of a Standing Committee in the initial stages. The Ministry of Human Resource Development is in the process of constituting this Standing Committee under my chairmanship.

CONCLUSION

While concluding I would like to quote Pandit Nehru:

"A University stands for humanism, for tolerance, for reason, for progress, for the adventure of ideas and for the search for truth. It stands for the onward march of the

40

human race towards even higher objectives. If the Universities discharge their duty adequately, then it is well with the nation and the people . . . ."

This should be the life breath of every university. It should be the guiding factor in all their activities and programmes. How many universities and institutes of higher learning in the country are able to measure up to Pandit Nehru's expectations? It calls for intensive and sincere introspection for identifying the reasons for not being able to fulfill this requirement. Let this also be integrated into the process of reorientation to fit into the changed environment.

ROLE OF SRI SATHYA SAI EDUCATION IN 21ST CENTURY

Om Shri Sai Ram Setha Koti Pranams at the Lotus Feet of Bhagwan Sri Sathya Sai Baba. My humble pranams to all the Sai devotees who have assembled here.

It is the greatest honour for me for having been invited to talk on the "Role of Sri Sathya Sai Education in 21ˢᵗ Century". I am blessed to do this pleasant task in the divine presence of Bhagwan. I am grateful to Shri Indulal Shahji for giving me this rare opportunity. It is needless to say that it is all Bhagwan's Sankalppa. Sri Sathya Sai Seva organisations and their international Chairman, Shri Indulal Shah deserve rich compliments for their thoughtful gesture to celebrate 1994 as Sathya Sai Education Year as a part of three year celebrations of the 70ᵗʰ year of Bhagwan Sri Sathya Sai Baba. What could be a better way of paying tribute and expressing gratitude to Bhagwan than this for His precious gift of a unique model of educational system to the world. I would also like to take this opportunity to offer my greetings to all the delegate teacher trainers from abroad and within India who have come to participate in this three-day Mini-Conference. I am sure you will have fruitful interaction and exchange of ideas, views and experiences which will enrich the EHV and Bal Vikas programmes.

God is birthless, limitless and infinite. Nothing can destroy Him. He is the Lord of all living beings. Yet He incarnates with his own divine energy whenever it is necessary.

In Bhagawad Gita, Lord Sri Krishna says to Arjuna:
"Yada yada hee dharmasya glanirbhavathi bharatha Abhyuthana madharmasya thadaatmaanam Srujamyaham".

It means:

"Ao Arjuna! Whenever Dharma declines and adharma rises, then I will incarnate myself."

He further says:

"Parithraanaaya Saadhoonaam vinashaya cha Dushkruthaam Dharma samsthapanarthaya sambhavaami yuge yuge."

It means:

"To protect the virtuous and to destroy the evil ones and to re-establish Dharma, I will incarnate in each Yuga."

In Thretha Yuga, God incarnated in the form of Sri Rama. In Dwapara Yuga, He incarnated as Sri Krishna. The purpose of these avatars was to destroy the evil, protect the good and re-establish the Dharma. Bhagwan Sri Sathya Sai Baba has incarnated in the Kali Yuga to re-establish Sanathana Dharma. During Thretha Yuga and Dwapara Yuga, the task of destroying evil people was resorted to because it was possible to identify them. In the Kali Yuga, the same thing cannot be adopted as evil seems to be all-pervasive. Therefore, Sai Avatar is adopting the path of love in transforming the whole of humanity. This is the difference between the previous avatars and the present one, which is the Poornavatar. He made 'Sanathana Dharma Samsthapana' as His mission, using education as a powerful tool. Human form is the superior creation of God on the earth and it is a rare opportunity to be born as a human being. Only human beings are endowed with discriminatory powers which other creations on this globe lack. The human being has a mission to fulfill in life. The mission is to seek self-realisation and ultimately merge with God. There are various paths which could be followed to achieve this. Gnana Yoga, Bhakti Yoga, Karma Yoga, Karma Sanyasa Yoga etc., are some of the paths indicated in the Bhagawad Gita. Bhagawan Sri Sathya Sai Baba is advocating 'Universal Love', which we may call 'Prema Yoga'. Baba's philosophy and message represents the quintessence of all great religions and have a continuing and growing relevance in modern times for all humanity. Bhagwan has declared that His objective is to bring about a global integration of the entire mankind where the human race will be united as one world-family, knit together by strong bonds of mutual love and respect, believing in the fatherhood of God and brotherhood of man. This would create conducive environment for the human beings to pursue their life mission. Whichever path one may opt for ultimately, one has to undertake the process of inner transformation and practice it all through. It is better if this transformation process starts early. This process of transformation is conditioned by the influence of parents, family environment, education and educational institutions, society around, the national perspectives and the world environment. Ultimately, it is the individual who is going to make up the society, nation and the world and therefore, if the individual is good, then the society, the nation and the world will be peaceful and a better place to live in. Thus the individual's frame of mind will ultimately decide the world peace.

What is happening around us today Violence, hatred, mistrust, growing divisive forces, narrow parochialism, separatist tendencies, considerable fall in moral, social, ethicaland national values both in personal and public life. Materialistic outlook is manifest in almost every dimension of man's life style and day-to-day living. Materialism has become a major force influencing his conduct and behaviour. It is shaping his character and personality and even determining his life's goal. Human dignity and self-respect founded on good character and integrity are overtaken by arrogance, conceit, hypocrisy and artificial postures. The erosion of character is noticed in social and national life. Personal ethics and moral responsibility towards society have become meaningless where there is dominance of selfinterest above everything. Man seems to have completely forgotten his true nature and spirit. Let me now focus on 'education', which is the most important factor in the process of transformation of man. Education should help a person for his total development—physical, intellectual and spiritual. It should help towards disciplined life, self-control, compassionate and humane approach, spontaneous sympathy, regard for all beings and keenness to serve the society. It should enable one not to become self-centred and narrow minded. Education should serve not only to develop one's intellect and skill but also help to broaden one's outlook and make him useful to society and the world at large. True education must humanise the person. The educational system must produce young men and women of character and ability, committed to national service and development.

Bhagwan Sri Sathya Sai Baba defines education as 'that which liberates man from bondage' and as 'that which leads man to immortality'. That which confers upon man light, liberation and life eternal is true education. Bhagwan Baba has unique views about *vidya* (education). He says "Vidya should teach unity, cooperation and equanimity. It should destroy the narrowness of the mind and promote world peace. One should learn such education which promotes good conduct, right mind, quest for truth, devotion, discipline and sense of duty". Education should be used to prepare a person for life in a meaningful way and not just train him for a job as the means of livelihood, He says. No present educational system in the world can boast of fulfilling the above requirement of education adequately.

Sri Sathya Sai education in human values programme is intended to draw out the best in a child and to enable his personality to develop towards perfection. The process of blossoming human excellence calls for excellence in each of the five aspects of human personality, namely intellectual, physical, emotional, psychic and spiritual. The five basic values—truth, righteous conduct, peace, love and non-violence correspond to the above five aspects of human personality. These values are universal and transcend all distinctions of country, religion, caste and creed. They embrace all beings, as their origin lies right within each individual. The five major objectives or ideals of education are knowledge, skill, balance, vision and identity. If one were to read through the reports of various Commissions and Committees on education with discerning eyes and in-depth analysis, a beautiful synthesis of five human values conforming to the five facets of human personality and the five ideals of education could be found. To my mind it is a beautiful merging based on deep analysis and study of human nature and promotion of human values through education fold facets of human personality with educational ideals and human values has been successfully worked out and implemented with practical bias at all the Sri Sathya Sai educational institutions. These pioneering efforts have been commended by leading academicians, scientists and policy makers in the country and the world over. We have this operational model before us which is dogma-free and has universal application irrespective of caste, creed, community, region or Country.

The whole approach to Value Orientation of Education is beautifully summed up by Bhagwan. He said:

> "The human values cannot be learnt by studying books and listening to lectures. These have to be cultivated by constant practice. Promotion of human values must become an integral part of the education process. National Unity and National Integration have to become a way of life. Students, Teachers and Educational Authorities should shed narrow and parochial loyalties and prepare themselves to serve society and the World. If all the educational institutions jointly strive to instill human values in students and faculty members, India

can become an ideal country and be an example to the whole World."

A lot of time and effort has gone into various aspects of development of education in terms of faculty, buildings, equipment etc., but not enough has been done in the area of 'manmaking'and 'people building'. This is a great task and a challenge. The Planning Commission, therefore, strongly felt that the time had come when, as a National policy and planning organisation at the apex level, it should study this aspect of human resources development. For the first time in the history of National planning in India, the Planning Commission felt it necessary to constitute a Core Group on Value Orientation of Education under my chairmanship. The Core Group has submitted its report. The Report referred extensively to the Sathya Sai Educational philosophy. It has been able to present a concrete Plan of Action relating to various levels of educational development, involving interdepartmental collaboration. Teacher has the most important role to play in the value development. The Group is of the view that teacher's personal, professional and social life is the crucial factor in the promotion of values. The most powerful influence of his personality lies in the 'hidden curriculum' of his personality and behaviour and the silent message which his students can and do get through his thinking, discipline of mind and refinement of taste.

The Group has recommended some reforms in the selection procedure of the teachers and a well thought-out programme of pre-service training of the newly recruited teachers and in-service orientation programme of the existing teachers with emphasis on Value Orientation of Education through direct, indirect and integrated methods. For this purpose, models of both pre-service teacher education and in-service teacher orientation have been suggested to be taken up by the Academic Staff Colleges of Universities, National Council for Educational Research and Training (N.C.E.R.T.) and Regional Colleges of Education and pace-setting training institutions even at the District level. As a follow-up of the recommendations of the Core Group, the Ministry of Human Resources Development has constituted a Standing Committee on Value Orientation of Education under my Chairmanship to oversee the implementation of value orientation of education at all levels right from the school to university level in the country. The Standing Committee is working out the detailed blue print for the implementation of Value Orientation of Education at school level, college level, university level and to use the electronic media and other organisations for promotion of value orientation of education. Sri Sathya Sai model of value based education is one of the major guiding factors for the Standing Committee. Advancement in science and technology certainly improved the materialistic quality of life of people. But it has also shown the way for destruction. There is a massive build up of deadly weapons in the world which can destroy the world many times over. Peaceful coexistence seems to have been threatened. Among nations, their mutual relations are seemed to be determined not on humanitarian considerations but on power domination and political expediency. The total scenario in the world, even in the 21st century, in terms of the need for man's balanced frame of mind and the need for good relations between nations for peaceful co-existence, in all probability, may remain the same unless some serious and sincere efforts are made to rectify the situation. The present and the future generations are to be helped to reorient themselves to be imbued with strong commitment to moral, ethical, spiritual and human values if we want to see peaceful world order. In this context, the only ray of hope for mankind is the teachings and the educational philosophy of Bhagwan Sri Sathya Sai Baba. His profound teachings and educational philosophy which are put to practice at the Prasanthinilayam are relevant to the whole world for all times to come. The role of Sri Sathya Sai education in 21st century is going to be vital for human development with value perception and the world peace.

The everlasting and universal values of life are given the primary and fundamental place in Bhagwan's system of education. Bhagwan established educational institutions to mould youngsters as better citizens and prepare them in all respects to be the torch bearers of future of the country and the world. If we can replicate or emulate the model of the Sri Sathya Sai value based education everywhere we would have prepared ourselves to meet the challenges of the 21st century. It will lead the humanity into the 21st century through sathya, dharma, shanti, prema and ahimsa.

CHANGED ECONOMIC SCENARIO— IMPERATIVES FOR HIGHER EDUCATION IN INDIA

INTRODUCTION

Soon after independence, the country had faced the greater challenge of rapidly industrialising the predominantly agricultural economy and in that process, it had to create wide-based infrastructure in higher and technical education institutions, research laboratories and industries covering a very wide spectrum of disciplines and capabilities. The higher education system has done a commendable job in fulfilling its role as a powerful tool for social, political and economic change in the country and also as a source of new knowledge, research and manpower generator for all sectors of the economy. During the 90's, the country is becoming progressively more integrated into the global economy. With the advent of the New Industrial Policy and liberalisation, the Indian industry is exposed to domestic and global competition. Knowledge-based industries will be on the increase. The levels of skills required are going to be high. In the changed situation, we need to have a work force having a scientific bent of mind and possess the much needed scientific temper and skill to maintain high quality of productivity at par with world standards. Commensurately, we have to gear up our R & D efforts. This changed scenario imposes two major imperatives on the higher education system. Firstly, the system has to cope with the resources inadequacy situation and secondly to respond to the demand of providing competent manpower and R & D capability to the industry in the changed environment. The system of higher education has to take up this challenge in the best possible manner.

HIGHER EDUCATION SYSTEM

There has been a spectacular growth in the higher education system in India during the post independence era. In 1950-51, there were 27 universities and 696 colleges with an enrolment of 3.68 lakhs students and a teaching faculty of 19,047. In 1990-91 there were 177 universities (including 'deemed' universities) and 7121 colleges with a student enrolment of 44.25 lakhs and a faculty strength of 2,13,125. Assuming even a steady rate of 4.2% growth in enrolment per year, the total student enrolment at the end of 1995 will be around 60 lakhs. Another heartening feature of the development of higher education in India is the steady growth in the enrolment of women students. In 1990-91, women were 32.5% of the total enrolment. If the upward trend in the enrolment of women continues, as it is expected to do, the demand for higher education will further increase. Expenditure on education as percentage of GNP varied from 1.2 in 1950-51 to 3.9 in 1986-87. Planwise approved outlays for education, including general, higher and technical education are shown in Table-1,1A,1B &1C (shown at pages 367-370). It may be seen that the percentage of higher education out of the total allocation for education varied from 20.89% in Sixth Plan to 11.20% in Eighth Plan.

CHANGED SCENARIO

Momentous changes have taken place on the international scene which are having a profound impact on both international relations and world economy. In India too historic changes have taken place on the economic front. The government has taken new initiatives and bold decisions to reorient and restructure the economy to meet the challenges of economic crisis in the country. The Eighth Five Year Plan has been launched from 1st April 1992 in the backdrop of certain strengths in the economy as well as certain concerns which have surfaced at the beginning of the Eighth Plan. During the nineties, the country is poised to become progressively more integrated into the global economy. Competition and pace of technological change are likely to intensify in almost all sectors of the economy.

IMPACT ON INDUSTRY

In the regime of new Industrial Policy and liberalisation, the Indian industry is exposed to more domestic and global competition. To meet these challenges it requires modernisation, upgradation of the competency of the work force, utilisation of modernmanagement techniques and increased efficiency and productivity while maintaining quality. The industries, in this context, need the help of universities and other institutes of higher learning more than ever before. They should build up confidence in the Indian Universities and other institutes of higher learning and utilise their expertise instead of looking for the soft options of consultancy and technology import.

IMPERATIVES ON HIGHER EDUCATION

In essence, the overall changed scenario could be viewed in terms of: (i) resources crunch, (ii) economic reforms with massive dose of liberalisation, (iii) globalisation of Indian economy, and (iv) Indian industry getting exposed to global competition. In this situation, higher education in this country is now being put to test. In the changed environment what are the imperatives on the higher education system and how it should cope? The system of higher education faces two major imperatives in the changed scenario. They are: (a) cope up with the resources inadequacy situation, and (b) respond to the demand of providing competent manpower and high quality R & D support. These imperatives could be tackled through proper reorientation and taking up measures such as : (a) optimal utilisation of resources, (b) resources mobilisation, (c) collaboration, networking andsharing of facilities, (d) seeking excellence and relevance in the R & D effort, (e) aiming at competent and relevant manpower development, and (f) undertaking inter-national interaction and collaboration. Universities should interact with business and industry sectors and national R & D organisations. The interaction will play a vital role in economic development. In the present day global situation, interaction and interdependence are well recognised. The need for interaction, collaboration and networking is more pronounced in the context of the resources crunch situation. The institutions of higher education and research should be able to interact with the outside world namely the society, the government, sister institutions, lower level institutions, industrial organisations etc. Through interaction, the institutes' excellence should be shared with others for national development. Higher and technical education institutions should move towards less dependence on government funding. Indian industry now being exposed to global competition needs reorientation. The national R & D laboratories need to generate funds at the present situation and allow to share their equipment and expertise of their manpower.

Time is ripe now for strong linkages between universities, industries and national R & D laboratories. This linkage will result in (i) sharing and optimising the use of resources, (ii) development of indigenous technology appropriate to our national priorities and resources, (iii) adapting the imported technology wherever needed for preparing the industries to meet global competitiveness, (iv) enriching teaching and research in universities with the back up of practical and field experience, (v) universities and R & D laboratories getting valuable clues for research orientation and (vi) fund generation. The process of interaction will contribute towards excellence, which in turn will contribute towards national development. A model for university, industry and R & D laboratory interaction has been proposed by me and published some time ago. The Model is shown in Annexure (Page 199).

EIGHTH PLAN

The approach to higher education as indicated in the Eighth Plan document suggests that keeping in view the present resources crunch, the expansion in higher education is to be accommodated in an equitable and cost effective manner mainly by large scale expansion of distance education system providing opportunities to larger segments of population particularly the disadvantaged groups like women and people living in backward and hilly areas and by measures for resources generation. The programme of distance education should absorb atleast 50 per cent of the additional enrolment during the Eighth Five Year Plan. Open universities should also start innovative programmes of a vocational nature for meeting the learning needs of rural areas. Opening up of new conventional universities and colleges should not be encouraged. Simultaneously, involvement of voluntary agencies and private sector participation in the opening and conduct of higher education institutions should be encouraged with proper checks to ensure maintenance of standards and facilities to make higher education as far as possible self financing, the Eighth Plan document says.

PROGRAMME OF ACTION (POA)

The Programme of Action related to the National Policy on Education (NPE) 1992, acknowledges the crucial role of higher education in training manpower for national development and indicates that it is necessary to provide it with adequate support and finances to maintain its infrastructure and establishment at an acceptable level; to keep abreast with latest developments; and meet future challenges. In this context, it has become necessary for the institutions of higher learning to consider measures for raising internal resources and improving their cost efficiency. While there is a case for raising tuition and other charges, which have remained more or less static for the past forty six years, an elaborate and effective system should be established for providing freeships, scholarships and loans to students belonging to the weaker sections of society. Efforts should also be made to evolve rational norms for providing grants to universities which should take into account per capita cost, teacher-student ratio, proportion of teaching and non-teaching staff, types of courses offered, costing of services and extent of their subsidisation, ratio of graduate and post-graduate / research students etc. There is need for a balanced distribution of resources between universities and research institutions, the Programme of Action goes on to add. A High Powered Committee has been constituted by the University Grants Commission to suggest measures for mobilisation of additional resources for higher education.

Similarly, for technical education, the Programme of Action indicates the following:

All institutions will be encouraged to achieve maximum self-reliance by generating resources through measures like enhancement of fees coupled with provision of soft loans to the needy students; consultancy; testing; sponsored projects; community contributions; institutional chairs; raising donations for infrastructural development with a provision for tax exemption; establishment of industrial foundations; charging fees for specific facilities such as laboratory, library, games, magazines, etc. The grant-in-aid institutions will be allowed to utilise the additional income generated for infrastructural and other developmental activities without linking it with the Governmental grants. As with higher education, a High Powered Committee would be set up to consider steps for mobilisation of additional resources for technical education, to bring about a better balance in the funding of institutions for technical and management education and research, and to improve the cost efficiency of the technical education system. Efforts will also be made to streamline the scheme of educational loans with a view to making it more customer-friendly.

A high powered committee on technical education has already been constituted by the Ministry of Human Resource Development under my Chairmanship. The Committee is going to finalise the report shortly.

TRUE AUTONOMY AND SELF-RELIANCE

Autonomy in its true sense should be the privilege of an educational institution so as to enable it to respond effectively in fulfilling its objectives and goals, especially in the changed environment. Considerable academic autonomy is already available. Towards achieving the objectives and the goals of an institution there should be ample financial autonomy as well. In the present day system of funding there is rigidity coupled with inadequacy. The inadequacy part is going to be more in the context of the resources crunch. Financial autonomy is vital for continuation of the institutions as real Centres of excellence. Therefore, the institutions should strive for fund generation and reduce their dependence on government gradually and thus pave the way towards self-reliance. Self-reliance should be understood in terms of building up of capabilities to bridge the gap between the fund requirement and the fund availability from the government through suitable measures for fund generation while at the same time not sacrificing their primary task of teaching and research.

CORPUS FUND

Creation of 'corpus fund' for each university or institution would be an appropriate mechanism to achieve the objective of self-reliance. The corpus will be in the form of an endowment fund. Revenue obtained from such fund can eventually be used to reduce the required support from the Government. The corpus fund could be created with contributions from industry, alumni, charitable trusts etc. as well as from the government. Indian Institutes of Technology, Indian Institute of Science and Indian Institutes of Management have already accepted the concept and they are in the process of creating corpus funds with the support of the government.

CONCLUSION

In the changed environment, the system of higher education should be able to show flexibility and resilience in reorienting itself to meet the challenges thrown out in the form of imperatives. While making these demands on higher education, however, one should keep in view that it is imperative to free the system from unnecessary constraints and political interference, thereby providing the needed academic, administrative and financial freedom. On the part of the system itself, it should be amenable to accountability

INAUGURAL ADDRESS AT THE 68TH ANNUAL MEETING OF THE ASSOCIATION OF INDIAN UNIVERSITIES

It gives me immense pleasure to be associated with you in the 68th Annual Meeting of the Association of Indian Universities. I am also glad that the Association is organising a one day Seminar on the subject "Environmental Challenges and the Universities". Perhaps this is the first time that the Vice-Chancellors of over 100 universities are meeting to discuss the environmental problems we face and to identify pathways to attain sustainable development through higher education. The concern over environmental issues have been expressed at various levels on different platforms and it is a welcome sign that the universities, as centres of knowledge come to the forefront to identify the course of action to be taken to assess the situation and to impart scientific inputs which could assist in taking positive steps to contain the environmental decay. I had the opportunity to go through some of the papers to be presented in the Seminar which clearly emphasise the role of universities to function as a training ground on environmental issues with a broad and sensitive understanding. I could feel the sense of urgency expressed in many of these papers to integrate environmental concerns into various disciplines of teaching at university level.

Right across the globe there is a growing concern on the need for preservation of environment which has a direct relationship with sustainable development. Extensive knowledge on the carrying capacity of the eco-systems and the impact of increased population pressure on nature and its ability to support life is required to promote the concept of sustainable development. It was at the Rio Conference that the issues of the extent of pollution caused by the rich North and the poorer South were brought into proper focus and the concept of 'one-worldism' with environment equally on everyone's agenda was evolved. The broad areas of human concerns like ecology and environment have started attracting the attention of many educational planners which can broaden the scope of various schools of thought. The role of universities with regard to environment essentially lies in evolving new teaching and research programmes covering various facets of physical sciences and synthesising these with the socio-economic and cultural environment of our country.

Environmental problems arise from diverse causes. These causes may be poverty, ignorance, customs, climate and geographic insufficiency, inadequacy of technology and development. The environmental problems of the developing countries may be attributable to the effects of poverty on one hand and the effects of economic development on the other. The threat to sustainability also comes from high levels of consumption of the rich nations. It is said that the industrialised countries with 24% of the world's population have a share of global consumption of various commodities extending from 50% to 90%. The consumption of food products by industrialised countries ranges from 48 to 72%. They consume 60% of fertilisers, 81% of paper, 85% of chemicals, 92% of cars and 75% of world's energy.

Environmental stress is proportional to these consumption levels. The industrialised world is responsible for 70% of the annual emissions of carbon di-oxide and 77% of cumulative carbon di-oxide emissions. Clearly, consumption patterns of the rich are unsustainable because of over use of non-renewable resources. Nevertheless, consumption patterns of the poor are also to some extent, unsustainable because of bad land use and degradation of the village commons. While environmental degradation causes diseases; poverty plays a major role in the sustenance of disease. Clean water, sanitation and cleaner energy systems can dramatically improve the health status of the poverty ridden people and contribute to their economic development. Population stabilisation should not be a forgotten issue on our environmental agenda. One issue where the Indian delegation had to face some uncomfortable moments at the Rio Summit was the issue of population. Literacy campaign, population education and involvement of Non Government Organisations in overcoming the cultural barriers in accepting the small family norm should complement the efforts of population control. There should be a strategic shift to clean and green technologies. Sustainable industrial development is not a matter of mere high-tech but of appropriate sci-tech. We have to phase out older and inappropriate technologies while simultaneously developing and disseminating a new generation of sophisticated and environmentally benign technologies. We have to encourage indigenous research effort to be directed at green technologies through a system of incentives and penalties.

Sustainable development demands technologies which are least polluting, uses natural resources optimally and also recycle wastes. These technologies should be compatible with the socio-economic, cultural, environmental and developmental priorities of our country. There is an urgent need to undertake human resource development and strengthen institutional capacities for research and development and conduct integrated assessment of available technologies and technological needs which suit the objectives and priorities of our national development. Therefore the need to stimulate research and development within the scientific and technological community is of prime importance. We have to build capacities to assess, develop and transfer appropriate technologies suitable to our physical as well as socio-economic and cultural systems.

An area that needs closer examination vis-à-vis environment is that of energy production. There is no denying the fact that the future energy scenario is grim. If the efficiency of energy production and consumption is not stepped up, there are going to be serious environmental implications in both energy producing and energy consuming regions. Increased R & D efforts in non-conventional sources of energy should be coupled with the national efficiency drive. A clear energy policy to prevent the country from being trapped in an oil incentive development pattern, is urgently needed.

The role of universities in taking up the challenges by providing adequate support to various institutions attempting to tackle environmental issues are enormous. However, the present day environmental education system at the university level encounters various problems. Even though the universities enjoy greater autonomy in framing their own curricula, paucity of funds and the extremely discipline oriented approach makes environmental education a complex issue at the university level. Along with the discipline oriented teaching the university education system at all levels must apply an understanding and appreciative approach to the environmental problems. It must be able to collect, analyse and integrate data on the linkages between the ecosystems and the adverse impact on environment like pollution and depletion of natural resources. They need to improve their existing infrastructure and infuse more knowledge so that priorities in teaching and research should orient towards identifying adequate tools for sustainable development. The research activities should be made adaptive and integrate scientific assessments with the indigenous knowledge.

Research programmes in the universities should be formulated in order to attain a better understanding of the carrying capacity of the earth which requires development of new analytical and productive tools. They should also aim at integrating physical, economic and social sciences in a broad frame so that the impact of economic and social behaviour on the environment is fully appreciated. To integrate the available information on all relevant sciences, the universities and the research institutions should interact and collaborate. The universities may take up the task of training scientists, decision makers and Non-Government Organisations to improve their capabilities and create public awareness on environment. Detailed studies are required to have a better understanding of our own resource base and ecological systems and also to monitor them in order to meet our environmental challenges. They must also equip themselves to provide the required information to decision makers and involve them alongwith teachers and scientists in research programmes. Several universities are offering post-graduate courses in environmental sciences, but perhaps serious attempts may be needed to evolve broad based courses with action oriented activities. Specialisation in environmental engineering, conservation and management, environmental health, social and cultural dimensions of ecology etc. are to be imbibed into the curricula for environmental education. The concerned university departments may attempt to impart education for community, children, rural youth and also organise ecodevelopment camps, foundation courses etc.

Various ministries, such as Environment & Forests, Human Resource Development, Science & Technology and Department of Biotechnology etc. are providing grants to various universities to promote environmental research for co-ordinated multi-disciplinary projects to study the dynamics, ecology and resource management of ecosystems and assessment of risks to them. The universities should come forward to utilise these grants in a big way and enhance their role in assisting to solve environmental problems. "Environment" is a term encompassing various facets of natural and human aspects and the environmental issues are so complex that the issues are embedded in wide matrix and, therefore, universities attempting to build new departments of environment should understand that a single department / university by itself will not be able to tackle many of these problems. Interaction and collaboration are essential. The role of the department of environment should not be restricted only to teaching and conducting sectoral issues of environment, but they should also act as co-ordinating agencies in integrating environmental concerns into various disciplines and also to imbibe the knowledge acquired by other disciplines so that proper insight is acquired to take up the new challenges.

I am sure the outcome of the Seminar will be valuable and I hope it would lead to concrete suggestions to meet the environmental challenges.

CONVOCATION ADDRESS AT THE 12TH CONVOCATION OF THE DAYALBAGH EDUCATIONAL INSTITUTE, AGRA

President, Prof. Satsangi, the Director, distinguished invitees, faculty members and the graduates of the year, I am greatly delighted to be with you on the happy occasion of the 12th Convocationof this reputed Deemed-to-be University, Dayalbagh Educational Institute. I am deeply honoured for being invited as the Chief Guest and to deliver the Convocation address and I am grateful to Prof. Satsangi, the Director for this. This is my second visit to Dayalbagh Institute; the first visit was some time during 1988, which was a very brief one. Now, I am happy to have another occasion to visit the Institute.

A glimpse into the essence of Dayalbagh—"The Garden of the Merciful" can be had from what Huzur Mehtaji Maharaj said in his welcome address to Pandit Jawaharlal Nehru when the latter visited the Institute during January 1956, which I quote "Dayalbagh, at a distance from the City of Agra, is quiet and peaceful like a village and yet there is perfect arrangement for sanitation and cleanliness as in cities. Students, scientists and devotees keep themselves peacefully engaged in their respective activities away from the turmoil of the world and unemployed educated youths, agriculturists and labourers get opportunities to earn their livelihood. Neither does wealth flow here, nor does anybody starve here; neither are there any big palaces and mansions here, nor are there any dilapidated huts here; neither is anyone great or high here, nor anyone small or insignificant, and if anybody here is honoured more than others, it is he who works better or more than others. Dayalbagh belongs to every resident, while no resident has any kind of property in anything here. In this small place, Dayalbagh, where nobody leads a life of laziness and indolence, which is neither a village nor a town, and which is both a village and a town . . . ." Dayalbagh has indeed an ideal atmosphere for serious pursuit of knowledge and character building.

The quality and relevance of education and training imparted to the students in the Institute was highly appreciated by Pandit Jawaharlal Nehru in his address during his above visit to the Institute. He said ". . . . the greatest problem of India today is how to educate and train our children and young men and make them fit for shouldering responsibilities, i.e. how to make them physically fit and prepare them mentally to shoulder the future responsibilities of the country, so that they may become fit in every way to discharge their duty. And if there is a good place where this work is done efficiently, naturally one feels happy about it. As a matter of fact, countries advance not on account of their size but by the manner its people lead their lives and by the character they possess and by the skill of their hands and intelligence they possess to do things. If India would make progress, it would do so because such people live here and not because thirty six crores of people live in this country. This is what makes me happy for having come to this place." Naturally everybody who visits this place should be happy looking at all the good things happening here and I am no exception to that.

It is heartening to note that the Institute has introduced a scheme of innovative and comprehensive education in the university and non-university technical education levels which aims at excellence and inculcate dignity of labour encouraging initiative and creative work. It will generate in the alumni the basic values of humanism, secularism and democracy by exposing them to the principles of all the major religions of the world and to their own cultural heritage, thus developing in them an integrated personality. This kind of value orientation of education is the need of the hour. The need has arisen in the context of degeneration in moral, social, ethical and national values, both in personal and public life. Personal ethics and moral responsibility towards society declined considerably. Man seems to have completely forgotten his true nature and spirit. Even the relationship between nations seems to be depending not on humanitarian considerations but on power domination and political expediency. Peaceful co-existence in the world seems to have been threatened. Under the circumstances, the only ray of hope seems to be the pursuit of Gandhian thought and values which are relevant to all the times to come and upholding the human value system through education.

Convocations are important moments in the life of a university and its graduates. They give us a sense of identity and continuity across the years and reaffirm the duty of each generation to transmit the best of its knowledge, wisdom and culture to the next. I know that you, the graduates, are leaving this Institute with a sense of fulfilment and gratitude. I have no doubt you have been well taught and trained and you learnt well. I offer you my sincere congratulations on your conferment of degrees and honours. I pray for your happiness and for the fulfilment of the promise as individuals and as a generation.

Today I would like to share with you some thoughts on higher education and technical education in the country and the imperatives for reorientation and innovative approaches. In the post-independence era there has been a spectacular growth in higher education and technical education. Soon after independence, in our attempts to rapidly change the then pre-dominantly agricultural economy into an industrial economy too, we have built a wide based infrastructure in higher education, technical education, industry and national R & D laboratories. There are about 200 universities and 7,958 colleges with a student enrolment of about 46 lakhs and a faculty strength of around 2,70,000. The estimated total students enrolment at the end of 1995 would be around 60 lakhs. Expansion of technical education, too, has been impressive. Now there are about 350 technical institutions at the degree level and 950 institutions at the diploma level with an intake of 68,000 and 1,26,000 students respectively. There are more than 90 institutions offering post-graduate courses in engineering and technology to about 8,500 students annually. In addition, there are around 50 institutions, including the four Indian Institutes of Management (IIMS) imparting management education to over 4,000 students annually. The higher education and technical education systems have done a commendable job in largely fulfilling their assigned role with all their limitations.

The percentage allocation of higher education out of the total allocation for education varied from 20.89% in the Sixth Plan to 11.20% in the Eighth Plan. The corresponding figures for technical education varied from 12.88% to 14.22%. The percentage of GNP for education is around 3.9%.

All of you are aware that momentous changes have taken place on the international scene. We have restructured our economy with a considerable dose of liberalisation. The result of the impact of the global changes and the national economic scenario is the emergence of an era of global consciousness. The Indian industry is exposed to global and indigenous competitiveness. To meet this challenge the industry requires modernisation, upgradation of the competence of the work force, utilisation of modern management techniques, increased efficiency and productivity and maintains quality. The situation thus requires a work force having a scientific bent of mind to maintain high quality and productivity at par with the world standards. Relevant R & D efforts should also be geared up. The higher and technical educational institutions have, therefore, to respond effectively to these emerging challenges to train men and women of calibre and competence of world standards and provide the needed R & D capability. Similarly the national R & D laboratories should develop and provide the needed R & D support to the industry for facing the global competition. On the part of Indian industries, they should build up confidence in the indigenous R & D capability and refrain from taking the easy option of importing technology. Leaving apart the impact of the changed economic scenario and the consequent imperatives, the higher and technical education systems are already suffering from several weaknesses and problems at present such as increase in demand for enrolment, proliferation of sub-standard institutions, dilution in quality and standard, failure to maintain academic calendar, out-dated curriculum, disparities in the quality of education, inadequate resources and lack of adequate support for research, out-dated management system etc. We need to give serious thought to the impact of the changed scenario and the deficiencies in the system and take remedial measures to make higher and technical education and research to be more purposeful. The higher and technical education systems in this country are now being put to test. They face two major imperatives in the changed scenario. They are : (a) to cope up with the resources inadequacy situation, and (b) to respond to the demand of providing competent manpower and high quality R & D support to industry and other related sectors of the economy. These imperatives could be tackled through proper reorientation and taking up some of the measures such as (a) optimal utilisation of resources, (b) resource mobilization efforts, (c) collaboration, networking and sharing of facilities, (d) seeking excellence and relevance in the R & D effort, (e) airing at competent and relevant manpower development, and (f) undertaking international interaction and collaboration.

Time is now ripe for the universities to interact with business and industry sectors and national R & D organisations. The interaction will play a vital role in economic development. In the present day global situation, interaction and interdependence are well recognised. The need for interaction, collaboration and networking is more pronounced in the context of the resources crunch situation. Through interaction, the institutes' excellence should be shared with others for national development. One of the ways of making higher and technical education more purposeful is to build up strong linkages between universities, industries and national R & D laboratories. This linkage will result in (i) sharing and optimising the use of resources, (ii) development of indigenous technology appropriate to our national priorities and resources, (iii) adapting the imported technology wherever needed for preparing the industries to meet global competitiveness, (iv) enriching teaching and research in universities with the backup of practical and field experience, (v) universities and R & D laboratories getting valuable clues for research orientation and (vi) fund generation. The process of interaction will contribute towards excellence, which in turn will contribute towards national development. A model for university, industry and R & D laboratory interaction has been proposed by me and published. The Model identifies areas of interaction between universities, national R & D laboratories and the industries.

The following measures will lead to optimal utilisation of resources for the university system:

a) Within the universities or institutions duplication and wastage should be avoided. Pooling and sharing of costly facilities should be followed.

b) Networking of facilities like computers and libraries could be resorted to locally. For example, within a city networking of computers and libraries of all the universities and research organisations could certainly lead towards optimal utilisation of resources. Similarly, national networking could also be thought of. In this context the University Grants Commission's project on Information and Library Networking (INFLIBNET) is quite relevant.

c) Establishing sound linkages between universities and national research laboratories, would facilitate sharing of facilities, exchange of faculty and experts and undertaking joint academic and research programmes.

d) Establishment of consortia of universities that can work in collaboration with higher institutions of learning such as TIFR, IISc, IITs, etc., would enable to utilise their superior resources, both human and material by the Universities.

e) According Deemed-to-be-University status to selected national laboratories to initiate post graduate programmes in certain special areas of Science, Engineering and Technology.
f) Establishing of joint centres to be run by the national laboratories and the Universities will provide better research and developmental facilities to the University sector.

As a part of resources mobilisation, establishing strong linkages with industries would go a long way. It would enable the industry to support the research and academic programmes in addition to dedicated financial contributions. The universities can also commercialise their research output, undertake consultancy and training programmes.

International linkages in science and technology could be a means to assist in the implementation of national programmes, as well as to open up avenues for collaborative interaction in the frontier areas or in those sectors which lead to the acquisition of knowledge not available within the country. The overall modalities of cooperation should be such that they should ensure the enhancement of self-reliance and at the same time, avoid impingement upon considerations of security and sensitivity of the country. International cooperation will also serve as a tool for sharing of India's experience and expertise in science and technology with other developing nations.

For achieving excellence, a university should have academic, financial and administrative autonomy. Considerable academic autonomy is available but there should be ample financial and administrative autonomy as well. In the present day system of government funding there is rigidity coupled with inadequacy. The inadequate situation is going to be worse in the context of the resources crunch. Financial autonomy is vital for continuation of the institutions as real Centres of excellence. Therefore, the institutions should strive for fund generation and reduce their dependence on government gradually and thus pave the way towards self-reliance.

Creation of 'corpus fund' for each university or institution would be an appropriate mechanism to achieve the objective of self-reliance. The corpus will be in the form of an endowment fund. Revenue obtained from such fund can eventually be used to reduce the required support from the Government. The corpus fund could be created with contributions from industry, alumni, charitable trusts etc., as well as from the government. Indian Institutes of Technology, Indian Institute of Science and Indian Institutes of Management have already accepted the concept and they are in the process of creating corpus funds with the support of the government.

I am aware that the young graduates present here may find my Convocation address a bit loaded. But I thought it is the right time to refer to the issues relating to higher and technical education for better appreciation, when some likeminded people are gathered here who have concern for education in the country and especially when you are leaving the portals of this University with great responsibility on your shoulders. I join today, along with your teachers and friends, in the hope that you who received the degrees and became the alumni of this university will contribute your share to the development of the country while pursuing your career. In this context, I would like to remind you about the four vital issues which need focussed attention in our country's progress. They are (i) population control, (ii) eradication of illiteracy, (iii) environmental protection and maintenance of ecological balance, and (iv) upholding the value system. I would like to stress the need for contribution from you, who are going into society with great hope, in tackling these problems. I am sure you will rise to the occasion.

INCREASING ACCESS TO DISTANCE EDUCATION: AN AGENDA FOR ACTION

I am happy to participate in the inaugural session of the Second National Conference of the Indian Distance Education Association (IDEA) being organised at Sri Venkateswara University, Tirupati. I am grateful to the Convenor Dr. Murali Manohar for inviting me to inaugurate the Conference. The main theme of the Conference is "Increasing Access to Distance Education: Agenda for Action" and I am happy to note that the Conference will examine the nature, scope and implications of distance education for future higher education and training needs of India, while evaluating the past and the present progress of distance education in India in relation to fulfillment of its desired goals and work out future projections. It also envisages to examine the steps required to be taken especially to achieve the Eighth Plan target of 50% enrolment of higher education students through distance education institutions. I would like to congratulate the organisers for choosing such a relevant theme for the Conference in the present day context of 'resources inadequacy situation' for higher education.

In the post-independence era there has been a spectacular growth in the number of higher education and technical education institutions. Soon after independence, in our attempts to rapidly change the then predominantly agricultural economy into an industrial economy too, we have built a wide based infrastructure in higher education, technical education, industry and national R & D laboratories. There are about 200 universities and 7,958 colleges with a student enrolment of about 46 lakhs and a faculty strength of around 2,70,000. The estimated total students enrolment at the end of

1995 would be around 60 lakhs. Expansion of technical education, too, has been impressive. Now there are about 350 technical institutions at the degree level and 950 institutions at the diploma level with an intake of 68,000 and 1,26,000 students respectively. There are more than 90 institutions offering postgraduate courses in engineering and technology to about 8,500 students annually. In addition, there are around 50 institutions, including the four Indian Institutes of Management (IIMs) imparting management education to over 4,000 students annually. In spite of such a spectacular growth in the number of higher and technical educational institutions, the system, however, is not able to cope up with the increased demand for enrolment.

The percentage allocation of higher education out of the total allocation for education varied from 20.89% in the Sixth Plan to 11.20% in the Eighth Plan. The corresponding figures for technical education varied from 12.88% to 14.22%. The percentage of GNP for education is around 3.9%. Now the government has taken a decision to increase the percentage of GNP for education to 6% during the Ninth Plan.

The higher and technical education systems in the country are now put to test in the context of the changed economic scenario. Brain storming sessions held in the Planning Commission underlined the following thrust areas for higher education: (1) integrated approach to higher education; (2) excellence in higher education; (3) expansion of education in an equitable and cost-effective manner in the process of making the higher education system financially self-supporting; (4) making higher education relevant in the context of changing socioeconomic scenario; (5) promotion of value education; and (6) strengthening of management system in the universities.

The additional enrolment in higher education during the Eighth Plan is estimated to be around 10 lakhs of which 9 lakhs will be at the undergraduate level. The approach to expansion of higher education in an equitable and cost-effective manner and making it self-supporting, will have distance education as one of its pointers. The Eighth Plan, rightly so, envisages that the expansion in higher education, keeping in view the present resource crunch, has to be accommodated in an equitable and cost-effective manner, mainly by large-scale expansion of Distance Education system and providing opportunities to larger segments of population, particularly the disadvantaged groups like women and people living in backward and hilly areas and by measures for resource generation. The programmes of Distance Education should absorb at least 50 per cent of the additional enrolment during the Eighth Plan and their cumulative enrolment should reach 15 lakhs, including 5 lakhs adult learners beyond the normal age group of

17-23 who have left school long back. The Eighth Plan document further says that the Open universities should also start innovative programmes of a vocational nature for meeting the learning needs of rural areas. If it is the aim to expand educational opportunities to cover a large proportion of the population in a country, distance education using modern communication technology is the solution. This need is more so in a developing country like India. Thus the 'distance education' concept assumes greater significance in the present day Indian context. Quality of education may be difficult to ensure with out-dated methods of teaching, poor laboratory facilities, uninspiring curricula etc. In addition, inequalities of quality and coverage of education among various regions and, various social and economic groups in the country pose problems. There is also need to provide educational outlets to those who could not get into the formal system of education due to either non-availability of seats, economic conditions or personal reasons. The solution for all these problems could well be distance education through multi-media approach. Satellite Instructional Television Experiment (SITE) conducted in India during 1975 demonstrated the potential of educational communication to large numbers at low cost through satellite.

The higher educational system must meet the challenge of increasing student population. The formal system with its limitations and rigidities in admission requirements may not alone be able to meet this challenge. The pressure could be relieved through an alternative system adopting a methodology which allows flexibility in operation, diversity in academic content not bound by time and space. This alternative approach is possible only through the open higher education adopting distance teaching.

The distance teaching approach in higher education is gaining more popularity because of its being less restrictive in terms of pre-requisites, namely educational qualifications and age. It accepts students from all walks of life without the rigid formalities of the conventional system. It adopts the learning process convenient to the learners own setting. A variety of teaching media are employed such as correspondence, print material, radio, television, telephone, audio and video cassettes. The Open Education is perhaps a 20th century concept even though its roots lie in the correspondence schools of the late 1800s. In 1922, in an American Radio magazine it appeared that the people's University of the Air will have a greater student body than all their universities put together. In 1926, in England, J.C. Stobart also mooted something similar. The Robbins Report on Higher Education mentioned about the potential value of 'the establishment by some universities for correspondence courses'. In about 20 countries, the Institutes of Open

Learning have been set up. Depending on the objectives and the level of clientele these institutions came to be known by different names, namely Open University, University without Walls, Open Schools, Correspondence Institutes etc. U.K.'s Open University, People's Universities in erstwhile USSR, Pakistan's Allama Iqbal Open University, Sri Lanka's Institute of Distance Education, China's Central Broadcasting and TV University, Australia's Deakin University, Japan's Broadcasting University, Thailand's Thammathirat Open University, India's Indira Gandhi National Open University and the Open University in Republic of Korea are some of the examples of higher educational institutions of distance learning. Distance education is also being tried out in countries like Malaysia, Philippines, Burma, New Zealand, Fiji and Papua New Guinea. Countries like USA, Canada, France, Sweden, Norway, Germany, also have adopted the open distance education approach. All these countries have adopted the multimedia approach for imparting open higher education. Most of these institutions arose from a pressing national need for education on a grand scale where an educational infrastructure was not well developed or where an existing system was perceived as elitist and closed.

An international organisation, namely, the Commonwealth of Learning, has been established by Commonwealth Governments in September, 1988 with its headquarters at Vancouver, Canada. The purpose of Commonwealth of Learning is to create and widen access to education and to improve its quality, utilising distance education techniques and associated communications technologies to meet the particular requirements of member countries. The concept of the Open University is not new to India. The Universities of Mysore, Madurai Kamraj (Madurai) and SNDT Women's University (Bombay) had set up the Open University learning system long back and the experiment has been rewarding. An Open University has been established in Andhra Pradesh during 1982 [since renamed as Dr. B.R. Ambedkar Open University (BRAOU)]. A National Open University named after the late Prime Minister Smt. Indira Gandhi i.e., Indira Gandhi National Open University (IGNOU) has been set up in September, 1985. Two more state open universities, namely the Kota Open University (KOU) and the Yashwantrao Chavan Maharashtra Open University in Maharashtra (YCMOU) have also been set up. The distance education institutions (open universities and institutes of correspondence education of conventional universities) accounted for about 11.5% of enrolment in higher education in 1990-91. The IGNOU has set up a Distance Education Council as a statutory body for the promotion, coordination and determination of standards of the Open University / distance education system in the country.

Distance education programmes offered are mostly in non-engineering, nontechnological or non-vocational areas in India. Attempts to provide distance education programmes in Engineering, Technology and vocational courses are rare. Courses which are suitably designed and developed could as well be offered through distance education mode in Engineering, Technology and vocational areas with success and acceptability.

India is now passing through a historic moment on the economic front. In the recent past, a series of policy measures to revitalise the economy have been initiated. Among them are the new Industrial and Trade Policies and various other development measures. With the advent of New Industrial Policy and liberalisation, the Indian industry is exposed to more domestic and global competition. To meet the challenge it requires modernisation, upgradation of the competence of the personnel, utilisation of modern management techniques and improved efficiency and productivity while maintaining quality. In view of the above, the need for upgradation of the competency of the personnel in industry and other sectors of the economy is paramount to increase efficiency and productivity to meet the global competitiveness and to meet the challenges of the resource crunch effectively. The existing facilities for continuing education and retraining are inadequate. There is a need to formalise the retraining programmes for engineering and technology personnel engaged in all sectors and to rake it mandatory. Increasing use of modern communication devices should be resorted to. Programme-learning packages need to be created and distance learning methodologies employed to enable self-development and training of all scientific and technical personnel. This would form part of the strategy to achieve the objectives relating to engineering and technical education during the Eighth Plan in the country. Hence the imperative need for encouraging distance education mode in Engineering and Technology.

The working engineers in the country, especially those who are in the far flung areas, need opportunities to upgrade their expertise and qualifications. Distance education mode can provide the needed opportunity. The Jawaharlal Nehru Technological University, Hyderabad is the first in the country to provide distance education opportunities in Engineering and Technology to working engineers. It is offering B.Tech. and M.Tech., Programmes through distance education mode.

Distance education at university level could be offered through two distinct modes. They are: A conventional university may offer distance education programmes in addition to traditional class room teaching (dual mode) or an institution may solely devote to teaching at a distance (single mode). Marian Croft, in one of his papers, raises the pertinent questions of how and where future educational needs can best be met. Does the conventional university provide us with the best hope? Or the open universities with their remarkable contributions to accessibility and equity? Or does the best answer lie somewhere between the two or in both? In many countries, distance education at the university level is already active in dual mode institutions. For example, in Canada the University of Waterloo, Laurentian University, the University of Ottawa and several others had distance education programmes before Athabasca University was founded as a single mode institution. Similar is the case with India. In other countries, like Australia, distance education has remained within the traditional universities. In the United Kingdom, the success of the Open University led to the creation of the Open College and now the Open Polytechnic, as well as to distance education programmes in other institutions. What would be the best approach for India? This is what the present Conference should deliberate and suggest formulation of a suitable approach. A mixture of the following approaches could be considered for discussion.

i. The existing dual mode universities could be encouraged and strengthened for Distance education.
ii. The other conventional universities may also be encouraged to take up distance educationProgrammes.
iii. More number of single mode institutions may be established. This is in consonance with the recommendation of the Central Advisory Board of Education (CABE) that each state should establish an open university. The IGNOU should provide technical and consultancy support to the State Governments for this purpose. The Distance Education Council should prepare guidelines for providing financial support to State Open Universities for their development. Such assistance should include support to develop new programmes and courses. The course materials already produced by the IGNOU and other open universities should be made available to new State Open Universities which could offer them through the languages of the region so that access to Open University programmes is widened. In order to promote the Open University system on a significant scale, the existing rules framed by the University Grants Commission

(UGC) for declaring open universities fit for central assistance should be reviewed.

iv. Providing for mobility and exchangeability between the formal and non-formal systems of education. The MOU signed between IGNOU and the Pondicherry University is the finest example in this regard.

I am sure the Conference will deliberate some of these issues and come out with fruitful suggestions. I now take pleasure in inaugurating the Conference and wish it a grand success.

CHALLENGES TO HIGHER EDUCATION AND RESEARCH IN INDIA

INTRODUCTION

After independence, we wanted to build a modern, strong, dynamic and self-reliant India which could stand abreast with the developed nations. While working towards this end, the country had faced the greater challenge of rapidly industrialising the then predominantly agricultural economy and in the process it had to create wide-based infrastructure in higher and technical education institutions, research laboratories and industries, covering a wide spectrum of disciplines and capabilities. During the 90's, the country is becoming progressively more integrated into the global economy. With the restructuring of the economy, new industrial and trade policies and liberalisation, the Indian industry is exposed to domestic and global competition. Knowledge based industries will be on the increase. The levels of skills and quality of R & D required are going to be high to maintain high quality of productivity at par with world standards. Technology plays an important role. We require a. high level of scientific capability too, as competitiveness in technology requires it. We have to increase our research efforts to catch up with the rest of the world in frontier areas of knowledge which will dominate and determine the course of the 21st century. We cannot also ignore basic research. Erosion in human values is another area causing concern. In this situation, the higher education system should identify the emerging challenges and respond to them adequately.

HIGHER EDUCATION DEVELOPMENT:

We have built a vast higher education system which is one of the largest in the world. There are at present 153 universities, 34 deemed to be universities, 7958 colleges and the total enrolment in higher education system is around 48 lakhs. It is estimated that the total student enrolment at the end of 1995 will be around 60 lakhs. The faculty strength is around 2.78 lakhs. In addition, there is a vast network of technical education, including colleges and institutions offering courses in engineering, medical sciences, management, pharmacology etc. It is on account of this extensive higher and technical education system and the human resource graduating from them that India is perceived to be among the biggest producers of scientific and technical manpower.

Planwise approved outlays for education including general higher and technical education are shown in Table-1 (page 367). It may be seen that the percentage of higher education out of the total allocation for education varied from 20.89% in the Sixth Plan to 11.20% in the Eighth Plan. Similarly, the corresponding percentages for technical education varied from 12.88% to 14.22%. The higher education system has done a commendable job with all its limitations, in fulfilling its role as a powerful tool for social, political and economic change in the country and also as a source of new knowledge, research and manpower generator for all sectors of the economy.

POLICY STATEMENTS ON HIGHER EDUCATION:

The National Policy on Education had stressed on: (1) creation of autonomous university departments and colleges; (2) State Councils of Higher Education (SCHE); (3) enhanced support to research; (4) strengthening of Open Universities (OUs) and Distance Education (DE); (5) consolidation of existing institutions and improvement of quality of teachers and teaching; (6) mechanism for delinking degrees from jobs; (7) establishment of a new pattern of Rural Universities; and (8) establishment of an apex body covering higher education in all areas.

The Eighth Five Year Plan document indicates the following thrust areas for higher education: (1) Integrated approach to higher education; (2) excellence in higher education; (3) expansion of education in an equitable and cost-effective manner and in the process making the higher education system financially self-supporting; (4) making higher education relevant in the context of changing socio-economic scenario; (5) promotion of value education; and (6) strengthening of management system in the universities. All these policy related approaches and programmes are being pursued for strengthening and development of higher education in general.

INDUSTRIAL DEVELOPMENT:

The country has been shifting from a predominantly agrarian economy towards an agro-industrial economy. While the industrial development, in quantitative terms, looks quite impressive, it is significant that industrial growth has fallen short of targets set in the five year plans. The conclusion must be that while we generated significant capabilities, the potential offered by the diversified industrial base has not been fully exploited. Among the plethora of reasons, inadequate access to the latest technology, implying a widening technological gap between India and the rest of the world, is one contributory factor in the under-exploitation of industrial capabilities. The Eighth Five Year Plan, while describing the growth of engineering industry, states that inadequate R & D is one of the weaknesses suffered by the industry. A sustained R & D effort has a strong bearing on industrial growth.

RESEARCH AND DEVELOPMENT:

A country such as USA invests upto US $ 150 billion on R & D while Japan invests US $ 100 billion per year. In India, we invest much less than $ 1 billion per year towards all our efforts in science and technology. India is investing about 0.9% of GNP for science and technology compared to 5 to 6% by some of the advanced countries. In Japan and USA, a high percentage of expenditure on science and technology comes from private industry. The Central Government accounted for about 76% of the total national R&D input in 1992-93, of which the major share went into applied research and experimental development.

It is worth examining the growth of R&D in industry. The Government has taken several measures to promote research in industry. By the end of 1992-93, there were 1361 in-house R & D units, in both the public and private sectors, and in the future it is likely to grow to around 1500 by the year 1995. The growth of R & D in industry remains, however, unimpressive.

R & D expenditure by industry, as a percentage of total R & D expenditure, is only21% in India, compared to 61% in U.K., 63% in Japan and 72% in U.S.A. The time has come for Indian industry to increase its contribution to R&D expenditure through either in-house R&D units or through supporting research in universities. This is essential if it is to survive against global competition. Research not only provides the best means of training and sharpening of intellect but also sows the seeds for newer application of science and technology. Three most important areas stated to be determining the course of the 21st century are: advanced materials, biotechnology and information technology. A country like India should make right efforts in building up of R & D in these areas. A good level of high quality research in basic sciences is characteristic of all developed economies. India cannot afford to neglect this aspect as well. We have a rather low ratio of R & D scientists per thousand population, which is lower than even some of the third world countries.

CHANGED SCENARIO:

Spectacular changes have taken place on the international scene which are having a profound impact on both international relations and world economy. In India too historic changes have taken place on the economic front. The government has taken new initiatives and bold decisions to reorient and restructure the economy to meet the challenges of economic crisis in the country. The Eighth Five Year Plan has been launched from 1st April, 1992 in the backdrop of certain strengths in the economy as well as certain concerns which have surfaced at the beginning of the Eighth Plan. During the nineties, the country is poised to become progressively more integrated into the global economy. Competition and pace of technological change are likely to intensify in almost all sectors of the economy. In essence, the overall changed scenario could be viewed in terms of: (i) resources crunch, (ii) economic reforms with considerable dose of liberalisation, (iii) globalisation of Indian economy, and (iv) Indian industry getting exposed to global competition. An area which needs urgent focussed attention is the 'upholding of the value system'. This is particularly because of the growing divisive forces, narrow parochialism, separatist tendencies, considerable fall in moral, social, ethical and national values, both in personal and public life. The "erosion in human values" aspect even though it has a global dimension, is to be considered either directly or indirectly as a part of the changed scenario.

IMPACT ON INDUSTRY:

In the regime of New Industrial Policy and liberalisation and in the context of globalisation of the Indian economy, the Indian industry is exposed to more domestic and global competition. Knowledge-based industries will be on the increase. The level of skills required is going to be high. Industries need to have a workforce having a scientific bent of mind and possess the much needed scientific temper and skill to maintain high quality of productivity at par with world standards. They also need a high quality R & D support. The industries, in this context, need the help of universities and other institutions of higher learning, the national R & D laboratories and the scientific bodies and academies much more than ever before. Industries should build up confidence in the indigenous capability and utilise it rather than looking for soft options of foreign consultancy and technology import.

CHALLENGES TO HIGHER EDUCATION AND RESEARCH:

The higher education system at present suffers from several weaknesses such as: (1) proliferation of sub-standard institutions, (2) failure to maintain academic calendar, (3) outdated curriculum, (4) disparities in the quality of education, and (5) lack of adequate support for research. This apart, the system of higher education and research faces three major challenges in the changed scenario. They are: (a) to cope up with the inadequate resources situation, and (b) to respond adequately to the demand of providing (i) competent manpower and (ii) high quality R & D support, (c) to uphold the value system. These challenges imply the following imperatives: (a) Optimal utilisation of resources, (b) resources mobilisation, (c) collaboration, networking and sharing of facilities, (d) undertaking international interaction, collaboration and consultancy activities, (e) seeking excellence and relevance in the R & D efforts, and (f) aiming at development of competent and relevant manpower, (g) implementation of value orientation of education programme.

RESPONDING TO THE CHALLENGES:

The higher education system should be prepared to respond adequately to the emerging challenges in the 90's. It should be made to be more vibrant, flexible, modern and relevance built into it. Some of the following measures suggested could help to cope up with the changed situation.

1. RISING UPTO THE EXPECTATIONS OF PANDIT NEHRU:

Pandit Nehru's vision of a university, reflected in his Convocation address at Allahabad University, is still relevant in the present day context. He said "A University stands for humanism, for tolerance, for reason, for progress, for the adventure of ideas and for the search for truth. It stands for the onward march of the human race towards ever higher objectives. If the Universities discharge their duty adequately, then it is well with the nation and the people . . . ." In the present day situation if the University system were to respond and measure up to the expectations of Nehru, it has to lay stress on and pursue four objectives: (1) excellence, (2) modernisation, (3) interaction (4) self-reliance. All these four are inter-related. A true pursuit of excellence in all spheres of activities of a university will help imbibing and nurturing in the university life the qualities of humanism, tolerance, reason and adventure of ideas, search for truth and thereby will help leading the humanity towards ever higher objectives. Modernisation in terms of courses, facilities, evaluation methods and faculty upgradation will in turn enrich the teaching, research, examination system and extension activities. Modernisation will equip the university better to play its role effectively. Interaction and inter-dependence are the well-recognised concepts in the present day global situation. Universities are no exception to this. They should come out of their ivory tower concept and interact with the outside world viz., the society, the government, sister institutions, lower level institutions, industrial organisations, national laboratories, national academies, professional bodies etc. Through interaction, the university's excellence should be shared for national development.

For achieving excellence, a university should have academic, financial and administrative autonomy. Considerable academic autonomy is already available. There should be ample financial and administrative autonomy as well. In the present day system of government funding there is rigidity coupled with inadequacy. The inadequate situation is going to be worse in the context of the resources crunch. Financial autonomy is vital for continuation of the institutions as real centres of excellence. Therefore, the institutions should strive for fund generation and reduce their dependence on government gradually and thus pave the way towards self-reliance.

CORPUS FUND

Creation of 'corpus fund' for each university or institution would be an appropriate mechanism to achieve the objective of self-reliance. The corpus will be in the form of an endowment fund. Revenue obtained from such fund can eventually be used to reduce the required support from the government. The corpus fund could be created with contributions from industry, alumni, charitable trusts etc., as well as from the government. Indian Institutes of Technology, Indian Institute of Science and Indian Institutes of Management have already accepted the concept and they are in the process of creating corpus funds with the support of the government.

2. RESOURCE MOBILISATION:

In the present inadequate resources scenario, it is incumbent on the universities and other institutions of higher learning to take up measures for resource generation. The time has come that the government alone cannot bear the total burden of financing the higher education. Additional resources are to be mobilised to share the cost. This is not peculiar to India alone and it is the case with many other countries too. If the universities have to manage their financial affairs more professionally, they will require finding ways and means of raising additional resources without government intervention.

A) COVERING RECURRING EXPENSES:

Some of the measures by which they can be made self-reliant for their recurring expenses are: (i) by increasing the fees to more realistic levels, (ii) by permitting to charge from foreign students (10% of the total strength) a reasonable tuition fees in foreign exchange, (iii) by increasing the over-head charges on the outside funded sponsored projects.

B) CONSULTANCY SERVICES:

With the best brains and high quality infrastructure available in some of the best universities of the country, it should be possible to take up consultancy services for the benefit of the Indian industry and other sectors of economy. One might even think offering of international consultancy. Educational consultancy would include institution building, establishment of specialised library facilities, development of curriculum, organizing continuing education programmes like seminars and short courses, joint research projects, faculty development and staff training. Through industrial consultancy a university can help closer interaction between the educational institutions and industry in the recipient country by sending experienced faculty and assisting them in taking up industrial consultancy assignments and extending the specialised analysis and testing facilities available at some of our most advanced universities. Universities can also extend consultancy services directly to industries abroad. The universities have to organise themselves to undertake consultancy effectively and at the same time make sure that the ongoing academic and research activities will not suffer because of the consultancy activities. Through publications and various other channels the universities have to project their capabilities for offering consultancy services. For this purpose, it would be helpful if a separate Consultancy Cell is established in the university for liaison activity and to coordinate consultancy assignments.

C) SHARING OF LIBRARY AND INFORMATION RESOURCES THROUGH NETWORKING:

The past few decades have witnessed knowledge and information explosion the world over. It has been increasingly realised that access to information holds the key to development. Libraries and information centres in India have been striving to do their best in terms of dissemination of knowledge and information with all their limitations. Internationalisation of business and global competition has led to a sudden increase in the international trans-border information flow. Information has become a saleable commodity with high inflationary trends on account of the sudden demand. This calls for heavy budgets in libraries even to maintain a reasonable level of acquisition of journals, books and reports. Similar is the case with the other information centres too. At the same time, they are also faced with the inadequate financial resources. Under these circumstances, resource sharing and cooperative functioning through networking becomes vital. Efficient resources sharing can be achieved by using the recent advances in information technology for realising a network of libraries and information centres. A number of Wide Area Networks (WANs) and metropolitan library networks have emerged in the country. The notable WANs are NICNET, ERNET, SIRNET, INDONET and INET. In addition, there is INFLIBNET, a major initiative from the University Grants Commission for inter-connecting universities, colleges and research institutes countrywide. There are also centres like INSDOC, National Centre for Science Information, Centre for Social Science Information etc. In the present day context of the limited resources, it is imperative that an integrated view is taken on these networks and centres and possibility of sharing resources among them is explored to avoid duplication and to maximise their resource utilisation, if necessary, through wider networking. It is also important to take simultaneously an integrated view of the library automation requirements at the university libraries and other centres, as they form the base for successful networking. Having seized with this problem, the Planning Commission organised a brain storming session on sharing of library and information resources through networking in the Planning Commission recently. The outcome of the brain storming session will be in the form of an Approach Paper on 'Sharing of Library and Information Resources through Networking', which is being finalised by a task group.

D) INTERACTION BETWEEN UNIVERSITIES-INDUSTRIES-NATIONAL R & D LABORATORIES-NATIONAL ACADEMIES AND PROFESSIONAL BODIES:

The need for interaction and linkages between universities-industries-national R & D laboratories-national academies and professional bodies is more pronounced now in the context of the resources crunch situation. The interaction will result in (i) sharing and optimising the use of resources, (ii) development of indigenous technology appropriate to our national priorities and resources, (iii) help adapting the imported technology wherever needed for preparing the industries to meet global competitiveness, (iv) enriching teaching and research in universities with the backup of practical and field experience, (v) universities and R & D laboratories getting valuable clues for research orientation and (vi) fund generation. The process of interaction will contribute towards excellence, which in turn will contribute towards national development. A Model for University-Industry-R & D Laboratory interaction has been formulated by me and published. The implementation of the model will go a long way in realising the fruits of interaction effectively. The Model has since been modified to include the scientific and other academies and institutions in the process of interaction (This Model is presented else where in this volume).

3. EDUCATION AND RESEARCH IN SCIENCE & TECHNOLOGY:

The premise that science and technology are intimately related to productivity, economic development and international competitiveness is all the more true in the present day changed scenario. A series of brain storming sessions were held in the Planning Commission on higher education and technical education, including management education, in the context of the changed economic scenario. Perspectives for development in Indian Institutes of Technology (IITs), Indian Institutes of Management (IIMs), Regional Engineering Colleges (RECs), Technical Teachers' Training Institutes (TTTIs) and Polytechnics and their imperative roles in the changed situation have been discussed in separate sessions and well documented. These documents spell out the reorientation needed in technical education at all levels. The brain storming sessions on higher education provided the inputs for the Eighth Plan.

As an outcome of the brain storming session on IITs, four areas were identified namely thrust area development in mission mode, international consultancy, industrial foundation and creation of corpus fund. Under thrust area development, the five IITs and IISc., Bangalore have identified eight generic areas for taking up focussed Technology Development Missions (TDM). List is shown in Table-1. The Missions include areas of strategic importance and export potential. They involve not only major research component but also commitment to technology development through innovation and its subsequent transfer to public or private sector industry. Developing, testing, and delivery of technology are very much part of the package. The Planning Commission has earmarked the required funds for these Technology Missions.

In addition to technology, certain science disciplines also need focussed attention as competitiveness in technology would require a high level of scientific capability. Some of these science disciplines are mathematical science (covering broadly mathematics, statistics, operations research, computer sciences) physical sciences, chemical sciences, biological sciences etc. Recently a brain storming session on "Mathematical Sciences in the context of changed economic scenario" has been organised in the Planning Commission and a Task Group has been constituted to prepare an approach paper on Mathematical Sciences, covering education, research and training aspects. Such brain storming sessions on the other prominent sciences / disciplines are also needed.

4. DISTANCE EDUCATION:

"Distance Education" concept assumes greater significance in the present day Indian context. The higher educational system must meet the challenge of increasing student population. The formal system with its limitations and rigidities in admission requirements may not alone be able to meet this challenge. The pressure could be relieved through an alternative system adopting a methodology which allows flexibility in operation, diversity in academic content not bound by time and space. This alternative approach is possible only through the open higher education adopting distance teaching. The distance education institutions accounted for about 11.5% of enrolment in higher education during 1991. The additional enrolment in higher education during the Eighth Plan is estimated to be around 10 lakhs of which 9 lakhs will be at the undergraduate level. The Eighth Plan envisages that this expansion, keeping in view the present resources crunch, has to be accommodated in an equitable and cost-effective manner, mainly by large scale expansion of distance education system. The programmes of Distance Education should absorb at least 50 per cent of the additional enrolment during the Eighth Plan. In many countries distance education at the university level is already active in dual mode institutions. In countries like Australia, distance education has remained within the traditional universities. What would be the best approach for India? For the Indian conditions, a proper mixture of the following approaches could be adopted.

i. The existing dual mode universities could be encouraged and strengthened for distance education.

ii. The other conventional universities may also be encouraged to take up distance education programmes.

iii. More number of single mode institutions may be established.

iv. Providing for mobility and exchangeability between the formal and non-formal systems of education. The MOU signed between IGNOU and the Pondicherry University is the finest example in this regard.

5. VALUE ORIENTATION OF EDUCATION:

There has been a growing concern in the country over the erosion of essential values which is reflected in the fall of moral, social, ethical and national values, both in personal and public life. It is worthwhile to quote two passages from the Report of the Education Commission (1964-66), which are still relevant. "India has a unique advantage with her great tradition of duty without self-involvement, unacquisitive temperament, tolerance, and innate love of peace and reverence for all living things. Too often are those precious assets forgotten and we tend to relapse into moods of pessimism, fears and forebodings, discord and destructive criticism. A new pride and a deeper faith expressed in living for the noble ideas of **peace** and **freedom, truth** and **compassion** are now needed".

"Modernisation did not mean—least of all in our national situation—a refusal to recognise the importance of or to inculcate necessary moral and spiritual values and self-discipline. While a combination of ignorance with goodness may be futile, that of knowledge with a lack of essential values may be dangerous".

The Planning Commission recognising the need for added focussed attention on value orientation of education felt it should be studied in-depth and in its totality in relation to various sectors of education and several developmental agencies. A Core Group on Value Orientation of Education was thus set up by the Planning Commission in January, 1992 under my Chairmanship with very wide terms of reference and with membership from various agencies and experts in the subject. The Core Group was able to present a concrete plan of action relating to various sectors of educational development, involving interdepartmental collaboration. As a follow-up of one of the recommendations of the Core Group, the

Ministry of Human Resources Development has constituted a Standing Committee on Value Orientation of Education under my Chairmanship to oversee the implementation of value orientation of education at all levels right from the school to university level in the country. The Standing Committee is working out the detailed blue print with specific time frames, for the implementation of value orientation of education at school level, college level, university level and to use the electronic and print media and to involve nongovernmental voluntary organisations for promotion of value orientation of education. At this stage, it is worthwhile to recall the concluding para of the Report of the Core Group on Value Orientation of Education. It says: "The urgent need for value orientation of education should not be merely a matter of brave declarations. The programme needs patience and careful and comprehensive planning. It needs to be built into our educational system, our media institutions, our cultural organisations, in the teachings of science and humanities, in all kinds of educational, social and political endeavours so that they have cumulative impact on the minds of our children and youth when they are receptive and uncorrupted by cynicism. If we have the necessary determination and firm commitment then 'we shall overcome'."

CONCLUSION:

The higher education system in the country is now being put to test. Universities should undertake intensive introspection and reorient themselves to respond adequately to the emerging challenges of the changed economic scenario in the country. In addition, it has the added responsibility in contributing to strengthen the value system in the society. At the same time, one should keep in view the imperative need to free the system from unnecessary constraints and political interference and provide the needed academic, administrative and financial freedom, and on the part of the system it should be amenable to accountability.

TABLE-1
TECHNOLOGY DEVELOPMENT MISSIONS AT IITs

No.	General Area	Coordinating IITs
1.	Food Process Engineering	Kharagpur, Bombay
2.	Integrated Design & Competitive Manufacturing (Engineering & Industrial Design, Fms)	Kanpur, Bombay
3.	Photonic Devices And Technology	Delhi, Kharagpur
4.	Energy Efficient Technology And Devices (Fuel Efficient Engines & Coal)	Madras, Delhi
5. *	Natural Hazards Mitigation (Use of Remote Sensing Applications)	Bombay, Madras
6.	Communication, Networking & Intelligent Automation	Kanpur, Kharagpur
7.	New Materials (Composites & Electronic Materials)	Madras, Delhi, Kanpur
8.	Biotechnology & Genetic Engineering	IISc, Bangalore In Collaboration with other IITs.

*This area was subsequently dropped.

ACCOUNTABILITY IN HIGHER EDUCATION

The importance of the theme of the Seminar "Accountability in Higher Education" needs no emphasis and it has a wide scope. It has come at a more appropriate time when new imperatives are added to higher education system in the context of the changed global scenario and the resources crunch situation in the country. I must congratulate the Association of Indian Universities for selecting such an important and relevant theme for the seminar. I am grateful for being invited to the seminar.

Accountability relates to the assigned responsibilities and tasks and funds received for that purpose. Accountability, when it is applied to higher education, could mean, in a broader sense, to what extent contributions have been made by it in realising the national goals, objectives and aspirations and also in meeting the requirements of the people with changing times.

While discussing 'accountability in higher education', one has to look at the total higher education system with all its various sub-systems. These are to be discussed relating their tasks to their accountability. Since this happens to be the inaugural session, I will make a brief reference to all major sub-systems.

CENTRAL AND STATE GOVERNMENTS:

The Central and State Governments formulate policies, programmes and guidelines for the development and expansion of higher education and provide financial resources. Accountability in this context relates to: (i) Formulation of NPE and POA and adoption by the Parliament (ii) Provide funding following the Government policy and keeping in view the resources situation. (iii) Being accountable to Parliament / Legislative Assemblies.

UNIVERSITY GRANTS COMMISSION (UGC):

The general duty of the University Grants Commission is to take such steps as it may deem fit for the promotion and coordination of university education and for the determination and maintenance of standards of teaching, examination and research in universities and allocate and disburse grants to the universities, deemed to be universities and colleges. The UGC, through its various general programmes and quality improvement programmes and schemes and through funding out of the resources made available by the government, has been striving to improve and promote quality of teaching, research and extension aspects of higher education in the country and to maintain standards. 'Determination' (of standards) aspect, perhaps, has been inadequately attempted. Now with the establishment of the Accreditation Council, this function gets activated and implemented. The areas in which it is standing helpless are the proliferation of sub-standard institutions, implementation of the code of ethics for teachers which is already linked with their increased pay scales package and make the university system work adhering to the norm of minimum number of working days. To tackle these problems it needs the political will and support too. Rejuvenation of the value system through education will go a long way to improve the situation.

NATIONAL ACCREDITATION AND ASSESSMENT COUNCIL:

Operationalisation of an effective system of accreditation in the country will gradually lead to the establishment of norms and criterion for institutional performance assessment and methodologies and tools for systematic institutional self-study and selfevaluation.

The institutions themselves will qualitatively benefit through integration of this element of assessment into the institutional culture.

The UGC has already initiated action to set up a National Assessment and Accreditation Council (NAAC). The Council has to attempt efforts towards determination of standards and assisting towards achieving quality and maintenance of standards in higher education through the accreditation process. Since the Accreditation Council is yet to begin its work the aspect of accountability needs to be looked at after the lapse of a reasonable time frame.

ASSOCIATION OF INDIAN UNIVERSITIES (A.I.U.):

The AIU is serving as an inter-university organisation with multiple objectives, with a view to promoting university activities, especially by way of sharing information and increasing cooperation in the field of education, culture, sports and allied areas. The Association has been striving to serve the cause of Indian universities. Involving the Vice-Chancellors of all the member-institutions in regular meetings to discuss matters of common interest, particularly at the annual meeting of the Association, has certainly been contributing to the cause of higher education. It's accountability has to be judged in relation to the fulfillment of its objectives.

INDIRA GANDHI NATIONAL OPEN UNIVERSITY (IGNOU):

IGNOU is a national University and three distinct functions are envisaged in its Act.
1. Promotion of open and distance education systems. 2. Coordination, determination and maintenance of standards in open and distance education systems. 3. Funding various distance education systems in the country.
The university is charged with the determination and promotion of distance education standards in the entire country besides its own function as an Open University. The accountability is to be judged in terms of its fulfillment of these responsibilities.

VARIOUS SCIENTIFIC COUNCILS / ORGANISATIONS / ACADEMIES:

The general objectives of these organisations are to promote research, training and continuing education programmes for professional upgradation. An intensive introspection is needed in assessing their success in fulfilling their objectives. The Institution of Engineers is preparing a 'Perspective Plan' document. Such attempts of clear thinking in drawing up perspectives are needed.

UNIVERSITIES / INSTITUTIONS / COLLEGES:

The higher education institutions have the following responsibilities:-
(i) Providing relevant and competent manpower (ii) Advancement of knowledge (iii) Undertaking relevant research (R & D) (iv) Taking up extension activities (v) In general, measuring up to Nehru's vision of a University, which states that "A University stands for humanism, for tolerance, for reason, for progress, for the adventure of ideas and for the search for truth. It stands for the onward march of the human race towards ever higher objectives. If the universities discharge their duty adequately, then it is well with the nation and the people . . . ."

In the present changed scenario in the global as well as national context, the levels of skills and quality of R & D required are going to be high to maintain high quality of productivity at par with the world standards. Technology plays an important role. We require a high level of scientific capability too as competitiveness in technology requires such a capability. We have to increase our research efforts to catch-up with the rest of the world in the frontier areas of knowledge which will dominate and determine the course of the 21st century. We cannot also ignore our basic research. Erosion of human values is another area causing concern. In addition, the higher education system suffers from several weaknesses such as: (1) proliferation of sub-standard institutions, (2) failure to maintain academic calendar, (3) out-dated curriculum, (4) disparities in the quality of education. The system of higher education and research faces three major challenges in the changed scenario. They are: (a) to cope up with the inadequate resources situation, and (b) to respond adequately to the demand of providing (i) competent manpower and (ii) high quality R & D support, (c) to uphold the value system. These challenges imply the following imperatives: (a) Optimal utilisation of resources, (b) resources mobilisation, (c) collaboration, networking and sharing of facilities, (d) undertaking international interaction, collaboration and consultancy activities, (e) seeking excellence and relevance in the research efforts, (f) aiming at development of competent and relevant manpower, (g) implementation of value orientation of education programme. The higher education system should be prepared to respond adequately to these emerging challenges in the 90's. It should be more vibrant, flexible, modern and relevance has to be built into it. For achieving excellence, a university should have academic, financial and administrative autonomy. Considerable academic autonomy is already available. There should be ample financial and administrative autonomy as well. In the present day system of government funding there is rigidity coupled with inadequacy. The inadequate situation is going to be worse in the context of the resources crunch. Financial autonomy is vital for continuation of the institutions as real centres of excellence. Therefore, the institutions should strive for fund generation and reduce their dependence on government gradually. Establishment of a 'corpus fund' will be a right step in this direction.

INDUSTRIES:

The country has been shifting from a predominantly agrarian economy towards an agro-industrial economy. While the industrial development, in quantitative terms, looks quite impressive, it is significant that industrial growth has fallen short of targets set in the five year plans. The conclusion must be that while we generated significant capabilities, the potential offered by the diversified industrial base has not been fully exploited. Among the plethora of reasons, inadequate access to the latest technology, implying a widening technological gap between India and the rest of the world, is one contributory factor in the under-exploitation of industrial capabilities. The Eighth Five Year Plan, while describing the growth of engineering industry, states that inadequate R & D is one of the weaknesses suffered by the industry. A sustained R & D effort has a strong bearing on industrial growth.

In Japan and USA, a high percentage of expenditure on science and technology comes from private industry. In India, there is a preponderance of Central Government expenditure on R&D in almost all spheres of activity. The Central Government accounted for about 76% of the total national R & D input in 1992-93, of which the major share went into applied research and experimental development.

R & D expenditure by industry, as a percentage of total R & D expenditure, is only 21% in India, compared to 61% in U.K., 63% in Japan and 72% in U.S.A. The time has come for Indian industry to increase its contribution to R&D expenditure through either in-house R&D units or through supporting research in universities. This is essential if it is to survive against global competition. The need for interaction and linkages between universities, industries, national R & D laboratories, national academies and professional bodies are more pronounced now in the changed scenario.

SOCIETY:

The society has also a responsibility, in shaping education according to its requirements and the changing times. Commensurate with the needs and aspirations of the people, the society around, the universities and colleges should interact actively in the formulation of the academic programmes. The society should help the institutions in fund generation activities. The achievement in this regard seems to be inadequate and needs to be boosted up.

The society's accountability could be measured in terms of: (i) Extending cooperation and interaction (ii) Offering feed back on the academic programmes (iii) Demand and help in formulating relevant academic programmes (iv) Philanthropic support Thus the accountability in higher education has to be viewed in its entirety, identifying the inter-connectivities of the various sub-systems for having a clear perspective.

STRATEGIES FOR UNIVERSITY-INDUSTRY COOPERATION IN ENGINEERING, SCIENCES AND TECHNOLOGY IN INDIA

I am indeed very happy to participate in this Forum on "Strategies for University—Industry Cooperation in Engineering, Sciences and Technology in India" being organised by UNESCO as a part of its Technical Support Services Programme to the Government of India.

I am grateful for being invited to Chair the Forum. I take this opportunity to congratulate UNESCO and UNDP, in particular Dr. John V. Kingston, Director, UNESCO, New Delhi.

The purpose of the Forum is to review the Report and Action Plan formulated by the UNESCO. The Action Plan is the synthesis of a study carried out in cooperation with 30 university departments and wide associated industries. The purpose of the Action Plan is to develop a set of policy recommendations for implementation for the government in order to stimulate an effective, mutually beneficial and self-sustaining interaction between universities and industries. It is indeed heartening to note that so many high ranking policy and decision makers, academics, scientists and industrialists are present here to participate in the Forum discussions. With the inputs of the Forum Members, the Report and the Action Plan will be finalised.

India has built a wide based infrastructure in higher and technical education, National R & D laboratories and industries covering a broad spectrum of disciplines and capabilities. Indian Professional Bodies and National Academies of Sciences and Engineering enjoy a high status and occupy commanding positions in the scientific and academic circles. However, interaction among these four has been inadequate or in some cases it is nil. Time is now ripe for meaningful interaction" and linkages among them in the changed global and national economic scenarios.

The result of the impact of the global changes and the national economic scenario is the emergence of an era of global consciousness. The Indian industry is exposed to global and indigenous competitiveness. To meet this challenge the industry requires modernisation, upgradation of the competence of the work force, utilisation of modern management techniques, increased efficiency and productivity and to maintain quality. The situation thus requires a work force having a scientific bent of mind to maintain high quality and productivity at par with the world standards. Relevant R & D efforts should also be geared up. The higher and technical educational institutions have, therefore, to respond effectively to these emerging challenges to train men and women of calibre and competence of world standards and provide the needed R & D capability. Similarly, the national R & D laboratories should develop and provide the needed R & D support to the industry for facing the global competition. The professional bodies and National academies should also contribute their own bit. On the part of Indian industries, they should build up confidence in the indigenous R & D capability and refrain from taking the easy option of importing technology.

The higher and technical education systems in this country are now being put to test.

They face two major imperatives in the changed scenario. They are : (a) to cope up with the resources inadequacy situation, and (b) to respond to the demand of providing competent manpower and high quality R & D support to industry and other related sectors of the economy.

One of the ways of making higher and technical education more purposeful is to build up strong linkages between universities, industries, national R & D laboratories and National academies. This linkage will result in (i) sharing and optimising the use of resources, (ii) development of indigenous technology appropriate to our national priorities and resources, (iii) adapting the imported technology wherever needed for preparing the industries to meet global competitiveness, enriching teaching and research in universities with the back up of practical and field experience, universities and R & D laboratories getting valuable clues for research orientation and, (vi) fund generation by the universities, R & D laboratories and the academies. The process of interaction will contribute towards excellence, which in turn will contribute towards national development. A Model for University, Industry, R & D Laboratory and National Academies Interaction has been proposed by me and published (shown in this book at page 154). The Model identifies areas of interaction between universities, industries, national R & D laboratories, professional bodies and National academies. A Standing Committee on University-Industry-National R & D Laboratories-Professional Bodies and National Academies Interaction has been constituted under my Chairmanship by the Planning Commission to promote and oversee the cooperation among these constituents. The Standing Committee is now in the process of preparing an Approach Paper on University-Industry—National R & D Laboratories-Professional Bodies and National Academies Interaction in India. I am sure the outcome of this UNESCO Forum will provide valuable inputs in this effort.

TECHNOLOGY DEVELOPMENT MISSIONS:

We have to encourage universities and Indian Institutes of Technology and other engineering institutions to take up technology development missions so as to boost up our indigenous R & D effort. The Indian Institutes of Technology (IITs) are the institutes of national importance and considered as centres of excellence in engineering and technology.

A series of Brain Storming Sessions were organised in the Planning Commission on IITs in the context of the changed economic scenario and in the context of the Prime Minister's observations relating to the need for modernising teaching, research and other facilities in the engineering institutions like IITs. The discussions in the brain storming sessions first resulted in the development of an approach paper dealing with new thrust areas for technology development, international consultancy, creation of corpus fund and industrial foundations.

As a result of further discussions, the five IITs and the Indian Institute of Science, Bangalore, have identified seven generic areas for taking up focussed technology development missions. The missions involve not only major research component but also a commitment to technology development through innovation and its subsequent transfer to public / private sector industry. Developing, testing and delivery of technology are very much part of the package. The missions include areas of strategic significance and export potential. It is envisaged that the funding of these projects should be through multiple agencies like Planning Commission / Ministry of Human Resource Development, other concerned ministries and industries. A National Steering Committee under my chairmanship has been constituted to monitor the progress of the technology development missions. These missions will set an example for the development of the required indigenous R & D through putting together some of best brains in the academic institutions in a cooperative mode and with the involvement of the Industries. If similar exercises are undertaken by the universities it will have a catalytic effect on University-Industry cooperation.

The UNESCO Report and the Plan of Action relate to the cooperation between the two constituents of national development, namely, Universities (including other Engineering and Technology Institutions) and the Industries. It is really an excellent attempt and they would certainly provide sound strategies for University-Industry cooperation in Engineering, Sciences and Technology in India.

Perhaps another attempt may be needed to build strategies for cooperation among all the four constituents i.e., Universities, Industries, National R & D Laboratories and National Academies taken together. This could possibly arise out of the Approach Paper being prepared by the Task Group of the Planning Commission's Standing Committee on University-Industry-National R & D Laboratories—Professional Bodies and National Academies interaction.

CHANGING TIMES—NEED FOR
UNIVERSITIES' REORIENTATION

INTRODUCTION:

"A University stands for humanism, for tolerance, for reason, for progress, for the adventure of ideas and for the search for truth. It stands for the onward march of the human race towards ever higher objectives. If the universities discharge their duty adequately, then it is well with the nation and the people . . . ."

Pandit Nehru

Traditionally the universities are contributing towards: (i) enrichment of human values (ii) development of the individual, (iii) national development, and (iv) world peace and progress—directly or indirectly. Pandit Jawaharlal Nehru's above quotation amply enshrines the essence of a university. While humanism, tolerance, reason, adventure of ideas and search for truth become its life supporting system, its sustained ability to discharge its duties adequately could form the bed-rock for progress and development of the nation. The higher education, including technical education is thus supposed to play an important role through facilitating individual's development, upholding and preserving the value system and providing relevant manpower and quality research outputs for national development. The question whether all the universities are fulfilling these objectives in recent times or not, is debatable. However, the system of higher and technical education should be flexible and resilient enough to absorb the effects of changing times and thereby should become adequately responsive through appropriate reorientation.

CHANGING TIMES:

Recently unconceivable changes have taken place right across the globe. Thou changes will have an impact on the international relations and the world economy in general Within the country also spectacular changes have taken place on the economic front through restructuring of the economy with considerable dose of liberalisation. The country is gradually getting integrated into the global economy. The result of globalisation is that the industries have to face global and indigenous competition. For this they should resort to modernisation, upgradation of technology and the competence of the work force, adopting modern management techniques, increasing efficiency and improving quality and productivity. There is resources inadequacy situation prevailing in the country. There is also a serious concern for erosion of the human values. All these present a changed setting for reorientation by all the major constituents in national development and a university is no exception to this.

IMPACT ON THE UNIVERSITY SYSTEM:

The impact of the changed scenario makes demands on the university system for the following, which are to be responded through necessary reorientation : (i) to provide competent and relevant manpower, (ii) to provide quality R & D support to industry, (iii) to uphold and enrich the value system, and (iv) to cope up with inadequate resources situation.

NEEDED REORIENTATION:

In the above changed situation, the university system has to reorient itself suitably and undertake the following: (i) bring in more relevance in teaching and research while maintaining quality (ii) provide quality R & D support to industry, (iii) work towards self-reliance, and (iv) take up value orientation of education.

RELEVANCE:

Presently there appears to be a structural imbalance between the requirements of the industry and business sectors and the curricula pursued by the universities. This gap is to be bridged through bringing in more relevance in the course contents as well as the research programmes. There should be a conscious effort to blend scholarship with relevance in respect of teaching and research. University-industry interaction can play a major role in this regard. The course content could be formulated with the active participation by the people from the industry. There should be exchange of faculty and experts and between the universities and the industries. Students should have access to industries for practical training. There should be a symbiotic relationship between university and *industry* for mutual benefit. Some of the areas of cooperation and benefits could be the following : *(a)* Curriculum development, (b) Mobility and exchange of faculty, (c) Training of students, (d) Funding of R & D projects, (e) Consultancy, (f) Ancillaries, (g) R & D collaboration, (h) Financial resources generation, (1) Relevant R & D, (j) Cost effectiveness, (k) Time bound programmes, (1) Improved and new technology, (m) Technology adaptation, (n) Quick adaptation of human resources, and (o) Training programmes. Swaminadhan Model for University-Industry-National R & D Laboratories-Professional Bodies and Academies Interaction for Country's Economic Development identifies the areas of interaction between these constituents. The model is presented elsewhere in this volume.

INDIGENOUS R & D EFFORT:

The Indian industries need quality R & D support to acquire superior technologies and face global competition. Acquisition of new technology can take place in the following ways: (i) Technology import related to foreign investment in India; (ii) Technology import by the Indian industry; and (iii) Indigenous R & D effort. The issue of technology import related to foreign investment in India needs serious attention. It should be carefully studied and assessed as to know whether the technology brought into the country is of the first rate or of third rate. It is essential to know the correct picture so that we can guard against their inferior quality.

Regarding the technology import by the Indian industry, it is logical to believe that the quality of technology imported may not suffer but one cannot be sure of getting the latest technology always . . . , Now what is importable is only purchasable technology which is out-of-date. To quote an example, Japan licenses out technology, relating to machine tools, which is almost one generation behind. Contemporary technology is not purchasable. The regimes of foreign technology denial already precluded the option of 'importing technology and will certainly do so increasingly in the future. In such a situation, if it Indian industry is to be globally competitive, the only option is of 'developing' our own technology.'

We have to encourage universities and Indian Institutes of Technology as other engineering institutions to take up technology development missions so as to boost up our indigenous R & D effort. The Indian Institutes of Technology (IITs) are the institute of national importance and considered as centres of excellence in engineering as technology.

A series of Brain Storming Sessions were organised in the Planning Commission on IITs in the context of the changed economic scenario and in the context of the Prime Minister's observations relating to the need for modernising teaching, research and other facilities in the engineering institutions like IITs. The discussions in the brain storming sessions first resulted in the development of an approach paper dealing with new thrust areas, international consultancy, creation of corpus fund and industrial foundation. As a result of further discussions, the five IITs and the Indian Institute of Science, Bangalore, have identified seven generic areas for taking up focussed Technology Development Missions (TDM).

The missions involve not only major research component but also a commitment to technology development through innovation and its subsequent transfer to public / private sector industry. Developing testing and delivery of technology are very much part of the package. The missions include areas of strategic significance and export potential. It is envisaged that the funding of these projects should be through multiple agencies like Planning Commission / Ministry of Human Resource Development, other concerned ministries and industries. A key factor of the missions is the participation by industry from the very beginning and a contribution equal to 25% of the government funding in terms of cash and services or manpower. Regional Engineering Colleges are also being encouraged to take up relevant R&D work through thrust area development and they are further encouraged to look into the R & D needs of the small scale industries sector. A National Steering Committee under my chairmanship has been constituted to monitor the progress of the technology development missions. These missions will set an example for the development of superior technology through indigenous R & D effort by putting together some of best brains in the academic institutions in a cooperative mode and with the involvement of the Industries. If similar exercises are undertaken by the universities it will have a catalytic effect on University-Industry cooperation for building up relevant and superior technological base.

SELF-RELIANCE:

Self-reliance should be interpreted in the sense that the gap between the fund requirement of the university and the fund availability from the government should be bridged by resource mobilisation through suitably reorienting the teaching and research activities. The following measures would help towards achieving self reliance : (i) Economy in expenditure, (ii) increasing cost effectiveness, (iii) mobilising resources, (iv) universityindustry interaction, and (v) corpus fund. Economy in expenditure could be achieved by "trimming the extra fat' wherever possible, by resorting to modem technology in management, sharing of facilities etc. Improving cost effectiveness involves optimisation of student intakes rationalization of staff structure and utilising the services of post-graduate students for instructional work.

Resources an be generated by rationalisation of fee structures, attracting foreign students, enhancing consultancy work and sponsored research and in offering revenue generating courses for the industry. University-industry interaction provides a major means of resource generation towards becoming self-reliant.

A corpus fund may be established in every institution and built-up to acts a steady internal source of revenue as return on investments. The corpus fund could be built up by the resources generated through consultancy, munificent contributions or donations contributions by alumni associations abroad and within the country and by matching grants from the government. The corpus fund concept would provide the needed finance autonomy to the university, in addition to the needed academic and administration autonomies.

Value Orientation of Education:

There has been a growing concern in the country over the erosion of essential values which is reflected in the fall of moral, social, ethical and national values, both in personal and public life. It is worthwhile to quote two passages from the Report of the Education Commission (1964-'66), which are still relevant. "India has a unique advantage with her great tradition of duty without selfinvolvement, Unacquisitive temperament, tolerance, and innate love of peace and reverence for all living things. Too often are those precious assets forgotten and we tend to relapse into moods of pessimism, fears and forebodings, discord and destructive criticism. A new pride and a deeper faith expressed in living for the noble ideas of peace and freedom, truth and compassion are now needed".

"Modernisation did not mean—least of all in our national situation—a refusal to recognise the importance of or to inculcate necessary moral and spiritual values and self-discipline. While a combination of ignorance with goodness may be futile, that of knowledge with a lack of essential values may be dangerous".

The Planning Commission recognising the need for added focussed attention on value orientation of education felt it should be studied in-depth and in its totality in relation to various sectors of education and several developmental agencies. A Core Group on Value Orientation of Education was thus set up by the Planning Commission in January, 1992 under my Chairmanship with very wide terms of reference and with membership from various agencies and experts in the subject. The Core Group was able to present a concrete plan of action relating to various sectors of educational development, involving interdepartmental collaboration.

As a follow-up of one of the recommendations of the Core Group, the Ministry of Human Resources Development has constituted a Standing Committee on Value Orientation of Education under my Chairmanship to oversee the implementation of value orientation of education at all levels right from the school to university level in the country The Standing Committee has been working out the detailed blue print with specific time frames, for the implementation of value orientation of education at school level, college level, university level and to use the electronic and print media and to involve nor governmental voluntary organisations for promotion of value orientation of education. The blue print for school education is already being implemented. The blue print for higher education which has been formulated, is now with the University Grants Commission. Every university and college, either general or technical, have to give serious thought to values an implement the value orientation programme with utmost concern.

CONCLUSION:

The higher education system in the country is now being put to test. Universities should undertake intensive introspection and reorient themselves to respond adequately the emerging challenges of the changed economic scenario in the country. In addition, it has the added responsibility in contributing to strengthen the value system in the society. At the same time, one should keep in view the imperative need to free the system from unnecessary constraints and political interference and provide the needed academic, administrative and financial freedom, and on the part of the system it should be amenable to accountability

RURAL HIGHER EDUCATION IN INDIA

INTRODUCTION:

"India lives in villages." These were the words of Mahatma Gandhi. The observation is still valid for the country where 75% population lives in rural India. The very basis of planning and development, the core of everything related to it is Man. An integrated package of services to the rural population must, therefore, include investments in Man. Education is the single most important factor in developing the human resources and in achieving rapid economic development. Education for the rural population gains importance in this context.

Gandhiji recognised the importance of education to the rural population and developed a revolutionary concept of education namely Basic Education or Nai Talim laying emphasis on making education conducive to the needs of our rural society. Gandhian basic education has survived in the country and represents a vital feature of our system. In the post-independence period, the University Education Commission set up by the Government of India under the Chairmanship of Dr. S. Radhakrishnan strongly urged the need for the general advancement of rural India "through an increasing range of quality, skill and training supplied through a system of rural colleges and universities". In the period followed the independence, there witnessed in the country a complementary system of education inspired by Gandhiji's idea of basic education along with the conventional system comprising primary, middle, secondary, higher secondary, degree level university institutions. As a deliberate policy of the Government, a large number of rural institutes were also set up during the Second Five Year Plan. Sri Niketan Rural Institute,

Jamia Milia Islamia, Gandhi Gram Rural Institute, Gujarat Vidya Peeth, Vidya Bhavan Rural Institute, Udaipur, Mouni Vidyapeeth, Gangotri and Sri Rama Krishna Mission Vidyalaya Rural Institute at Coimbatore were premier rural institutions developed for the mission in view. However, to meet the requirements of the time, most of these institutions faced transformations during the course of the period. Institutions like Sri Niketan Rural Institute, Jamia Milia, Gandhigram Rural Institute and Gujarat Vidyapeeth got absorbed in the traditional system of education. The others like the Vidya Bhavan Rural Institute, Mouni Vidyapeeth and Sri Rama Krishna Mission got co-opted within the formal system through affiliation with the universities. However, institutions like Gujarat Vidyapeeth and Gandhigram Institute could retain their distinct character of rural oriented and extension education. The new Rural Institutes to be set up in the future should retain this character.

NATIONAL POLICY ON EDUCATION:

The National Policy on Education 1986 strongly recommended a new pattern of rural universities on the lines of Gandhian ideas on education. To quote NPE, "to take up the challenges of micro planning at grassroots level for the transformation of rural areas". As per the Programme of Action (POA), 1992, these institutions are not envisaged as a conventional institution for award of diplomas and degrees based on terminal examinations. Rather a complex of institutions is envisaged which seeks to integrate all aspects of education with life and needs of community. These may include training with productive and creative activities, horizontally across disciplines of science, technology, humanities and social sciences and vertically across all stages of education—primary to higher education. This would help reduce the deep-rooted alienation of the conventional education from the people. The NPE 1986 and POA, 1992 also emphasised the need for a "Central Council of Rural Institute" for the formulation and implementation of a well-coordinated programme for the development of rural institutes. The Council would identify the rural institutes and other voluntary agencies engaged in Gandhian basic education of rural education which have potential for growth and are primarily meant for the rural areas but have not received sufficient support and encouragement from the Government and its agencies over the years.

RURAL HIGHER EDUCATION:

The scheme for the development of rural institutes would provide a new pattern of education based on the concept of correlation between socially useful productive work and academic study. The institutes would provide to the country well trained persons seeking new avenues of employment in rural economy, thereby improving the quality of life of rural people. The new pattern of education imparted at these institutes will go a long way in preventing exodus of rural trained manpower to urban settlement and in accelerating the development process in the rural areas.

A refreshing recent development is that the Government of India has set up a National Council of Rural Institutes (NCRI) at Hyderabad to promote rural higher education on the lines of Mahatma Gandhi's revolutionary ideas so as to take up challenges of micro planning for transformation of rural areas as envisaged in the present National Policy on Education. The Government of Andhra Pradesh also has set up Swami Ramananda Tirtha Rural Institute at Jalalpur Village in Nalagonda District, Andhra Pradesh based on the ideals and philosophy of Mahatma Gandhi and Swami Ramananda Tirtha on education and rural development. Many more such institutions are likely to come in the near future.

RURAL INSTITUTES:

The rural institutes should be developed on the following lines:

i)   To be distinct and different from the conventional universities and institutions;

ii) To serve the local rural needs and aspirations and to integrate with the life around;

iii) To offer programmes to be in tune with Gandhiji's ideals.

iv) To be a conduit for transfer of modern technology to the rural areas.

In the above context, the following should be the activities of the rural institutions:

a.   Education and training should be related to life situations in the rural areas;

b.   They should encompass horizontally across all disciplines and vertically across all the stages of education—primary to higher education level;
c.   They should offer a pattern of education based on the concept of co-relation between socially useful productive work and academic study. The education and training should be integrated with productive and creative activities;
d.   They should help the rural economy;
e.   They should facilitate encouragement to rural youth to stick on to rural areas.
f.   Integration of educational activities with production centres should take place. For this tie ups with local industries, ITIs, Community Polytechnics in the neighbourhood should be formed.
g.   Make use of the expertise and skill in the unorganised sector, e.g., artisans, craftsmen etc. of villages for training of the students.
h.   Value inculcation in the rural youth.

NATIONAL COUNCIL OF RURAL INSTITUTES:

The Council should take up the following major activities:

i.   Coordination, promotion and determination of standards in rural higher education;
ii.   Consolidation and development of the existing institutions;
iii.   Encourage establishment of new rural institutions through its involvement;
iv.   Encourage voluntary social action in rural areas in a big way.

AREAS OF OPERATION FOR THE COUNCIL:

A) EDUCATION AND RESEARCH:

a)   Organise courses relating to rural development, such as rural health and sanitation, rural industrial entrepreneurship programmes, management of cooperative institutions, micro planning etc.
b)   Facilitate linkages between technical institutions and rural institutions for rural development;

c) To carry on research studies, surveys, evaluation etc. on the use of appropriate technologies.

d) In furtherance of the objectives of the Council:

    i. publish reports, papers, periodicals, monographs and books;

    ii. Organise lectures, meetings, conferences, seminars, discussions, exhibitions etc.

B) R & D AND INNOVATION:

The Council should encourage and facilitate the following:

Agriculture and Allied Areas:
- Development of appropriate technologies for preservation of vegetables, flowers and fruits for both domestic and export market.
- Organising cool chains like pre-cooler, refrigeration, controlled atmosphere, cold storage etc.
- Development of agricultural tools and implements to reduce drudgery for rural men and women.
- Organising agro-centres.
- Organising tissue culture centres in rural areas.
- Organising embryo transfer technology centres in rural areas.

Environment:
- Focus on conservation of the environment and natural resources.
- Wasteland development and social forestry.

Energy:
- Carry on research and organise low-cost and energy-efficient cooking devices for rural people.

Water Management:
- Development of location-specific technologies for watershed development.
- Development of technologies for irrigation water management for both surface as well as ground water.

Rural Housing:
- Development and promotion of technologies for low-cost housing using local materials.

Health Care:
- Community based low-cost comprehensive health care programmes for mothers, children and disabled.
- Development of low-cost diagnostic kits.

C) TRAINING:

- Upgradation of the skills of the village artisans, who are in the unorganised sector.
- Organising village industries entrepreneurship programmes.
- Organising training programmes for health and development workers.
- Offering training programmes and short-term courses for farmers and agricultural labourers.
- Conducting training programmes for the trainers, particularly in the voluntary sectors, so that improved technologies are disseminated for the proper development of the rural areas.
- Conducting training programmes, conferences, lectures, seminars on rural development activities of particular interest to women, with an accent on improved technologies appropriate to their role in rural development.

D) SOCIAL ACTION:

- Work for the economic, social, educational and cultural development of the rural poor people.
- Build up social approaches for technology development.
- Promotion of value orientation of education and inculcation of values in the society.
- Economic empowerment of the poor through technology empowerment and gender equity.
- Work towards developing model villages.
- Service and rehabilitation activities.

- Popularise family planning.
- Take up integrated rural development programmes.
- Build up voluntary efforts in rural development with a focus on injecting new technological inputs.

E) WOMEN'S STUDIES AND GENDER EQUITY:

- Undertake women's studies programmes.
- Evolve and implement appropriate gender equity based programmes and schemes for the welfare and empowerment of women.

The National Council of Rural Institutes, in carrying out its operation in all the above areas may take the help of other established rural institutions as well as technical institutions and organisations. In the initial stages it may be desirable to have small '*Think Tank*' group formed to help the Council.

Convocation Address On The Occasion Of The Golden Jubilee Convocation Of The D.A.V. (PG) College, Dehradun

Dr. Nigam, Principal, D.A.V. College, Respected Prof. Nautiyal, Vice-Chancellor of H.N.B. Garhwal University, Shri Jagendra Swarup, Secretary, Dayanand Shiksha Sansthan, distinguished invitees, recipients of the awards and degrees and ladies and gentlemen, I am highly delighted to be present on this happy occasion of the Golden Jubilee Convocation of the DAV (PG) College. I am grateful for being invited to be the Chief Guest on this occasion. Convocations are important moments in the life of a university or a college and its graduates. They give us a sense of identity and continuity across the years and reaffirm the duty of each generation to transmit the best of its knowledge, wisdom and culture to the next. I know that you, the graduates, are leaving this college with a sense of fulfillment and gratitude. I have no doubt you have been well taught and trained and you learnt well. I offer you my sincere congratulations on your conferment of degrees and honours. I pray for your happiness and for the fulfillment of the promise as individuals and as a generation.

The D.A.V. College has a long tradition. Founded in 1892 in the sacred memory of Maharishi Dayanand Saraswati as a night school in Meerut, was subsequently transferred to Dehradun in 1904, where the school was developed under Thakur Puran Singh Negi. It became an intermediate college in 1922 and elevated to a degree college in 1946 and finally became a post-graduate college since 1948. Thus the college has its roots in the pre-independence days. I am sure, the Hemavati Nandan Bahuguna Garhwal University is extending its full support to the college in its academic reforms as the country is catching up with globalisation. The college has got illustrious alumni like Sir Shiv Sagar Ram Goolam, Former President, Mauritius and Shri Lokendra Bahadur Chand, Former Prime Minister of Nepal.

Today I would like to share some of the national and international concerns with you, the young graduates leaving the portals of this college. Recently unconceivable changes have taken place right across the globe. These changes are having an impact on the international relations and the world economy in general. Within the country also spectacular changes have taken place on the economic front through restructuring of the economy with considerable dose of liberalisation. The country is gradually getting integrated into the global economy. The result of globalisation is that the industries have to face global and indigenous competition. For this they should resort to: modernisation, upgradation of technology and the competence of the work force, adopting modern management techniques, increasing efficiency and improving quality and productivity. There is a situation of inadequate resources. There is also a serious concern for erosion of the human values. All these present a changed setting for reorientation by all the major constituents in national development and a university or a college is no exception to this.

This changed scenario makes demands on the university system for the following, which are to be responded through necessary reorientation : (i) to provide competent and relevant manpower, (ii) to provide quality R & D support to industry, (iii) to uphold and enrich the value system, and (iv) to cope with inadequate resources situation. In the above changed situation, the university system has to reorient itself suitably and undertake the following: (i) bring in more relevance in teaching and research while maintaining quality (ii) undertake quality R & D with support from industry, (iii) work towards self-reliance, and (iv) take up value orientation of education. However, the following aspects should be kept in view: Firstly, while items (i) and (iv) applying to all the institutions, the degree of response in case of items (ii) and (iii) varies depending upon the degree of development, nature of courses offered and research potential and the location of the University or College, secondly, complete cessation from government financial support cannot be anticipated. Self-reliance could be achieved through bridging the gap between the fund requirement and the fund availability from the government by adopting suitable fund generation methods.

An area that caught up the imagination of the planners and the policy makers right across the globe is that looking at development and ecology in an integrated manner. No doubt that the twentieth century has seen some spectacular changes of social, scientific and political significance and tremendous developments in Science and Technology and their application in agriculture, industry, improvement in longevity and quality of life and in many other areas of human activity, have been the landmark of this century. However, these achievements have extracted their own price, resulting in large scale indiscriminate damage to life support systems. Yet, we can see now a silver line of hope in the greater realization among nations to look at ecology and development in an integrated manner. Sustainable development concepts thus gained importance. Pro-poor and gender equity approaches have also become real imperatives for true development and voluntary social action is a major contributor in this process.

Human development should be at the centre stage of the development process in a country with a large population, like India. Towards this goal, generation of adequate employment opportunities, building up of peoples institutions, population control, universalisation of elementary education, eradication of illiteracy, provision of safe drinking water and primary health facilities to all, and growth and diversification of agriculture to achieve self-sufficiency in food grains, are some of the areas which need attention on priority basis. A third of our population lives in condition of poverty, denied of the basic minimum needs and the worst sufferers are the women, children and the old among them. We have to enable the under-privileged sections also to derive full benefits of the developmental process.

All these signal towards a process of development which has to be inter-woven into ecofriendly, pro-poor and gender equity based approaches.

With this perspective, the task of the country's development becomes formidable in view of its vastness, large population and inadequacy of resources. Government alone cannot tackle this task and voluntary effort and people's whole-hearted participation are needed to complement the efforts of the Government. 'The strategy, therefore, should rely on building up and strengthening peoples institutions, making people active participants in the development process, and encouraging and supporting voluntary effort through the wholehearted involvement of innovative and socially dedicated scientists, technologists and scholars as well as committed non-governmental and voluntary organisations who can play a meaningful and constructive role through their 'Voluntary Social Action'.

Sustainable development implies a model of development in which both the present and the future are taken into consideration. The main engineering and technological areas that have bearing on sustainable development are : environmental infrastructure (water supply, sanitation, drainage, solid waste management), pollution control, shelter, urban planning and development, transport, energy, communications, computers and information systems, space technology and remote sensing, ocean development, bio-technology, biomedical engineering, agriculture, irrigation, food processing, industries and engineering constructions. Sustainable development demands technologies which are least polluting, uses natural resources optimally and also facilitates recycle of wastes. These technologies should be compatible with the socio-economic, cultural, environmental and developmental priorities of our country. There should be a strategic shift to cleaner and green technologies for a better tomorrow. Sustainable industrial development is not a matter of mere high-tech but also of appropriate sci-tech. We have to phase out older and inappropriate technologies while simultaneously developing and disseminating a new generation of sophisticated and environmentally benign technologies. We have to encourage indigenous research effort to be directed at green technologies through a system of incentives and penalties.

Acquisition of new technology can take place in the following ways: (i) Technology import related to foreign investment in India; (ii) Technology import by the Indian industry; and (iii) Indigenous R & D effort. The issue of technology import related to foreign investment in India needs serious attention. It should be carefully studied and assessed as to know whether the technology brought into the country is of the first rate or of third rate. Regarding the technology import by the Indian industry, it is logical to believe that the quality of technology imported may not suffer but one cannot be sure of getting the latest technology always: Now what is importable is only purchasable technology which is out-of date. To quote an example, Japan licenses out technology relating to machine tools, which is almost one generation behind. Contemporary technology is not purchasable. The regimes of foreign technology denial already precluded the option of 'importing' technology and will certainly do so increasingly in the future. In such a situation, if the Indian industry is to be globally competitive, the only option is of 'developing' our own technology. There has been a growing concern in the country over the erosion of essential values which is reflected in the fall of moral, social, ethical and national values, both in personal and public life. It is worthwhile to quote two passages from the Report of the Education Commission (1964-66), which are still relevant.

"India has a unique advantage with her great tradition of duty without self-involvement, unacquisitive temperament, tolerance, and innate love of peace and reverence for all living things. Too often are those precious assets forgotten and we tend to relapse into moods of pessimism, fears and forebodings, discord and destructive criticism. A new pride and a deeper faith expressed in living for the noble ideas of **peace** and **freedom, truth** and **compassion** are now needed". Another para says: "Modernisation did not mean—least of all in our national situation—a refusal to recognise the importance of or to inculcate necessary moral and spiritual values and self-discipline. While a combination of ignorance with goodness may be futile, that of knowledge with a lack of essential values may be dangerous". The Planning Commission recognising the need for focussed attention on value orientation of education felt it should be studied in-depth and in its totality in relation to various sectors of education and several developmental agencies. A Core Group on Value Orientation of Education was thus set up by the Planning Commission under my Chairmanship. The Core Group was able to present a concrete plan of action relating to various sectors of educational development, involving inter-departmental collaboration. As a follow-up of one of the recommendations of the Core Group, the Ministry of Human Resources Development has constituted a Standing Committee on Value Orientation of Education under my Chairmanship to oversee the implementation of value orientation of education at all levels right from the school to university level in the country. The Standing Committee is working out the detailed blue print with specific time frames, for the implementation of value orientation of education at school level, college level, university level and to use the electronic and print media and to involve non-governmental voluntary organisations for promotion of value orientation of education. At this stage, it is worthwhile to recall the concluding para of the Report of the Core Group on Value Orientation of Education. It says: "The urgent need for value orientation of education should not be merely a matter of brave declarations. The programme needs patience, careful and comprehensive planning. It needs to be built into our educational system, our media institutions, our cultural organisations, in the teachings of science and humanities, in all kinds of educational, social and political endeavours so that they have cumulative impact on the minds of our children and youth when they are receptive and uncorrupted by cynicism. If we have the necessary determination and firm commitment then 'we shall overcome'."

Before I conclude, I join today, along with your teachers and friends, in the hope that you, who received the degrees and became the alumni of this college, will contribute your share to the development of the country while pursuing your career. In this context, I would like to remind you about the four vital issues which need focussed attention in our country's progress. They are: (i) population control, (ii) eradication of illiteracy, (iii) environmental protection and maintenance of ecological balance, and (iv) upholding the value system. I would like to stress the need for contribution from you, who are going into society with great hope, in tackling these problems. I am sure you will rise to the occasion.

HIGHER EDUCATION AND RESEARCH IN INDIA—PERSPECTIVES AND INNOVATIONS

"Our Education Policy must focus on making ours a fully literate Country with a modern and world class Educational System that makes India a Super Power of the knowledge economy"

—Dr. Man Mohan Singh

I feel privileged for being invited to deliver the Sree Sankara Lecture as a part of Sri Sankara jayanti Celebrations being organised by Sri Sankaracharya University, Kalady. I would like to express my gratitude to the Vice-Chancellor, Dr. K.S. Radhakrishnan for affording me this wonderful opportunity of delivering the prestigious Sri Sankara Lecture.

I am happy to visit this great Sri Sankaracharya University of Sanskrit established at Kalady which was once upon a time purified and glorified by the birth of that great Soul, Sri Adi Sankaracharya. It is heartening to note that the University is a premier institution imparting education in Sanskrit along with modern subjects. The vast knowledge and wisdom enshrined in our ancient scriptures like Vedas, Upanishads, Puranas, Sastras, Agamas, Tantras and Samhitas are unlimited and many secrets and mysteries of scientific theories and developments are hidden in them. We seem to have been ignoring the bounty of knowledge, a treasure trove of scientific excellence—unaware and leaving them without a care. Even foreigners have recognized the importance of our scriptures e.g., a Nobel Laureate, Mr. Schrodinger who propagated the Quantum Theory has stated that he

118

was inspired by the study of Upanishads and was guided in his quest by the theories mentioned therein. And our own scientist, Sir Jagadeesh Chandra Bose attributed his thesis on plants as living things to the study of Vedas. There appears to be many such instances. It is high time we encourage the scholars versed with Vedas and other scriptures so that we will be able to recapture our limitless ancient knowledge for the well being of our people. Concerted efforts are needed for bringing out the vast knowledge hidden in the ancient scriptures through studies and research. I am sure this great University is doing its best in bringing out such vast knowledge and wisdom hidden in our ancient scriptures.

"Only Wisdom is greater than Wisdom" is an old proverb. "The purest of the pure is Wisdom" is the dictum pronounced by Lord Krishna in Bhagavadgeeta. "Wisdom and Wisdom alone is the ultimate goal of an evolved soul" is the thesis established by Sri Adi Sankaracharya, The Great.

Sri Adi Sankaracharya is an outstanding personality with a multi faceted spark and creativity. His doctrine of non-duality evoked enthusiasm from great stalwart scientists of the world like Albert Einstein, Schrodinger and others. The world knows him as an unparalleled philosopher, poet, organizer and Guru. But, when we look at his wonderful achievements from the angle of modern education systems, I am sure a great educationist can be seen in him.

Even though Sri Adi Sankaracharya is a born genius, he received systematic education in a regular schooling system of those days. But, it is said that a vedic learning which normally takes 30 to 40 years for a brilliant student, was finished by Sri Adi Sankaracharya within a period of 3 years or so. And he took his Sanyasa Ashrama at the age of eight and authored the great Brahma Sutra Bhashya at the age of twelve. It is said that Sri Adi Sankaracharya began his Vijaya Yatra around his Sixteenth year and before that he finished writing of all major books. That means, he had put his theories into black and white first and then set out to teach the same to his disciples and encounter the opponents to make them realize the truth.

Even though Sri Adi Sankaracharya is a born genius and logistician par excellence, he never assumed that his disciples also can understand things with the same ease and speed. So, he broadly divided his teaching techniques into three categories.

The Prakarana Grandhas: These are the books which target an ordinary follower with an average level of intelligence. In these the exact theory of Advaitha Siddantha is explained in uncomplicated and fair bits and methods of contemplating and Sadhana are also given. All the Prakarana Grandhas are totally his own creations.

Next category is called **Laghu Vyakhyas.** These are the simple commentaries on great works of popular authors like Sanathsujatha, Apastambha etc. These Laghu Vyakhyas target scholars of an average standard and they tackle the logical paradoxes that an average scholar gets confronted with.

The third and the main category is called **Bhashyas.** Bhashya means a thorough commentary. Sri Adi Sankaracharya wrote Brahma Sutra Bhashya, Upanishad Bhashya and Bhagavadgita Bhashya with an unparalleled expertise. These Bhashyas target scholars of excellence and opponents of ferocious scholarship. The real glow of Sri Adi Sankaracharya's logic and imagination can be vividly seen here. But, even in such high flown argumental stages Sri Adi Sankaracharya never loses his clarity either in thought or expression. This made Sri Sankaracharya not only a great propagator of a religion, but also a Great guru and a great educationist.

Another greatness of Sri Adi Sankaracharya, as an educationist can be seen in his foresight about the writings of his disciples. There were instances in history to prove that when Gurus did not allow his disciples to put their understanding on paper and when such disciples wrote books about their Guru and his teachings after his demise, then all the disciples expressed totally divergent opinions and theories which finally resulted in the distortion of the teachings of their Guru.

Sri Adi Sankaracharya did not allow this to happen. First, he put all his thoughts into black and white before he came out for the purpose of propagation. And when he gathered disciples he commanded his main disciples to write commentaries on his own works and he actually checked them up before they were allowed to be released to the society. Padmapadacharya's 'Panchapaduka', Sureswaracharya's 'Nishkarmya Siddi' and such works come under this category. Sri Adi Sankaracharya's spiritual and scholarly attainments are unfathomable.

Since I am not a Sanskrit scholar and being an educationist, engineer-scientist and a planner, I have chosen the topic of my lecture as "Higher Education and Research in India—Perspectives and Innovations"

I. INTRODUCTION

Education provides a means for personality development and livelihood support. It facilitates imbibing the qualities of humanism, tolerance, reason and adventure of ideas and contributes to the onward march of the humanity towards ever-higher objectives. The Education Policy while promoting the above qualities, should have liberal values and principles, academic freedom, Institutional autonomy, social Justice and intellectual excellence as the guiding principles. The System of Higher Education and Research in India is subjected to stresses and strains during the past one-decade or so with the advent of globalization and economic reforms in India. To meet these emerging challenges and future demands, the system needs reorientation infused with innovations and long-term perspectives.

II. HIGHER EDUCATION AND RESEARCH—STATUS

(A) HIGHER EDUCATION

India has developed a wide based infrastructure in Higher and Technical Education, National R & D Laboratories and Industries covering a wide range of disciplines and capabilities in the post independence era. The number of Universities rose from 25 in 1950 to 360 at present. Similarly, the number of Colleges have increased from 700 in 1950 to 16000 at present, out of which 60 percent are in the urban areas and the remaining 40% are in the rural areas. The number of Teachers increased from 15,000 to 4.8 lakhs during the same period. The number of students increased from 1.00 lakh in 1950 to 94.00 lakhs at present.

The role of higher education is many fold. It fulfills its role towards social responsibility, which is in the nature of shaping the individual into a good citizen and serve as a tool for gainful employment leading to a better life for the individual and the people dependent on him/her. It provides manpower for Industry, science and technology and contributes towards the creation of basic social infrastructure viz., education, health, nutrition, food and shelter etc., It contributes towards economic infrastructure as well viz., agriculture, energy, water, transport, communication etc. It also contributes for better social and administrative governance.

The world and inevitably India, have been in the throes of major economic and technological changes. The process affected not only the market economy of the nation, but also, the whole system of higher education which has to prepare its graduates for participation in the social and economic development of the country and the type of cultural environment and ethos it needs to foster. Moreover, education is itself being internationalized, universities are losing their territorial boundaries. Information Technology is further contributing to this change and will have a major impact on the structure, management and mode of delivery of the educational system. We are living through a period of social and economic revolution which cannot leave our educational system untouched. These major challenges have come at a time when the system has been facing an enormous economic crunch. Yet, within their limited resources, universities are striving to meet the requirements of change.

(B) TECHNICAL EDUCATION

Technical education (which includes engineering and management education as well) is one of the most potent means for creating skilled and technical manpower required for the developmental tasks of various sectors of the economy. It forms one of the most important and crucial components of human resources development with great potential for adding value to products and services, for contributing to national economy and for improving the quality of life of the people. It incorporates a technological dimension which is a vehicle for development. Technical education may itself imply high costs, but such high costs, being directly related to development, should be viewed as an essential productive investment, yielding valuable returns to society and contributing to socio-economic development. The Scientific Policy Resolution (1958) rightly states that 'The key to national prosperity, apart from the spirit of the people, lies, in the modern age, in the effective combination of three factors—technology, raw materials and capital—of which the first is perhaps the most important, since the creation and adoption of new scientific techniques can, in fact, make up for a deficiency in natural resources and reduce the demands on capital.'

Keeping in view the requirements of the country, we needed four levels of technical education: (i) Programmes / courses offered by ITIs whose products work as skilled workers, (ii) Diploma level programmes offered by Polytechnics whose products work as Supervisors, (iii) Degree level programmes offered by IITs, Engineering Colleges and Universities, whose products function as engineers and technologists, and (iv) Post-graduate programmes like MBA and other PG Diplomas, M.Tech and Ph.D offered by IITs, IIMs, Universities, etc whose products will become Management Personnel, teachers, scientists and researchers.

There has also been exponential expansion in Technical Education especially with establishment of a number of private engineering colleges and polytechnics in the Southern and Western Regions of India. Facilities of Masters and Doctoral programmes in engineering and technology have also been created in a number of institutions. The vast network of institutions include Indian Institutes of Technology (IITs), Regional Engineering Colleges (RECs) (some of them have been upgraded into National Institutes of Technology (NITs)) technical universities, deemed universities, university departments of engineering and technology, State and private engineering colleges recognized by the AICTE, specialized institutions in the field of mining, architecture, industrial engineering, foundry and forge technology, etc. The Indian Institutes of Management, University departments and professional bodies cater to the needs of managerial manpower.

Technical Education has to play an important role in developing highly skilled middle level technical manpower for the organized as well as the unorganized sectors. Necessary steps will have to be taken to make technician education flexible, modular and credit-based with provisions for multi-point entry to achieve this goal. The upgradation of the technical education system in terms of capacity, quality and efficiency is being ensured through the World Bank assisted project throughout the country. Laying down norms for minimum qualifying contact-hours, guidelines for design of curricula containing elements of computer education and new emerging technologies and rationalizing nomenclatures of courses throughout the country is the responsibility of the All India Council for Technical Education (AICTE). The AICTE has to initiate action to launch the National Testing Service for admissions to the Under—Graduate courses.

(C) PROBLEMS AND WEAKNESSES

The higher and technical education systems are already suffering from several weaknesses and problems at present such as increase in demand for enrolment, proliferation of sub-standard institutions, dilution in quality and standards, failure to maintain academic calendar, out-dated curriculum, disparities in the quality of education, inadequate resources and lack of adequate support for research, out-dated management system etc. We need to give serious thought to the impact of the changed scenario and the deficiencies in the system and take remedial measures to make higher and technical education and research to be more purposeful.

(D) SCIENCE & TECHNOLOGY

Science and technology have been an integral part of Indian civilization and culture over the past several millennia. Few are aware that India was the fountainhead of important foundational scientific developments and approaches. These cover many great scientific discoveries and technological achievements in mathematics, astronomy, architecture, chemistry, metallurgy, medicine, natural philosophy and other areas. A great deal of this traveled outwards from India. Equally, India also assimilated scientific ideas and techniques from elsewhere, with open-mindedness and a rational attitude characteristic of a scientific ethos. India's traditions have been founded on the principles of universal harmony, respect for all creation and an integrated holistic approach. This background is likely to provide valuable insights for future scientific advances. During the century prior to Independence, there was an awakening of modern science in India through the efforts of a number of outstanding scientists. They were responsible for great scientific advances of the highest international caliber.

India has been committed to the task of promoting the spread of science. The key role of technology as an important element of national development is also well recognized. The Scientific Policy Resolution of 1958 and the Technology Policy Statement of 1983 enunciated the principles on which the growth of science and technology in India has been based over the past several decades. These policies have emphasized self-reliance, as also sustainable and equitable development. They embody a vision and strategy that are applicable today, and would continue to inspire us in our endeavours.

There is today a sound infrastructural base for science & technology. These include research laboratories, higher educational institutions and highly skilled human resource. Indian capabilities in science and technology cover an impressive range of diverse disciplines, areas of competence and of applications. India's strength in basic research is recognized internationally. Successes in agriculture, health care, chemicals and pharmaceuticals, nuclear energy, astronomy and astrophysics, space technology and applications, defence research, biotechnology, electronics, information technology and oceanography are widely acknowledged. Major national achievements include very significant increase in food production, eradication or control of several diseases and increased life expectancy of our citizens.

The rapidity with which science and technology is moving ahead is mind-boggling. Science is becoming increasingly inter- and multi-disciplinary, and calls for multi-institutional and, in several cases, multi-country participation. Major experimental facilities, even in several areas of basic research, require very large material, human and intellectual resources. The continuing revolutions in the field of information and communication technology have had profound impact on the manner and speed with which scientific information becomes available, and scientific interactions take place.

Science and technology have had unprecedented impact on economic growth and social development. Knowledge has become a source of economic might and power. This has led to increased restrictions on sharing of knowledge, to new norms of intellectual property rights, and to global trade and technology control regimes. Scientific and technological developments today also have deep ethical, legal and social implications. There are deep concerns in society about these. The ongoing globalisation and the intensely competitive environment have a significant impact on the production and services sectors.

Since Independence, the country has established a large number of national laboratories dealing with a variety of areas in Science and Technology (S&T) including Agriculture and Medicine. A number of institutions are also involved in research in social sciences and management studies. There are several agencies and departments of the government such as Council of Scientific and Industrial Research (CSIR), Department of Bio-Technology (DBT), Indian Council of Agricultural Research (ICAR), Indian Council of Medical Research (ICMR), Department of Electronics (DOE), Department of Science and Technology (DST) etc. dealing with science and technology. In order to support social sciences and humanities, several councils such as the Indian Council of Social Science Research (ICSSR) have been established.

Major scientific departments with their research laboratories/institutions in the Central Government are the main vanguards of the research efforts being carried out in the country. Besides, there are other Central Government Ministries/Departments who have a number of research institutions under their administrative and financial control. In addition, there are inhouse R & D units of public sector industries, which are mostly under the administrative control of the Central Government but a few public sector industries are either under State Governments or in the joint sector of Central and State Governments. Some private sector industries have established their own inhouse R & D units. The inhouse Research and Development units are responsible for undertaking R & D activities for the respective industrial organizations. The State Governments have their own research institutions, which mainly comprise of agricultural universities and their research stations besides having other research institutions directly under different departments of the State Governments.

The higher education sector undertakes research activities mostly of basic (fundamental) and applied research through their own funds and funds from U.G.C. as well as through projects sponsored by the major scientific departments of the Central Government.

There are non-profit research associations/institutions which carry out R&D activities and these are supported by either industry or government or both.

The Government has taken several measures towards promoting industrial research in industry itself. The growth of R&D in industry still remains to be inadequate.

The R&D expenditure by Industry, as a percentage of total R&D expenditure, is only 21% in India compared to 61% in U.K., 63% in Japan and 72% in U.S.A. The time has come now that the Indian industry should increase their share of contribution towards R&D expenditure through either their own R&D units or through supporting research in universities, if they want to survive against global competition.

III. GLOBALISATION AND CONTEMPORARY SITUATION

We are living in an era of change. Momentous changes have taken place on the international scene, which have a profound impact on both international relations as well as the world economy. In India too, tremendous changes have taken place on the economic front. The government has been launching new initiatives buttressed by bold decisions to reorient and restructure the economy. The country is poised to become progressively more integrated into the global economy. Competition and the pace of technological change are intensifying in almost all sectors of the economy. Knowledge-based industries are on the upswing.

The impact of these changes on Indian industry has been considerable and it is exposed to global as well as indigenous competition. To meet these challenges, it has to resort to modernization, upgrade technology and competence of the workforce, adopt modern management techniques and increase efficiency and productivity. Structural adjustments aim at increasing Indian exports and this would be possible through, among other things, Indian enterprises acquiring global levels of expertise in developing and producing high quality products and marketing them internationally. It equally applies to agriculture sector. Under such circumstances, we need to have a workforce having scientific bent of mind and possess the much needed scientific temper and skills to maintain high quality of productivity on par with world standards. In addition we have to assume a position of technological superiority.

The impact of globalization and the contemporary policy shifts in financing of higher education and technical education system, is two-fold:

The system is called upon:

(a) i) to develop technology through indigenous R&D effort and
   ii) to provide quality man power to industry
(b) to seek avenues for supplementary fund generation.

The Universities have to strengthen their capabilities and undertake the following measures to face the challenges:

(a) optimal utilization of resources
(b) resource mobilization efforts
(c) collaboration, networking and sharing of facilities
(d) seeking excellence and relevance in the R&D effort
(e) aiming at competent and relevant manpower development, and
(f) undertaking international interaction and collaboration

The responsibility on the R&D Labs is also increased and they have to respond adequately to meet the technology needs of the industry. They are also called upon to generate funds for their sustainability and development.

IV. PERSPECTIVES AND INNOVATIONS IN HIGHER EDUCATION

The following are the key issues to be addressed to strengthen the higher and technical education system in the country:

a. Access
b. Equity
c. Relevance
d. Quality and Excellence
e. Governance
f. Resources

A. ACCESS

Presently there are 94.00 lakhs students in formal and informal system. The formal system is sharing 83% of the burden and the non-formal is sharing 17%. The clubbed access parameter (Formal + Non-Formal) is 6.9 and it is 5.75 for Formal System alone.

The factors, which have resulted in tremendous pressures on **access to higher education,** are: **(a)** the demographic expansion of population; **(b)** rising social expectations; **(c)** increasing expansion of primary, secondary and higher secondary education, impacting on admission to higher education; **(d)** economic development coupled with the belief that the social and economic mobility of persons is more likely to be assured by achieving higher levels of education and **(e)** the principle of equity enshrined in our Constitution, based on the principles of democracy.

To respond to the issue of Access in the present day context, the following options suggested in the approach paper of the U.G.C. for the Tenth Plan, would be worth while to note:

1. Expand open and distance education mode to meet the entire demand.
2. Increase both physical and academic infrastructure in conventional mode and run teaching programs in present full time mode as well as allow students to combine conventional and open structure, i.e. partial full-time and partial distance-education mode, to get degree. Enhance open system appropriately.
3. Use present physical infrastructure in double shifts with additional full time teachers and other staff strengths as well as allow students to combine conventional and open structure, i.e. partial full-time and partial distance-education mode, to get degree. Enhance open system appropriately.

4. Increase in a limited manner both the present physical and academic structure and use the enhanced structure in double shifts with added human support from contracted retired teachers and other staff and recognized persons from industry, research laboratories and other sectors as well as allow students to combine conventional and open structure, i.e. partial full-time and partial distance-education mode, to get degree. Enhance open system appropriately.

INNOVATIONS

(a) One also needs to create and use information and communication network linking all the colleges and universities. This would ensure uniformity in access to teaching material and help to maintain standards of education.

(b) The information network would help teachers to supplement their teaching in the classroom by cleverly blending it with multi-media support material on a particular topic, or giving feel of demonstration experiments through computer simulation, or watching experiments being done in well equipped laboratories, or listening to experts form India and abroad.

(c) The innovative use of information network would "virtually enhance the academic infrastructure" in the classroom and that too in a cost effective way. We need to train and encourage teachers to develop multi-media material.

(D) MANAGING KNOWLEDGE SOCIETY

During the last century, the world has undergone a change from agriculture society, where manual labour was the critical factor, to industrial society where the management of technology, capital and labour provided the competitive advantage. Then the information era was born in the last decade, where connectivity and software products are driving the economy of a few nations. In the 21st century, a new society is emerging where knowledge is the primary production resource instead of capital and labour. The Knowledge Society is powered by innovation capacity. Efficient utilization of this existing knowledge can create comprehensive wealth of the nation and also improve the quality of life—in the form of better health, education, infrastructure and other social indicators. Ability to create and maintain the knowledge infrastructure, develop knowledge workers and enhance their productivity through creation, growth and exploitation of new knowledge will be the key factors in deciding the prosperity of this Knowledge Society. Whether a nation has arrived at a stage of knowledge society is judged by the way the country effectively deals with knowledge creation and knowledge development in all sectors like IT, Industries, Agriculture, Health Care etc.

Higher education should play an active role in this transformation process of the society in to a knowledge society and manage the change. This could be done also through value added formal as well as distance education systems. There has been considerable effort to apply technology for improving the delivery of distance education system over the years. With the availability of an exclusive education satellite (EDUSAT), the time is ripe for making intense use of ICT to create an interactive virtual class rooms in all remote areas.

(E) INNOVATION SYSTEM

Knowledge is converted into wealth for social good through the process of innovation. Innovation is an important factor for the competitiveness of both service and manufacturing sectors. Innovation tends to emanate less from R&D and more from other sources including organizational change. Hence there is an urgent need to establish an innovation system in the country. Such a system would involve creation of clusters, which are networks. This network can include inter dependent firms, knowledge producing institutions / universities, colleges / institutes, research institutes, technology providing firms / bridging institutions, (for example think tanks, providers of technical and consultancy services) and customers linked in a value addition creating production chain. The concept of clusters goes beyond that of a firm network, as it captures all forms of knowledge sharing and exchange. Thus, an innovative system with its clusters would tap into the growing stock of global knowledge, assimilate and adopt it to local needs and finally create new knowledge and technology.

(F) Approach for Making Distance Education Programme Viable

A three-pronged approach is essential to make distance education programme viable and a successful proposition through the universal tele-education system to all remote parts of the country. Since the EDUSAT is providing the connectivity the other two essential components which are vital for the success of the programme are Tele-Education System and the Quality Content Generation and deployment.

I) Tele—Education Delivery System

This universal tele-education delivery system works via heterogeneous network platform through IP protocol. It provides virtual classrooms in a multi class and studio environment with seamless two-way interaction between the teachers and students in a collaborative framework. It provides seamless, one-to-one, one-to-many connectivity, through the broadcasting network in a multicasting mode of delivery. It seamlessly enables a remote teacher to become a teacher to all the students in a session. Unlike the other video conferencing system and multimedia tools currently in use for tele-education purposes, this Interactive Universal Tele-education delivery system creates a virtual classroom. It enables the teacher to take the student to a live virtual tour of the subject. This provides a cost effective solution for interactive content delivery. In a comparative basis we can create 250 nodes tele-education system for interactive delivery at a cost of establishing 4 multi-station video conferencing systems.

II) Quality Content Generation

There are three components for education: lectures, practical or laboratory and library. The content includes all the above three. Content can be generated in many ways. The first one is the assimilation of the subject by an expert teacher through research study of many books and articles leading to the generation of quality and creative content in a presentable format. The teacher presents in a unique and innovative way to make the content appealing and easily understandable to the students. The second form of content could be on a self-learning method by breaking down the content into a series of question answer models. Third may be from various books, which can be extracted through a digital library and presented just in time to all the remote students. Fourth may be from Internet, where wealth of information is available. Teacher may search the information on the Internet and push the content live through the tele-education system.

The content should have supportive animations, which may even bring virtual laboratories and virtual immersion effects to the remote students. When the content is generated, it should be a sharable learning object across the nation and across all platforms.

(G) DIGITAL LIBRARY INITIATIVE

India has a mission of digitizing million books through a digital library programme. This programme is progressing well and already 90,000 books are digitized, out of which 50,000 are already on the web **http://www.dli. ernet.in.** Many of the books are in Indian languages. This Digital Library of India Initiative had also become test bed for many Indian Language Technology Researches including the development of Machine Translation Systems, OCRs, Summarizers and so on in Indian languages. More than 21 centres spanning academic institutions, social organizations and Government agencies including the Rashtrapati Bhavan have partnered in creating this huge repository of knowledge. This programme is fully supported by the Ministry of Communication and Information Technology. The Distance Education Centres can utilize the facilities of the digital library initiative and digitize all the course material available with them for different disciplines. This will enable them to offer large number of e-learning courses and design web based education.

B. EQUITY

The Indian Constitution provides to secure to all its citizens justice, liberty, equality and to promote among all 'fraternity'. Therefore equity and social justice are to be reflected in higher education and research too. The focus should be on the weaker sections of the society including women.

Within the country also disparities exist. These include the locational disparities resulting from regional imbalances such as rural areas, hill and desert areas and islands. Specific groups which show such backwardness are also women whose participation is only 33 per cent in higher education, the reserved categories, some of the educationally disadvantaged minorities and the disabled.

Education for women's equality is a vital component of the overall strategy of securing equity and social justice in education. There is the need for institutional mechanisms to ensure that gender sensitivity is reflected in the implementation of all educational programmes across the board. It is being increasingly recognized that the problem of Universal Elementary Education (UEE) is, in essence, the problem of the girl child. It is imperative that participation of girls is enhanced at all stages of education, particularly in streams like science, vocational, technical and commerce education where girls are grossly under represented. The education system as a whole should be re-oriented to promote women's equality in education.

The overall strategy of securing equity and social justice in education should also include the educational needs of Scheduled Castes/Scheduled Tribes, minorities and the physically and mentally handicapped. The educational system should be geared up to promote equalization of educational opportunities.

C) RELEVANCE

Relevance in Higher Education has to be looked at various levels and disciplines. There appears to be a structural imbalance between the requirement of the industry and business sector and the curricula pursued by the universities and colleges. It is also not conducive for entrepreneurship and self-employment. This should be corrected through bringing in more relevance in course contents as well as research programmes.

At undergraduate level bulk of student population, around 83%, in formal education is in traditional disciplines like Arts, Science, Humanities & Social Sciences, Law and Commerce. Out of total number colleges existing today, there are nearly 75% of the colleges in the disciplines of Arts, Commerce, Science, Humanities & Social Sciences. Attempts to bring in relevance have been to club vocational subjects in conventional education system. This has the drawback of eating on the core subjects and introducing professional subject matter at a marginal level.

Thus, the output is neither sound in core subjects nor is skilled in vocational subjects, thereby they are neither accepted by the industry nor can they become entrepreneurs.

As indicated in the UGC approach paper one can think of a flexible education approach where students can pursue simultaneously a degree and add-on utility oriented programs that would allow the student to acquire an advanced diploma along with a degree or go for one more year of intensive professional subject learning and get two degrees at the end of four years. The convergence of open and conventional education is going to be of help in this aspect also.

Relevance has a greater significance at postgraduate level. The postgraduate teaching in colleges needs special attention. We need to evolve master degrees with sound foundation and relevance. This means no compromise should be made in respect of teaching in core subjects. In addition, training in emerging inter disciplinary fields with acceptance of credit based 'cafeteria' approach with modular structure is most desirable.

University-Industry interaction can play an important role towards achieving relevance. The course content could be formulated with the active participation by the experts from the industry. There should be exchange of faculty and experts between universities and industries. Students should have access to industries for practical training.

At research level there should be a conscious effort to blend scholarship with relevance. New emerging areas like biotechnology, genomic sciences, defence and strategic studies which includes national security affairs, insurance and banking with special reference to economics and world trade etc., should be given due importance.

D) QUALITY AND EXCELLENCE

In the context of globalisation and the concomitant challenges, the higher education system should respond in terms of producing trained manpower of caliber and competence and also in terms of providing the needed R & D capability. In addition, it has to produce highly talented men and women whose vast grasp of knowledge would enable them to take up innovations in advancing frontiers of knowledge and know-how. The implication of this is that the system should build up excellence and maintain quality.

In this context some of the following measures suggested by the U.G.C for quality improvement are worth noting:

i) Improvement in the quality of under-graduate education and specially colleges in backward, hilly, desert, island areas and colleges serving women, reserved categories, minorities and the differently abled. A cluster approach may be utilized by identifying one college as focal for development in a district, and the other colleges sharing the assets.

ii) Greater interaction between educational institutions, industry, trade, agriculture and rural development,

iii) Emphasis on value education through raising students' social awareness, within the overall framework of sustainable development and raising the quality of life, human development, issues pertaining to environment, human rights, and the rights of vulnerable groups (gender, age, social groups). These must be linked to the Constitutional goals of distributive justice, and equity in a pluralistic, secular, society.

iv) Greater use of information technology for teaching, and multi-media approach.

v) Cafeteria approach in curricular structural arrangements—courses to be choice, credit based, with core and optional, modular with several terminal points. This can be specially implemented in post-graduate courses, autonomous colleges and unitary universities.

vi) Interdisciplinary emphasis and greater support to them such as women's studies, ethnic studies, water studies, environment studies, and involving humanities, social sciences as well as science and technology.

vii) Improving the quality of post-graduate education through more independent, project oriented, individual work and continuous internal assessment.

viii) Improving the quality of the Ph.D. through a preparatory Ph.D. programme.

ix) Examination reforms especially in post-graduate programmes, autonomous colleges and unitary universities, and setting up examination boards for affiliated colleges to remove their burden on examinations.

x) Inter-University Centres, which offer qualitative front-line facilities to teachers and research scholars, require better inputs; and setting up of new centers in areas not covered.

xi) For teacher development, need for infrastructure support—library and access through INFLIBNET, individual workspace, rest rooms, child care facilities; university based programmes for faculty development besides Academic Staff Colleges; study/sabbatical leave; increase in the fellowships under the Faculty Improvement Programme and Research Awards; strengthening of Academic Staff Colleges.

xii) Changes in the method of recruitment of teachers in colleges through a university level Teacher Recruitment Board.

xiii) Incentives for performance of teachers.

xiv) Implementation of the Reports of the Curriculum Development Centres.

xv) Promoting Internal Quality Assessment Cells and accreditation through NAAC and introducing incentive based development grant to universities and colleges (at least one-third of the grant).

The quality improvement can be brought about by modernization of syllabi, increased research, networking of universities and departments and also increase the allocation of funds. The University system should move to the center stage. It should utilize the autonomy for innovations in teaching and pursuing high quality research. Emphasis should be given to facilitate interaction across the boundaries of institutions; provision of better infrastructure, more rationalized funding of research, integration of teaching, research and evaluation. There is need for better networking among institutions. Mutual collaboration and cooperation among universities is needed for optimal utilization of available resources.

Excellence can only be nurtured selectively. The concept of identification of "Universities with Potential for Excellence" proposed by the U.G.C. would add to nurturing excellence. Some universities should be funded at higher level so as to enable them to attain excellence in teaching and research. Such universities would have to put graduate education in pure sciences at a priority level as indicated by U.G.C. It is also a laudable proposition by U.G.C., that the status of "Excellence" would also be awarded to a few colleges. U.G.C. would identify few hundred colleges and fund them at a higher level to improve their academic infrastructure. These colleges would have academic freedom allowing them to do experimentation in curriculum and introduce innovations in teaching. They will have responsibility to conduct their own examinations and of declaration of results. The university would award degree with the name of the college on the degree certificate. This sharing of responsibility of conferring degree jointly would make colleges more responsible.

E) GOVERNANCE

The Indian higher education is big, in fact huge. It also has to manage demands and aspirations of extreme nature. The quality in education is primarily dependent on what happens in classrooms and laboratories but it also goes beyond the wall-boundaries of classrooms; it is imbibed on sport grounds, in libraries, in hostels, in central administrative office, in principals' room, the list is endless. The point to recognize is that we have to think of Total Quality Management in higher education. And this is where governance takes a center-stage. The huge and multi-faceted Indian education system needs to embrace Management Information System approach to achieve efficiency. The approaches being suggested in earlier pages to meet the challenge of enhanced number, relevance, excellence and so on, need professional management of higher education institutions. In the tenth plan UGC is planning to go for creation of generic MIS for running of colleges and universities and implement it. One more dimension, to be added, is to go for intensive training for administrators of higher education.

The management and the governance of universities have to be improved to enforce better financial and administrative discipline. Decentralisation of the university system, greater powers to departments, student nomination to university bodies on basis of merit or excellence is some of the issues, which need attention.

F) RESOURCES

In the backdrop of the changed economic scenario and the policy approaches, it is evident that:

(i) the subsidy component in higher and technical education is being reduced and

(ii) there is need for mobilization of additional resources by the universities and other institutions.

It should, however, be recognized that there will be variations in the potential for fund generation between university to university, institution to institution and even between department to department within a university or institution. Mostly departments of sciences, engineering and management have the scope for fund generation whereas the other departments like humanities and social sciences have little such scope and, therefore, it would be logical to view the university as a whole as a 'unit' for fund generation and financing. In the present situation the government alone cannot bear the total burden of financing the higher and technical education. Additional resources are to be mobilized to share the costs in an innovative manner. The Programme of Action (POA) 1992, while acknowledging the crucial role of higher education in training manpower for national development, indicates that it has become necessary for the institutions of higher learning to consider measures for raising internal resources and improving their cost efficiency. While there is a case for raising tuition fee and other charges which have remained more or less static for the past fifty years, an elaborate and effective system should be established for providing freeships, scholarships and loans to students belonging to the weaker sections of society. Efforts should also be made to evolve rational norms for providing grants to universities which should take into account per capita cost, teacher-student ratio, proportion of teaching and non-teaching staff, types of courses offered, costing of services and extent of their subsidization, ratio of graduate and post-graduate/research students etc. There is need for a balanced distribution of resources between universities and research institutions; the programme of Action goes on to add. Similarly, for technical education, the programme of Action indicates that all institutions will be encouraged to achieve maximum self-reliance by generating resource through various measures. The eighth plan document suggested that the involvement of voluntary agencies and private sector participation in the opening and conduct of higher education institutions should be encouraged with proper checks to ensure maintenance of standards and facilities to make higher education as far as possible self financing.

(i) **SELF RELIANCE**

Self-reliance should be interpreted in the sense that the gap between the fund requirement of the university and the fund availability from the government to be bridged by resource mobilization effort through suitably reorienting the teaching and research activities. The following measures would help towards achieving self-reliance:

(ii) ## ECONOMY IN EXPENDITURE

Economy in expenditure could be achieved by "trimming the extra fat" wherever possible, by resorting to modern technology in management, sharing of facilities etc.

(iii) ## INCREASING COST EFFECTIVENESS

Improving cost effectiveness involves optimization of student intakes, rationalization of staff structure and utilizing the services of post-graduate students for instructional work.

(iv) ## MOBILISING RESOURCES

Resources can be generated by rationalization of fee structures, attracting foreign students enhancing consultancy work and sponsored research and in offering revenue-generating courses for the industry.

(v) ## UNIVERSITY-INDUSTRY PARTNERSHIP

University-Industry interaction provides a means of resource generation for becoming self-reliant.

(vi) ## OPTIMAL UTILIZATION OF RESOURCES

(a) Within the universities or institutions duplication and wastage should be avoided. Pooling and sharing of costly facilities should be followed.

(b) Networking of facilities like computers and libraries could be resorted to locally. For example, within a city networking of computers and libraries of all the universities and research organizations could certainly lead towards optimal utilization of resources. Similarly, national networking could also be thought of. In this context, the University Grants Commission's project on Information and Library Networking (INFLIBNET) is quite relevant.

(c) Establishing sound linkages between universities and national research laboratories, would facilitate sharing of facilities, exchange of faculty and experts and undertaking joint academic and research programmes.

(d) Establishment of consortia of universities that can work in collaboration with higher institutions of learning such as TIFR, IISc., IITs, etc., would enable to utilize their superior resources, both human and material by the Universities.

(e) Deemed-to-be-University status could be accorded to selected national laboratories to initiate postgraduate programmes in certain special areas of Science, Engineering and Technology.

(f) Establishing of joint Centres to be run by the national laboratories and the universities will provide better research and developmental facilities to the university sector.

(vii)   CORPUS FUND

A corpus fund may be established in each university and built up to act as a steady internal source of revenue as returns on investments. The corpus fund could be built up by the resources generated through consultancy, munificent contributions or donations, contributions by alumni associations abroad and within the country and by matching grants from the government. The corpus fund concept would provide financial autonomy to the university, in addition to academic and administration autonomies.

RECOMMENDATIONS OF THE HIGHER POWER COMMITTEES ON RESOURCES:

The Punnayya Committee (UGC) and Swaminadhan Committee (AICTE) on financing of higher education and technical education respectively, made in depth analysis of the present financing pattern and made very constructive recommendations on the subject. These two reports taken together present an integrated approach to the problems of financing of higher education in the country. They spell out the need for various new strategies in funding higher and technical education that have serious short, medium and long term implications.

Swaminadhan Committee made some innovative recommendations, which will set in motion reforms not only in technical education funding but also in higher education, if implemented. These are:

i) The Central Government should examine the feasibility of levying an **educational cess** on industries for funding technical education and R & D activities in technical institutions.

ii) The Government of India may set up an **Educational Development Bank of India (EDBI)** for financing soft loans for establishment of institutions and also to assist students to meet their fee and living requirements.

iii) A **National Loans Scholarship Scheme (NLSS)** may be set up under EDBI to provide soft loans to needy students.

iv) Wherever necessary, the State Governments may also set up a **State Education Fund**, supplementing the **NLSS**, to give assistance to needy students in the form of loan scholarships at nominal interest rates and easy repayment terms.

v) The Plan allocation for technical education sector, both Central and State should be based and related to the plan outlays in the industrial and service sectors and as a matter of policy, these sectors should have an appropriate share earmarked for technical manpower development and this share be made available to Ministry of Human Resource Development to be used exclusively for the development of technical manpower.

vi) The tuition fees in all government funded and aided institutions in all the States should be revised to a rational level of at lease 20% of the annual recurring cost per student.

vii) A corpus fund is to be established in every institution.

Some of the recommendations made by the Punnayya Committee are:

i) The basis of funding of a Central University may be linked to its Specific objectives and to its pursuit of excellence, innovativeness, all-India character and ability to provide access to weaker sections.

ii) From the Ninth Plan onwards, grants should be related to unit cost of activities as a rule expect for new programmes for which unit costs are not determined or would be difficult to determine.

iii) Development grants should be linked to an academic audit system and performance indicators to be developed by each university.

iv) Each university must have a perspective plan which must be linked to its objectives, environment and potential.

v) On the pattern of the U.K., the Indian universities should adopt academic audit system and UGC may give highest priority to it as this will not only promote academic efficiency but also cost effectiveness.

vi) With a view to mobilizing resources from within the country and abroad, an Alumni Association may be set up in each university with the assistance of an advisory body consisting of the well wishers of the university.

If the recommendations of the Punnayya Committee and Swaminadhan Committee are implemented it will contribute a lot towards planning and management of higher education and technical education in the country.

V. PERSPECTIVES AND INNOVATIONS IN SCIENCE & TECHNOLOGY

In recent decades the world has been witness to the phenomenal impact made by Science & Technology (S&T) in shaping the lifestyle of the common man. In the coming decade, S&T must surely play a pivotal role in all the important tasks that lie ahead of us if India has to really forge ahead in the new century. Deployment of S&T as an effective instrument of growth and change becomes an imperative strategy, if we have to meet the goal of providing a better quality of life to a much larger percentage of our population than we have done so far, be generally self-reliant and self-sufficient in strategic areas, become internationally competitive in at least some of the areas where we have unique needs or advantages, and be in the fore-front in our strong areas and stand on our own as a nation in the fast-changing global situation.

In addition to the above major thrusts all effort should be made to spread the culture of science in the community at large and promote rural development through the application of S&T for it is only when our entire population has the right attitudes and a better quality of life that there will be overall development providing a higher quality of life and social justice. In order to achieve this it is necessary that voluntary agencies and educational institutions, government machinery should work together.

When viewed in the context of the pace of development in S&T in other parts of the world, the nature and dimensions of the problems of national development confronting us and the immense potential of S&T to help solve current problems, it is found that, despite significant advances, the gap between India and other advanced countries has significantly widened in terms of scientific and technological capabilities. There is, therefore, a greater urgency for promoting Science and Technology, both for internal development and for international competitiveness. It would also be worthwhile to note that within the country there are enormous gaps in the infrastructural facilities and capabilities between what obtains in specialized scientific agencies and national laboratories, in the industrial undertakings, and in the educational system. This situation needs to be remedied rapidly if those emerging from our educational system have to be effective in our national research and production systems.

One of the weaknesses of the S&T infrastructure has been its weak linkage with the production system. This has led to an insufficient use of science generated, and the lack of appreciation of capabilities in the universities, national laboratories, scientific agencies and the higher education system in general. The total resource of S&T personnel in the country compared to the population and the magnitude of the task before us is small in comparison to what obtains elsewhere in the world. The quality of these personnel varies very widely. Furthermore, large numbers of these are not actually engaged in activities that can be construed as scientific or technical. A clear effort for development of R&D Manpower is called for in order to match the number and quality of training, to the needs of the country. Despite increasing allocation for S&T activities, allocation for development of R&D manpower remains meager. There is also concern in the S&T community that the very best talent with the potential to be leaders of S&T is being lost either to opportunities available abroad or to other areas of endeavour in the country. There is need for determined effort to attract some of the best amongst our students to take research as a career.

Despite the seemingly large infrastructure created for S&T the quality of the infrastructure is not entirely satisfactory in the educational institutions. There are not many educational institutions in the country with R&D facilities and infrastructure comparable to those available in similar institutions in advanced countries. It is, therefore, becoming difficult for educational institutions to carry out competitive R&D work. Although our educational institutions produce large manpower, the absorptive capacity of the educational institutions for R&D is not very high. There are brilliant individuals, young and old, in our educational institutions who have produced high quality work and yet the overall quality of research from the education sector needs to be improved.

Although all the post-graduate students and Ph.D.s in the country have been produced by our educational institutions, there is hardly any budget actually ear marked for R & D in these institutions. Not more than 50 crores of rupees per annum are available in the regular budget of the university sector, earmarked for research. In general the universities do not have a research budget and much of the money received from UGC is used for mere survival. Without support for innovation, the educational institutions will not be able to contribute to national development. It is necessary to orient R & D efforts in educational institutions to national needs and this effort can be made only when adequate support is provided. Almost all the funding that the scientists and others in the universities get for research is based on research projects from scientific agencies. The total money available for this purpose from these agencies is also not very high and is not commensurate with the size of the country and the large number of educational institutions. All the support for higher education and research comes from the government. Industry is yet to contribute its mite in this direction.

A rational approach to basic research, especially long-term support in some areas must take into account the new scenario. Similarly the technology policy must go beyond technology import, absorption, adaptation or assimilation. The benefits emerging from S&T must reach all sections of the society including the weaker sections.

Despite various shortfalls, limitations and missed opportunities, India has made substantial progress in a number of areas. We have now achieved high rates of economic growth; reasonable level of food sufficiency; substantial increase in the average life expectancy; and growth of literacy and success in higher education. However, there are many un-achieved aspirations, in the food sector, economic growth, literacy, health and especially in achieving greater internal technological strength.

Recognising that today's science is tomorrow's technology and that a strong science base is a prerequisite for achieving technological competence, efforts should be continued to build and maintain a strong science base. Scientists with exceptional capabilities should be nurtured and supported fully. Facilities comparable with international standards should be offered so as to enable them to carry out outstanding research within the country. More Centres of excellence should be created and they must be encouraged to function in close coordination with Institutions of Higher Learning to supply future manpower needs for the national science and technology programmes. While pursuing the S&T programmes, the existing Centres of excellence should be involved so that the expertise and infrastructure available in various disciplines of S&T is utilized in planning and development of S&T programmes.

It is essential to dispense with hierarchical bureaucracy in the R&D institutions. There should be adequate delegation of powers. Science auditing should be professionalised with the concept of time accountability on decision makers and administrators in addition to the evaluation of achievement of goals/targets. Decision making powers and authority for implementation should be decentralized. Flexibility in finance and administrative procedures are of utmost importance to develop interactive linkages with industries and user groups. Participative decision-making processes must be introduced urgently in the S&T institutions to achieve better team effort. Creation of conducive environment for S&T personnel for research promotion and management of science are very essential. The activities pertaining to scientific management, promotion and development must be performed by scientists and technologists. They must take all necessary steps to raise the morale of working level scientists and technologists.

In a country of India's size and endowments, self-reliance is inescapable and must be at the very heart of technological development. We should develop indigenous technology appropriate to national priorities and resources. Rightly, the basic objectives of the Technology Policy Statement of 1983 are: development of indigenous technology and efficient absorption and adaptation of imported technology appropriate to national priorities and resources. The Universities and the R&D Organisations (including National Laboratories) have an important role to play in this regard.

There should be greater emphasis on clean technologies in the coming years. In order to face such emerging future challenges without being reactive, S&T programmes need to have a goal of achieving zero toxicity, zero environmental impact and should be oriented to full eco-friendliness.

Allocation of adequate resources for the S&T sector is a complex issue. At the macro level, the R&D expenditure as a percentage of GNP is close to 0.9. The target for this percentage by the end of the Tenth five year plan should be, at least close to 2%. While the role of the government in supporting basic research, technology development and its application as well as the promotion of S&T infrastructure must continue at an accelerated scale, efforts must be made to generate maximum resources for R&D from the production and service sectors.

TECHNOLOGY FORECAST AND ASSESSMENT

Technology forecast (TF) and technology assessment (TA) assume an important role. Since Universities and IITs are familiar with frontiers of knowledge it is but natural that they should play an important role in technology forecast (TF) and technology assessment (TA) to help the country to select right areas of action.

For a situation where global competitiveness is being driven by technology as an important element, TF/TA studies and their continuing updates with special stress on the assessment of domestic and global markets are essential. Market driven technology development will now onwards be crucial for industry and government. Indicators available from TF/TA studies with assessment of markets, provides valuable clues for the Universities, R&D laboratories and IITs to plan in advance their research orientation. Concerned Universities and IITs should have a TF/TA group with the thrust areas they are specializing. These groups may also be encouraged to make specific TF/TA and techno market surveys for the industry. In addition to TF/TA studies, Universities and IITs could also conduct tailored courses under continuing education programmes for industry personnel regarding some new results of TF/TA studies and also enabling industry personnel to do some studies themselves.

Technology Information, Forecasting and Assessment Council (TIFAC) has done some TF/TA studies and it is also building up an information base to continue the TF/TA studies in more quantitative manner with continual updates.

A common dialogue between Universities/IITs, TIFAC and Indian Trade & Industry Associations will bear fruit towards the development of right type of indigenous technologies.

Human Resource Development in Science and Technology

Although there has been a phenomenal growth in the number of universities and colleges imparting science education, there has been a consistent decline in the percentage of school students opting for science after passing the higher secondary examinations, from 32 percent in 1950 to 15 percent now. There has also been a marked change in the profile of students taking up the science stream. Today, high school students opting for science are often those with low scores while in the past, those with high scores would opt for science. Even the majority of the meritorious 150 students selected for the mathematics, physics, chemistry and biology Olympiads do not opt for careers in the sciences. The drop-out rate among the research fellows qualifying the National Entrance Test (NET) is also a fairly high at 35 percent.

Human resource / manpower development assumes a special significance in the process of developing technological innovations as well as implementation of new technologies and finding solutions to problems arising during the process of modernization. It is also a measure of the strength of the country as it contributes to socio-economic development. Development of S&T manpower depends on the quality of higher education in science and technology. Considerable strengthening of the scientific and technical manpower will be needed with the liberalization of the economy and the thrust on science and technology programmes. This should be done by selectively nurturing excellence in S&T education; identifying talented students and motivating them to take up science and technology as a career; providing avenues and opportunities for those engaged in the science and technology field to update and enhance their knowledge and skills; devising strategies to retain the best talents in active scientific work and involve the corporate sector in science education and R&D. All this could be achieved through setting up of specialized science institutes as centres of excellence on par with the Indian Institute of Technology (IITs) and Indian Institutes of Management (IIMs); adoption of at least one school and one undergraduate college by each national laboratory; attracting talented students to R&D through an assured career opportunity scheme; and upgrading the knowledge base of teachers through the concept of floating academics on a regional basis in new emerging areas like genomics, bio-informatics, conducting polymers etc. Other measures will include: liberalization of travel grants for attending conferences / seminars abroad, co-joint appointments with universities abroad; getting the corporate sector to sponsor chairs in specialized institutes and to adopt a school or college; providing graduate-level and postgraduate-level merit scholarships / fellowships from a central fund for netting young talented scientists etc.

University-Industry R & D Laboratory-Scientific Bodies and Academies Interaction

As stated earlier, India has built a wide based infrastructure in higher and technical education, national R & D laboratories and industries covering a broad spectrum of disciplines and capabilities. Indian Professional Bodies and National Academies of Sciences and Engineering enjoy a high status and occupy commanding positions in the scientific and academic circles. However, interaction among these four has been inadequate. Time is ripe for greater meaningful interaction and linkages among them in the changed global and national economic scenarios.

This linkage, inter-alia, will result in (i) development of indigenous technologies appropriate to our national priorities and resources, (ii) facilitate adapting the imported technology by the industries to meet global competitiveness, (iii) enriching teaching and research in universities with the backup of practical and field experience, (iv) universities and R & D laboratories getting valuable clues for research orientation (v) sharing and optimizing the use of resources and (vi) fund generation by the universities and R & D laboratories. A Model for University, Industry, R & D Laboratory and National Academies Interaction has been formulated by me and published (Annexure-I). The Model identifies areas of interaction between universities, industries, national R & D laboratories, professional bodies and National academies. Planning Commission took the initiative in convening a meeting to discuss how to strengthen linkages and interaction covering the above four constituents and based on one of its recommendations, a Standing Committee on University-Industry-National R & D Laboratories-Professional Bodies and National Academies Interaction has been constituted under the Chairmanship of Dr. D. Swaminadhan, the then Member, Planning Commission, Govt. of India to promote and oversee the cooperation among these constituents. The Standing Committee prepared an Approach Paper on University—Industry-National R & D Laboratories-Professional Bodies and National Academies Interaction in

India. The Approach Paper contains valuable recommendations for promotion of the interaction and the co-operation need among the four constituents for National development.

HUMANITIES & SOCIAL SCIENCE RESEARCH

What was said about the quality of research in science would also apply to social sciences. In spite of a large number of universities in the country carrying out social science research, there are not many centers of real excellence in these fields. Without under-estimating the value of fundamental research there is a felt need for social science research scholars to deal with research of national relevance and to disseminate this information to policy makers and planners in a form which is useful.

University Grants Commission (UGC), the Indian Council of Social Science Research (ICSSR) and other Councils dealing with Humanities and Social Sciences have to make a coordinated effort to highlight and link Humanities and Social Science research achievements to national development.

There is also need for dove-tailing of research findings into the syllabi and for linkages between social science research and other sectors of research. It is rightly said that there is a real danger of creating a unidimensional man in the absence of such linkages.

VALUE ORIENTATION OF EDUCATION

India is a great country with its rich cultural heritage, tradition, ethos and human values. **Swamy Vivekananda** said "if there is any land on this earth that can lay claim to be the blessed Punyabhoomi, the land where humanity has attained its highest towards gentleness, towards generosity, towards calmness, above all, the land of introspection and spirituality—it is India".

India's freedom movement was mostly through non-violence methods spearheaded by **Mahatma Gandhi** who firmly believed in truth, righteous conduct, peace, non-violence and love for all. The integrity of the nation, it rich cultural heritage and its compositeness, Indian ethos and values, equal respect for all citizens irrespective of caste, creed, colour, region, religion and march towards a bright future, were some of the basic considerations which the constitution makers had in mind while framing the Constitution of India.

The Report of the Education Commission (1964-66) states:

> "India has a unique advantage with her great tradition of duty without self-involvement, unacquisitive temperament, tolerance and innate love of peace and reverence for all living things. Too often are those precious assts forgotten and we tend to relapse into moods of pessimism, fears and forebodings, discord and destructive criticism. A new pride and a deeper faith expressed in living for the noble ideas of peace and freedom, truth and compassion are now needed".

> "Modernisation did not mean—least of all in our national situation—a refusal to recognize the importance of or to inculcate necessary moral and spiritual values and self-discipline. While a combination of ignorance with goodness may be futile, that of knowledge with a lack of essential values may be dangerous".

What is happening around us now is a great cause for concern for all of us. There are growing divisive forces, narrow parochialism, separatist tendencies, considerable fall in moral, social, ethical and national values both in personal and public life. It is time that we deeply introspect, review, identify the root causes and arrive at remedies to arrest erosion of our value system and to uphold the Indian ethos.

Education is a major vehicle for value inculcation. The Planning Commission recognizing the need for focussed attention on value orientation of education felt it should be studies in-depth and in its totality in relation to various sectors of education and several developmental agencies. A Core Group on Value Orientation of Education was thus set up by the Planning Commission in January, 1992 under the Chairmanship of Prof. Dr. D. Swaminadhan, the then Member, Planning Commission, with very wide terms of reference and with membership from various agencies and experts in the subject. The Core Group was able to present a concrete plan of action relating to various sectors of educational development, involving interdepartmental collaboration.

As a follow-up of one of the recommendations of the Core Group, the Ministry of Human Resource Development has constituted a Standing Committee on Value Orientation of Education under the Chairmanship

Prof. Dr. D. Swaminadhan, the then Member, Planning Commission, to oversee the implementation of value orientation of education at all levels right from the school to university level in the country. The Standing Committee had worked out the detailed blue print with specific time frames, for the implementation of value orientation of education at school level, college level, university level and to use the electronic and print media and to involve non-governmental voluntary organizations for promotion of value orientation of education. The blue print for school education is already being implemented. The blue print for higher education, which has been formulated, had to be cleared by the University Grants Commission. Every university and college, either general or technical, have to give serious thought to human values and implement the value orientation of education programme with utmost concern.

International scenario also does not seem to be better in respect of human values. Peaceful co-existence seems to be difficult. International relations seem to be devoid of humanitarian considerations. The overall scenario in the world even in the 21st century, in terms of the need for man's balanced frame of mind and the need for good relations between nations for peaceful co-existence, in all probability, may remain the same unless serious and sincere efforts are made to improve the situation. The present and the future generations are to be helped to reorient themselves to be imbued with strong commitment to ethical, spiritual and human values. In such a state of affairs, cross cultural and global dialogue, international understanding, exchange of views and ideas, studies and research in the area of human values will be helpful not only in the national but also in the international context for remedying the situation. A sound foundation for international understanding, peace and progress for the humanity on this globe could be built through such an exercise.

CONCLUSION

The demands on the higher educational system have grown phenomenally. In an environment of increasing competition, the need of reconciling the new global emphasis on the market economy with the United Nation's pronouncements on promoting sustainable development, and the survival of its human population at an adequate level of the quality of life—all these demand a whole range of skills from the graduates of humanities, social sciences, sciences and commerce, as well as from the various professional disciplines such as agriculture, law, management, medicine and engineering. We can no longer continue with the model of general education as we have been pursuing for the large bulk of the student population. Rather, it will require a major investment to make this large human resource productive by coupling the older general disciplines of humanities, social sciences, sciences and commerce to their applications in the new economy, and having adequate field based experience, to enhance knowledge with skills and develop appropriate attitudes. This is how 'relevance' can be brought into higher education system.

If we wish to achieve our national goals of sustainable development with equity and social justice, education must get its context and relevance from these goals. Our human resource development will depend on our planning strategies for social and economic development. Neglect of this most important national wealth, human resources, through the neglect of the educational infrastructure and its identified deficits, including higher education, which is the cutting edge of development, will imperil these national goals.

Excellence needs to be nurtured, supported and encouraged. Attaining excellence needs selective approach through school, college and university level. For this, short term and long term strategies may have to be worked out. Inter-linkages between the school education, higher education and research should well be recognized and necessary reorientation should be undertaken. The trend of de-emphasis on creativity should be arrested and conducive atmosphere for creative work and innovations should be created in schools and the university system. Policies for science and technology, humanities and social sciences are to be properly oriented for achieving research excellence in India. It is time we formulated a new Science & Technology policy for the Country.

A number of committees have been appointed in the past to review our education and research systems. Excellent reports have been prepared and submitted to the authorities. This equally applies to report on value orientation of education. Many times their recommendations have not been acted upon and it is high time that these recommendations are critically looked into and where they are appropriate, they should be implemented.

Finally, education should be an instrument for developing not only an economically prosperous society, but one which can live comfortably in the context of pluralism and democracy as also provide for equity and social justice with respect for gender, caste, clan and creed. If we desire to maintain high ethical values in our public life, in the professions, in business, and foster the development of the most backward and marginalized who form a major proportion of our population, considerable rethinking and specific policy directions, with needed fiscal support, would have to be provided for education and research. Greater political and national will is needed for implementation of the accepted policies in school education and in the areas of science and technology, humanities and social sciences so as to facilitate implementation in the right earnest.

If changes are not brought in an expeditious manner in the country, there will be lot of migration of brainpower to other countries as it is happening already at present. There is a need for changing the priorities in our education system, in the sense we should follow the dictum **"Quality education for all is more important than education of all"**.

The National Policy on Education of 1986 which was reviewed in 1992 may need another review now.

REFERENCES

1. University Grants Commission.1996. *Policy Frame and Programmes of the University Grants Commission in the IXth Five Year Plan:* Working Group Report on Higher Education Planning Commission, Government of India, June, 1996.
2. Planning Commission, Government of India.2001.*Report of the Steering Committee on Secondary, Higher & Technical Education for the Xth Five Year Plan*: December, 2001. India.
3. University Grants Commission. 2002 *Philosophy & Approach During Tenth Five Year Plan in Higher Education*, April, 2002.
4. Education Commission.1966.*Report of the Education Commission*: Government of India,1964-66.
5. Government of India.1992. *National Policy on Education, 1986-Programme of Action 1992*: Govt. of India, Ministry of Human Resources Development.
6. Dr. Swaminadhan. D. 1996. *Address at the UNESCO Forum on "Strategies for University—Industry Cooperation in Engineering, Sciences and Technology in India"* January 1996, New Delhi.
7. Dr. Swaminadhan. D. 1997. *"Higher Education, Technical Education and Management Education: A Draft Approach Paper for Ninth Plan"*: Included in the book "Knowledge through our life time" published by Prof. M. Madaiah Felicitations Committee, Mysore 1997.

8. MGNIRSA.1998. *Round Table Conference on "Education"*: organized by Mahatma Gandhi International Research Centre for Indian Freedom Movement and National Reconstruction (Mahatma Gandhi Centre) of MGNIRSA—May 1998.

9. Planning Commission.1996. *An approach paper "Promotion of Interaction between University-Industry-National R&D Labs—National Academies"*: The standing committee on Industry—Institution interaction. Planning Commission, Govt. of India, May 1996.

10. Dr. Abdul Kalam. A. P.J. 2005. *Convocation Address*: The Sixteenth Convocation of Indira Gandhi National Open University, March 5, 2005.

Annexure I

* SWAMINADHAN MODEL FOR UNIVERSITY – INDUSTRY – NATIONAL R&D LABORATORIES – PROFESSIONAL BODIES AND ACADEMIES INTERACTION FOR COUNTRY'S ECONOMIC DEVELOPMENT

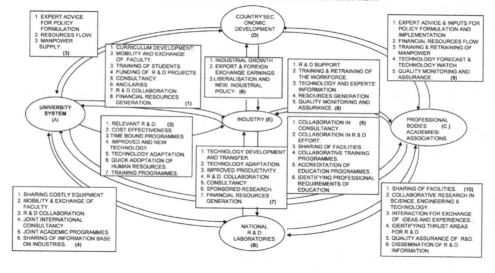

Note: 1. 'Country's Economic Development caption may include all the sectors of the Economy and the Government.
2. 'University System' includes professional Institutes of Higher Learning in Engineering, Technology, Medicine, Pharmacy, Agriculture, Management, etc.
3. Professional Bodies/Academies/Associations include INSA, IASc, NASc, INAE, the Institution of Engineers (India), ICAR, ICMR, UGC, AICTE, FCCI, CII, ASSOCHAM, etc.
*Formulated by Prof.Dr.D. Swaminadhan, Member Planning Commission, New Delhi (September 1 994).

Note: 1. 'Country's Economic Development caption may include all the sectors of the Economy and the Government.

2. 'University System' includes professional Institutes of Higher Learning in Engineering, Technology, Medicine, Pharmacy, Agriculture, Management, etc.

3. Professional Bodies/Academies/Associations include INSA, IASc, NASc, INAE, the Institution of Engineers (India), ICAR, ICMR, UGC, AICTE, FCCI, CII, ASSOCHAM, etc.

*Formulated by Prof. Dr. D. Swaminadhan, Member Planning Commission, New Delhi (September 1 994).

TECHNICAL
EDUCATION

TECHNICAL EDUCATION IN INDIA— PROBLEMS AND PROSPECTS

Dr. Jagadeesh, Sri Sambasiva Rao, Sri Ratheish, distinguished invitees, ladies and gentlemen,

It is indeed a great privilege for me for having been invited to deliver the Fourth Prof. Y. Nayudamma Memorial Lecture. I am grateful to Dr. Jagadeesh, President, Society of Science for the People for giving me this splendid opportunity. Prof. Nayudamma was a brilliant scientist and the country should be proud of his achievements. The people of Andhra should be especially proud of him as he belonged to Andhra. His contributions to scientific field, growth of science and technical education in the country are well known. His foresightedness was evident in his ideas and programmes like open Houses (leather fairs, fashion parades), Retainership schemes, Research-Industry Linkages (Leather Club), starting of an industry based on R & D, training of manpower and technology transfer mechanism based on the principle technology is best transferred along with the man'. One of his best remembered ideas, being continued at CLRI even now, is the annual Tanners' Get-Together, in which scientists and industrialists get together and exchange information. The Indian Leather industry owes a lot to this man of great foresight, vision and unquestionable R & D managerial capability for having placed it on the road to progress.

The topic I have chosen for the Memorial Lecture is **'Technical Education in India—Problems and Prospects'**. I have settled for this topic after considering various topics in science and technology, as I felt that technical education has to play an important role in the present day changed economic scenario in the country and abroad.

Technical education is one of the most potent means for creating skilled and technical manpower required for the developmental tasks of various sectors of economy. It incorporates a technological dimension which is a vehicle for development. Technical education may itself imply high costs, but such high costs, being directly related to development, should be viewed as an essential productive investment yielding valuable returns to society and contributing to socio-economic development. The Scientific Policy Resolution (1958) rightly states that "The key to national prosperity, apart from the spirit of the people, lies, in the modern age, in the effective combination of three factors—technology, raw materials and capital of which the first is perhaps the most important, since the creation and adoption of new scientific techniques can, in fact, make up for a deficiency in natural resources and reduce the demands on capital".

The science and technology education and research in India has made significant contributions to the overall development of the country. From a very merely agriculture based society in the early forties, India is today rated among the biggest industrialised nations having a sound base of industries along side with a highly developed agriculture sector. As we march towards the 21st century and with our policies of economic liberalisation, it is imperative that our developmental efforts are supported by the relevant science and technology inputs on one hand and relevant human resources on the other. The technical education has thus, to play a very significant role in the changed economic scenario.

DEVELOPMENT OF TECHNICAL EDUCATION IN INDIA

The growth of technical education depends on the socio-economic and industrial conditions of a country and its development is controlled by the needs and requirements of the economy. After Independence, the country was faced with the great challenge of rapidly industrialising the predominantly agricultural economy and in this process it had to build up its technical education system within a short period.

Major efforts have been made to create a wide-based infrastructure of higher education institutions, research laboratories and industry, covering a broad spectrum of disciplines and capabilities. There are now over 185 Universities and academic institutions of national importance and over 5700 colleges with a total enrolment of about 4 million students for graduate, post-graduate and research degrees and diplomas, with over 2,70,000 teachers. The higher education institutes include those offering programmes in Arts, Science, Commerce, Engineering, Technology, Management, Finance, Humanities, Social Sciences, etc.

With regard to technical education, there were only 38 institutions at the degree level with an intake of 2940 students and 53 institutions at the diploma level with an intake of 3670 students in the year 1947. Today there are over 350 technical institutions at the degree level and nearly 950 technical institutions at the diploma level with an annual intake of 68,000 and 1,26,000 students respectively. These include regular engineering colleges, polytechnics, Indian Institutes of Technology, Indian Institute of Science, Bangalore, Regional Engineering Colleges and other institutions. For training craftsmen, there are over 2500 Industrial Training Institutes/ centres admitting over three lakh students per year. About 1900 institutions conduct vocational courses at the higher secondary school level (10+2 level), admitting about 95,000 students per year. There are over 50 centres, including Indian Institutes of Management, imparting management education to over 4,000 students. There are over 90 centres offering post-graduate programmes in engineering and technology with an annual intake of over 85-n students. The government has set up about 450 m. or S & T research laboratories under its various departments and ministries. There are also about 1075 recognised in-house R & D laboratories in public and private sector undertakings. More than 200 consultancy firms are engaged in engineering design, analysis and research. Expenditure on education as percentage of GNP varied from 1.2 in 1950-51 to 3.9 in 1986-87.

STRUCTURE OF TECHNICAL EDUCATION:

Keeping in view the requirements of the country, we needed four levels of technical education. (i) Programmes / courses offered by ITIs whose products will be working as skilled workers, (ii) Diploma level programmes offered by Polytechnics whose products will be working as Supervisors, (iii) Degree level programmes offered by IITs, Engineering Colleges and universities, whose products will function as engineers and technologists and (iv) Post graduate Programmes like M.B.A. and other P.G. Diplomas, M.Tech. and Ph.D. offered by IITs, IIMs, Universities etc., whose products will become Management Personnel, teachers, scientists and researchers.

The Indian Institutes of Technology are established as institutions of national importance to initiate and nurture indigenous effort for technological development. The Regional Engineering Colleges are established with the objective of bringing a major quality change in educational programmes and to train personnel to handle and manage engineering activities in the country.

The four Indian Institutes of Management are autonomous societies set up with government support. These four represent a potent force for professionalising management in India. Collectively they have graduated nearly 8000 MBAs whose annual earning capacity of around Rs. 100 crores indicates the kind of contributions they are making to Indian industry. A significant number have become chief executives of enterprises and some have become entrepreneurs; a larger number occupy senior managerial positions in Indian private and public sector enterprises. The IIMs have also shown a considerable capacity for adding to the teaching, training and research capability of the nation in the field of management.

Four Technical Teacher Training Institutes were established during 1960's to function as resource centres for the development of polytechnics in the respective regions. Their duties include curriculum development, teacher training, development of learning resource material, educational research and other activities related to diploma level education.

DEFICIENCIES IN THE SYSTEM:

The Technical Education system suffers from certain weaknesses and deficiencies. No doubt there has been a considerable quantitative expansion in technical education but quality suffered and there is lack of relevance. There exists a structural imbalance of skill requirements of business and industry sectors and the traditional curricula followed by educational institutions. This is resulting in unemployment, under-employment and wastage in the system. The wastage in the system is enormous, being 30% at the degree level, 35% at the diploma level and 45% at the post-graduate level. The infrastructural facilities available in the vast majority of technical education institutes are extremely inadequate. There is an acute shortage of faculty with about 25 to 40% of the faculty positions remaining unfilled. In most of the institutions there is hardly any R & D activity. The technical education institutions are functioning in isolation. Linkages and interaction between technical education institutions and user agencies such as industries,

R & D and design organisations and development sectors are not sufficiently strong. Neither is there a strong interaction among institutions by way of sharing of facilities like equipments, libraries, teaching faculty and other resources. Little attention has been paid to the strategies for raising non-budgetary resource and maximum people's participation.

SEVENTH PLAN EFFORTS:

The Seventh Plan focussed on consolidation and optimum utilisation of existing infrastructural facilities; upgradation and modernisation, identification of critical areas, creation of infrastructure in new areas of emerging technologies, effective management of the overall system and institutional linkages between technical education and other development sectors. Some new schemes like continuing education, institution-industry interaction, research and development in technical education were initiated as part of implementation of the National Policy of Education.

THRUST AREAS FOR THE EIGHTH PLAN:

Taking a lead from the Prime Minister's two important observations made during one of the Planning Commission meetings regarding the need for modernising the. teaching and research activities in engineering institutions like Indian Institutes of Technology, who are considered as centres of excellence, and the need for adopting futuristic approaches to meet the emerging challenges of science and technology, a series of Brain Storming Sessions were organised in the Planning Commission to identify directions for further growth of technical education in the country.

The following thrust areas have been suggested:

(i)   Modernisation and upgradation of infrastructural facilities,
(ii) Quality improvement in technical and management education,
(iii) Responding to New Industrial Policy and Institution-Industry-R & D Laboratories Interaction, and
(iv) Resource mobilisation.

I) MODERNISATION AND UPGRADATION OF INFRASTRUCTURAL FACILITIES:

Modernisation relates to both technical equipment and teaching methods. We have to adopt futuristic approaches for achieving modernisation and self-reliance in a sustained manner. Coordinated and concerted efforts are needed to upgrade and consolidate the infrastructural facilities in the existing institutions. The process of removal of obsolescence would include enhancement of computer facilities and establishment and inter-linking of large computer systems with educational and research institutions through appropriate telecommunication facilities. Steps should be taken to strengthen and create facilities in crucial areas of technology where weaknesses exist, in areas of emerging technologies and in the new specialised fields.

II) QUALITY IMPROVEMENT IN TECHNICAL AND MANAGEMENT EDUCATION:

A holistic and need based approach will have to be adopted to reorient the technical and management education. A more broad based flexible system with provision for multipoint entry is required to enable us to offer a better response to the unspecified demands of the future. At the micro level, the curriculum should be developed to encourage creativity and innovation in experimental work by introducing problem or process oriented laboratory exercises. New technology oriented entrepreneurship and management courses are to be introduced in selected institutions having adequate infrastructural facilities. There should be greater emphasis on production engineering and towards design and product development. It would be desirable to couple the technology forecasting with the system of manpower forecasting and planning. Universities and the IITs should play an important role in technology forecast and assessment with the fruitful involvement of Technology Information, Forecasting and Assessment Council (TIFAC), Institute of Applied Manpower Research (IAMR), and Indian Trade and Industries Associations. This would enable to develop the right type of indigenous technologies, to assess related manpower requirements and to produce related trained manpower. Existing facilities for continuing education and retraining are inadequate. There is a need to formalise the training programmes for engineering and technology personnel engaged in all sectors and to make them mandatory. Programme learning packages need to be created and distance learning methodologies employed to enable self-development and training of scientific and technical personnel.

III) RESPONDING TO THE NEW INDUSTRIAL POLICY AND INSTITUTION-INDUSTRY-R & D ORGANISATIONS INTERACTION:

Momentous changes are taking place on the international scene which will have a profound impact on international relations and the world economy. Most developing countries have also embarked on bold measures of reform and restructuring their economies and opening up to forces of competition, both domestic and foreign. The Government of India also have taken new initiatives and bold decisions to reorient and restructure the economy to meet the challenges of the economic crisis in the country through its policy—of liberalisation, new Industry and Trade Policy etc. The impact of these changes on Indian industry is considerable and it is exposed to global as well as indigenous competition. To meet these challenges, it has to resort to modernisation, upgrading technology and competency of the work force, adopting modern management techniques and increasing / efficiency and productivity. In this context the universities, engineering institutions and national P & D laboratories have a greater role to play. A strategy may have to be evolved for effective interaction between industry, universities and national R & D laboratories. For this purpose, considerable organisational mechanisms such as Industry Liaison Board, Industry—Institution Cells, Industrial Foundations, etc. will have to be set up. The industry should support R & D activities through the institutions. To bring about meaningful interaction, Swaminadhan Model for University-Industry-R & D Organisations interaction could be suitably adopted / adapted.

RESOURCE MOBILISATION:

One of the features of the restructuring of the economy is the decrease in the levels of government subsidy. It would naturally affect the technical education sector also as the Government is under financial constraints. This brings into focus the need for Technical Education system to generate funds to supplement the funding from the government through suitable means, which will not, at the same time, affect their primary task of teaching and research. There are a number of measures which could be taken to tackle the resources inadequacy and lessen its impact. The following measures could be adopted:

1. Avoidance of duplication of investment in Technical Education institutions located close to each other and proper maintenance of available facilities and instruments.
2. Developing institution-wise specialisation in respect of courses and Technical manpower so that the institutions can have the most Sophisticated an d modern library and laboratory facilities in their chosen fields.
3. Weeding out of outdated and stereotyped courses and introduction of relevant courses in emerging areas.
4. Multiple uses of infrastructural facilities through part-time courses, continuing education programmes, consultancy and testing services.
5. Marginal increase in intake capacities in areas of scarce manpower and decrease in intake of low demand areas.
6. Introduction of multiple or at least double shifts in Technical Education institutions.
7. Maximum use of non-monetary inputs, like better planning, advanced technologies and practices, better system of supervision an administration, monitoring and review etc.
8. Commercialisation of the research output of the institutions.
9. Raising of fees in relation to Government, Government-aided and unaided institutions on a graduated scale. The measure of raising fees, however, should be coupled with scholarships for SCs / STs and for students below poverty line and a loan scheme to other students.
10. Creation of a corpus fund with contributions from industry, alumni, charitable trusts etc. as well as from Government.
11 (a) Pursuing the idea indicated in National Policy on Education / Programme of Action of requiring development departments

to allocate a fixed percent of their annual budgets for the development of Technical Education institutions (TEIs).

(b)   The question of (i) collection of education cess from the industry, and (ii) giving tax exemption to industry for contributions made by it for the development of technical education should receive serious consideration.

12. Implementing the Institution / University-Industry-National R & D Laboratories Interaction with all seriousness which will not only help towards national development but also help towards fund generation by the universities and other technical institutions.

POLYTECHNIC EDUCATION:

Polytechnic Education catering to the middle level technician education is equally suffering from lack of quality and relevance. During 70's, the complaint was that the polytechnic courses were mostly theoretical with very little practical bias. The diploma courses were a poor imitation of the degree courses and, therefore, they did not really serve the middle level technical personnel requirements. Further, the complaint was that no attempt had been made towards specialisation that is no attempts were made to produce specialised technicians. Perhaps the situation has not changed much even now due to the proliferation of substandard institutions.

The Central Government had launched a massive project with the assistance of the World Bank to enable the state governments to upgrade their polytechnics in capacity, quality and efficiency, which is quite laudable.

The Brain Storming Session held in the Planning Commission on Polytechnic Education discussed in depth and suggested to bring out a document 'An Approach Paper on Perspectives for Development of Polytechnic Education-during the 90's and Beyond', covering the following areas: Meeting the increasing demand through (i) manpower assessment and planning, (ii) optimal utilisation of capacities, and (iii) adopting distance education mode, 2.Relevance and quality, 3. Resource generation, 4.Private participation, 5. Institution-Industry interaction and institution-society interaction (Community polytechnics), 6.Women's participation, 7.Entrepreneurial development programmes which will help reduction in unemployment, 8. Curriculum development, 9. Quality improvement of teachers: (i) Pedagogy (ii) Industrial / field exposure, 10. Accreditation of Polytechnics, 11.Management of Polytechnics, 12. Linkages between Polytechnics, vocational institutions and Industrial Training Institutes and Engineering Colleges, 13. Networking and collaboration among polytechnics, 14. Role of institutions like Indian Institutes of Technology, Regional Engineering Colleges, other engineering colleges and universities in the development of polytechnics. The document is being drafted by a Committee in the light of the discussions held during the Brain Storming Session.

TECHNICAL TEACHERS' TRAINING INSTITUTES (TTTIS):

The Technical Teachers' Training Institutes have been doing pioneering work in the areas of technical teachers training, curriculum development, institutional model development, research and development, consultancy and extension services related to technician education. The objectives of TTTIs have become all the more relevant in the context of the National Education Policy, the recent World Bank assisted project for strengthening technician education in India and also in the context of the changed economic scenario. As observed by the Review Committee on TTTIs (1990), in spite of high internal efficiency exhibited by these institutes in undertaking various programmes and activities, their external efficiency in terms of improving the quality of technical education system is less significant. A major reason for this is the constraints and limitations imposed on these institutes because of their present status and because of the lack of authority required to introduce, modify and close down programmes depending upon the changing context of technician education in the country. To overcome the above constraints and to ensure that TTTIs are able to play the role of bringing about excellence in technician education, the recommendation of the Review Committee that these institutes are accorded some kind of exalted status and dignity, is quite relevant.

REGIONAL ENGINEERING COLLEGES (RECs):

The Regional Engineering Colleges are national institutions established as joint and cooperative ventures of the Government of India and the concerned state governments. They have a national character. They are expected to provide academic leadership to the other technical institutions in the respective regions. As such it is imperative that proper conditions are created which will be conducive for free academic growth and to become real Centres of excellence. It is more so in the present changed Indian economic scenario wherein the industries have to meet the new challenges of global competition. As a result of the Brain Storming Session on Regional Engineering Colleges held in the Planning Commission, a document on 'Perspective for Excellence in Regional Engineering Colleges' has been brought out. The Report identifies several priority activities for RECs during the Eighth Plan and beyond. There are some deficiencies in the present system. The most important of these are lack of academic freedom, dual funding and multiple controls. Removal of these deficiencies would require some structural changes in the Regional Engineering Colleges set up. The question of granting 'deemed to be universities' status for some of the well developed RECs and for the rest granting 'autonomous status' initially, by University Grants Commission, could be seriously considered. With these measures, it should be possible for the RECs to blossom into Centres of excellence and play a leading role in helping the Indian industries and revitalising technical education in the country.

INDIAN INSTITUTES OF TECHNLOGY (IITs)

The IITs are the institutes of national importance and considered as Centres of excellence in engineering and technology. A series of Brain Storming Sessions were organised in the Planning Commission on IITs in the context of the changed economic scenario and in the context of the Prime Minister's observations relating to the need for modernising teaching research and other facilities in the engineering institutions like IITs. The discussions in the Brain Storming Session firstly resulted in the development of an approach paper dealing with new thrust areas, international consultancy, creation of corpus fund and industrial foundation. As a result of further discussions, the five IITs and the Indian Institute of Science, Bangalore have identified eight generic areas for taking up focussed technology development missions, as indicated in Annexure V. The missions involve not only major research component but also a commitment to technology development through innovation and its subsequent transfer to public / private sector industry. Developing, testing and delivery of technology are very much part of the package. The missions include areas of strategic significance and export potential. It is proposed that the funding of these projects should be through multiple agencies like Planning Commission / Ministry of H.R.D., other concerned ministries and industries. The Planning Commission has already allocated for the year 1993-94 Rs. 1 crore as seed money for each generic area proposed by the IITs and Indian Institute of Science, Bangalore for technology development in a mission mode.

INDIAN INSTITUTES OF MANAGEMENT (IIMS)

The role of management in the development process is widely recognised. Similarly, management education is perceived as being important for building managerial competence. The rapid growth of industrial and commercial enterprises in the 50's produced a demand for more and better trained managers in India. During 'this decade, management development took place largely through short management programmes for senior administrators and managers. Four Indian Institutes of Management were subsequently established—two during 60's at Ahmadabad and Calcutta, one during 70's at Bangalore and one during 80's at Lucknow and these four represent a potent force, professionalising management in India.

Two Review Committees were appointed on the Indian Institutes of Management. The first one, the Nanda Committee, was appointed in 1979 which submitted its report in 1981. The other Review Committee, the Kurien Committee, was appointed in 1991, and its report has been submitted recently. The Nanda Committee recommended that the objectives should include training and education of (i) Managers for public utilities and services and (ii) Management teachers. The Kurien Committee reaffirmed the Mission of the IIMs to strengthen management in business, industry and commerce. It further recommended that the mission statement needs to be expanded to emphasise IIM's commitment to public service and public management.

The University Grants Commission is providing assistance to about 40 universities / institutes for conducting programmes in Management Studies. The IITs also decided to develop management education programmes which started during the late 70's. The thrust of the programmes is on the management of technology. A-number of other private institutes of management like XLRI, Jamshedpur, are also doing good work in the field of management education and research.

During the nineties, the country is likely to become progressively more integrated into the global economy. Rapid economic growth with social justice and a reasonable balance of payments position are likely to remain over-riding priorities. Competition and pace of technological change are likely to intensify in most sectors of economy. As indicated earlier, with the advent of new Industrial Policy and liberalisation, the Indian industry is exposed to more domestic and global competition. 'Professional Management' becomes a vital component in industry. It equally applies to other sectors of economy especially, in the context of the financial resources crunch and the need for better and effective management, of available resources.

With the above situation, management education, training and research assumes greater significance and the Indian Institutes of Management, Schools or Departments of Management in Universities and other Institutes have to play a greater role in helping to formulate management strategies for the changing scenario. Unless management of public and private sector enterprises respond to greater competition in an effective manner, there will be large scale sickness especially among smaller enterprises. The management institutes should disseminate to competing enterprises through teaching, training, publishing and consultancy, the expertise to cope effectively with competition.

In the context of changing domestic and global economic scenario, the Planning Commission has taken the initiative to convene meetings of the IIM Directors and other experts to discuss and formulate new approaches in the management education, training and research. The discussions resulted in identifying some vital issues and areas which would contribute towards strengthening management education, research and training in the country.

It has also resulted in identifying certain priorities for the IIMs during Eighth Plan and beyond. Some of such priorities which will help the IIMs to play a systemic role in nineties are:

(i) To develop expertise in management of competition, quality management and international, management and .disseminate it to Indian industry. For this purpose IIMs industry linkages will need to be strengthened. Special efforts will need to be made to enable the more vulnerable, smaller enterprises to cope with competition, and to develop the expertise in dynamic forms of entrepreneurial management.

(ii) To identify strategic priority sectors that are currently poorly managed, and develop strategies for revitalizing them, involving orchestrated research, case studies, training, teaching and consultancy and also institution building in sectoral institutes of research / training.

(iii) To contribute to the effort at estimating the size and composition of the nation's managerial corps, its training needs now and in the future, and to a national strategy of catering to these needs.

(iv) To strengthen the management teaching and research apparatus in the country through stepping up the output of Ph.D.s in management, faculty development, materials development, and strengthening of other institutions providing management training.

(v) To network with academic institutions imparting professional education in other fields in order to strengthen their management systems and facilitate their attempts to add managerial competence to the professionals they produce.

Financial autonomy is vital for continuation of the IIMs as Centres of excellence and in this context the need is to initiate steps for fund generation by the IIMs and reduce their dependence on the Government to the extent possible, thus paving the way towards self-reliance. Creation of a substantial corpus fund for each IIM can be explored.

Focus on innovations in management education, is needed. Issues and problems relating to organisational culture and commitment, productivity and quality and processes of internal change, new initiatives in the social responsibility of management, globalisation of industry and trade and relevant strategies for India are to be addressed and solutions sought. In this context, the IIMs, Universities, other institutions of management, professional bodies like the Association of Indian Management schools have a responsible role to play.

DISTANCE EDUCATION MODE IN ENGINEERING AND TECHNOLOGY:

Education imparted through the Open University System is not a rival but a complimenting approach to formal system. Distance learning system facilitates democratisation of adult education process. Many countries in Asia and elsewhere have provided opportunities for adult education by adopting the open education system and set up, for this purpose, higher educational institutions of distance learning. There have been significant developments in the field of communication technology like use of satellites for telecast of educational programmes and computers for learning. Adopting such new technologies in distance education can help to cut cost and improve quality, equity and participation. Even though distance-teaching may tend to prove to be the most flexible and the most easily adapted alternative approach, it demands lot of efforts to maintain quality and standard in the basic disciplinary content of a degree programme or an enrichment programme meant for competency upgradation or a vocational programme for that matter.

Distance teaching also needs an innovative approach for its success. India having its own multipurpose satellite is well set for using electronic media for distance learning. Distance education programmes offered are mostly in non-engineering, non-technological or non-vocational areas in India. Attempts to provide distance education programmes in Engineering, Technology and vocational courses are rare. Courses which are suitably designed and developed could be offered through distance education mode in Engineering, Technology and Vocational areas with success and acceptability.

The working engineers in the country, especially those who are in the far flung areas, need opportunities to upgrade their expertise and qualifications. Distance education mode can provide the needed opportunity. The Author recalls as its once Vice-Chancellor, the Jawaharlal Nehru Technological University, Hyderabad is the first in the country to provide distance education opportunities in Engineering and Technology for working engineers and scientists to remove obsolescence and provide opportunities for updating, upgrading, broadening and diversifying their knowledge and skills. The University is offering Distance Education Programmes in B.Tech. and M.Tech. through correspondence-cum-contact mode. The university has already opened its doors for external registration for M.S. and Ph.D. programmes for working engineers in the country. Such an 'open' concept in engineering and technological education should be encouraged.

MANAGEMENT OF TECHNICAL EDUCATION:

The Technical education system should be dynamic and capable of responding to the changes in the socio-economic system of the country, national aspirations, objectives and goals. For this, the system should be efficient and the concerned people should have freedom for operation and innovation.

In the Indian Technical education system, there are two levels of organisation—at the Central and state levels, with a complex interface between them depending more on convention and precedents for interaction rather than on formal and recognised authority.

The All India Council for Technical Education (A.I.C.T.E.) is responsible for planning and co-coordinated development of technical education, promotion of qualitative improvement and regulation and maintenance of norms and standards. The University Grants Commission (UGC) has also a role to play in the development of technical education, as it finances about 32 university departments dealing with Higher education and engineering. It has also the authority to recommend "Deemed University" status to institutions to the Central government.

Most of the state governments have established Directorates of Technical Education for effective administration of technical education. However, the academic control of state level engineering colleges vests in the universities to which they are affiliated. Each state has set up a State Board of Technical Education for giving proper direction to the development of technical education in the state. At the diploma level the academic control is also exercised by the State Board of Technical Education. In case of government engineering colleges and polytechnics full administrative control and financing of institutions is exercised by the government. Aided private institutions are managed by a Board of Governors with representation from the government. It is essential that the management system should be effective and functional with sufficient decentralisation. Even more important, the system itself should be responsive to changes as indicated earlier. It is imperative on the part of the AICTE to evolve suitable management structure for different types of institutions.

Autonomy to selected Engineering Institutions will help towards freedom and Innovation in academic activities. 'Corpus fund' concept will facilitate reaching towards 'financial freedom' as well. These approaches and ideas deserve all the support when we are aiming at excellence in technical education.

CONCLUSION:

The impact of the change in global and national economic scenarios is the emergence of an era of global consciousness. This situation, among other things, requires a workforce having a scientific bent of mind and possessing the much desired temper and skills to maintain high quality and productivity at par with the world standards. Our R & D efforts should also be geared up accordingly. The Science and Technology education and research has, therefore, to respond to these emerging challenges to train men and women of caliber and competency of world standards and provide the needed R & D capability. In addition, the explosion of knowledge in Science and Technology sectors requires highly talented men and women whose fast grasp of knowledge could enable them to respond to the desired innovations in advancing the frontiers of knowledge and know-how. However, the success in this regard will depend upon our abilities to cope up with the emerging pressures of resources crunch on the one hand and the need for up gradation of the quality of Science and Technology education on the other.

IMPERATIVES OF UNIVERSITY-INDUSTRY—R & D ORGANISATION INTERACTION FOR NATIONAL DEVELOPMENT

Distinguished Vice-Chancellor, Faculty Members, Students, Invitees, ladies and Gentlemen,

It is a great privilege for me to have been invited by Sri Venkateswara University to deliver the Sri Rebala Lakshminarsa Reddy Endowment Lecture this year. I express my gratitude to the Vice-Chancellor, Prof. Jayarama Reddy for giving me this opportunity. Having given the choice, I have deliberated over many topics and ultimately settled with the topic **'Imperatives of University-Industry-R & D Organisation Interaction for National Development'** for the lecture, keeping in view the urgent need for optimising the use of resources in view of the country's economic crisis.

Momentous changes are taking place on the international scene. The end of the cold war, the transformations in Eastern Europe, the disintegration of the Soviet. Union and the imminent emergence of a common market in Western Europe are events of truly historic significance. These changes will have a profound impact on both the international relations and the world economy. Simultaneously, most developing countries have embarked on bold measures of reform in restructuring their economies and opening up to forces of competition, both domestic and foreign. All these changes will certainly have an impact on the Indian economy.

India is passing through a historic moment on the economic front. The Eighth Five Year Plan is being launched in the backdrop of certain Strengths in the economy as well as certain concerns which have surfaced over the recent years. The Government have taken new initiatives and bold decisions to reorient and restructure the economy to meet the challenges of the present economic crisis in the country.

The above scenario necessitates bringing in certain imperatives in the approach to Planning and these include—providing for more decentralisation; enlisting people's cooperation and participation in the National Programmes and Schemes; striving to achieve targets with less financial outlays through improved efficiency and productivity, optimizing the utilisation of resources and encouraging greater involvement of private sector etc.

In the process of increasing efficiency and productivity in a situation of resourcescrunch, pooling, sharing and optimising the use of available resources assumes importance. It applies to all sectors and there should be greater cooperation and interaction. Interaction and interdependence are well recognised concepts in the present day world. Universities, Industries and R & D Organisations are no exception to this.

R & D EFFORTS IN THE COUNTRY:

Research activity in Science and Technology in India are undertaken by universities and institutions / units / departments which can be classified under the various sectors as—Central Government, State Governments, Higher Education Sector, Public Sector Industry, Private Sector Industry, and Non-profit Institutions / Associations.

Major scientific departments with their research laboratories / institutions in the Central Government are the main vanguards of the research efforts being carried out in the country. Besides, there are other Central Government Ministries / Departments who have a number of research institutions under their administrative and financial control. In addition, there are in-house R & D units of public sector industries which are mostly under the administrative control of the Central Government but a few public sector industries are either under State Governments or in the joint sector of Central and State Governments. Some private sector-industries have established their own in-house R & D units. The in-house research and development units are responsible for undertaking R & D activities for the respective industrial organisations. The State Governments have their own research institutions which mainly comprise of agricultural universities and their research stations besides having other research institutions directly under different departments of the State Governments.

In the Higher Education system there are 193 Universities and University level institutions and about 7000 colleges. The higher education sector undertake research activities mostly of basic (fundamental) and applied research through their own funds and funds from U.G.C. as well as through projects sponsored by the major scientific departments of the Central Government.

There are non-profit research associations / institutions which carry out R & D activities and these are supported by either industry or government or both.

With the advent of the new Industrial Policy and liberalisation, the Indian industry is exposed to more domestic and global competition. To meet the challenge it requires modernisation, upgradation of the competency of the personnel, utilisation of modern management techniques and increased efficiency and productivity while maintaining quality.

TECHNOLOGY POLICY AND THE ROLE OF UNIVERSITIES AND R & D ORGANISATIONS:

In a country of India's size and endowments, self-reliance is inescapable and must be at the very heart of technological development. We should develop indigenous technology appropriate to national priorities and resources. Rightly, the basic objectives of the Technology Policy Statement of "1983 are: development of indigenous technology and efficient absorption and adaptation of imported technology appropriate to national priorities and resources. The Universities and the R & D Organizations (including National Laboratories) have an important role to play in this regard.

The Prime Minister of India recently observed that "A poor country like India cannot go on changing technology every year. We must adopt a futuristic approach". This has a special relevance for maintaining excellence, modernisation and self-reliance in a sustained manner. In this context, technology forecast (TF) and technology assessment (TA) assume an important role. Since Universities and IITs are familiar with frontiers of knowledge, it is but natural that they should play an important role in technology forecast (IF) and technology assessment to help the country to select right areas.

For a situation where global competitiveness is being driven by technology as an important element, TF / TA studies, and their continuing updates with special stress on the assessment of domestic and global markets are essential. Market driven technology development will now onwards be crucial for industry and government. Indicators available from TF / TA studies with assessment of markets, provides valuable clues for the Universities, R &D laboratories and IITs to plan in advance their research orientation. Concerned Universities and IITs should have a TF / TA group with the thrust areas they are specialising. These groups may also be encouraged to make specific TF / TA and technology market surveys for the industry. In addition to TF / TA studies, Universities and IITs could also conduct tailored courses under continuing education programmes for industry personnel regarding some new results of TF / TA studies and also enabling industry personnel to do some studies themselves.

Technology Information, Forecasting and Assessment Council (TIFAC) has done some TF / TA studies and it is also building up an information base to continue the TF / TA studies in more quantitative manner with continual updates.

A common dialogue between Universities / IITs, TIFAC and Indian Trade & Industry Associations will bear fruit towards the development of right type of indigenous technologies.

NEED FOR UNIVERSITY-INDUSTRY-R & D ORGANISATION INTERACTION

The new National Policy on Education points out the need for a networking system between technical education on the one hand and industry, R & D organisations and other related sectors on the other. This will become possible only if a process of polarisation and networking are initiated as suggested by the Working Group on Technical and Management Education set up by the Ministry of Human Resource Development.

The need of the hour is to forge strong linkages for interaction between universities industries and R & D organisations, which will result in: (i) pooling, sharing and optimizing the use of resources, (ii) development of indigenous technology appropriate to our national priorities and resources, (iii) adapting the imported technology wherever needed for preparing the industries to meet global competitiveness, (iv) enriching teaching and research in universities with practical and field experience, and (v) universities and R & D laboratories getting valuable clues for research orientation. The process of interaction will not only lead to mutual benefit of the partners but also contribute to national development.

UNIVERSITY-INDUSTRY INTERACTION

Excellence, modernisation, interaction and self-reliance are the four crucial elements in the development of Higher Education in general and Technical Education in particular. These factors should not be viewed in isolation but in relation to each other with the ultimate objective of attaining excellence.

The universities and the professional institutions should come out of their ivory towers and interact with the outside world. Similarly the industries should build up confidence in the capabilities of the universities and the Institution and interact with them for mutual benefit. It should be recognised that the academic world, industries and R & D Organisations together hold the key to the technology development in many of the core sectors of our country's economy. Through interaction the University gains insight into the problems of industry and it provides a base for research and education. Survival of industry largely depends on the improved, innovative and new technologies and for this purpose it needs the support of the academic institutions. Unfortunately, in our country Universities including technological institutions and the industry have been run on parallel lines without interaction.

The lack of strong linkage between Universities and the industry has led to the present situation where:

– the faculty, in general, have no industrial experience or exposure;
– there is not much provision for continuing education in the Universities and Institutions for practicing engineers to update their technology competence;
– State-of-art in the industry prevents flow between organised research in the Universities and institutions and evolution of Industrial R & D;
– there is no suitable mechanism available for interaction in most of the departments of the Universities and Institutions;
– some of the Universities and Institutions feel constrained to accept contracts with time bound results;
– there is chronic dependence of our industry on foreign collaboration.

The remedy to this situation lies in forging strong interaction between the academic world and the industries. In this connection, I may mention that a Symbiotic Model, which is known as **'Swaminadhan Model for University-Industry Symbiosis'** has been proposed by me in the recent past, as the Vice-Chancellor of the Jawaharlal Nehru Technological University, Hyderabad.

The Universities and the professional institutions must so develop their capabilities as to be looked upon by the industry and by entrepreneurs as their technology brain trust, reservoir of technology know-how and technological human resource, which they can tap with confidence, The academic institutions should be sources of information and advise on technology choice by keeping a constant tab on an updated data base with adequate knowledge of technology change, technology innovation, technology transfer, technology adaptation and model plans whose technologies have earned recognition and acclaim. They should become a clearing house for all information on the technological developments taking place in the country.

Universities must enter the country's industrial life and become a part of it and thereby become a partner in progress and a frontline organisation in technology and technological human resource development for the industry, its promoters and the entrepreneurs as well as the technological trouble shooter for industry. It should also become a conduit between industry and technology experts in various fields in the country and abroad.

The Universities should prepare a comprehensive Directory of Technology Experts (DITEX) in different fields of Technological expertise and know-how and forge continuing links with them through various means of involvement like seminars, talks, lectures, research collaborations, research guidance, sharing consultancy work with them and offering awards, honours, recognitions, honorary degrees, Visiting Professorships, positions like adjunct Professorship, guest faculty positions, etc.

The Universities should conduct industry survey to know:

a) Processes technology and equipment being used in the industry
b) The areas in which the University could contribute to industry in matters of research and consultancy and human resource development.
c) Technology choices: technology change, technology import, technology innovations, technology transfers etc

The IITs have initiated several measures and programmes towards interaction with the industry like establishment Industrial Foundations working on commercial lines.

Establishment of such a professional unit may lead to ease the chronic dependence of industry on foreign collaboration. The Industry should involve the Universities and academic institutions in project identification, formulation, appraisal, implementation, monitoring and evaluation.

UNIVERSITY-R & D ORGANISATIONS INTERACTION

Major scientific departments and defence Organisations in their research laboratories / institutions have costly equipment and expert resource personnel. The utilisation may not be optimal and they could be shared the University system which is mostly under-financed and exposed to obsolescence. The interaction between the Universities including professional institutions of higher learning, and R & D Laboratories will lead to mutual benefit.

The following interactions could be identified:

i) SHARING OF COSTLY EQUIPMENT:

The costly equipment available in National research laboratories could be thrown open to the university system through a suitable Memorandum Of Understanding. The UGC has been successful to some extent in this regard through signing Memoranda Of Understanding with the Atomic Energy Commission and Council for Scientific and Industrial Research (CSIR) for making available their facilities to the University system. Efforts were made by the Jawaharlal Nehru Technological University, Hyderabad to enter into Memorandum Of Understanding with some of the National laboratories situated at Hyderabad to use their facilities for teaching and research.

ii) MOBILITY AND EXCHANGE OF FACULTY

It is desirable to provide for free exchange of faculty, experts and scientists among universities, industries and. R & D laboratories. It will enrich teaching and research in universities with practical and field experience and enable the university faculty to get exposed to industrial and R & D environments.

As also recommended by the Working Group on Technical and Management. Education set up by the Ministry of Human Resource Development, mobility and exchange of faculty between academic institutions, national laboratories and industry should be encouraged to prevent inbreeding. To facilitate such free mobility and exchange of personnel, the existing rules and regulations regarding inter-departmental deputations etc. should be modified and liberalised.

iii) R & D COLLABORATION:

The Universities and the R & D Laboratories can take up R & D collaboration activities combining their research potential and resources.

iv) JOINT INTERNATIONAL CONSULTANCY:

The Universities / IITs and R & D Laboratories may have their own strengths and deficiencies for consultancy. Coming together, they can cover up the deficiencies of each other with their mutual strengths and forge a cohesive and strong partnership for International Consultancy.

Joint educational International Consultancy could be offered, which may include institution building, establishment of specialised laboratory facilities, development of curriculae, organising continuing education programmes like seminars and short courses, joint research projects, faculty development and technical staff training. Through industrial consultancy, we can help foster closer interaction between the educational institutions and industry in the recipient country by sending our experienced faculty and scientists and assisting them in taking up industrial consultancy assignments and extending the specialized analysis and testing facilities available at the universities, institutes and national laboratories in India. Consultancy services could also be extended directly to industries abroad. International consultancy will result in better appreciation of the technology and industrial capabilities of India in the receiving country, finally leading to mutually beneficial commercial relations.

v) JOINT ACADEMIC PROGRAMMES

Joint academic programmes in emerging areas of technology could be offered using the combined potential of the teaching faculty and the scientific personnel and infrastructural facilities of the universities and the R & D laboratories. The finest example of this approach is the M.O.U. between the Jawaharlal Nehru Technological University and the Indian Institute of Chemical Technology at Hyderabad to offer an M.Tech. programme in Chemical Technology, mostly using the facilities of the Institute, R & D Laboratories could also be recognised by the universities for Ph.D. programme.

INDUSTRY-R & D ORGANISATIONS / LABORATORIES INTERACTION:

The Government has taken several measures towards promoting industrial research in industry itself. By the end of 1988-89, there were nearly 1075 in-house R & D units which are likely to grow around 1500 by the year 1995. The growth of R & D in industry is, however, still remains to be unimpressive. The R & D expenditure by Industry, as a percentage of total R & D expenditure, is only 21% in India compared to 61% in U.K., 63% in Japan and 72% in U.S.A. Indian industry is ushering in a new era of high technology covering micro electronics, space technology, special materials, biotechnology, fine chemicals, life saving drugs and so on. In this context, launching work for acquiring exclusive technologies assume special significance as in many of these areas technologies may be denied to us. To meet the challenge of technology obsolescence and for the related technology development aspects, the industry needs the support of R & D laboratories as much as it does from the universities.

The specific areas of interaction between Industry and R & D Organisations are:—(1) Technology development and transfer, (2) Technology adaptation, (3) Productivity improvement, (4) R & D Collaboration, (5) Consultancy, and (6) Sponsored Research.

The Council of Scientific & Industrial Research (CSIR) is assigned the functions of promotion, guidance and coordination of scientific and industrial research in the country.

C.S.I.R. laboratories hold the overall 3 charge of fostering industrial development of the country. Its Technology Utilisation Division (TUD) is concerned with promoting the marketing and utilisation of CSIR knowledge-base, expertise and facilities through enhanced linkages with industrial organisations, counselling and design organisations, financial institutions and other potential users. Polytechnology Transfer Centres are set up in some State capitals to assist the local industrial units in identification and solving of their scientific and technological problems.

Greater efforts with widened scope are needed by all the national laboratories and scientific institutions to help the Indian industry. The Indian industry should on its part build up more confidence in the national laboratories and institutions (and universities) and utilise their expertise and resources for technology innovation and development, technology transfer and adaptation, productivity improvement, consultancy etc. In turn, the requirements of industry will provide the base for R & D activities in the national laboratories. Thus there is greater need for symbiotic relationship between Industry and R & D Organisations.

MODEL FOR UNIVERSITY-INDUSTRY-R & D ORGANISATION INTERACTION:

For realising effective symbiotic relationship between universities, R & D Organisations and Industries, a Model is formulated by the author (presented elsewhere in this Volume). The word 'University System' in the Model may include professional institutions of higher learning in Engineering, Technology, Medicine, Pharmacy, Agriculture, Management etc., and similarly the word 'Industry' may include any other related sectors of economy. To bring about effective interaction, there should be specific cells / units in the Universities, R & D laboratories and Industry to act as contact points and for coordination. For example, I have established a Bureau of Industrial Consultancy and R & D Activities (BICARD) in the Jawaharlal Nehru Technological University, Hyderabad to interact with the Industry and other sectors to acquaint with their problems, to boost their confidence in the University's capabilities, to receive consultancy assignments and to coordinate with the concerned schools and departments of the University in executing the work. Finally, I feel that the financial and promotional agencies have their own role to play to get closer own role interaction between the academic institutions, R & D organizations and the industry which ultimately is going to benefit the funding agencies in tackling industrial sickness. In this context, there is a need for creation of National

Cell to promote and coordinate the linkages a between the promotional agencies, university, industry and. R& D organisations.

CONCLUSION

It is believed that the Swaminadhan Model for University-Industry-R & D Organisation Symbiosis presented now if implemented will result in pooling, sharing and optimising the use of resources in terms of men, material and finance in these sectors and help towards national development through industrial growth. Teaching and research activities in universities gets enriched. There would be better and relevant industrial R & D output and the industries will thus be well prepared to face the global competition. For effective realisation of the desired results implementation of the Model through the suggested National Cell for promotion and coordination, appears to be a logical course of action.

INAUGURAL ADDRESS AT THE FOURTH ANNUAL MANAGEMENT EDUCATION CONVENTION OF THE ASSOCIATION OF INDIAN MANAGEMENT SCHOOLS

Prof. Philip, President of the Association of Indian Management Schools and Convention Chairman, Dr. Abraham, Convention Coordinator, Delegates to the Convention, Distinguished invitees, ladies and gentlemen,

I consider it as a privilege to be with you this morning to participate in the inaugural session of the Fourth Annual Management Education Convention of the Association of Indian Management Schools. I would like to express my deep sense of gratitude to Professor Philip and his colleagues for inviting me to inaugurate the Convention.

I am happy to note the Association of Indian Management Schools, established as the professional body of Indian Management Schools in August 1988, is doing yeoman service in the cause and promotion of management education in the country, with focus on quality and management, manpower training and development, management research and curriculum development.

I should congratulate the Association for choosing such an appropriate and relevant theme like "Management Strategies for the Changing Scenario" for this year's Convention which will cover vital issues like Emerging international management scenarios, The global revolution of privatisation, Economic liberalisation and its impact on Indian industry, Strategic linkages for international business, Research in Management education and New

Directions in Indian management education. I am happy to note that in addition to Indian participation, fraternal delegates from Canada, England and South East Asia are also participating in the Convention.

The role of management in the development process is widely recognised. Similarly, management education is perceived as being important for building managerial competence. The rapid growth of industrial and commercial enterprises in the 50's produced a demand for more and better trained managers in India. During this decade, management development took place largely through short management programmes for senior administrators and managers. Four Indian Institutes of Management were subsequently established—two during 60's at Ahmedabad and Calcutta, one during 70's at Bangalore and one during 80's at Lucknow and these four represent a potent force, professionalising management in India. Two Review Committees were appointed on the Indian Institutes of Management. The first one, the Nanda Committee, was appointed in 1979 which submitted its report in 1981. The other Review Committee, the Kurien Committee, was appointed in 1991, and its report is submitted recently. The Nanda Committee recommended that the objectives should include training and education of (i) Managers for public utilities and services and (ii) Management teachers. The Kurien Committee reaffirmed the Mission of the IIMs to strengthen management in business, industry and commerce. It further recommended that the. Mission statement needs to be expanded to emphasise IIM's commitment to public service and public management.

The University Grants Commission is providing assistance to about 40 universities / institutes for conducting programmes in Management Studies. The IITs also decided to develop management education programmes which started during the late 70's. The thrust of the programmes is on the management of technology. A workshop of the Directors of IITs held earlier at Delhi had recommended that IIT Management Programmes should be oriented towards management of technology, diagnostic research, human resource development and the teachers of IITs should be deployed to IIMs to study management techniques, undertake collaborative researches and carry out applied research activities. Off late, momentous changes have taken place on the international scene. The end of the cold war, the transformations in Eastern Europe, the disintegration of the Soviet Union and the imminent emergence of a common market in Western Europe are events of truly historic significance. These changes will have a profound impact on both international relations and the world economy. Most of the developing countries also embarked on bold measures and reforms in restructuring their economies and opening up to forces of competition both domestic and foreign. All these changes will certainly have an impact on the Indian economy.

In India too, historic changes on the economic front are taking place. The Eighth Five Year Plan is launched from April, 1992 in the backdrop of certain strengths in the economy as well as certain concerns which have surfaced over the recent years. The government has taken new initiatives and bold decisions to reorient and restructure the economy to meet the challenges of economic crisis in the country.

During the nineties, the country is likely to become progressively more integrated into the global economy. Rapid economic growth with social justice and a reasonable balance of payments position are likely to remain over-riding priorities. Competition and pace of technological change are likely to intensify in most sectors of economy. With the advent of new Industrial Policy and liberalisation, the Indian industry is exposed to more domestic and global competition. To meet these challenges it requires modernisation, upgradation of competency of the workforce, utilisation of modern management techniques and increased efficiency and productivity while maintaining quality. Thus 'Professional Management' becomes a vital component in industry. It equally applies to other sectors of economy especially, in the context of the financial resources crunch and the need for better and effective management of available resources.

With the above situation, management education, training and research assumes greater significance and the Indian Institutes of Management, Schools or Departments of Management in Universities and Institutes have to play a greater role in helping to formulate management strategies for the changing scenario. Unless management of public and private sector enterprises respond to greater competition in an effective manner, there will be large scale sickness especially among smaller enterprises. The management institutes should disseminate to competing enterprises through teaching, training, publishing and consultancy, the expertise to cope effectively with competition.

Structural adjustment aims at increasing Indian exports and this will be possible mostly through Indian enterprises acquiring global levels of expertise in developing and producing high quality products and marketing them internationally. The Institutes of Management and the Schools of Management have to develop the management expertise to meet this requirement and disseminate it widely to Indian enterprises. This implies the development of expertise in international management and in catalysing in Indian industry global levels of quality, productivity and innovativeness.

In the context of changing domestic and global economic scenario, the Planning Commission has taken the initiative to convene meetings of the IIM Directors and other experts to discuss and formulate new approaches in the management education, training and research. The discussions resulted in identifying some vital issues and areas which would contribute towards strengthening management education, research and training in the country.

The Eighth Plan envisages an annual growth rate in exports of 13.6% and an incremental capital output ratio of 4.1% which required upgrading of the management skills not just to enterprises but also of government ministries, departments and agencies and other organisations providing human capital and infrastructural services like education, health, environmental management, transportation, energy, communications etc. It is, therefore, imperative that IIMs and other Schools of Management identify strategic priority sectors that are currently not properly managed and develop the needed management expertise and diffuse it effectively to them. In this exercise close collaboration will be needed between IIMs, Schools of Management, government organisations and other priority sectors. The Planning Commission may provide an umbrella under which dialogue and cooperation between strategic priority sectors, and IIMs could be initiated.

The four IIMs together should be able to offer short and long duration training to all the management teachers in the country. Besides strengthening the teaching and research skills of the management academics, exposing them to innovative pedagogies and providing them with depth in their areas of specialisation, a part of the training should be towards institution building so that they can develop their home schools / departments, taking advantage of some of the values and practices that have contributed to the excellence of the IIMs. IIMs should also disseminate to other management teaching / training institutions in the country, course materials, cases, research findings etc. They can utilise for this purpose the Board of Management Studies of All India Council for Technical Education (AICTE) and Association of Indian Management Schools. They can also use their leverage in these bodies to raise accreditation standards.

There is a need for the IIMs to network with other academic institutions such as IITs, Universities, sectoral research / training institutions to facilitate their attempts to impart managerial skills to their students. IIMs can contribute to the entrepreneurship, technology management and industrial management programmes offered by the IITs. Management content of the B.Com. and other degree programmes offered by Indian universities could be enriched through interaction with IIMs.

The number of managers without any formal managerial training in the country is large. Even though there is no reliable estimate available about the number of personnel with supervisory and managerial responsibilities in the country, their number must be too large. There are an estimated 1 lakh managers in Central Government Public Sector Undertakings; and possibly there may be twice that number in private corporate sector. The number of managers in the governmental administration may exceed half-a-million. There are two million small scale manufacturing units headed by entrepreneur-managers. The services sector, academic institutions, NGOs, etc. too have a very large number of managers. A rough estimate is that there may be some three million managers in the country directing, coordinating and motivating a workforce of about 60 million.

This managerial army of say 3 million is highly differentiated by function, level, sector, and organisation. A significant improvement in the skills, drive, efficiency, innovativeness, quality orientation, and customer service orientation of this group of our society can generate incalculable benefits for the nation. As suggested during discussions in the Planning Commission, it is vitally important that a 'research effort' is mounted during the Eighth Plan to study the size and composition of our managerial corps, understand the roles different types of managers in different organisations, industries, and sectors are required to play and the knowledge-base, skills, attitudes needed, now and in the future, to play these roles effectively. IIMs should play a role, along with Institute of Applied Manpower Research, various trade, industry and sectoral associations etc., in this research task. The Association of Indian Management Schools can also be involved. Here, too, the Planning Commission could play a catalytic role. When once the above estimates become available, a strategy can be formulated for providing the nation's managerial class access to the needed knowledge-base, skills, and attitudes. Formal training provided at the IIMs would be a small though important catalytic component of this strategy. The IIMs' effort would be a pace setter and innovator in nature. Much larger extension work will need to be done, through strengthening and enlarging distance learning programmes provided by such institutions as IGNOU and others and starting of many more management training programmes both public and in-house. Preparation of educative audio-visual and other material for mass dissemination, such as through industry and sectoral bodies, AIR and Doordarshan could be undertaken. The IIMs can play both catalytic and expertise providing roles in this effort. The discussions in the Planning Commission with Directors of IIMs and other experts resulted also in identifying certain priorities of the IIMs during Eighth Plan and beyond.

Some of such priorities which will help the IIMs to play a systemic role in nineties are:

(i) To develop expertise in management of competition, quality management and international management and disseminate it to Indian industry. For this purpose IIMs—industry linkages will need to be strengthened. Special efforts will need to be made to enable the more vulnerable, smaller enterprises to cope with competition, and to develop the expertise in dynamic forms of entrepreneurial management.

(ii) To identify strategic priority sectors that are currently poorly managed, and develop strategies for revitalising them, involving orchestrated research, case studies, training, teaching and consultancy and also institution building in sectoral institutes of research / training.

(iii) To contribute to the effort at estimating the size and composition of the nation's managerial corps, its training needs now and in the future, and to a national strategy of catering to these needs.

(iv) To strengthen the management teaching and research apparatus in the country through stepping up the output of Ph.D.s in management, faculty development, materials development, and strengthening of other institutions providing management training.

(v) To network with academic institutions imparting professional education in other fields in order to strengthen their management systems and facilitate their attempts to add managerial competence to the professionals they produce.

Autonomy in its true sense should be the privilege of institutions of higher and technical education, including Management Institutes like IIMs so as to enable them to respond with full vigour for the fulfillment of their objectives and goals. Already considerable academic autonomy relating to offering courses, evolving evaluation methods, teaching, research and training is available in IIMs. Since finance is one of the important factors in achieving the goals of IIMs, there should be ample financial freedom as well. In the present system of funding by the Government, there is rigidity coupled with deficiency. The deficiency part is going to be more in the present situation of financial resources crunch. Financial autonomy is vital for continuation of the IIMs as Centres of excellence and in this context the need is to initiate steps for fund generation by the IIMs and reduce their dependence on the Government to the extent possible, thus paving the way towards self-reliance. Creation of a substantial corpus fund for each IIM can be explored. Revenue obtained from such fund can eventually be used to reduce the required support from the Government. Rigorous efforts should be made by IIMs to increase their revenues by increased teaching, training and consulting fees, search for large endowments to support specific activities, pursuit of better paying international teaching and training programmes, research and consultancy etc. A major effort will have to be made by IIMs to make their post-graduate programmes pay for themselves. Adequate rise in admission, placement, tuition and other fees should be made. International MBA programmes or international student participation charging the fees at international rates may have to be considered. India has a large scientific and technical manpower, being about one-third in the world and endowed with rich natural resources, which could, if effectively utilised, considerably contribute to the country's economic growth and social development. Achievements in areas like converting ideas into action, transfer of technology for improved productivity and performance, transforming human energy into synergy and optimizing resources for generating wealth and promoting the well being of the teeming millions in the country are, no doubt, impressive, but a lot more is desired. The role of professional management is paramount in this regard. The management system, however, cannot be borrowed and transplanted from elsewhere. Even though management theories and principles are universal, their application has to be contextually rooted in the local ethos and milieu. Focus on innovations in management education, is needed. Issues and problems relating to organisational culture and commitment, productivity and quality and processes of internal change, new initiatives in the social responsibility of management, globalisation of industry and trade and relevant strategies for India are to be addressed and solutions sought. In this context, the IIMs, Universities, other institutions of management, professional bodies like the Association of Indian Management Schools have a responsible role to play.

I am sure that the Convention will have fruitful discussions and the outcome will lead to valuable clues and recommendations for management strategies in the changing scenario, globally and nationally, on the economic front. I take great pleasure in inaugurating the Convention and wish it all success.

Inaugural Address At The National Seminar And I.S.T.E. Silver Jubilee Celebrations

Professor Hegde, Professor George, participants of the Seminar, distinguished invitees, ladies and gentlemen:

It is indeed a great privilege for me for having been invited to inaugurate the National Seminar on "Role of Central Government / State Governments / All India Council for Technical Education / University Grants Commission/ Universities / Directorates of Technical Education in Technical Education" and also to inaugurate the Indian Society for Technical Education (ISTE) Silver Jubilee activities. I am grateful to Prof. George and Prof. Hegde for giving me this opportunity.

I am happy to note that the Indian Society for Technical Education has completed 25 years and is celebrating its Silver Jubilee during 1992-93. The ISTE, the only national professional association of educators in Engineering and Technology in India, is doing a yeoman service in the cause of improving standards and quality of technical education. It is indeed heartening to note that the Society has been engaged in a variety of programmes and actions leading to upgradation and modernisation of curriculum, faculty and the education infrastructure. It has also been taking up Continuing Education Programmes for working engineers in order to avoid technical obsolescence. It is creditable that the society has an impressive membership base of over 24,000 professionals.

Momentous changes are taking place on the international scene, which have aprofound impact on both international relations and the world economy. In India too historic changes on the economic front have taken place. The Eighth Five Year Plan has been launched from 1st April, 1992 in the backdrop of certain strengths in the economy as well as certain concerns which surfaced over the recent past. The Government has taken new initiatives and bold decisions to reorient and restructure the economy to meet the challenges of economic crisis in the country.

During the 90's, the country is likely to become progressively more integrated into the global economy. Competition and pace of technological change are likely to intensify in almost all sectors of the economy. With the advent of New Industrial Policy and liberalisation, the Indian industry is exposed to more domestic and global competition. To meet these challenges, it requires modernisation, upgradation of the competency of the work force, utilisation of modern management techniques and increased efficiency and productivity, while maintaining quality. In this context, the role of technical education and training is paramount. In turn, the Indian Institutes of Technology (IIT), Indian Institutes of Management (IIM), Regional Engineering Colleges (REC), Technical Teachers Training Institutes (TTTI), Polytechnics and even Industrial Training Institutes (IIT) have distinct roles to play in shaping Technical Education and training to suit the changed scenario. Professional bodies like I.S.T.E. and Institution of Engineers have also their own roles to play. Contributions from Universities and private engineering and Management institutions are also imperative in this regard. In this context, the Central and State governments and organisations like U.G.C. and A.I.C.T.E. should create conducive atmosphere for education and training in these institutions and provide sound policy support.

Due to financial resources constraint, technical education institutions have to think in terms of pooling, sharing and optimising the available resources, realise that interaction and inter-dependence as an accepted concept and pursue collaboration and networking. Upgradation of the competency of the teachers, updating the curriculum and reviewing the evaluation system, the Institution-Industry Interaction and University-Industry-R & D Organisation interaction are also some of the issues which need focussed attention. The concept of the institutions of higher and technical education gradually progressing towards becoming less dependent on Government is also gaining momentum.

The Prime Minister referred to two important issues in the first Full Planning Commission meeting held in September, 1991. The first one relates to the need for modernising teaching, research and other facilities in engineering institutions like IITs which are regarded as centres of excellence and the second one stressing the need for adopting futuristic approaches in meeting the emerging challenges in science and technology.

Taking a lead from the Prime Minister's above observations, the Planning Commission assumed a new role of looking in depth into the development of higher and technical education in addition to its role of resources allocation. In this new role, in order to have free exchange of views, ideas and approaches on some of the issues indicated above which would help in making the institutions of higher and technical education move towards becoming real centres of excellence, the Planning Commission organised a series of Brain Storming Sessions on higher education, Universities, IITs, IIMs and RECs recently. The Brain Storming Session for Polytechnics is scheduled to be held shortly.

The Brain Storming Session on higher education underlined the following thrust areas:

i.   integrated approach to higher education;
ii. Excellence in higher education;
iii. expansion of education in an equitable and cost-effective manner, and making the higher education system financially self-supporting;
iv. making higher education relevant in the context of changing Socioeconomic scenario;
v.   promotion of value education; and
vi. Strengthening of management system in the universities scenario.

The Brain Storming Session on IITs resulted in developing an Approach Paper by the IITs covering issues related to (i) new thrust areas, (ii) international consultancy, (iii) creation of corpus fund and (iv) industrial foundation. With regard to new thrust areas, the IITs have identified seven generic areas to take up focussed technology development missions. These missions involve not only major research component but also a commitment to technology development through innovation and its subsequent transfer to private sector industry. Developing, testing and delivery of technology are very much part of the package and the Missions include areas of strategic significance or having export potential. The Report on the missions indicate that the funding of the projects in a mission mode should be through multiple agencies namely, Planning Commission, Ministry of Human Resource Development, other concerned Ministries and industries.

India has a large scientific and technical manpower, being about one-third in the world and endowed with rich natural resources, which could, if effectively utilised, considerably contribute to the country's economic growth and social development. Achievements in areas like converting ideas into action, transfer of technology for improved productivity and performance, transforming human energy into synergy and optimizing resources for generating wealth and promoting the well being of the teeming millions in the country are, no doubt, impressive, but a lot more is desired. The role of professional management is paramount in this regard.

The Brain Storming Sessions on IIMs organised to discuss and formulate new approaches in the Management Education, training and research resulted in identifying some vital issues and areas which would contribute towards strengthening management education, research and training in the country. It was found imperative that IIMs and other schools of management should identify strategic priority sectors that are currently not properly managed and develop the needed management expertise and diffuse it effectively to them. In this exercise, close collaboration will be needed between IIMs, Schools of Management, University Departments, Government organisations and other priority sectors. The Planning Commission will provide an umbrella under which dialogue and cooperation between strategic priority sectors and IIMs could be initiated. The four IIMs together should be able to offer short and long duration training to all the management teachers in the country. There is need for the IIMs to network with other institutions such as IITs, Universities, Central research / training institutions to facilitate their attempts to impart managerial skills to their students. The discussions on IIMs resulted also in identifying certain priorities of the IIMs to be pursued during the Eighth Plan and beyond.

The first Brain Storming Session on RECs in September, 1992 resulted in recognizing the need for creating proper atmosphere and conditions conducive to academic and financial autonomy so as to enable them to grow into real centres of excellence. The RECs have been asked to collectively prepare a document on "Perspectives for RECs for the Eighth Plan and Beyond".

Technical education, including management education, is one of the most potent means for creating skilled manpower required for the developmental tasks of various sectors of the economy. Technical education incorporates the technological dimension which is a vehicle for development. While this implies high costs of construction, laboratory equipment, library books and journals and high rate of obsolescence, such high cost, being directly related to development, should be viewed as an essential productive investment, yielding valuable returns to the society and contributing to socio-economic development.

During the past four decades, there has been a phenomenal expansion of technical education in the country. Today, we have over 200 recognised technical education institutions (TEIs) at the first degree level and more than 560 polytechnics at the diploma level with annual admission capacities of 40,000 and 80,000 students, respectively. About 140 institutions offer facilities for postgraduate studies and research in several specialized areas with an annual capacity of 9,400 students. The quantitative expansion has resulted in the lowering of the standards and there exists a structural imbalance of skill requirement of the business and industry sector and the traditional curricula transacted by the educational institutes. These factors give rise to problems of unemployment and under-employment. The wastage in the system is enormous, being 30 per cent at the degree level, 35 per cent at the diploma level and 45 per cent at the post-graduate level.

The infrastructural facilities available in the vast majority of technical education institutions (TEIs) are extremely inadequate. There is an acute shortage of faculty with about 25 to 40 per cent of faculty positions remaining unfilled. In most of the institutions, there is hardly any R & D activity.

The following thrust areas need to be pursued in technical education during the Eighth Plan: (1) modernisation and upgradation of infrastructural facilities. (2) quality improvement in technical and management education. (3) responding to new industrial policy and Industry-University / Institution-R & D Laboratories interaction. (4) resources mobilisation.

Modernisation relates both to technical equipments and teaching methods. Technology development is a capital intensive process. It is, therefore, imperative to adopt futuristic approaches in meeting the emerging challenges in science and technology. Coordinated and concerted efforts would have to be made to upgrade and consolidate the infrastructural facilities in the existing institutions. The process of removal of obsolescence would include enhancement of computer facilities and establishment and interlinking of large computer systems with educational and research institutions through appropriate telecommunication facilities. Steps should be taken to strengthen and create the facilities in crucial areas of technology where weaknesses exist, in the areas of emerging technologies and in new specialised fields.

A holistic and need-based approach would have to be adopted to reorient the technical and management education. A more broad-based flexible system with provision of multi-point entry is required to enable a better response to the unspecified demands of the future. At the micro-level, the curriculum should be developed to encourage creativity and innovation in experimental work by introducing problem / process-oriented laboratory exercises. New technology-oriented entrepreneurship and management courses are to be introduced in selected institutions having adequate infrastructural facilities. There should be greater emphasis on production engineering and towards design and product development.

Since technical education is inherently expensive, concrete steps to ensure cost effectiveness as an aspect of resource mobilisation are of vital importance.

It would be desirable to couple the technology forecasting system with the system of manpower forecasting and planning. Universities and IITs are familiar with the frontier areas of knowledge and hence should play an important role in technology forecast and technology assessment with the fruitful involvement of Technology Information Forecasting and Assessment Council (TIFAC), Institute of Applied Manpower Research (IAMR) and the Indian Trade and Industries Associations. It should be possible to develop the right type of indigenous technologies, assess the related manpower requirements and to produce the right type of trained manpower.

A strategy may have to be evolved for effective linkages between the industry, institutions and R & D laboratories. This linkage will help in : (i) pooling, sharing and optimising the use of resources, (ii) development of indigenous technology appropriate to our national priorities and resources, (iii) adapting the imported technology wherever needed for preparing the industries to meet global competitiveness, (iv) enriching the teaching and research in the universities with the component of practical and field experience, and (v) universities and R & D laboratories getting valuable clues for research orientation. The process of interaction will not only lead to mutual benefit of the partners but also contribute to national development. For realising an effective symbiotic relationship between the universities, R & D organisations and industries, a Model has been suggested by me in the recent past.

The existing facilities for continuing education and retraining are inadequate. There is a need to formalise the retraining programme for engineering and technology personnel engaged in all sectors and to make them mandatory. Programme-learning packages need to be created and distance learning methodologies employed to enable self-development and training of all scientific and technical personnel. In some of these areas professional bodies like I.S.T.E. can play a vital role in collaboration with Engineering Institutions.

The working engineers in this country, especially those who are in far-flung areas, need opportunities to upgrade their expertise and qualifications. Distance education mode can provide the needed opportunity. Distance education programmes now offered are mostly in non-engineering, non-technological or non-vocational areas in India. Attempts to provide distance education programmes in engineering, technology and vocational courses are rare. Courses which are suitably designed and developed could be offered through distance education mode in engineering, technology and vocational areas with success and acceptability. The distance education programmes for B.Tech. and M. Tech. Degree courses offered at Jawaharlal Nehru Technological University, Hyderabad bears ample testimony for its success.

Teacher education should need focussed attention when we are aiming at excellence in technical education. At polytechnic level, the Technical Teachers' Training Institutes are fulfilling this requirement. At higher education level, the University Grants Commission has established Academic Staff Colleges in some universities which are catering to the teacher education requirements limited to general disciplines only. However, with regard to higher technical education, there does not seem to be any specific mechanism available for teacher education. Therefore, suitable mechanisms are to be identified for this purpose. The Academic Staff Colleges of University Grants Commission could also have an added component of teacher education in engineering technology. Similarly, the Technical Teachers' Training Institutes could be adequately strengthened to offer teacher education facilities for the engineering faculty at graduate and post-graduate level. Some time ago, the project proposal submitted by the Jawaharlal Nehru Technological University, Hyderabad to establish a National Academy of Pedagogy in Engineering Technology and Management was approved in principle by A.I.C.T.E. and this could be pursued further to have one more mechanism available for teacher education in engineering technology and management.

With these observations, I take pleasure in inaugurating the National Workshop and wish it a fruitful outcome.

It is also my privilege to inaugurate the I.S.T.E. Silver Jubilee activities, which I am sure, will also include intensive and meaningful programmes throughout the year and wish all success. I am confident that the I.S.T.E. will continue to play its role well as a professional Society committed to achieving excellence in technical education in the country, especially in the changed

A MODEL FOR UNIVERSITY-INDUSTRY-R & D ORGANISATIONS INTERACTION

SYNOPSIS:

Higher Education, Technical Education, business and industry sectors and R & D Organisations have vital roles to play in the economic development. In India time is ripe for strong interaction between them in the context of the resources crunch in the country and the new initiatives taken by the Government in restructuring the economy. The universities and institutes of technical education should move towards becoming less dependent on Government for funding and, therefore, take measures for fund generation through interaction. The industries now being exposed to global competition due to liberalisation of the economy, need modernisation and upgradation of the competency of the workforce. The National R & D Organisations are also required to generate funds to some extent and, therefore, need interaction with Industries and Universities. The R & D Organisations, through interaction, will not only be able to generate resources but also get valuable inputs for research orientation and put their manpower and equipment to optimal utilisation. The paper discusses the Indian situation and offers a Model for University-Industry-R & D Organisation Interaction.

INDIAN HIGHER EDUCATION SYSTEM:

In India there are 193 Universities and University level Institutions and about 7000 Colleges. The enrolment of students in 1991-92 was 44,25 lakhs (36.93 lakhs in the affiliated colleges and 7.32 lakhs in the university departments). The number of women students was 14.37 lakhs (32.4 percent). The total number of teachers was 2.63 lakhs. The enrolment in correspondence courses and Open Universities at the end of the Seventh Plan (1985-90) was approximately 5 lakh students.

There has also been a phenomenal expansion of technical education in the country.

Today, there are over 200 recognised technical education institutions (TEIs) at the first degree level and more than 500 polytechnics at the diploma level with annual admission capacities of 40,000 and 80,000 students, respectively. About 140 institutions offer facilities for post-graduate studies and research in several specialised areas with an annual capacity of 9,400 students. The corresponding number of teachers is 27,000. However, there exists a structural imbalance of skill requirement of the business and industry sector and the traditional curriculum transacted by the educational institutions.

These factors give rise to problems of unemployment and under-employment. The wastage in the technical education system is considerable, being 30 per cent at degree level, 35 per cent at diploma level and 45 per cent at post-graduate level. One of the reasons for this is that the TEIs are functioning mostly in isolation. Linkage and interaction between TEIs and user agencies, such as industries, R & D an, design organisations and development sectors are not sufficiently strong.

CHANGES IN GLOBAL AND INDIAN SCENARIOS:

Momentous changes have taken place on the international scene. These changes will have a profound impact on both the international relations and the world economy.

Simultaneously, most developing countries have embarked on bold measures of reform in restructuring their economies and opening up to forces of competition, both domestic and foreign. All these changes will certainly have an impact on the Indian economy too.

India is also passing through a historic moment on the economic front. TheGovernment has taken new initiatives and bold decisions to reorient and restructure the economy to meet the challenges of the present economic crisis in the country. The Eighth Five Year Plan has been launched in the backdrop of certain strengths in the economy as well as certain concerns which have surfaced over the recent years.

NEED FOR UNIVERSITY-INDUSTRY-R & D ORGANISATION INTERACTION:

The above changed scenario necessitates measures for mobilisation of resources by higher education and technical education systems. They include avoiding duplication and wastage, increasing the efficiency of the system, optimising utilisation of the resources through pooling and sharing and resorting to generation of resources while at the same time not neglecting their primary task of teaching & research. The need for fund generation by universities is in the context of both seeking for financial autonomy and the present resources crunch. This added role of fund generation brings into sharp focus the need for interaction with other agencies.

During the 90's, India is likely to become progressively more integrated into the global economy. Competition and pace of technological change are likely to intensify in almost all sectors of the economy. With the advent of New Industrial Policy and liberalisation, the Indian industry is exposed to more domestic and global competition. To meet these challenges, it requires modernisation, upgradation of the competency of the work force, utilisation of modern management techniques and increased efficiency and productivity, while maintaining quality. Thus it needs interaction with Universities/ Institutions and R & D Organisations / Laboratories.

The National R & D Organisations / Laboratories are also affected due to the present resources crunch and so they are also expected to generate certain amount of resources for their maintenance which will be possible through interaction with Industries and other agencies.

There is thus need for forging strong linkages for interaction between universities, industries and R & D organisations. The interaction will not only lead to mutual benefit of the partners but also contribute to national development. The linkages between Universities, Industries and R & D Laboratories will help towards : (i) pooling, sharing and optimising the use of resources, (ii) development of indigenous technology appropriate to national priorities and resources, (iii) adapting the imported technology wherever needed for preparing the industries to meet global competitiveness, (iv) enriching teaching and research in universities with practical and field experience, and (v) universities and R & D laboratories getting valuable clues for research orientation.

UNIVERSITY-INDUSTRY-INTERACTION

Excellence, modernisation, interaction and self-reliance are the four crucial elements in the development of Higher Education in general and Technical Education in particular. Self-reliance should be viewed in terms of bridging the gap between fund requirement and fund availability from the Government, through suitable self fund generation mechanisms. These four elements should not be viewed in isolation but in relation to each other with the ultimate objective of attaining excellence.

The universities and the professional institutions should come out of their ivory towers and interact with the outside world. Similarly, the industries should build up confidence in the capabilities of the universities and the Institutions and interact with them for mutual benefit. It should be recognised that the academic world, industries and R & D Organisations together hold the key to the technology development in many of the core sectors of the country's economy. Through interaction the University gains insight into the problems of industry and it provides a base for research and education. Survival of industry largely depends on the improved, innovative and new technologies and for this purpose it needs the support of the academic institutions.

Thus there is a need for forging strong interaction between the academic world and the industries. For this purpose the author suggested a Symbiotic Model, which is known as **Swaminadhan Model for University-Industry Symbiosis(1)** when he was the Vice-Chancellor of the Jawaharlal Nehru Technological University, Hyderabad.

The Universities and the professional institutions must so develop their capabilities as to be looked upon by the industry and by entrepreneurs as their technology brain trust, reservoir of technology know-how and technological human resource, which they can tap with confidence. The academic institutions should be sources of information and advice on technology choice by keeping a constant tab on an updated data base with adequate knowledge of technology change, technology innovation, technology transfer, and technology adaptation. They should become a clearing house for all information on the technological developments taking place in the country.

Universities must enter the country's industrial life and become a part of it and thereby become a partner in progress and a frontline organisation in technology and technological human resource development as well as the technological trouble shooter for industry. It should also become a conduit between industry and technology experts in various fields in the country and abroad.

The Universities should prepare a comprehensive Directory of Technology Experts (DITEX) in different fields of Technological expertise and know-how and forge continuing links with them through various means of involvement like seminars, talks, lectures, research collaborations, research guidance, sharing consultancy work with them and offering awards, honours, recognitions, honorary degrees, Visiting Professorships, positions like adjunct Professorship, guest faculty positions, etc.

The Universities should conduct industry survey to know:

(a) Technology processes and equipment being used in the industry.
(b) The areas in which the University could contribute to industry in matters of research and consultancy and human resource development.
(c) Technology choices technology change, technology import, technology innovations, technology transfers etc.

The Indian Institutes of Technology (IITs) have initiated several measures and programmes towards interaction with the industry and they are in the process of establishment of Industrial Foundations working on commercial lines. Establishment of such a professional unit may lead to ease the chronic dependence of industry on foreign **collaboration.**

The industry and the other sectors of economy should involve the Universities and academic institutions in project identification, formulation, appraisal, implementation, monitoring and evaluation.

UNIVERSITY-R & D ORGANISATIONS-INTERACTION

Major national scientific departments and defence R & D Organisations / Laboratories in their research laboratories / institutions have costly equipment and expert resource personnel. The utilisation may not be optimal and they could be shared with the University system which is mostly under-financed and exposed to obsolescence. There could be fruitful interaction between the Universities, including professional institutions of higher learning, and R & D Organisations / Laboratories.

The following areas could be identified for interaction:

I) SHARING OF COSTLY EQUIPMENT:

The costly equipment available in National research laboratories could be thrown open to the university system through a suitable Memorandum Of Understanding. The University Grants Commission (UGC) has been successful to some extent in this regard through signing of a Memoranda Of Understanding (MOU) with the Atomic Energy Commission and Council for Scientific and Industrial Research (CSIR) for making available their facilities to the University system. Efforts were made by the Jawaharlal Nehru Technological University, Hyderabad to enter into a Memorandum Of Understanding with some of the National laboratories situated at Hyderabad to use their facilities for teaching and research.

II) MOBILITY AND EXCHANGE OF FACULTY:

It is desirable to provide for free exchange of faculty, experts and scientists among universities, industries and R & D laboratories. It will enrich teaching and research in universities with practical and field experience and enable the university faculty to get exposed to industrial and R & D environments. Mobility and exchange of faculty between academic institutions, national laboratories and industry should be encouraged to prevent inbreeding. To facilitate such free mobility and exchange of personnel, the existing rules and regulations regarding inter-departmental deputations etc. should be modified and liberalised.

III) R & D COLLABORATION:

The Universities and the R & D Laboratories can take up R & D collaboration activities combining their research potential and other resources.

iv) JOINT INTERNATIONAL CONSULTANCY:

The Universities / IITs and R & D Laboratories may have their own strengths and deficiencies in their expertise. Coming together, they can cover up the deficiencies of each other with their mutual strengths and forge a cohesive and strong partnership for not only consultancy work within the country but also International Consultancy.

Joint educational International Consultancy could be offered, which may include institution building, establishment of specialised, laboratory facilities, development of curricula, organising continuing education programmes like seminars and short courses, joint research projects, faculty development and technical staff training. Through industrial consultancy, it could be assisted to foster closer interaction between the educational institutions and industry in the recipient country by sending experienced faculty and scientists and assisting them in taking up industrial consultancy assignments and extending the specialised analysis and testing facilities available at the universities, institutes and national laboratories in India. Consultancy services could also be extended directly to industries abroad.

International consultancy will result in better appreciation of the technology and industrial capabilities of India in the receiving country, finally leading to mutually beneficial commercial relations.

v) JOINT ACADEMIC PROGRAMMES:

Joint academic programmes in emerging areas of technology could be offered using the combined potential of the teaching faculty and the scientific p personnel and infrastructural facilities of the universities and the R & D laboratories.

The finest example of this approach is the M.O.U. signed between the Jawaharlal. Nehru Technological University and the Indian Institute of Chemical Technology, a national laboratory at Hyderabad to offer an M.Tech. programme in Chemical Technology, mostly using the facilities of the Institute. R & D Laboratories could also be recognised by the universities for Ph.D. programmes.

INDUSTRY-R & D ORGANISATIONS / LABORATORIES INTERACTION

The Government has taken several measures towards promoting industrial research in industry itself. By the end of 1988-89, there were nearly 1075 in-house R & D units which are likely to grow around 1500 by the year 1995. The growth of R & D in industry is, however, still remains to be unimpressive. The R & D expenditure by Industry, as a percentage of total R & D expenditure, is only 21% in India compared to 61% in U.K., 63% in Japan and 72% in U.S.A.

Indian industry is ushering in a new era of high technology covering micro electronics, space technology, special materials, biotechnology, fine chemicals, life saving drugs and so on. In this context, launching work for acquiring exclusive technologies assume special significance as in many of these areas technologies may be denied to India.

To meet the challenge of technology obsolescence and for the related technology development aspects, the industry needs the support of R & D laboratories as much as it does from the universities.

The specific areas of interaction between Industry and R & D Organisations are:—(1) Technology development and transfer, (2) Technology adaptation, (3) Productivity improvement, (4) R & D Collaboration, (5) Consultancy, and (6) Sponsored Research.

Greater efforts with widened scope are needed by all the national laboratories and scientific institutions to help the Indian industry. The Indian industry should on its part build up more confidence in the national laboratories and institutions (and universities) and utilise their expertise and resources for technology innovation and development, technology transfer and adaptation, productivity improvement, consultancy etc. In turn, the requirements of industry will provide the base for R & D activities in the national laboratories. Thus there is greater need for symbiotic relationship between Industry and R & D Organisations.

MODEL FOR UNIVERSITY-INDUSTRY-RD ORGANISATION INTERACTION:

For realising effective symbiotic relationship between Universities, R & D Organisations and Industries, a Model has been formulated and the Model is shown in the Annexure. The word 'University System' in the Model may include professional institutions of higher learning in Engineering, Technology, Medicine, Pharmacy, Agriculture, Management etc., and similarly the word 'Industry' may include any other related sectors of economy.

There should be specific cells / units in the Universities, R & D Laboratories and Industry to act as contact points and for coordination. For example, the author has established a Bureau of Industrial Consultancy and R & D Activities (BICARD) at the Jawaharlal Nehru Technological University, Hyderabad to interact with the Industry and other sectors to acquaint with their problems, to boost their confidence in the University's capabilities, to receive consultancy assignments and to coordinate with the concerned schools and departments of the University in executing the work.

The financial and promotional agencies have also their own role to play to get closer interaction between the academic institutions, R & D organisations and the industry which ultimately is going to benefit the funding agencies in tackling industrial sickness. In this context, there is a need for creation of a National Cell to promote and coordinate the linkages between the promotional agencies, university, industry and R & D organisations.

REFERENCES:

1. Dr. Swaminadhan. D. 1989. *Swaminadhan Model for University-Industry Symbiosis:* Proceedings of the Workshop held on August 29, 1989 at Jawaharlal Nehru Technological University, Hyderabad, India and published in the University News dated 14th May, 1990 of Association of Indian Universities, New Delhi.
2. Dr. Swaminadhan. D. 1992. *Imperatives of University-Industry-R & D Organisation Interaction for National Development:* Published in the "University News" dated May 18, 1992, Association of Indian Universities, New Delhi.

SWAMINADHAN MODEL FOR UNIVERSITY- INDUSTRY-
R & D ORGANISATION SYMBIOSIS

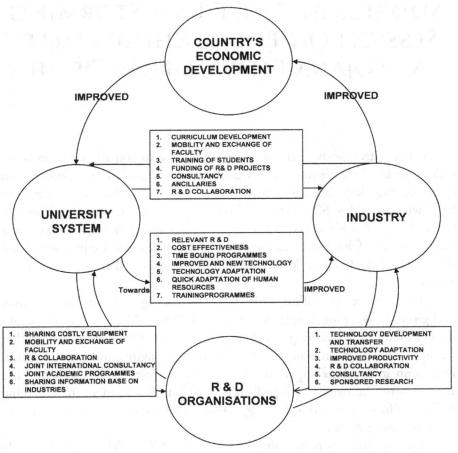

Note:
1. 'University System' includes professional institutes of Higher Learning in Engineering, Technology, Medicine, Pharmacy, Agriculture, Management etc.
2. 'Industry' may also include other sectors of the economy.

ADDRESS AT THE BRAIN STORMING SESSION ON POLYTECHNICS HELD AT YOJANA BHAVAN, NEW DELHI

At the outset, let me extend a warm welcome to you all and express my thanks for kindly accepting out invitation to come to Planning Commission to attend this Brain Storming Session on Polytechnics. We are privileged to have with us today Shri Pranab Mukherjee, Deputy Chairman, Planning Commission to address the Brain Storming Session. His presence here is a manifestation of his keen interest in the field of technical education. I am very grateful to him for kindly accepting to address this Brain Storming Session.

The purpose in calling this Brain Storming Session has its own background. We took inspiration from the Prime Minister's observations in one of the full Planning Commission meetings where he observed that we have to look to the needs of modernising Engineering and Technical Education institutions, especially those which are centres of excellence and also stressing the need to adopt futuristic approaches to meet the emerging challenges in science and technology. Hence the need to arrange a number of Brain Storming Sessions.

First we had Brain Storming Sessions on IITs, IIMs and then lastly during the month of September, 1992 we had the Brain Storming Session on RECs. The main idea in organising these Sessions is to discuss in-depth the prospects and the problems in Technical Education so that we can identify if there are any linkages among the various levels of education and at the same time looking at the prospective of Technical Education.

This is the background in which this Brain Storming Session is convened and for this Session I would like to identify the main purposes as (1) To look at the present Technician Education at the Polytechnic level and some of the related problems. (2) To discuss how to make it more responsive to the changing scenario in domestic and global economy. (3) To draw up perceptive for the development of Polytechnic Education during the 90's and beyond. These are the specific purposes for which we are here. And, incidentally we may also discuss Industrial Training Institutes education and also the general vocational courses offered at tenth standard and the ten plus two stage, possibilities of linkage between Polytechnics, the ITIs and the vocational education.

I would like to spend a few minutes of time to set the tone for the discussion. If you look at the technical education system, we can find that its growth is dependent upon the socio-economic and industrial conditions prevailing in the country. And its development, of course is related to the requirements of the economy of the country. That being so, naturally the growth of technical education during the pre-independence days has not been much. But the moment we attained independence, we had to take quick strides to develop technical education keeping in view the needs of the changing and rapidly industrialising nation, which was predominantly agricultural to start with.

Now, keeping in view the requirements of the country and the economy, we need four levels of technical education. (1) Programmes / courses offered by ITIs whose products will be working as skilled workers (2) Diploma level programmes offered by Polytechnics whose products will be working as Supervisors (3) Degree level programmes offered by IITs, Engineering Colleges and universities, whose products will function as engineers and technologists and (4) P.G. Programmes like M. Tech. and Ph. D. offered by IITs, IIMs, universities etc., whose products will become Management Personnel, Teachers, Scientists and Researchers.

Looking at the statistics on Polytechnic education, in 1947, there were 53 institutions at diploma level with an intake of 3670 students. Today there are nearly 950 technical institutions with an annual intake of about 1,26,000 students. For training craftsmen, there are about 2500 Industrial Training Institutes with over 3 lakh students annually. About 1900 institutions conduct vocational courses at 10+2 level admitting about 95,000 students annually. Still there is greater demand for technical education. This point is to be noted.

Now, what are the general problems we face or criticisms we hear normally? During 70's the criticism was that the Polytechnic courses were mostly theoretical with very little practical bias. The diploma courses were a poor imitation of the degree courses and, therefore, they did not really serve the middle level technical personnel requirements. And lastly, no attempt had been made towards specialisation i.e., no attempts were made to produce specialist technicians. Perhaps the situation has not changed much even now due to the proliferation of sub-standard institutions.

Now, in the 90's there are several other issues adding to the above situation. As you are aware, momentous changes have taken place on the international scene which will have a profound impact on the international relations and world economy. And also within the country, there have been changes in the economic scenario and the Government has taken new initiatives and bold decisions to reorient and restructure the economy through introducing the new Industrial Policy, Trade Policy, and liberalisation and so on. We have launched the Eighth Five Year Plan from 1st April, 1992 in the backdrop of certain strengths in the economy as well as certain serious concerns which have surfaced over the recent past. And the country is likely to become progressively more integrated into global economy. Competition and pace of technological change are likely to intensify in all sectors of the economy. What is the impact of these changes, especially on industry? It is exposed to global competitions. The result is to add greater responsibility to technical education to cater to the industry's needs in the wake of the liberalised policies of the Government of India.

Looking at these deficiencies and problems it boils down to three main problems facing the technical education, which are equally applicable to polytechnic education also. They are: (1) Increasing demand for technical education (2) Resources crunch for education in general and technical education in particular (3) The question of relevance of technical education. Now, how to tackle these problems to maintain access, equity, quality and cost effectiveness? These have to be discussed and arrive at certain conclusions and recommendations.

How to tackle the increasing demand? Firstly, to meet this demand we need to have manpower projections and planning instead of trying blindly to cater to the demand. Secondly, optimal utilisation of existing capacity through sharing and shift systems. Thirdly, encourage private participation with proper checks; checks on standards, checks on infrastructural facilities and on the faculty available in these institutions and above all we have to safeguard the interests of weaker sections of the society who have to be protected. The other way of meeting this demand is through distance education mode in technician education. However, proper care is to be taken in designing the courses with sufficient in built practical component as it is different from the distance education programmes in general disciplines.

Then, how to meet this resources crunch? We have to think in terms of pooling, sharing and optimising the available resources through networking, collaboration and so on within the system itself. Secondly, encouraging institution-industry interaction. They get mutually benefited and the institution may earn some funding through this process. Thirdly, discarding outmoded courses and programmes. Fourthly, striving to move towards achieving cost-effectiveness which might lead gradually to becoming less dependent on government. In these days of resources crunch, this idea is catching up and we have to look into this seriously.

Then there is the question of relevance of the output of engineering colleges and polytechnics. There is 30 per cent wastage at Undergraduate level, 35 per cent at diploma level and 45 per cent at post graduate level. One of the reasons for this wastage is due to the structural imbalance between the skill and knowledge requirements of industry and the traditional curricula transacted by the institutions. This has to be corrected to bring about relevance. We have to conduct studies on the needs of industries and other user agencies and identify the gap between the knowledge requirement and curricula transacted and then restructure the curricula involving the people from the industry. Then we will be able to provide adequate practical and industrial training in collaboration with industries. These are some measures to be taken to see that the present approaches are modified to bring about relevance. But what about those who have already passed out and working? For them we have to provide continuing educational facilities through either part-time programmes or through distance education mode. I am referring to the non-degree programmes also through distance education mode.

There are certain externally aided projects in addition to the programmes initiated by the government for polytechnics. They should be properly dovetailed for optimal results.

Now, as I said in the beginning, at the end of this Session, we expect a kind of framework to prepare a document-an approach paper on Perspectives for Development of Polytechnic education during the 90's and beyond. We should discuss and arrive at a consensus, conclusions and suggestions on the following areas, which will be helpful in preparing the approach paper.

1. Meeting the increasing demand through:
    a. manpower assessment and planning
    b. optimal utilisation of capacities and
    c. adopting distance education mode.

2. Relevance and quality
3. Resources generation
4. Private participation
5. Institution-industry interaction and institution-society interaction. Community Polytechnics to be strengthened so that they will become more responsive to societal needs
6. Women's participation
7. Entrepreneurial development programmes which will help reduction in unemployment
8. Curriculum development
9. Quality improvement of teachers
    a. Pedagogy
    b. Industrial / field exposure

10. Accreditation of Polytechnics
11. Management of Polytechnics
12. Linkages between polytechnics, vocational institutions and it is
13. Networking and collaboration among polytechnics
14. Role of Institutions like IITs, RECs, other engineering colleges and universities in the development of polytechnics.

ADDRESS AT THE CONFERENCE OF VICE-CHANCELLORS AT UNIVERSITY OF POONA

If higher education has to contribute effectively towards fulfilling the national objectives, goals and aspirations and the requirements of the people with changing times, we have to create conditions for achieving excellence, quality, relevance, access and equity. While excellence, quality and relevance are more 'within', access and equity which have a wider context, are 'without' in relation to a university or an institution of higher learning. Quality being an all time objective, relevance relates to requirements of changing times. The changed economic scenario brings-in interaction and self-reliance to the extent possible, as further imperatives. Added to this, the higher education system at present suffers from some weaknesses such as proliferation of sub-standard institutions, failure to maintain academic calendar, out-dated curriculum. As a result quality suffered.

UNIVERSITY GRANTS COMMISSION

The general duty of the University Grants Commission is to take such steps as it may deem fit for the promotion and coordination of university education and for the determination and maintenance of standards of teaching, examination and research in universities and allocate and disburse grants to the universities, deemed to be universities and colleges.

The UGC, through its various general programmes and quality improvement programmes and schemes and through funding out of the

215

resources made available by the government, has been striving to improve and promote quality of teaching, research and extension aspects of higher education and to maintain standards. However, 'determination of standards' aspect has been inadequately attempted. In these circumstances, establishment of a National Accreditation and Assessment Council (N.A.A.C.) assumes greater significance. The efforts of the Accreditation and Assessment Council would, directly or indirectly, help in improving the above situation to a large extent. I must congratulate the U.G.C. for establishing the Accreditation and Assessment Council, which fulfils implementation of the statements made in the N.P.E., P.O.A. and the Eighth Plan document. I do not intend to refer to the various practices prevailing abroad as they are already referred to in the Theme Paper. We have to keep in view that we need to evolve a mechanism suited to our own conditions.

An institution of higher learning, when it commits itself to excellence, quality and relevance, has to, among other things, be amenable to self-assessment, self-improvement and assessment by outside agencies. In this context, a mechanism like National Accreditation and Assessment Council, inter-alia should: (a) be more of a catalytic agent, (b) help in clearly defining of the institute's primary missions or goals, which are to be realistic and appropriate, (c) encourage self-assessment, (d) undertake assessment and accreditation in an un-biased manner, (e) constantly monitor and improve the quality process, participation, achievements etc., and (f) also be able to provide information on the quality of institutions and programmes to migrating students and the society. The National Assessment and Accreditation Council should be truly autonomous so that it could be fairly objective in carrying out its assigned tasks.

Assessment and accreditation could be for an institution as a whole or any of its departments, schools or any programme or scheme. Institutional accreditation should embrace all educational endeavours conducted by an institution, regardless of its complexity. While evolving the qualitative criterion for the assessment of institutions, in addition to the principal areas of institutional activities and responsibilities, due weightage should be given to 'relevance', that is relevance in teaching, research and extension activities. Blending 'scholarship' and 'relevance' should be an important factor.

The Report of the Committee on Accreditation and Assessment Council brought out during 1987 by UGC and the present Theme Paper on Accreditation and Assessment Council provide enough material on N.A.A.C. and I must say that the envisaged objectives, criterion and responsibilities for

N.A.A.C. are quite comprehensive and there should be room for flexibility to absorb changes.

The system of higher education should be able to show flexibility and resilience in reorienting itself to meet the emerging challenges of the changed global and national economic scenarios. Such a situation demands that the system should be free from unnecessary constraints and political interference and have the needed academic, administrative and financial freedom. On the part of the system itself, it should be amenable to accountability. In all these areas, except political interference, I am confident that the N.A.A.C., in the course of a reasonable time frame, will be able to make significant contributions and help the higher education system in the country.

ENGINEERING EDUCATION—
AN INDIAN PERSPECTIVE

Technical education (which includes engineering and management education as well) is one of the most potent means for creating skilled and technical manpower required for the developmental tasks of various sectors of the economy. It forms one of the most important and crucial components of human resource development with great potential for adding value to products and services, for contributing to national economy and for improving the quality of life of the people. It incorporates a technological dimension which is a vehicle for development. Technical education may itself imply high costs, but such high costs, being directly related to development, should be viewed as an essential productive investment, yielding valuable returns to society and contributing to socio-economic development. The Scientific Policy Resolution (1958) of India rightly states that "The key to national prosperity, apart from the spirit of the people, lies, in the modern age, in the effective combination of three factors— technology, raw materials and capital of which the first is perhaps the most important, since the creation and adoption of new scientific techniques can, in fact, make up for a deficiency in natural resources and reduce the demands on capital".

The science and technology education and research in India have made significant contributions to the overall development of the country. From a merely agriculture based society in the early forties, India is today rated among the biggest industrialised nations having a sound base of industries along side with a highly developed agriculture sector. As we march towards the 21st century and with our policies of economic liberalisation, it is imperative that our developmental efforts are supported by the relevant science and technology inputs on one hand and relevant human resources on the other. Technical education and research have thus, to-play a very significant role in the changed economic scenario. For this, they need proper reorientation.

DEVELOPMENT OF HIGHER AND TECHNICAL EDUCATION IN INDIA

Growth of technical education depends on the socioeconomic and industrial conditions of a country and its development is controlled by the needs and requirements of the economy. After Independence, the country was faced with the greater challenge of rapidly industrialising the predominantly agricultural economy and in this process major efforts had been made to create a wide-based infrastructure of higher and technical education institutions, research laboratories and industry, covering a broad spectrum of disciplines and capabilities. There are now over 185 Universities and academic institutions of national importance and 7958 colleges with a total enrolment of about 4.8 million students for graduate, postgraduate and research degrees and diplomas, with over 2,70,000 teachers. The higher education institutes include those offering programmes in Arts, Science, Commerce, Engineering, Technology, Management, Finance, Humanities, Social Sciences etc.

With regard to technical education institutions, there were only 38 institutions at the degree level with an intake of 2940 students and 53 institutions at the diploma level with an intake of 3670 students in the year 1947. Today there are 372 technical institutions at the degree level and 958 technical institutions at the diploma level with an annual intake of 88,930 and 1,52,554 students respectively. These include regular engineering colleges, polytechnics, Indian Institutes of Technology, Regional Engineering Colleges and other institutions. For training craftsmen, there are over 2650 Industrial Training Institutes/ centres admitting over 3.8 lakh students per year. About 2000 institutions conduct vocational courses at the higher secondary school level (10+2 level), admitting about one lakh students per year. There are 306 centres, including institutions conducting part-time and correspondence courses and Indian Institutes of Management, imparting management education to over 27,440 students. There are about 100 centres offering postgraduate programmes in engineering and technology with an annual intake of over 9000 students. The government has set up about 450 major S & T research laboratories under its various departments and ministries. There are also about 1360 recognised in-house R & D laboratories in public and private sector undertakings. More than 200 consultancy firms are engaged in engineering design, analysis and research.

STRUCTURE OF TECHNICAL EDUCATION:

Keeping in view the requirements of the country, we needed four levels of technical education. (i) Programmes/ courses offered by ITIs whose products will be working as skilled workers, (ii) Diploma level programmes offered by Polytechnics whose products will be working as Supervisors, (iii) Degree level programmes offered by IITs, Engineering Colleges and universities whose products will function as engineers and technologists and (iv) Post graduate programmes like M.B.A. and other P.G. Diplomas, M.Tech. and Ph.D. offered by IITs, IIMs, Universities etc., whose products will become Management Personnel, teachers, scientists and researchers.

The Indian Institutes of Technology are established as institutions of national importance to initiate and nurture indigenous effort for technological development. The Regional Engineering Colleges are established with the objective of bringing a major quality change in educational programmes and to train personnel to handle and manage engineering activities in the country.

The four Indian Institutes of Management represent a potent force for professionalising management in India. Collectively they have graduated nearly 8000 MBAs whose annual earning capacity of around Rs. 100 crores indicates the kind of contributions they are making to Indian industry. The IIMs have also shown a considerable capacity for adding to the teaching, training and research capability of the nation in the field of management.

Four Technical Teacher Training Institutes were established during sixties to function as resource centres for the development of polytechnics in the respective regions. Their duties include curriculum development, teacher training, development of learning resource material, educational research and other activities related to diploma level education.

Deficiencies and Distortions in the System:

The Technical Education system suffers from certain weaknesses and deficiencies. No doubt there has been a considerable quantitative expansion in technical education but quality suffered and there is lack of relevance. The following are the major imbalances and distortions which need focussed attention:

i. The quantitative expansion has resulted in the lowering of standards and there exists a structural imbalance of skill requirement of the industry and business sectors and the traditional curriculum transacted by the educational institutions. These factors give rise to problems of unemployment and under—employment.
ii. Wastage in the system is enormous. An analysis of the intake and Out-turn figures of recognised institutions shows that wastage is of 30% at degree level, 35% at diploma level and 45% at post-graduate level.
iii. The infrastructural facilities available in the vast majority of technical educational institutions are extremely inadequate.
iv. There is an acute shortage of faculty with about 25-40% of faculty positions remaining unfilled.
v. In most of the institutions there is hardly any R & D activity.
vi. The technical educational institutions are functioning in isolation. Linkage and interaction between technical educational institutions and user-agencies such as industries, R & D and design organisations and development sectors are not sufficiently strong.
vii. There has been an enormous increase in public expenditure on education but little attention has been paid to the strategies for raising non-budgetary resources and maximising people's Participation.

POLICY STATEMENTS:

(A) NATIONAL POLICY ON EDUCATION, 1986 (AS MODIFIED IN 1992):

The National Policy on Education, inter-alia, underlined the need for re-organising the technical and management education system to effectively deal with the changes in the economy, social environment, production and management processes and rapid expansion of knowledge and advances in science and technology.

It laid specific guidelines for the qualitative and quantitative development of the technical and management education sectors; establishment of linkages amongst the concerned agencies; manpower assessment and technical education forecasting; increasing effectiveness of technical education management system; proper delivery systems, measures to achieve greater cost effectiveness and generation of resources through suitable means. It further states that technician education has to play an important role in developing highly skilled middle level technical manpower for the organised as well as the unorganised sectors and necessary steps will be taken to make technician education flexible, modular and credit based with provisions for multi-point entry to achieve this goal. Programme of Action (POA) 1992 spells out the steps for implementation of the National Policy on Education.

(B) EIGHTH FIVE YEAR PLAN:

The perspectives for development of technical education during the eighth plan have the following thrust areas:

i. Modernisation and upgradation of infrastructural facilities,
ii. Quality improvement in technical and management education,
iii. Responding to New Industrial Policy and Institution Industry-R & D Laboratories interaction, and
iv. Resource mobilisation.

The strategies envisaged to achieve the objectives related to these thrust areas are:

I) MODERNISATION:

Modernisation relates to both technical equipment and teaching methods. We have to adopt futuristic approaches for achieving modernisation and self-reliance in a sustained manner. Coordinated and concerted efforts are needed to upgrade and consolidate the infrastructural facilities in the existing institutions. The process of removal of obsolescence would include enhancement of computer facilities and establishment and inter-linking of large computer systems with educational and research institutions through appropriate telecommunication facilities. Steps should be taken to strengthen and create facilities in crucial areas of technology where weaknesses exist, in areas of emerging technologies and in the new specialised fields.

II) QUALITY IMPROVEMENT:

A holistic and need based approach will have to be adopted to reorient the technical and management education. A more broad based flexible system with provision for multipoint entry, is required to enable us to offer a better response to the unspecified demands of the future. At the micro level, the curriculum should be developed to encourage creativity and innovation in experimental work by introducing problem or process oriented laboratory exercises. New technology oriented entrepreneurship and management courses are to be introduced in selected institutions having adequate infrastructural facilities. There should be greater emphasis on production engineering and towards design and product development. It would be desirable to couple the technology forecasting with the system of manpower forecasting and planning. Universities and the IITs should play an important role in technology forecast and assessment with the fruitful involvement of Technology Information, Forecasting and Assessment Council (TIFAC), Institute of Applied Manpower Research (IAMR), and Indian Trade and Industries Associations. This would enable to develop the right type of indigenous technologies, to assess related manpower requirements and to produce related trained manpower. Existing facilities for continuing education and retraining are inadequate. There is a need to formalise the training programmes for engineering and technology personnel engaged in all sectors and to make them mandatory. Programme learning packages need to be created and distance learning methodologies employed to enable self-development and training of scientific and technical personnel.

III) RESPONDING TO THE NEW INDUSTRIAL POLICY:

Momentous changes have taken place on the international scene which will have a profound impact on international relations and the world economy. Most developing countries have also embarked on bold measures of reform, restructuring their economies and opening up to forces of competition, both domestic and foreign. The Government of India also have taken new initiatives and bold decisions to reorient and restructure the economy to meet the challenges of the economic crisis in the country through its policy of liberalisation, new Industry and Trade Policies etc. The impact of these changes on Indian industry is considerable and it is now exposed to global as well as indigenous competition. To meet these challenges, it has to resort to modernisation, upgrading technology and competence of the work force, adopting modern management techniques and increasing efficiency and productivity. In this context, the various constituents of national development like universities, engineering institutions, national R & D laboratories and the professional bodies and academies have greater roles to play. A. strategy may have to be evolved for effective interaction between them. To bring about such a meaningful interaction, a Model for University-Industry-National R & D Laboratories-Professional Bodies and Academies Interaction for country's economic development has been formulated by me. The model identifies the areas of interaction between the various above constituents leading to country's economic development. It is imperative that each of these constituents have a Consultancy Unit / Cell and there is a national coordination mechanism for promoting effective interaction.

IV) RESOURCE MOBILISATION:

Now the time has come where the government alone cannot bear the burden of financing the technical education and, therefore, additional resources are to be mobilised to share the cost. This is not peculiar to India alone and it is the case with many other countries too. This brings into focus the need for Technical Education system to generate funds to supplement the funding from the government through suitable means, which will not, in any way, affect their primary task of teaching and research. There are a number of measures which could be taken up to tackle the inadequate resources situation and lessen its impact.

The following measures could be adopted:

1. Avoidance of duplication of investment in Technical Education institutions located close to each other and proper maintenance of available facilities and instruments.
2. Developing institution-wise specialisation in respect of courses and technical manpower so that the institutions can have the most sophisticated and modern library and laboratory facilities in their chosen fields.
3. Weeding out of outdated and stereotyped courses and introduction of relevant courses in emerging areas.
4. Multiple use of infrastructural facilities through part-time courses, continuing education programmes, consultancy and testing services.
5. Marginal increase in intake capacities in areas of scarce manpower and decrease in intake of low demand areas.
6. Introduction of multiple or at least double shifts in Technical Education institutions.
7. Maximum use of non-monetary inputs, like better planning, advanced technologies and practices, better system of supervision and administration, monitoring and review etc.
8. Commercialisation of the research output of the institutions.
9. Raising of fees in Government-run, Government-aided and unaided institutions on a graduated scale. The measure of raising fees, however, should be coupled with scholarships for SCs / STs and for students below poverty line and a loan scheme to other students.
10. Creation of a corpus fund with contributions from industry, alumni, charitable trusts etc., as well as from Government.
11. Implementing the Institution / University-Industry-National R & D Laboratories—Professional Bodies and Academies Interaction with all seriousness which will not only help towards national development but also help towards fund generation by the universities and other technical institutions.

The All India Council for Technical Education had appointed a High Power Committee on Mobilization of Additional Resources for Technical

Education under my chairmanship and the report of the Committee was submitted in May, 1994. Some of the important recommendations of the High Power Committee are i) The Central Government should examine the feasibility of levying an **educational cess** on industries for funding technical education and R & D activities in technical institutions. ii) The Government of India may set up an **Educational Development Bank of India (EDBI)** for financing soft loans for establishment of institutions and also to assist students to meet their fee and living requirements. iii) A **National Loan Scholarship Scheme (NLSS)** may be set up under EDBI to provide soft loans to needy students. iv) Wherever necessary, the State Governments may also set up a **state Education Fund,** supplementing the NLSS, to give assistance to needy students in the form of loan scholarships at nominal interest rates and easy repayment terms. v) The plan allocation for technical education sector, both central and state, should be based and related to the plan outlays in the industrial and service sectors and as a matter of policy, these sectors should have an appropriate share earmarked for technical manpower development and this share be made available to Ministry of Human Resource Development to be used exclusively for the development of technical manpower. vi) The tuition fees in all government funded and aided institutions in all the states should be revised to a rational level of at least 20% of the annual recurring cost per student. vii) A corpus fund is to be established in every institution.

BRAIN STORMING SESSIONS:

Taking a lead from the Prime Minister's two important observations made during one of the Planning Commission meetings regarding the need for modernising the teaching and research activities in engineering institutions like Indian Institutes of Technology, who are considered as centres of excellence, and the need for adopting futuristic approaches to meet the emerging challenges of science and technology, a series of Brain Storming Sessions were organised in the Planning Commission to formulate perspectives for achieving excellence and relevance in technical education in the country. As a result of the Brain Storming sessions, documents relating to an Approach Paper for IITs and their Technology Development Missions, development of Indian Institutes of Management, perspectives for excellence in Regional Engineering Colleges, Polytechnics and Technical Teachers' Training Institutes, were prepared. These documents contain valuable recommendations and suggestions for reorientation of technical education and research.

MANAGEMENT EDUCATION, TRAINING AND RESEARCH:

The role of management in the development process is widely recognised. Similarly, management education is perceived as being important for building managerial competence. During the nineties, the country is heading towards becoming progressively more integrated into the global economy. As indicated earlier, with the advent of new Industrial Policy and liberalisation, the Indian industry is exposed to more domestic and global competition. Competition and pace of technological change are likely to intensify in most sectors of economy. 'Professional Management' becomes a vital component in industry. It equally applies to other sectors of economy especially, in the context of the financial resources crunch and the need for better and effective management of available resources.

With the above situation, management education, training and research assumes greater significance and the Indian Institutes of Management, Schools or Departments of Management in Universities and other Institutes have to play a greater role in helping to formulate management strategies for the changing scenario. Unless management of public and private sector enterprises respond to greater competition in an effective manner, there will be large scale sickness especially among smaller enterprises. The management institutes should disseminate to competing enterprises through teaching, training, publishing and consultancy, the expertise to cope effectively with competition.

Focus on innovations in management education and training and quality in research are needed. Issues and problems relating to organisational culture and commitment, productivity and quality, processes of internal change, new initiatives in the social responsibility of management, globalisation of industry and trade and relevant strategies for India are to be addressed and solutions sought. In this context, the IIMs, Universities, other institutions of management, professional bodies like the Association of Indian Management schools have a responsible role to play.

DISTANCE EDUCATION MODE IN ENGINEERING AND TECHNOLOGY:

Distance education programmes offered are mostly in non-engineering, non-technological or non-vocational areas in India. Attempts to provide distance education programmes in Engineering, Technology and vocational courses are very few except by some of the professional bodies like the Institution of Engineers (India). Courses which are suitably designed and developed could be offered through distance education mode in Engineering, Technology and vocational areas with success and acceptability.

The working engineers in the country, especially those who are in the far flung areas, need opportunities to upgrade their expertise and qualifications. Distance education mode can provide the needed opportunity. The Jawaharlal Nehru Technological University, Hyderabad is the first university in the country to provide distance education opportunities in engineering and technology for working engineers and scientists to remove obsolescence and provide opportunities for updating, upgrading, broadening and diversifying their knowledge and skills. The University is offering Distance Education Programmes in B.Tech. and M.Tech. The university has already opened its doors for external registration for M.S. and Ph.D. programmes for working engineers in the country. Such an 'open' concept in engineering and technological education should be encouraged.

CONCLUSION:

The impact of the change in global and national economic scenarios is the emergence of an era of global consciousness. The industries require, among other things, a workforce having a scientific bent of mind and possess the much desired temper and skills to maintain high quality and productivity at par with the world standards. Our R & D efforts should also be geared up commensurately. The Science and Technology education and research have, therefore, to respond to these emerging challenges to train men and women of calibre and competence of world standards and provide the needed R & D capability. In addition, the explosion of knowledge in Science and Technology sectors requires highly talented men and women whose fast grasp of knowledge could enable them to respond to the desired innovations in advancing the frontiers of knowledge and know-how. However, the success in this regard will depend upon our abilities to cope up with the emerging pressures of resources crunch on the one hand and the need for upgradation of the quality of Science and Technology education and research on the other, through proper reorientation.

KEY NOTE ADDRESS
AT THE SEMINAR ON
"INDUSTRY—MANAGEMENT
INSTITUTION INTERFACE"

Prof. Kapoor, the Vice-Chancellor, participants of the Seminar, Ladies and Gentlemen,

Indeed, I am very happy to participate in the inaugural session of the Seminar on **"Industry-Management Institution Interface"** being organised by the Department of Commerce and Business Management of the Panjab University. I am grateful for being invited to inaugurate the Seminar and to deliver the Keynote address, which gives me an opportunity to share my thoughts on management education in the country and the need for interaction with the industry.

The role of management in the development process is widely recognised. Similarly, management education is perceived as being important for building managerial competence. The rapid growth of industrial and commercial enterprises in the 50's produced a demand for more and better trained managers in India. During this decade, management development took place largely through short management programmes for senior administrators and managers. Four Indian Institutes of Management were subsequently established—two during 60's at Ahmedabad and Calcutta, one during 70's at Bangalore and one during 80's at Lucknow and these four represent a potent force, professionalising management in India. Two Review Committees were appointed on the Indian Institutes of Management. The first one, the Nanda Committee, was appointed in 1979 and other Review

Committee, the Kurien Committee, was appointed in 1991. The Nanda Committee recommended that the objectives should include training and education of (i) Managers for public utilities and services and (ii) Management teachers. The Kurien Committee reaffirmed the Mission of the IIMs to strengthen management in business, industry and commerce. It further recommended that the mission statement needs to be expanded to emphasise IIM's commitment to public service and public management.

The University Grants Commission is providing assistance to about 40 universities / institutes for conducting programmes in Management Studies. IITs also decided to develop management education programmes which started during the late 70's. The thrust of the programmes is on the management of technology. A number of other private institutes of management are also doing good work in the field of management education and research.

Recently momentous changes have taken place on the international scene which will have a profound impact on international relations and the world economy. Most developing countries have also embarked on bold measures of reform, restructuring their economies and opening up to forces of competition, both domestic and foreign. The Government of India also have taken new initiatives and bold decisions to reorient and restructure the economy to meet the challenges of the economic crisis in the country through its policy of liberalisation, new Industry and Trade Policies etc. The impact of these changes on Indian industry is considerable and it is now exposed to global as well as indigenous competition. To meet these challenges, it has to resort to modernisation, upgrading technology and competence of the work force, adopting modern management techniques and increasing efficiency and productivity. In this context, the various constituents of national development like universities, engineering and management institutions, national R & D laboratories and the professional bodies and academies have greater roles to play. A strategy may have to be evolved for effective interaction between them. In this context, organising the present Seminar is timely and I would like to congratulate the organisers for their thoughtful gesture. To bring about such a meaningful interaction, a Model for University-Industry-National R & D Laboratories-Professional Bodies and Academies Interaction for country's economic development has been formulated by me. The model is shown else where in this volume. The model identifies the areas of interaction between the various above constituents leading to country's economic development. It is imperative that each of these constituents have a Consultancy Unit / Cell and there is a national coordination mechanism for promoting effective interaction.

During the nineties, the country is heading towards becoming progressively more integrated into the global economy. As indicated earlier, with the advent of new Industrial Policy and liberalisation, the Indian industry is exposed to more domestic and global competition. Competition and pace of technological change are likely to intensify in most sectors of economy. 'Professional Management' becomes a vital component in industry. It equally applies to other sectors of economy especially, in the context of the financial resources crunch and the need for better and effective management of available resources.

With the above situation, management education, training and research assumes greater significance and the Indian Institutes of Management, Schools or Departments of Management in Universities and other Institutes have to play a greater role in helping to formulate management strategies for the changing scenario. Unless management of public and private sector enterprises respond to greater competition in an effective manner, there will be large scale sickness especially among smaller enterprises. The management institutes should disseminate to competing enterprises through teaching, training, publishing and consultancy, the expertise to cope up effectively with competition.

Structural adjustments aim at increasing Indian exports. This would be possible, through, among other things, Indian enterprises acquiring global levels of expertise in developing and producing high quality products and marketing them internationally. The management institutes can develop the management expertise for doing this and disseminate it widely to the Indian enterprises. A high priority for the management institutes should therefore be the development of expertise in international management and in catalysing in Indian industry global levels of quality, productivity and innovativeness.

In the context of changing domestic and global economic scenario, the Planning Commission has taken the initiative to convene meetings of the IIM Directors and other experts to discuss and formulate new approaches in the management education, training and research. The discussions resulted in identifying some vital issues and areas which would contribute towards strengthening management education, research and training in the country. A document titled "IIMs and the Eighth Plan" was brought out, which identified certain priorities for the IIMs during the Eighth Plan and beyond.

The MBA level programmes and the management development programmes offered by the IIMs and other management institutions need to be refocussed to emphasise dynamic leadership', change agentry, and entrepreneurial skills, capacity to integrate various management functions and develop effective competitive strategies with the help of computer based MIS, and expertise relating to international management and total quality management so that the participants in these programmes can play a transformational role in Indian industry. In this context it may be desirable to insist on some work experience as a prerequisite for admission to the MBA level programmes, to ensure greater maturity, receptivity to this sort of expertise, and placement at higher levels so that the graduates have the opportunity to play change agent roles in the organisations they join.

Liberalisation also implies step up of entrepreneurship. Although, there already exists an impressive infrastructure for training entrepreneurs, the IIMs and other management institutions could specialise in training growth oriented, high technology, pioneering, innovative entrepreneurs and/or in helping existing entrepreneurs to become more dynamic. IIMs and other management institutions and university departments can also strengthen existing entrepreneurship training institutions and train entrepreneurship trainers.

Several mechanisms need to be developed or strengthened to disseminate the management institutions expertise to Indian industry. Managerial training and consultation are already going on but need to be increased. MoUs between IIMs, other management institutions and leading industry and trade associations like FICCI, ASSOCHAM, IMC, CII, and AIMA can be entered into for collaboration in research, training, consultation, etc. The IIMs and other management institutions could set up an all India Committee with representation from the IIMs, other management institutions, industry bodies, Ministry of Industry, financial institutions, etc., for dialogue, collaboration and dissemination.

The targets of the Eighth Plan are likely to rest on two crucial assumptions: an incremental capital output ratio of 4.1 and an annual growth rate in exports of 13.6%. Both these assumptions require upgrading of the management skills not just of enterprises but also of government ministries, departments, and agencies, and also of a host of other organisations providing human capital and infrastructural services like education, health, environmental management, transportation, energy, communications, etc. Increasingly therefore IIMs and other management institutions must identify strategic priority sectors that are currently

DR. DEVARAKONDA SWAMINADHAN

inappropriately managed and develop the needed management expertise and diffuse it effectively to them. Already much work of this type has been done but much more needs to be done in an orchestrated and sharply focussed manner. Close collaboration will be needed between the IIMs and other management institutions and government organizations and other components of strategic priority sectors, especially sectoral institutes like NCERT, NIEPA, NIHM, NIRM. IRMA, NIBM, etc. Strengthening of the functioning of these institutes can have large mutiplier effects for the sectors they serve. The Planning Commission could provide an umbrella under which dialogue and cooperation between strategic priority sectors, their institutes, IIMs and other management institutions could be catalysed.

The number of managers without any formal managerial training in the country is vastly greater than the number with even a modicum of training. There are no reliable estimates of the number of personnel with supervisory and managerial responsibilities in the country. A guess estimate is that there may be some three million managers in the country directing, coordinating, and motivating a workforce of perhaps 60 million.

This managerial army of say three million is highly differentiated by function, level, sector, and organisation. A significant improvement in the skills, drive, efficiency, innovativeness, quality orientation, and customer service orientation of this group of our society can generate incalculable benefits for the nation. It is vitally important therefore that a research effort is mounted to study the size and composition of our managerial corps, understand the roles different types of managers in different sorts of organisations, industries and sectors are required to play and the knowledge—base, skills, attitudes needed, now and in the future, to play these roles effectively. The management institutes can play a role, along with Institute of Applied Manpower Research, various trade, industry and sectoral associations etc., in this research task. Here, too, the Planning Commission could play a catalytic role.

Once even crude estimates become available, a strategy can be formulated of providing the nation's managerial class access to the needed knowledge-base, skills and attitudes. Formal training provided at the IIMs and other management institutions would be a small though important catalytic component of this strategy. Much larger extension work will need to be done, through strengthening and enlarging distance learning programmes provided by such institutions as IGNOU and AIMA, the starting of many more management training programmes both public and in-house, and the preparation of educative audiovisual and other material for mass dissemination, such as through industry and sectoral bodies, AIR and Doordarshan. The IIMs and other management institutions can play both catalytic and expertise providing roles in this effort.

An important systemic role for the IIMs and other management institutions in management education would be to strengthen the management teaching and research apparatus in the country. Given the escalating need for quality management scholars, the IIMs and other management institutions will need to increase sharply their output of Ph.D.s, to say 50 per year by the end of the Eighth Plan.

Faculty development and institution building in other management training and teaching institutions should also be a high priority for the IIMs and other reputed management institutions. The four IIMs and other well developed management institutions together should be able to offer short and/or long duration training to all the management teachers in the country by the end of the Eighth Plan. Besides strengthening the teaching and research skills of management academics, exposing them to innovative pedagogies and providing them with depth in their areas of specialisation, an ingredient of their training should be institution building and change agentry so that they can transplant into their home schools / departments some of the values and practices that have contributed to the excellence of the IIMs and other reputed management institutions. These management institutions should also disseminate to other management teaching / training institutions in the country course materials, cases, research findings, etc. They should utilise for this purpose such umbrella organisations as the Board of Management Studies of AICTE and Association of Indian Management Schools. They should use their leverage in these bodies to raise accreditation standards.

Similarly, another important role for the IIMs and other management institutions should be to network with other academic or quasi-academic institutions such as IITs, universities, sectoral research / training institutions etc., to help them function more effectively and also to facilitate their attempts to impart managerial skills to their graduates. IIMs and other management institutions can contribute, for example, to the entrepreneurship, technology management, and industrial management programmes operated by or contemplated by the IITs. The management content of B.Com and other degree programmes offered by Indian universities could be enriched with the help of the IIMs and other management institutions. The IIMs and other management institutions could help in the dissemination of innovative pedagogies that bring the process of learning alive in many pedagogically fossilised academic institutions.

Focus on innovations in management education and training and quality in research are needed. Issues and problems relating to organisational culture and commitment, productivity and quality, processes of internal change, new initiatives in the social responsibility of management, globalisation of industry and trade and relevant strategies for India are to be addressed and solutions sought. In this context, the IIMs, Universities, other institutions of management, professional bodies like the Association of Indian Management schools have a responsible role to play.

I am sure the Seminar deliberations will be fruitful and the outcome will go a long way towards the attempts to build up strong linkages between management institutions and industry. I take pleasure in inaugurating the Seminar and wish it a grand success.

REMOTE SENSING AND GIS ICORG—94

Professor Gopal Reddy, the Vice-Chancellor, participants of the International Conference, distinguished invitees, ladies and gentlemen,

It is a great pleasure for me to participate in the Inaugural Session of the International Conference on Remote Sensing and GIS being organised by the Jawaharlal Nehru Technological University, Hyderabad. I am grateful to the Vice-Chancellor for inviting me to be the Chief Guest and to inaugurate the Conference.

I am tempted to recall my association with this University where I spent nearly two and a half years in the past as its Vice-Chancellor. I have fresh and pleasant memories of those days when we all of us used to work in a team mode with a commitment to build and transform the University into one of the Centres of excellence in engineering and technology. That cooperative spirit gave me the strength and boldness to establish ten schools of excellence to serve as the nucleus for the University which could provide academic guidance, support and inspiration to all the constituent units of the University. In addition to the schools of excellence, a number of centres of excellence were initiated in the constituent colleges for taking up post-graduate and research programmes in emerging areas. Faced with the resources crunch, a novel and unconventional approach had been adopted through involving the industry, national R & D laboratories and other organisations in teaching and research programmes. The University has set the most outstanding example of university-industrynational R & D laboratories interaction. Most of the new post graduate programmes are supported by industry through sponsorship of their employees to pursue M.Tech and MBA programmes. Sharing and optimising the use of available resources—both men and material—has been the-main stay in the teaching and research programmes. The University has also been making pioneering efforts in continuing and distance education in engineering and technology for working engineers.

I am delighted to note that the School of Water Resources, Environment and Remote Sensing has evolved itself on the lines on which it was visualised and it is making a mark at the national and international level. The Centre for Remote Sensing, having started with a humble beginning around 1990 has grown rapidly to its present status and the credit should go to all those concerned in the school and the centre for their commitment. The very fact that it could organise such an important international Conference as ICORG-94, itself is an ample demonstration of its achieved level of academic status.

Remote sensing from Space has already established its usefulness in solving several intricate problems and hidden anomalies affecting environment, pollution, water resources, irrigation, floods, ground water targeting, soil salinity determination, forest rapping, urban sprawl coverage, crop acreage estimation, charting sea-surface temperature for exploring potential fish zones etc.

Remote sensing is now taught in many universities and institutions as a full-fledged degree course or as part of the curriculum on geology, agriculture, water resources, forestry, etc. About 12 universities are offering remote sensing courses at the post-graduate and doctoral levels. The Indian Institute of Remote Sensing, Dehradun, National Remote Sensing Agency, Hyderabad, Space Applications Centre, Ahmedabad, Regional Remote Sensing Service Centres and other user organisations are offering remote sensing courses in the country. So far, about 6,300 scientists /engineers have been trained in the country and about 800 persons are being trained every year. Special training courses for the faculty of universities / schools are continued to be organised. Efforts are also being made to introduce remote sensing at the senior secondary level curriculum as well with the help of National Council for Educational Research and Training (NCERT).

The level of growth and application of modern science and technology determines the status of a nation as developed or developing. There is a growing concern about the increasing gap between the poor and the rich, the North and the South in the world. It was repeatedly noticed by the U.N. Agencies that more than 80% of the wealth, two-thirds of the metals, three-fourths of the energy produced the world over, goes to the possession of the industrialised countries, who are termed as developed and they make up only 20 per cent of the world population. This advantage is mainly due to their mastery and utilisation of modern science and technology.

Pandit Jawaharlal Nehru, the first Prime Minister and the architect of modern India, assigned to Science and Technology a pivotal role in national development. This has been reflected in the formulation and adoption of the Scientific Policy Resolution of 1958. It recognised science and technology as the key to national prosperity besides cultivating scientific spirit and scientific temper. It envisaged effective combination of technology, raw materials and capital to achieve national prosperity. With scarce capital and critical materials, India has to heavily depend on modern technology to overcome such limitations. In response to the need for guidance on a wide ranging and complex set of inter-related areas of science and, technology, industry, economy and trade, the Technology Policy Statement (TPS) was announced by the Government in 1983. Its main objectives are to develop indigenous technologies and help absorption of the imported ones wherever needed. Now a new Technology Policy is being contemplated in view of the new economic policy and the changed global scenario.

India is in a unique position as far as science and technology are concerned. Science and technology are to be utilised for solving the basic needs of the people such as food, shelter, clothing, health etc. The country's large S & T manpower should take up the tasks of not only contributing to the frontiers of science and technology, but also help to use these tools for modernising our economic and commercial sectors. In this context, we are endeavouring not only to plan for science and technology development but also for integrating science and technology in the economic planning.

In economic planning, conservation and efficiency have big roles to play. We have to combine efficient use of natural as well as human resources to achieve growth. In this process, Remote Sensing and GIS can play an important role. The modern technology of Remote Sensing integrated with collateral information forms a viable and powerful tool for planning and decision making through creation of Geographical Information System (GIS). GIS are used to assist decision makers by indicating various alternatives in development and conservation planning and modelling the potential outcomes of a series of scenarios. Basic knowledge on the location, quantity and availability of natural resources is thus indispensable for more rational planning.

The importance of natural resources and socio-economic data in planning is increasingly being recognised by the decision makers at different levels. Integration of all the information and depiction of the same in spatial format would facilitate identification of the regional disparities in development. Spatial planning can be effectively achieved by using the modern tools and methods like the remotely sensed data from satellite and developing Geographical Information System (GIS) alongside.

The World Commission on Environment and Development (1987) called for the achievement of necessary growth rates in economic development without harm to the life supporting systems of the planet. It defined sustainable development as "a process of change in which the exploitation of resources, the direction of investments, the orientation of technological development and institutional change are all in harmony and enhance both current and future potential to meet human needs and aspirations". Sustainable development involves more than growth. It requires a change in the content of growth, to make it less material and energy-intensive and more equitable in its impact. These changes are required in all countries as a part of the package of measures to maintain the stock of ecological capital, to improve the distribution of income and to reduce the degree of vulnerability to economic crises.

The basic framework for the Indian space programme is the 1990-2000 Decade profile. A self-reliant and integrated programme, with indigenous building and launching of satellites with maximal utilisation of Indian industry has been envisaged in this profile for providing and sustaining two operational space systems namely, INSAT System and IRS System for meeting the various application needs in communications, broadcasting, meteorology, disaster management and resources management, maximum utilisation of space technology for socio-economic development of the country and the rural areas in particular has been envisaged in this profile.

The second generation Indian Remote Sensing Satellites viz., IRS-IC and IRS-ID are planned to be launched and operationalised during the Eighth Plan period. A satellite system using Microwave Remote Sensing Censors has been proposed to be initiated. The major goal of achieving an operational Natural Resources Information System (NRIS) based on Geographical Information System (GIS) and with modelling capabilities is targeted for the Eighth Plan period. With the emphasis shifting in favour of optimal exploitation of natural resources on an environmentally benign and sustainable basis, there is need for taking a holistic approach towards resources management. Towards this, integrated study of land and water resources at micro-level is envisaged at national level. These studies will help in preparing a comprehensive plan of action for sustainable development.

There is export potential for providing ground systems/ products, satellite and launch vehicle systems, satellite services and launch services on a commercial basis to other countries, which will make the Indian space engineering industry a more viable proposition in the years to come. The setting up of the Corporate Front, a techno-managerial corporate body will facilitate ploughing back the corporate earnings for sustained product development and market promotion efforts, besides promotion of partnership between Space Department and industries. The expertise and experience gained in carrying out complex space technology projects in academic institutions and universities will be harnessed further for enhanced participation of these institutions in the national space effort.

Scientific exploration was essentially the prime mover for space and technology development initiatives in India. However, the remarkable developments in technology and its applications during the last three decades or so have firmly established the immense potential of space to transform the life style of human society as a whole. With this potential, the perceptions of development have undergone significant alterations with space technology providing unique solutions in the areas of communications, meteorology and natural resources. In the present day changed scenario, space could also be viewed as a medium for strengthening the country's global economic competitiveness. It is rightly said that space activities can be viewed as a technology drive for entire economy benefiting a wide range of space and non-space related industries.

The Indian space programme has made great strides in using the sophisticated remote sensing technology to maximally benefit the grassroots of the nation in a timely and cost-effective manner. The nation has established a self-reliant base in this technology which is now playing a crucial role in the management of natural resources. India is one 'of the very few countries to have its own indigenous operational space and ground segment as well as necessary expertise and infrastructure for implementing various remote sensing application projects. The indigenous state-of-the-art Indian Remote Sensing Satellites—IRS series, provide the space segment for the remote sensing services in the country. We have now IRSIA and IRS-1B Remote Sensing satellites operational. IRS-IC is in the making. IRS-P2 space craft has been launched recently. Process on IRS-P3 has been started.

A unique management system, National Natural resources Management System (NNRMS) has been evolved in the country for the past decade to address specific problems related to remote sensing technology and to enhance its utilisation. The NNRMS now cover diverse fields such as agriculture, crop acreage and yield estimation, drought warning and assessment, flood control and damage assessment, land use / land cover, mapping for agroclimatic planning, wasteland management, water resources management, ocean / marine resources survey and management, urban development, mineral prospecting, forest resources survey and management etc.

Integrated Mission for Sustainable Development (IMSD) has been launched in 157 districts of the country. These space remote sensing-based integrated studies provide a unique example of the use of space technology in planning for sustainable development of a region. The methodology involves generation of various thematic maps based on space derived information and combining them with socio-economic data of relevance to arrive at optimal strategies for development. Set of maps showing the land capability, land irrigability, soil erosion status, vegetation and agriculture status, wasteland information, underground and surface water resources, meteorological parameters etc., are derived from space remote sensing and integrated with socio-economic, socio-cultural and demographic information, using Geographic Information System to delineate priority watersheds or blocks based on their degradation status and are further sub-divided into a number of micro level spatial units, which are unique in terms of their resource potential. For each of those units, Specific developmental action plans and the recommendations for optimum management practices for land and water resources development efforts are arrived at. While doing so, the cultural acceptability of the developmental plans by the local habitat and environmental compatibility of the recommended plans are also given due weightage.

Massive land degradation and urban migration, large scale deforestation, unhealthy industrial practices, poor management of land and water resources and large scale emission of green house gases are already causing, not only great hardships to the people but also irreversibly changing our ecology and climate. The solution calls for utilising the best technological tools available to achieve sustainable, integrated development that would meet the minimum needs of the present and growing demands of the future generations, ensuring the conservation of ecology and the natural environment. Sustainable development thus involves a multi-dimensional approach, comprising not only technology but also socioeconomic an d environmental parameters. In this context, remote sensing and GIS would afford us a powerful tool. I am sure the focal theme of the seminar focussing on environmental planning would provide us valuable insights and inputs for planning.

I take great pleasure in inauguration the International Conference and I wish the Conference a grand success.

TECHNOLOGY FOR A
BETTER TOMORROW

I am privileged to participate in the inaugural session of the International level Seminar on the topical theme of the 9th Indian Engineering Congress "Technology for a Better Tomorrow" being organised in this great city of Calcutta. It adds to the jubilation that it also happens to be the occasion of the Platinum Jubilee celebrations of the Institution of Engineers (India). I am grateful to Shri P.M. Chacko, President, I.E.I., for inviting me to attend this inaugural session and to inaugurate the seminar. It is indeed heartening to note that the topical theme is being discussed through various seminars with sub-themes related to it, which include Energy and Environment, Conformable Technology and Adaptation, Eco-Management, Technology for Sustenance, Technology Education and Information and Communication Technology and Remote Sensing. These sub-themes selected for the seminars cover vital areas of development, education and management of technologies in the context of sustainable development. I must congratulate the organisers for choosing such a vital and relevant theme for the Seminar.

The premise that science and technology are intimately related to productivity, economic development and international competitiveness is all the more true in the present changed global and national scenarios on the economic front. Science and technology are inter-dependent. Scientific advances help develop new technologies and the need for new technologies provide the impetus for new scientific discoveries. Global competitiveness in technology would require a high level of scientific capability as well.

The level of creation and application of science and technology would determine the status of a nation as developed or developing. UN studies indicate that more than 80 per cent of the wealth, two-thirds of the metals, three-fourths of the energy produced in the world over, goes to the possession of the industrialised countries who are termed as 'developed' and they only make up 24 per cent of the world population. The remaining 76 per cent of the world's population belong to the developing or less developed or under-developed category. It is obvious that the distinction between developed and developing countries is due to their differing capabilities in the creation, mastery and utilisation of modern science and technology.

Pandit Jawaharlal Nehru, the first Prime Minister and the architect of modern India, assigned to Science and Technology a pivotal role in national development. This had been reflected in the formulation and adoption of the Scientific Policy Resolution of 1958. It recognised science and technology ac the key to national prosperity besides cultivating scientific spirit and scientific temper. It envisaged effective combination of technology, raw materials and capital to achieve national prosperity. With scarce capital and critical materials, India has to heavily depend on modern technology to overcome such limitations. Technology Policy Statement (TPS) was announced by the Government of India in 1983, whose main objectives are to develop indigenous technologies and help absorption of the imported ones wherever needed. Now a new Technology Policy is being contemplated in view of the new economic policy and the changed global scenario.

The Prime Minister, in the first Full Planning Commission meeting held in September, 1991, referred to two important issues. The first one was related to the need for modernising teaching, research and other facilities in engineering institutions especially at I.I.T.s, which are regarded as Centres of excellence. The second stressed the need to adopt futuristic approaches in meeting the emerging challenges in science and technology. He said, "A poor country like India cannot go on changing technology every year. We must adopt futuristic approaches". This calls for a rigorous technology forecasting and assessment effort involving all the constituents in the technology development.

We are all living now in an era of change. Momentous changes have taken place right across the globe, which have an impact on the international relations and world trade. Changes have also taken place in India due to restructuring of its economy and liberalization policies. The result is globalisation and global competition. The country is progressively becoming more integrated into the global economy. Knowledge-based industries will be on the increase. Levels of skills required are going to be high. Competition and pace of technological change are going to intensify in most sectors of the economy. Industries need: modernisation, upgradation of technology and competence of their work force, increased efficiency and productivity and to maintain quality. Professional management becomes a vital component in industry.

Structural adjustments aim at increasing Indian exports and this would be possible through, among other things, Indian enterprises acquiring global levels of expertise in developing and producing high quality products and marketing them internationally. Under such circumstances, we need to have a workforce having a scientific bent of mind and possess the much needed scientific temper and skills to maintain high quality of productivity on par with world standards. We have to boost up our indigenous R & D effort and develop high quality indigenous technologies. A symbiotic relationship between industry—university—national R & D laboratories—scientific and professional bodies would help to a great extent in meeting this challenge.

Technology plays a very important role as the trend catches up with the knowledge-based industries. The process of upgradation or acquiring new technologies can take place in the following manner: (i) Indigenous R & D effort to help the Indian industry; (ii) Technology import by the Indian Industry; and (iii) Technology import related to foreign investment in India.

With regard to the indigenous R & D effort, the Planning Commission initiated Technology Development in a mission mode in eight generic areas, involving the five I.I.T.s and the Indian Institute of Science, Bangalore. The missions involve not only a major research component but also a commitment to technology development through innovation and the subsequent transfer to the Indian industries. Developing, testing and delivery of technology are very much a part of the package. A key factor of the missions is the participation by industry from the very beginning and a contribution equal to 25% of the government funding in terms of cash and services or manpower. Regional Engineering Colleges are also being encouraged to take up relevant R & D work through thrust area development and they are also encouraged to look into the R & D needs of the small scale industries sector. The national laboratories and some of the universities are also striving to contribute considerably towards indigenous R & D efforts in the present day changed scenario.

Regarding the technology import by the Indian industry, it is logical to believe that the quality of technology imported may not suffer but one cannot be sure of getting the latest technology always. In the process of adaptation they may need assistance from the higher and technical education institutions and the national R & D laboratories.

The issue of technology import related to foreign investment in India needs serious attention. It should be carefully studied and assessed to know whether the technology brought into the country is of the first rate or of third rate. It is essential to know the correct picture so that we can guard against their inferior quality.

Today technological changes are taking place at a greater pace and the world is passing through an exciting stage of technological progress in several fronts. Technology is perhaps the most important resource to any nation. Invention, innovation, investments-in risky ventures, adoption of new technologies and new products, etc., are the major processes in. wealth creation and making the countries technologically superior.

But what is the consequence of all this? Prosperity? Yes. But massive land degradation and urban migration, large scale deforestation, unhealthy industrial practices, poor management of land and water resources, large scale emission of green house gases and global warming are already causing, not only great hardships to the people but also irreversibly changing our ecology and climate. The solution calls for utilising the best technological tools available to achieve sustainable, and integrated development that would meet the minimum needs of the present and growing demands of the future generations, ensuring the conservation of ecology and the natural environment. Sustainable development thus involves a multi-dimensional approach, comprising not only technology but also socioeconomic and environmental parameters. This does not mean environment and development need to be at loggerheads with each other. The positive links between efficient income growth and the environmental need to be exploited. The key to sustainable growth is not to produce less but to produce differently. Economic development and ecological balance have to be fused together into the same developmental strategy.

The World Commission on Environment and Development (1987) called for the achievement of necessary growth rates in economic development without harm to the life supporting systems of the planet. It refers to sustainable development as "a process of change in which the exploitation of resources, the direction of investments, the orientation of technological—development and institutional change are all in harmony and enhance both current and future potential to meet human needs and aspirations". Sustainable development, therefore, involves more than growth. It involves paying concurrent attention to problems of intra and inter-generational equity.

The threat to sustainability comes also from high levels of consumption of the rich nations. It is said that the industrialised countries with 24% of the world's population have a share of global consumption of various commodities extending from 50% to 90%. The consumption of food products by industrialised countries ranges from 48 to 72%. They consume 60% of fertilisers, 81% of paper, 85% of chemicals, 92% of cars and 75% of world's energy. Environmental stress is proportional to these consumption levels. The industrialised world is responsible for 70% of the annual emissions of carbon di-oxide. Clearly, consumption patterns of the rich are unsustainable because of over use of nonrenewable resources.

Teeming millions of the developing countries and their peasant practices may have been proje cted as taxing the eco-harmony and bio-resources but the fact is the consumption levels of the rich endanger the eco-balance far more than the subsistence needs of the poorer masses. While environmental degradation causes diseases, poverty plays a major role in their sustenance. Clean water, sanitation and cleaner energy systems can dramatically improve the health status of the poverty ridden people in the third world countries and contribute to their economic development. In the Indian context, population stabilisation also should be an important issue on the environmental agenda. Literacy campaign, population education and involvement of Non-Government Organisations in overcoming the cultural barriers in accepting the small family norm should complement the efforts of population control.

There should be a strategic shift to cleaner and green technologies for a better tomorrow. Sustainable industrial development is not a matter of mere high-tech but also of appropriate sci-tech. We have to phase out older and inappropriate technologies while simultaneously developing and disseminating a new generation of sophisticated and environmentally benign technologies. We have to encourage indigenous research effort to be directed at green technologies through a system of incentives and penalties.

Sustainable development demands technologies which are least polluting, uses natural resources optimally and also recycle wastes. These technologies should be compatible with the socio-economic, cultural, environmental and developmental priorities of our country. There is an urgent need to undertake human resource development and strengthen institutional capacities for research and development and conduct integrated assessment of available technologies and technological needs which suit the objectives and priorities of the country's development.

The space and remote sensing technology is perhaps the most potent tool in the process of achieving sustainable development, contributing towards a better tomorrow.

Scientific exploration was essentially the prime mover for space technology development initiatives in India. However, the remarkable developments in technology and its applications during the last three decades or so have firmly established the immense potential of space to transform the life style of human society as a whole. With this potential, the perceptions of development have undergone significant alterations with space technology providing unique solutions in the areas of communications, meteorology and natural resources. In the present day changed scenario, space could also be viewed as a medium for strengthening the country's global economic competitiveness. It is rightly said that space activities can be viewed as a technology drive for entire economy benefiting a wide range of space and nonspace related industries.

The Indian space programme has made great strides in using the sophisticated remote sensing technology to maximally benefit the grassroots of the nation in a timely and cost-effective manner. The nation has established a self-reliant base in this technology which is now playing a crucial role in the management of natural resources. India is one of the very few countries to have its own indigenous operational space and ground segment as well as necessary expertise and infrastructure for implementing various remote sensing application projects. The indigenous state-of-the-art Indian Remote Sensing Satellites—IRS series, provide the space segment for the remote sensing services in the country.

Three most important areas stated to be determining the course of the 21st century is advanced materials, bio-technology and information technology. A country like India cannot afford to lag behind and should make right efforts in building up of R & D in these areas. A good level of high quality research in basic sciences is characteristic of all developed economies. India cannot afford to neglect this aspect as well. A country such as U.S.A. invests upto US $150 billion on R & D while Japan invests US $100 billion per year. In India, we invest less than US $ 1 billion per year towards all our efforts in science and technology. India is investing about 0.9 per cent of GNP for science and technology, compared to 5 to 6 per cent by some of the advanced countries. In some of the advanced countries, a high percentage of expenditure on science and technology come from private industry.

R & D expenditure by industry, as a percentage of total R & D expenditure, is only 21% in India, compared to 61% in U.K., 63% in Japan and 72% in U.S.A. The time has come for Indian industry to increase its contribution to R&D expenditure through either in-house R&D units or through supporting research in universities. This is essential if it is to survive against global competition.

I am sure the outcome of the deliberations on the topical theme through its various seminars will provide us with valuable inputs into the development of technologies for a better tomorrow and also towards the formulation of a new technology policy for India. I take pleasure in inaugurating the seminar and wish it a great success.

TECHNICAL EDUCATION AND RESEARCH IN INDIA—NEED FOR REORIENTATION

I feel greatly honoured for being invited to deliver the Seventh A.N. Khosla Memorial Lecture at the Ninth Indian Engineering Congress being organised in this great city of Calcutta. It is heartening to note that this happens to be the Platinum Jubilee year for the Institution of Engineers (India). I would like to express my gratitude to Shri P.M. Chacko, President, the Institution of Engineers (India) for affording me this wonderful opportunity of addressing such a galaxy of engineers and scientists through this lecture instituted in the memory of that great engineer, statesman and educationist Dr. A.N. Khosla. Dr. Khosla had many creditable achievements. He was considered to be the father of river valley projects and a doyen of Indian Water Resources Engineers. He had the credit of being the first Indian Vice-Chancellor of the University of Roorkee and the first engineer to be appointed as the Governor of a State. His engineering achievements were remarkable. His close association with several major river valley projects like Hirakud, Bhakra Nangal and Ram Ganga will be remembered for a long time to come. The invention of Khosla Disc for Precision Levelling across rivers and wide valleys, his theory for design of Barrages and Weirs on permeable foundations are important contributions to civil engineering. I draw great pleasure and pride in that he was a Member of the Planning Commission too. I am delighted to note that he was also dealing with the subject of education in the Planning Commission as I am doing now—of course, confining myself to higher and technical education.

I must be the second person with engineering background to become a Member of the Planning Commission after Dr. Khosla. I could see that he made valuable contributions to education while being in the Planning Commission. He commanded high respect from Pandit Nehru who was the Chairman of the Planning Commission at that time. I am told that Dr. Khosla prepared a scheme of providing loan scholarships to the poor but meritorious students for pursuing higher education and sent it to Pandit Nehru in 1962. It was the time of the Chinese aggression. Even amidst such a situation, Nehru appreciated Dr. Khosla's proposal and it was cleared in the meeting of the Planning Commission held soon after the Chinese aggression. Perhaps the realisation that the real defence of the country could be ensured through the promotion of higher education, making it available to all meritorious students irrespective of their income, might' have weighed in favour of its approval even under such an extraordinary situation. Such was the foresight of that great engineer-cum-educationist, who felt that the boundaries of the country could be made safe through excellence in higher technical education and research.

Keeping in view Dr. Khosla's association with the subject of education (including technical education), in the Planning Commission and also the theme of the Ninth Engineering Congress "Technology for a Better Tomorrow", I have selected the topic of my lecture as **'Technical Education and Research in India—Need for Reorientation'**.

INTRODUCTION:

Technical education (which includes engineering and management education as well) is one of the most potent means for creating skilled and technical manpower required for the developmental tasks of various sectors of the economy. It forms one of the most important and crucial components of human resource development with great potential for adding value to products and services, for contributing to national economy and for improving the quality of-,life of the people. It incorporates a technological dimension which is a vehicle for development. Technical education may itself imply high costs, but such high costs, being directly related to development, should be viewed as an essential productive investment, yielding valuable returns to society and contributing to socio-economic development. The Scientific Policy Resolution (1958) rightly states that "The key to—national prosperity, apart from the spirit of the people, lies in the modern age, in the effective combination of three factors—technology, raw materials and capital of which the first is perhaps the most important,— since the creation and adoption of new scientific techniques can, in fact, make up for a deficiency in natural resources and reduce the demands on capital".

The science and technology education and research in India have made significant contributions to the overall development of the country. From a merely agriculture based society in the early forties, India is today rated among the biggest industrialised nations having a sound base of industries along side with a highly developed agriculture sector. As we march towards the 21st century and with our policies of economic liberalisation, it is imperative that our developmental efforts are supported by the relevant science and technology inputs on one hand and relevant human resources on the other. Technical education and research have thus, to play a very significant role in the changed economic scenario. For this, they need proper reorientation.

DEVELOPMENT OF TECHNICAL EDUCATION IN INDIA

Growth of technical education depends on the socioeconomic and industrial conditions of a country and its development is controlled by the needs and requirements of the economy. After. Independence, the country was faced with the greater challenge of rapidly industrialising the predominantly agricultural economy and in this process major efforts had been made to create a wide-based infrastructure of higher and technical education institutions, research laboratories and industry, covering a broad spectrum of disciplines and capabilities. There are now over 185 Universities and academic institutions of national importance and 7958 colleges with a total enrolment of about 4.8 million students for graduate, postgraduate and research degrees and diplomas, with over 2,70,000 teachers. The higher education institutes include those offering programmes in Arts, Science, Commerce, Engineering, Technology, Management, Finance, Humanities, and Social Sciences etc.

With regard to technical education institutions, there were only 38 institutions at the degree level with an intake of 2940 students and 53 institutions at the diploma level with an intake of 3670 students in the year 1947. Today there are 372 technical institutions at the degree level and 958 technical institutions at the diploma level with an annual intake of 88,930 and 1, 52,554 students respectively. These include regular engineering colleges, polytechnics, Indian Institutes of Technology, Regional Engineering Colleges and other institutions. For training craftsmen, there are over 2650 Industrial Training Institutes/ centres admitting over 3.8 lakhs students per year. About 2000 institutions conduct vocational courses at the higher secondary school level (10+2 level), admitting about one lakh students per year. There are 306 centres, including institutions conducting part-time and correspondence courses and Indian Institutes of Management, imparting management education to over 27,440 students. There are about 100 centres offering postgraduate programmes in engineering and technology with an annual intake of over 9000 students. The government has set up about 450 major S & T research laboratories under its various departments and ministries. There are also about 1360 recognised in-house R & D laboratories in public and private sector undertakings. More than 200 consultancy firms are engaged in engineering design, analysis and research.

STRUCTURE OF TECHNICAL EDUCATION:

Keeping in view the requirements of the country, we needed four levels of technical education. (i) Programmes/ courses offered by ITIs whose products will be working as skilled workers, (ii) Diploma level programmes offered by Polytechnics whose products will be working as Supervisors, (iii) Degree level programmes offered by IITs, Engineering Colleges and universities, whose products will function as engineers and technologists and (iv) Post graduate programmes like M.B.A. and other P.G. Diplomas, M.Tech. and Ph.D. offered by IITs, IIMs, Universities etc., whose products will become Management Personnel, teachers, scientists and researchers.

The Indian Institutes of Technology are established as institutions of national importance to initiate and nurture indigenous effort for technological development. The Regional Engineering Colleges are established with the objective of bringing a major quality change in educational programmes and to train personnel to handle and manage engineering activities in the country.

The four Indian Institutes of Management represent a potent force for professionalising management in India. Collectively they have graduated nearly 8000 MBAs whose annual earning capacity of around Rs. 100 crores indicates the kind of contributions they are making to Indian industry. The

IIMs have also shown a considerable capacity for adding to the teaching, training and research capability of the nation in the field of management.

Four Technical Teacher Training Institutes were established during sixties to function as resource centres for the development of polytechnics in the respective regions. Their duties include curriculum development, teacher training, development of learning resource material, educational research and other activities related to diploma level education.

DEFICIENCIES AND DISTORTIONS IN THE SYSTEM:

The Technical Education system suffers from certain weaknesses and deficiencies. No doubt there has been a considerable quantitative expansion in technical education but quality suffered and there is lack of relevance. The following are the major imbalances and distortions which need focussed attention:

i.   The quantitative expansion has resulted in the lowering of standards and there exists a structural imbalance of skill requirement of the industry and business sectors and the traditional curriculum transacted by the educational institutions. These factors give rise to problems of unemployment and under-employment.

ii. Wastage in the system is enormous. An analysis of the intake and out-turn figures of recognised institutions shows that wastage is of 30% at degree level, 35% at diploma level and 45% at post-graduate level.

iii. The infrastructural facilities available in the vast majority of technical educational institutions are extremely inadequate.

iv. There is an acute shortage of faculty with about 25-40% of faculty positions remaining unfilled.

v.   In most of the institutions there is hardly any R & D activity.

vi. The technical educational institutions are functioning in isolation. Linkage and interaction between technical educational institutions and user—agencies such as industries, R & D and design organisations and Development sectors are not sufficiently strong.

vii. There has been an enormous increase in public expenditure on education but little attention has been paid to the strategies for raising non-budgetary resources and maximising people's participation.

POLICY STATEMENTS:

(A) NATIONAL POLICY ON EDUCATION, 1986 (AS MODIFIED IN 1992):

The National Policy on Education, inter-alia, underlined the need for re-Organizing the technical and management education system to effectively Deal with the changes in the economy, social environment, production and management processes and rapid expansion of knowledge and advances in science and technology. It laid specific guidelines for the qualitative and quantitative development of the technical and management education sectors; establishment of linkages amongst the concerned agencies; manpower assessment and technical education forecasting; increasing effectiveness of technical education management system; proper delivery systems, measures to achieve greater cost effectiveness and generation of resources through suitable means. It further states that technician education has to play an important role in developing highly skilled middle level technical manpower for the organised as well as the unorganised sectors and necessary steps will be taken to make technician education flexible, modular and credit-based with provisions for multi-point entry 166 to achieve this goal. Programme of Action (POA) 1992 spells out the steps for implementation of the National Policy on Education.

B) EIGHTH FIVE YEAR PLAN:

The perspectives for development of technical education during the eighth plan have the following thrust areas: (i) Modernisation and upgradation of infrastructural facilities, (ii) Quality improvement in technical and management education, (iii) Responding to New Industrial Policy and Institution—Industry—R & D Laboratories interaction, and (iv) Resource mobilisation. The strategies envisaged to achieve the objectives related to these thrust areas are :

I. MODERNISATION:

Modernisation relates to both technical equipment and teaching methods. We have to adopt futuristic approaches for achieving modernisation and self-reliance in a sustained manner. Coordinated and concerted efforts are needed to upgrade and consolidate the infrastructural facilities—in the existing institutions. The process of removal of obsolescence would include enhancement of computer facilities and establishment and inter-linking of large computer systems with educational and research institutions through appropriate telecommunication facilities. Steps should be taken to strengthen and create facilities in crucial areas of technology where weaknesses exist, in areas of emerging technologies and in the new specialised fields.

II. QUALITY IMPROVEMENT:

A holistic and need based approach will have to be adopted to reorient the technical and management education. A more broad based flexible system with provision for multipoint entry is required to enable us to offer a better response to the unspecified demands of the future. At the micro level, the curriculum should be developed to encourage creativity and innovation in experimental work by introducing problem or process oriented laboratory exercises. New technology oriented entrepreneurship and management courses are to be introduced in selected institutions having adequate infrastructural facilities. There should be greater emphasis on production engineering and towards design and product development. It would be desirable to couple the technology forecasting with the system of manpower forecasting and planning. Universities and the IITs should play an important role in technology forecast and assessment with the fruitful involvement of Technology Information, Forecasting and Assessment Council (TIFAC), Institute of Applied Manpower Research (IAMR), and Indian Trade and Industries Associations. This would enable to develop the right type of indigenous technologies, to assess related manpower requirements and to produce related trained manpower. Existing facilities for continuing education and retraining are inadequate. There is a need to formalise the training programmes for engineering and technology personnel engaged in all sectors and to make them mandatory. Programme learning packages need to be created and distance learning methodologies employed to enable self-development and training of scientific and technical personnel.

III. RESPONDING TO THE NEW INDUSTRIAL POLICY:

Momentous changes have taken place on the international scene which will have a profound impact on international relations and the world economy. Most developing countries have also embarked on bold measures of reform, restructuring their economies and opening up to forces of competition, both domestic and foreign. The Government of India also have taken new initiatives and bold decisions to reorient and restructure the economy to meet', the challenges of the economic crisis in the country through its policy of liberalisation, hew Industry and Trade Policies etc. The impact of these changes on Indian industry is considerable and it is now exposed to global as well as indigenous competition. To meet these challenges, it has to resort to modernisation, upgrading technology and competence of the work force, adopting modern management. techniques and increasing efficiency and productivity. In this context, the various constituents of national development like universities, engineering institutions, national R & D laboratories and the professional bodies and academies have greater roles to play. A strategy may have to be evolved for effective interaction between them. To bring about such a meaningful interaction, a Model for University-Industry-National R & D Laboratories-Professional Bodies and Academies Interaction for country's economic development has been formulated by me.(The model is shown elsewhere in this Volume). The model identifies the areas of interaction between the various above constituents leading to country's economic development. It is imperative that each of these constituents have a Consultancy Unit / Cell and there is a national coordination mechanism for promoting effective interaction.

IV. RESOURCE MOBILISATION:

Now the time has come where the government alone cannot bear the burden of financing the technical education and, therefore, additional resources are to be mobilised to share the cost. This is not peculiar to India alone and it is the case with many other countries too. This brings into focus the need for Technical Education system to generate funds to supplement the funding from the government through suitable means, which will not, in any way, affect their primary task of teaching and research. There are a number of measures which could be taken up to tackle the inadequate resources situation and lessen its impact.

The following measures could be adopted:

1. Avoidance of duplication of investment in Technical Education institutions located close to each other and proper maintenance of available facilities and instruments.
2. Developing institution-wise specialisation in respect of courses and technical manpower so that the institutions can have the most sophisticated and modern library and laboratory facilities in their chosen fields.
3. Weeding out of outdated and stereotyped courses and introduction of relevant courses in emerging areas.
4. Multiple use of infrastructural facilities through part-time courses, continuing education programmes, consultancy and testing services.
5. Marginal increase in intake capacities in areas of scarce manpower and decrease in intake of low demand areas.
6. Introduction of multiple or at least double shifts in Technical Education institutions.
7. Maximum use of non-monetary inputs, like better planning, advanced technologies and practices, better system of supervision and administration, monitoring and review etc.
8. Commercialisation of the research output of the institutions.
9. Raising of fees in Government-run, Government-aided and unaided institutions on a graduated scale. The measure of raising fees, however, should be coupled with scholarships for SCs / STs and for students below poverty line and a loan scheme to other students.
10. Creation of a corpus fund with contributions from industry, alumni, charitable trusts etc., as well as from Government.
11. Implementing the Institution / University—Industry—National R & D Laboratories—Professional Bodies and Academies Interaction with all seriousness which will not only help towards national development but also help towards fund generation by the universities and other technical institutions.

The All India Council for Technical Education had appointed a High Power Committee on Mobilization of Additional Resources for Technical Education under my chairmanship and the report of the Committee was submitted in May, 1994. Some of the important recommendations of the

High Power Committee are i) The Central Government should examine the feasibility of levying an educational cess on industries for funding technical education and R & D activities in technical institutions. ii) The Government of India may set up an Educational Development Bank of India (EDBI) for financing soft loans for establishment of institutions and also to assist students to meet their fee and living requirements. iii) A National Loan Scholarship Scheme (NLSS) may be set up under EDBI to provide soft loans to needy students. iv) Wherever necessary, the State Governments may also set up a State Education Fund, supplementing the NLSS, to give assistance to needy students in the form of loan scholarships at nominal interest rates and easy repayment terms. v) The plan allocation for technical education sector, both central and state, should be based and related to the plan outlays in the industrial and service sectors and as a matter of policy, these sectors should have an appropriate share earmarked for technical manpower development and this share be made available to Ministry of Human Resource Development to be used exclusively for the development of technical manpower. vi) The tuition fees in all government funded and aided institutions in all the states should be revised to a rational level of at least 20% of the annual recurring cost per student. vii) A corpus fund is to be established in every institution.

BRAIN STORMING SESSIONS:

Taking a lead from the Prime Minister's two important observations made during one of the Planning Commission meetings regarding the need for modernising the teaching and research activities in engineering institutions like Indian Institutes of Technology, who are considered as centres of excellence, and the need for adopting futuristic approaches to meet the emerging challenges of science and technology, a series of Brain Storming Sessions were organised in the Planning Commission to formulate perspectives for achieving excellence and relevance in technical education in the country. As a result of the Brain Storming sessions, documents relating to an Approach Paper for IITs and their Technology Development Missions, development of Indian Institutes of Management, perspectives for excellence in Regional Engineering Colleges, Polytechnics and Technical Teachers' Training Institutes, were prepared. These documents contain valuable recommendations and suggestions for reorientation of technical education and research.

POLYTECHNIC EDUCATION:

Polytechnic Education catering to the middle level technician education is equally suffering from lack of quality and relevance. In the past, the complaint was that the polytechnic courses were mostly theoretical with very little practical bias and they were a poor imitation of the degree courses and, therefore, they did not really serve the middle level technical personnel requirements. Further, the complaint was that no attempt had been made towards specialisation i.e. is no attempts were made to produce specialised technicians. Perhaps the situation has not changed much even now due to the proliferation of substandard institutions. The Central Government had launched a massive project with the assistance of the World Bank to enable the state governments to upgrade their polytechnics in capacity, quality and efficiency, which is quite laudable.

The Brain Storming Session held in the Planning Commission on Polytechnic Education discussed in depth as how to reorient polytechnic education and the discussions resulted in bringing out a document titled "Towards Excellence in Polytechnic Education—Perspectives for the Year 2000 and Beyond". This document, among other things, discusses a new concept of polytechnic education, which envisages new goals and missions for the polytechnic education system and its operation.

REGIONAL ENGINEERING COLLEGES (RECs):

The Regional Engineering Colleges are national institutions established as joint and cooperative ventures of the Government of India and the concerned state governments. They have a national character. They are expected to provide academic leadership to the other technical institutions in the respective regions. As such it is imperative that proper conditions are created which will be conducive for free academic growth and to become real Centres of excellence. It is more so in the present changed Indian economic scenario wherein the industries have to meet the new challenges of global competition. As a result of the Brain Storming Session on Regional Engineering Colleges held in the Planning Commission, a document on "Perspective for Excellence in Regional Engineering Colleges" has been brought out. The Report identifies several priority activities for RECs during the Eighth Plan and beyond. There are some deficiencies in the present system. The most important of these are lack of academic freedom, dual funding and multiple controls. Removal of these deficiencies would require some structural changes in the Regional Engineering Colleges set up. The question of granting 'deemed to be universities' status for some of the well developed RECs and for the rest granting 'autonomous status' initially, by University Grants Commission, could be seriously considered. With these measures, it should be possible for the RECs to blossom into Centres of excellence and play a leading role in helping the Indian industries and revitalising technical education in the country.

INDIAN INSTITUTES OF TECHNOLOGY (IITs) AND TECHNOLOGY DEVELOPMENT MISSIONS:

The IITs are the institutes of national importance and considered as Centres of excellence in engineering and technology. A series of Brain Storming Sessions were organised in the Planning Commission on IITs in the context of the changed economic scenario and in the context of the Prime Minister's observations relating to the need for modernising teaching research and other facilities in the engineering institutions like IITs. The discussions in the Brain Storming Session firstly resulted in the development of an approach paper dealing with new thrust areas, international consultancy, creation of corpus fund and industrial foundation. As a result of further discussions, the five IITs and the Indian Institute of Science, Bangalore have identified eight generic areas for taking up focussed Technology Development Missions. The missions involve not only major research component but also a commitment to technology, development through innovation and its subsequent transfer to public / private sector industry. Developing, testing and delivery of technology are very much part of the package. The missions include areas of strategic significance and export potential. It is envisaged that the funding of these projects should be through multiple agencies like Planning Commission / Ministry of H.R.D., other concerned ministries and industries. A National Steering Committee under my chairmanship has been constituted to monitor the progress of the technology development missions. These missions will set an example for the development of the required indigenous R & D efforts through putting together some of the best brains in the academic institutions in a cooperative mode and with the involvement of the user agencies.

MANAGEMENT EDUCATION, TRAINING AND RESEARCH:

The role of management in the development process is widely recognised. Similarly, management education is perceived as being important for building managerial competence.

The rapid growth of industrial and commercial enterprises in the 50's produced a demand for more and better trained managers in India. During this decade, management development took place largely through short management programmes for senior administrators and managers. Four Indian Institutes of Management were subsequently established—two during 60's at Ahmedabad and Calcutta, one during 70's at Bangalore and one during 80's at Lucknow and these four represent a potent force, professionalising management in India. Two Review Committees were appointed on the Indian Institutes of Management. The first one, the Nanda Committee, was appointed in 1979 and other Review Committee, the Kurien Committee, was appointed in 1991. The Nanda Committee recommended that the objectives should include training and education of (i) Managers for public utilities and services and (ii) Management teachers. The Kurien Committee reaffirmed the Mission of the IIMs to strengthen management in business, industry and commerce. It further recommended that the mission statement needs to be expanded to emphasise IIM's commitment to public service and public management. The University Grants Commission is providing assistance to about 40 universities / institutes for conducting programmes in Management Studies. The IITs also decided to develop management education programmes which started during the late 70's. The thrust of the programmes is on the management of technology. A number of other private institutes of management like XLRI, Jamshedpur, are also doing good work in the field of management education and research.

During the nineties, the country is heading towards becoming progressively more integrated into the global economy. As indicated earlier, with the advent of new Industrial I and liberalisation, the Indian industry is exposed to more domestic and global competition. Competition and pace technological change are likely to intensify in most sectors of economy. 'Professional Management' becomes a vital component in industry. It equally applies to other sectors of economy especially, in the context of the financial resources crunch and the need for better and effective management of available resources. With the above situation, management education, training and research assumes greater significance and the Indian Institutes of Management, Schools or Departments of Management in Universities and other Institutes have to play a greater role in helping to formulate management strategies for the changing scenario. Unless management of public and private sector enterprises respond to greater competition in an effective manner, there will be large scale sickness especially among smaller, enterprises. The management institutes should disseminate to competing enterprises through teaching, training, publishing and consultancy, the expertise to cope effectively with competition. In the context of changing domestic and global economic scenario, the Planning Commission has taken the initiative to convene meetings of the IIM Directors and other experts to discuss and formulate new approaches in the management education, training and research. The discussions resulted in identifying some vital issues and areas which would contribute towards strengthening management education, research and training in the country. A document titled "IIMs and the Eighth Plan" was brought out, which identified certain priorities for the IIMs during the Eighth Plan and beyond. Focus on innovations in management education and training and quality in research are needed. Issues and problems relating to organisational culture and commitment, productivity and quality, processes of internal change, new initiatives in the social responsibility of management, globalisation of industry and trade and relevant strategies for India are to be addressed and solutions sought. In this context, the IIMs, Universities, other institutions of management, professional bodies like the Association of Indian Management schools have a responsible role to play.

TECHNICAL TEACHERS' TRAINING AND ORIENTATION:

Technical teachers' competence and updating of knowledge are crucial for the improvement of the quality and excellence in technical education. Teacher is the pivotal in the teaching and learning process. As such, it is important that suitable facilities are provided for teacher training and orientation.

The Technical Teachers' Training Institutes have been doing pioneering work in the areas of technical teachers training, curriculum development, institutional model development, research and development, consultancy and extension services related to technician education. The objectives of

TTTIs have become all the more relevant in the context of the National Education Policy, the recent World Bank assisted project for strengthening technician education in India and also in the context of the changed economic scenario. As observed by the Review Committee on TTTIs (1990), in spite of high internal efficiency exhibited by these institutes in undertaking various programmes and activities, their external efficiency in terms of improving the quality of technical education system is less significant. A major reason for this is the constraints and limitations imposed on these institutes because of their present status and because of the lack of authority required to introduce, modify and close down programmes depending upon the changing context of technician education in the country. To overcome the above constraints and to ensure that TTTIs are able to play the role of bringing about excellence in technician education, the recommendation of the Review Committee that these institutes are accorded some kind of exalted status and dignity, is quite relevant. A major consequence of the brain storming session organised in the Planning Commission on TTTIs is the preparation of a document "Perspectives for Excellence in Technical Teachers' Training Institutes". The document indicates a set of clear directions for TTTIs to be pursued in the future during the turn of the century. This new design should benefit technician education and many other related constituencies.

At higher technical education level there do not seem to be any concerted effort for teacher orientation and training. The Academic Staff Colleges established by the University Grants Commission at some of the universities are mainly catering to the general disciplines of higher education. Therefore, there is every need to establish mechanisms for teacher training and orientation at higher technical education level. In this context, it would be desirable to pursue the project proposal formulated by the Jawaharlal Nehru Technological University, Hyderabad, with which I was associated as its Vice-Chancellor in the past, for establishment of a National Academy of Pedagogy in the engineering, technology and management, which was already approved in principle by the AICTE, is worth pursuing. In addition, the Academic Staff Colleges of the UGC should also be strengthened for covering the needs of the technical teachers training and orientation. Distance education mode could also be utilised for technical teachers' orientation.

DISTANCE EDUCATION MODE IN ENGINEERING AND TECHNOLOGY:

Education imparted through the Open University System is not a rival but a complimenting approach to formal system. Distance learning system facilitates democratisation of adult education process. Many countries in Asia and elsewhere have provided opportunities for adult education by adopting the open education system and set up, for this purpose, higher educational institutions of distance learning. There has been a significant development in the field of communication technology like use of satellites for telecast of educational programmes and computers for learning. Adopting such new technologies in distance education can help to cut costs and improve quality, equity and participation. Even though distance-teaching may tend to prove to be the most flexible and the most easily adapted alternative approach, it demands lot of efforts to maintain quality and standard in the content of a degree programme or an enrichment programme meant for competence upgradation or a vocational programme for that matter. Distance teaching also needs an innovative approach for its success. India having its own multipurpose satellite is well set for using electronic media for distance learning.

Distance education programmes offered are mostly in non-engineering, nontechnological or non-vocational areas in India. Attempts to provide distance education programmes in Engineering, Technology and vocational courses are very few except by some of the professional bodies like the Institution of Engineers (India). Courses which are suitably designed and developed could be offered through distance education mode in Engineering, Technology and vocational areas with success and acceptability.

The working engineers in the country, especially those who are in the far flung areas, need opportunities to upgrade their expertise and qualifications. Distance education mode can provide the needed opportunity. The Jawaharlal Nehru Technological University, Hyderabad is the first university in the country to provide distance education opportunities in engineering and technology for working engineers and scientists to remove obsolescence and provide opportunities for updating, upgrading, broadening and diversifying their knowledge and skills. The University is offering Distance Education Programmes in B.Tech. and M.Tech. The university has already opened its doors for external registration for M.S. and Ph.D. programmes for working engineers in the country. Such an 'open' concept in engineering and technological education should be encouraged.

266

MANAGEMENT OF TECHNICAL EDUCATION:

The Technical education system should be dynamic and capable of responding to the changes in the socio-economic conditions of the country, national aspirations, objectives and goals. For this, the system should be efficient and the concerned people should have freedom for operation and innovation.

In the Indian Technical education system, there are two levels of organisations—at the Central and State levels, with a complex interface between them, for the management of technical education, in addition to institutional management. The All India Council for Technical Education (A.I.C.T.E.) is responsible for planned and co-coordinated development of technical education, promotion of qualitative improvement and regulation and maintenance of norms and standards. The University Grants Commission (UGC) has also a role to play in the development of technical education, as it finances about 32 university departments dealing with Higher education and engineering. It has also the authority to recommend "deemed university" status to institutions to the Central Government. Most of the state governments have established Directorates of Technical Education for effective administration of technical education. However, the academic control of state level engineering colleges vests in the universities to which they are affiliated. Each state has set up a State Board of Technical Education for giving proper direction to the development of technical education in the state. At the diploma level the academic control is also exercised by the State Board of Technical Education. In case of government engineering colleges and polytechnics full administrative control and financing of institutions is exercised by the government. Aided private institutions are managed by a Board of Governors with representation from the government.

It is essential that the management system should be effective and functional with sufficient decentralisation. Even more important, the system itself should be responsive to changes as indicated earlier. It is imperative on the part of the AICTE to evolve suitable management structure for different types of institutions. Autonomy to selected Engineering institutions will help towards freedom and innovation in academic activities. 'Corpus fund' concept will facilitate reaching towards 'financial freedom' as well. These approaches and ideas deserve all the support when we are aiming at excellence in technical education.

EXTRA MURAL LECTURE AT
THE ROORKEE UNIVERSITY

INTRODUCTION:

"A University stands for humanism, for tolerance, for reason, for progress, for the adventure of ideas and for the search for truth. It stands for the onward march of the human race towards ever higher objectives. If the universities discharge their duty adequately, then it is well with the nation and the people . . ."

Pandit Nehru.

Traditionally the universities are contributing towards: (i) enrichment of human values (ii) development of the individual, (iii) national development, and (iv) world peace and progress—directly or indirectly. Pandit Jawaharlal Nehru's above quotation amply enshrines the essence of a university. While humanism, tolerance, reason, adventure of ideas and search for truth become its life supporting system, its sustained ability to discharge its duties adequately could form the bed-rock for progress and development of the nation. The higher education, including technical education is thus supposed to play an important role through facilitating individual's development, upholding and preserving the value system and providing relevant manpower and quality research outputs for national development. The question whether all the universities are fulfilling these objectives in recent times or not, is debatable. However, the system of higher and technical education should be flexible and resilient enough to absorb the effects of changing times and thereby should become adequately responsive through appropriate reorientation.

Changing Times:

Recently unconceivable changes have taken place right across the globe. These changes will have an impact on the international relations and the world economy in general. Within the country also spectacular changes have taken place on the economic front through restructuring of the economy with considerable dose of liberalisation. The country is gradually getting integrated into the global economy. The result of globalisation is that the industries have to face global and indigenous competition. For this they should resort to: modernisation, upgradation of technology and the competence of the work force, adopting modern management techniques, increasing efficiency and improving quality and productivity. There is resources inadequacy situation prevailing in the country. There is also a serious concern for erosion of the human values. All these present a changed setting for reorientation by all the major constituents in national development and a university is no exception to this.

Impact on the University System:

The impact of the changed scenario makes demands on the university system for the following, which are to be responded through necessary reorientation: (i) to provide competent and relevant manpower, (ii) to provide quality R & D support to industry, (iii) to uphold and enrich the value system, and (iv) to cope up with inadequate resources situation.

Needed Reorientation:

In the above changed situation, the university system has to reorient itself suitably and undertake the following: (i) bring in more relevance in teaching and research while maintaining quality (ii) provide quality R & D support to industry, (iii) work towards self-reliance, and (iv) take up value orientation of education.

269

RELEVANCE:

Presently there appears to be a structural imbalance between the requirements of the industry and business sectors and the curricula pursued by the universities. This gap is to be bridged through bringing in more relevance in the course contents as well as the research programmes. There should be a conscious effort to blend scholarship with relevance in respect of teaching and research. University-industry interaction can play a major role in this regard. The course content could be formulated with the active participation by the people from the industry. There should be exchange of faculty and experts and between the universities and the industries. Students should have access to industries for practical training. There should be a symbiotic relationship between university and industry for mutual benefit. Some of the areas of cooperation and benefits could be the following : (a) Curriculum development, (b) Mobility and exchange of faculty, (c) Training of students, (d) Funding of R & D projects, (e) Consultancy, (f) Ancillaries, (g) R & D collaboration, (h) Financial resources generation, (i) Relevant R & D, (j) Cost effectiveness, (k) Time bound programmes, (l) Improved and new technology, (m) Technology adaptation, (n) Quick adaptation of human resources, and (o) Training programmes. Swaminadhan Model for University-Industry-National R & D Laboratories-Professional Bodies and Academies Interaction for Country's Economic Development identifies the areas of interaction between these constituents (Annexure-I).

INDIGENOUS R & D EFFORT:

The Indian industries need quality R & D support to acquire superior technologies and face global competition. Acquisition of new technology can take place in the following ways:

(i) Technology import related to foreign investment in India; (ii) Technology

(ii) Import by the Indian industry; and (iii) Indigenous R & D effort. The issue of technology import related to foreign investment in India needs serious attention. It should be carefully studied and assessed as to know whether the technology brought into the country is of the first rate or of third rate. It is essential to know the correct picture so that we can guard against their inferior quality. Regarding the technology import by the Indian industry, it is logical to is out-of-date. To quote an example, Japan licenses out technology, relating to machine tools, which is almost one generation behind? Contemporary technology is not purchasable. The regimes of foreign technology denial already precluded the option of 'importing' technology and will certainly do so increasingly in the future. In such a situation, if the Indian industry is to be globally competitive, the only option is of 'developing' our own technology.

We have to encourage universities and Indian Institutes of Technology and other engineering institutions to take up technology development missions so as to boost up our indigenous R & D effort. The Indian Institutes of Technology (IITs) are the institutes of national importance and considered as centres of excellence in engineering and technology.

A series of Brain Storming Sessions were organised in the Planning Commission on IITs in the context of the changed economic scenario and in the context of the Prime Minister's observations relating to the need for modernising teaching, research and other facilities in the engineering institutions like IITs. The discussions in the brain storming sessions first resulted in the development of an approach paper dealing with new thrust areas, international consultancy, creation of corpus fund and industrial foundation. As a result of further discussions, the five IITs and the Indian Institute of Science, Bangalore, have identified seven generic areas for taking up focussed technology development missions (Annexure II).

The missions involve not only major research component but also a commitment to technology development through innovation and its subsequent transfer to public / private sector industry. Developing, testing and delivery of technology are very much part of the package. The missions include areas of strategic significance and export potential. It is envisaged that the funding of these projects should be through multiple agencies like Planning Commission / Ministry of Human Resource Development, other concerned ministries and industries. A key factor of the missions is the participation by industry from the very beginning and a contribution equal to 25% of the government funding in terms of cash and services or manpower. Regional Engineering Colleges are also being encouraged to take up relevant R & D work through thrust area development and they are further encouraged to look into the R & D needs of the small scale industries sector. A National Steering Committee under my chairmanship has been constituted to monitor the progress of the technology development missions. These missions will set an example for the development of superior technology through indigenous R & D effort by putting together some of best brains in the academic institutions in a cooperative mode and with the involvement of the Industries. If similar exercises are undertaken by the universities it will have a catalytic effect on University-Industry cooperation for building up relevant and superior technological base.

SELF-RELIANCE:

Self-reliance should be interpreted in the sense that the gap between the fund requirement of the university and the fund availability from the government should be bridged by resource mobilisation through suitably reorienting the teaching and research activities. The following measures would help towards achieving self reliance: (i) Economy in expenditure, (ii) increasing cost effectiveness, (iii) mobilising resources, (iv) university-industry interaction, and (v) corpus fund.

Economy in expenditure could be achieved by "trimming the extra fat" wherever possible, by resorting to modern technology in management, sharing of facilities etc. Improving cost effectiveness involves optimisation of student intakes, rationalization of staff structure and utilising the services of post-graduate students for instructional work.

Resources can be generated by rationalisation of fee structures, attracting foreign students, enhancing consultancy work and sponsored research and in offering revenue generating courses for the industry. University-industry interaction provides a major means of resource generation towards becoming self-reliant.

A corpus fund may be established in every institution and built-up to act as a steady internal source of revenue as return on investments. The corpus fund could be built up by the resources generated through consultancy, munificent contributions or donations, contributions by alumni associations abroad and within the country and by matching grants from the government. The corpus fund concept would provide the needed financial autonomy to the university, in addition to the needed academic and administrative autonomies.

VALUE ORIENTATION OF EDUCATION:

There has been a growing concern in the country over the erosion of essential values which is reflected in the fall of moral, social, ethical and national values, both in personal and public life. It is worthwhile to quote two passages from the Report of the Education Commission (1964-66), which are still relevant.

"India has a unique advantage with her great tradition of duty without selfinvolvement, unacquisitive temperament, tolerance, and innate love of peace and reverence for all living things. Too often are those precious assets forgotten and we tend to relapse into moods of pessimism, fears and forebodings, discord and destructive criticism. A new pride and a deeper faith expressed in living for the noble ideas of **peace** and **freedom, truth** and **compassion** are now needed".

"Modernisation did not mean—least of all in our national situation—a refusal to recognise the importance of or to inculcate necessary moral and spiritual values and self-discipline. While a combination of ignorance with goodness may be futile, that of knowledge with a lack of essential values may be dangerous".

The Planning Commission recognising the need for added focussed attention on value orientation of education felt it should be studied in-depth and in its totality in relation to various sectors of education and several developmental agencies. A Core Group on Value Orientation of Education was thus set up by the Planning Commission in January, 1992 under my Chairmanship with very wide terms of reference and with membership from various agencies and experts in the subject. The Core Group was able to present a concrete plan of action relating to various sectors of educational development, involving interdepartmental collaboration.

As a follow-up of one of the recommendations of the Core Group, the Ministry of Human Resources Development has constituted a Standing Committee on Value Orientation of Education under my Chairmanship to oversee the implementation of value orientation of education at all levels right from the school to university level in the country. The Standing Committee has been working out the detailed blue print with specific time frames, for the implementation of value orientation of education at school level, college level, university level and to use the electronic and print media and to involve non-governmental voluntary organisations for promotion of value orientation of education. The blue print for school education is already being implemented. The blue print for higher education which has been formulated is now with the University Grants Commission. Every university and college, either general or technical, have to give serious thought to values and implements the value orientation programme with utmost concern.

FOUNDATION DAY LECTURE
"TECHNOLOGICAL SUPERIORITY— PRE-REQUISITE FOR ECONOMIC SURVIVAL IN THE CHANGED GLOBAL SCENARIO"

I consider it as a privilege for having been invited to deliver this year's Foundation Day Lecture of the Central Building Research Institute, Roorkee. I am grateful to Dr. R.N. Iyengar, Director of the Institute for inviting me to deliver this lecture. It gives me added pleasure to visit this premier Institute because its work relates to Civil Engineering, which happens to be my basic discipline. Foundation Day celebrations should provide an opportunity to introspect into to what extent the objectives for which the Institute has been established are fulfilled and to focus into the future activities. I am sure that this year's Foundation Day celebration have fulfilled this objective.

I am happy to note that the Central Building Research Institute, being a constituent unit of the C.S.I.R., has been vested with the responsibility of generating, cultivating and promoting Building Sciences and Technology in the service of the country. I could see from the information brochure that the Institute has been assisting the building construction and building material industries in finding timely, appropriate and economical solutions to the problems of materials, rural and urban housing, energy conservation, efficiency, fire hazards, structural and foundation problems and disaster mitigation. The Institute seems to have well-developed R & D facilities in all the above areas. I believe that the Institute is doing its own bit towards national economic development in the present context of changing global and national economic scenarios, through their programmes and activities.

Since I was given the freedom to choose any topic for the lecture, I considered a few themes and ultimately decided to settle down to one that should deal with the economic strengthening of the country. This prompted me to choose the topic "**Technological Superiority—Pre-requisite for Economic Survival in the Changed Global Scenario**" for the Foundation Day Lecture.

"TECHNOLOGICAL SUPERIORITY—PRE-REQUISITE FOR ECONOMIC SURVIVAL IN THE CHANGED GLOBAL SCENARIO"

INTRODUCTION:

Technology is perhaps the most important resource to any nation. Technology plays a very important role as the trend catches up with the knowledge-based industries. Today technological changes are taking place at a greater pace and the world is passing through an exciting stage of technological progress in several fronts. Invention, innovation, investment in risky ventures, adoption of new technologies and new products etc., are the major process in wealth creation and making the countries technologically superior. India cannot afford to lag behind and should make every effort needed to be in the forefront in achieving technologic superiority.

R & D EFFORT IN INDIA:

A year after independence, India was able to spend a meagre Rs. 11 million (R & D activity in the central sector. Four decades later, the figure grew to more than 30,000 million. According to the latest available statistics, in the year 1992-93, Rs. 38,910 millions were spent on R&D by the Central government. The corresponding figures for the states sect and the private sector are 4788 million and 7718 million bringing the total expenditure on R&D in 1992-93 to Rs. 51416 million. Sector-wise percentage share of national expenditure for 1992-93 was 64.3% by the Central Government institutions, 9.3% by State Government 11.4% public sector industries and 15.0% by the private sector industries. Plan allocation for S & T increased from Rs. 1420 million in the Fourth Plan to Rs. 91800 million during the Eighth Plan.

Another significant factor is the multiplicity of R&D agencies in the country leading to a particular agency specialising in a particular type of activity. It can be seen that Central Government accounted for about 76% of the total national R&D input in 1992-93 out of which the major chunk went into applied research and experimental development.

A country such as U.S.A. invests upto US $150 billion on R & D while Japan **invests** US $100 billion per year. In India, we invest less than US $ 1 billion per year towards all our efforts in science and technology. India is investing about 0.83 per cent of GNP for science and technology, compared to 5 to 6 per cent by some of the advanced countries. Obviously, higher investments are needed. In some of the advanced countries, a high percentage of expenditure on science and technology comes from private industry.

CHANGED GLOBAL SCENARIO AND ITS IMPACT:

We are living in an era of change. Momentous changes have taken place on the international scene which are having a profound impact on both international relations as well as the world economy. In India too, a tremendous change has taken place on the economic front. The government has launched new initiatives buttressed by bold decisions to reorient and restructure the economy and to meet the challenges of the economic crisis facing the country. During the nineties, the country is poised to become progressively more integrated into the global economy. Competition and the pace of technological change are likely to intensify in almost all sectors of the economy. In the coming years, knowledge-based industries will be on the upswing.

The impact of these changes on Indian industry is considerable and it is now exposed to global as well as indigenous competition. To meet these challenges, it has to resort to modernisation, upgrading technology and competence of the workforce, adopting modern management techniques and increasing efficiency and productivity. Structural adjustments aim at increasing Indian exports and this would be possible through, among other things, Indian enterprises acquiring global levels of expertise in developing and producing high quality products and marketing them internationally. It equally applies to agriculture sector. Under such circumstances, we need to have a workforce having a scientific bent of mind and possess the much needed scientific temper and skills to maintain high quality of productivity on par with world standards. In addition we have to assume a position of technological superiority.

NEED FOR DEVELOPING INDIGENOUS TECHNOLOGIES:

Acquisition of new technology can take place in the following ways: (i) Technology import related to foreign investment in India; (ii) Technology import by the Indian industry; and (iii) indigenous R & D effort. The issue of technology import related to foreign investment in India needs serious attention. It should be carefully studied and assessed as to know whether the technology brought into the country is of the first rate or of third rate. It is essential to know the correct picture so that we can guard against their inferior quality.

Regarding the technology import by the Indian industry, it is logical to believe that the quality of technology imported may not suffer but one cannot be sure of getting the latest technology always. Now what is importable is only purchasable technology which is out-of-date. To quote an example, Japan licenses out technology relating to machine tools which is almost one generation behind. Contemporary technology is not purchasable. The regimes of foreign technology denial already precluded the option of 'importing' technology and will certainly do so increasingly in the future. In such a situation, if the Indian industry is to be globally competitive, the only option is of 'developing' our own technology.

TECHNOLOGIES FOR SUSTAINABLE DEVELOPMENT:

Sustainable development implies a model of development in which both the present and the future are taken into consideration. The main engineering and technological areas that have bearing on sustainable development are: environmental infrastructure (water supply, sanitation, drainage, solid waste management), pollution control, shelter, urban planning and development, transport, energy, communications, computers and information systems, space technology and remote sensing, ocean development, bio-technology, bio-medical engineering, agriculture, irrigation, food processing, industries and engineering constructions. Sustainable development demands technologies which are least polluting, uses natural resources optimally and also facilitates recycle of wastes. These technologies should be compatible with the socio-economic, cultural, environmental and developmental priorities of our country. There should be a strategic shift to cleaner and green technologies for a better tomorrow. Sustainable industrial development is not a matter of mere high-tech but also of appropriate sci-tech. We have to phase out older and inappropriate technologies while simultaneously developing and disseminating a new generation of sophisticated and environmentally benign technologies. We have to encourage indigenous research effort to be directed at green technologies through a system of incentives and penalties.

SOME INITIATIVES FOR ACHIEVING TECHNOLOGICAL SUPERIORITY:

Farsightedness and imaginative initiatives are needed to achieve technological superiority in the present day context. The following initiatives and attempts should contribute towards achieving that objective.

A. STRENGTHENING RESEARCH EXCELLENCE:

It is absolutely crucial that we do not ignore basic research. If we wish to have a competitive edge in technology, which plays such an important role in the present day context, we will also require a high level of scientific capability. We will have to gear up our research efforts not only to catch up with the world in frontier areas of knowledge but also to acquire a leadership role in some of the areas which will dominate and determine the course of the 21st century. The emerging situation demarcates a prominent role for higher education, especially in relation to the realms of science, technology and management. Higher education is being put to a test at the moment. In the changed environment of the day, the system of higher education faces two major imperatives. These are: (a) need to cope up with inadequacy of resources, and (b) need to respond to the demand for providing competent manpower and high quality R & D support. In this backdrop, the system of higher education should orient itself and be prepared to respond adequately to these emerging challenges. The Planning Commission organised a Brain Storming Session on **"Research Excellence in India"** in January, 1996 under my Chairmanship. Many eminent scientist researchers and Vice-Chancellors participated in the discussions. The Brain Storming Session introspected on the research excellence in India and the following suggestions were made which could help in formulating a broader framework for a plan of action for strengthening research excellence in India.

i. A comprehensive and integrated view may be taken on the strengthening of research excellence in India covering sciences, humanities and social sciences.

ii. Attaining excellence needs selective approach through school, college and university level. For this, short term and long term strategies may have to be worked out.

iii. Inter linkages between the school education, higher education and research should well recognised and necessary reorientation should be undertaken.

iv. There is every need for maximising use of resources by way of sharing especially library and computer resources, through networking and using existing national facilities like NICNET, ERNET etc.

v. The interaction between university, industry, national R&D labs and national academies should be promoted and the industry should play a greater role in supporting reseal excellence.

vi. Expand catchment area of potential scientists and researchers through strengthening the school education and covering uncovered regions.

vii. About 100 colleges could be selected and supported for providing a better catchment area of scientists and researchers.

viii. The trend of de-emphasis on creativity should be arrested and conducive atmosphere for creative work and innovations should be created in the school and university system.

ix. Merit and potential for research at individual level should be recognised and support in the universities.

x. Adequate and timely support to identified research groups in universities should be provided.

xi. Promote genuine team work for research among institutions.

xii. 'Accountability' aspect of academic and research organisations as well as individual researchers should be stressed.

xiii. Policies for science and technology, humanities and social sciences are to be properly oriented for achieving research excellence in India.

xiv. It was felt that there is need of political and national will for implementation of the accepted policies in the areas of science and technology, humanities and social sciences so as to facilitate implementation in right earnest As an outcome of this brain storming session, a Planning Commission Task Group has been appointed under the chairmanship of Dr. M.S. Swaminadhan to formulate an Approach Paper on "Strengthening Research Excellence in India". Similar Task Groups have been constituted by the Planning Commission for preparing approach papers on "Mathematical Sciences" and on "Sharing of Library and Information Resources" as a result of brain storming sessions held in the Planning Commission. These approach papers will provide valuable inputs for strengthening research excellence in India.

B. UNIVERSITY-INDUSTRY-R & D LABORATORY-SCIENTIFIC BODIES AND ACADEMIES INTERACTION:

India has built a wide based infrastructure in higher and technical education, national R & D laboratories and industries covering a broad spectrum of disciplines and capabilities. Indian Professional Bodies and National Academies of Sciences and Engineering enjoy a high status and occupy commanding positions in the scientific and academic circles. However, interaction among these four has been inadequate. Time is now ripe for greater meaningful interaction and linkages among them in the changed global and national economic scenarios.

This linkage, inter-alia, will result in (i) development of indigenous technologies appropriate to our national priorities and resources, (ii) facilitate adapting the imported technology by the industries to meet global competitiveness, (iii) enriching teaching and research in universities with the back up of practical and field experience, (iv) universities and R & D laboratories getting valuable clues for research orientation (v) sharing and optimising the use of resources, and. (vi) fund generation by the universities and R & D laboratories. A Model for University, Industry, R & D Laboratory and National Academies interaction has been proposed by me and published (Annexure 1 shown at page 154). The Model identities areas of interaction between universities, industries, national R & I) laboratories, professional bodies and National academies. Planning Commission took the initiative in convening a meeting to discuss how to strengthen linkages and interaction covering the above four constituents and based on one of its recommendations, a Standing Committee on University-Industry-National R & D Laboratories-Professional Bodies and National Academies interaction has been constituted under my Chairmanship to promote and oversee the cooperation among the constituents. The Standing Committee is now in the process of preparing an Approach Pap on University-Industry-National R & D Laboratories-Professional Bodies and Nation Academies Interaction in India.

During January, 1996, the UNESCO organised a Forum on Strategies University-Industry Cooperation in Engineering, Sciences and Technology in India at New Delhi, which I happened to chair. The purpose of the Forum was to review the Report an Action Plan formulated by the UNESCO. The Action Plan was the synthesis of a study carried out in cooperation with 30 university departments and wide associated industries and'—purpose was to develop a set of policy recommendations for implementation, for Government of India in order to stimulate an effective and mutually beneficial self-sustaining interaction between universities and industries. The discussions at the Forum contributed al to enrich the Action Plan. The Action Plan contains valuable recommendations relating promotion of cooperation between universities and industries, which would help towards building up of indigenous R & D capability. This action plan will also provide valuable inputs to the preparation of the above referred approach paper by the Planning Commission Standing Committee.

C. TECHNOLOGY DEVELOPMENT MISSIONS:

We have to encourage universities and Indian Institutes of Technology and other engineering institutions to take up technology development missions so as to boost up our indigenous R & D effort. The Indian Institutes of Technology (IITs) are the institutes of national importance and considered as centres of excellence in engineering and technology. A series of Brain Storming Sessions were organised in the Planning Commission on IITs in the context of the changed economic scenario and in the context of the Prime Minister's observations relating to the need for modernising teaching, research and other facilities in the engineering institutions like IITs. The discussions in the brain storming sessions first resulted in the development of an approach paper dealing with new thrust areas, international consultancy, creation of corpus fund and industrial foundation. As a result of further discussions, the five IITs and the Indian Institute of Science, Bangalore, have identified seven generic areas for taking up focussed technology development missions (Table 1 shown at page 87). The missions involve not only major research component but also a commitment to technology development through innovation and its subsequent transfer to public / private sector industry. Developing, testing and delivery of technology are very much part of the package. The Missions include areas of strategic significance and export potential. It is envisaged that the funding of these projects should be through multiple agencies like Planning Commission / Ministry of Human Resource Development, other concerned ministries and industries. A key factor of the missions is the participation by industry from the very beginning and a contribution equal to 25% of the government funding in terms of cash and services or manpower. Regional Engineering Colleges are also being encouraged to take up relevant R&D work through thrust area development and they are also encouraged to look into the R & D needs of the small scale industries sector. A National Steering Committee under my chairmanship has been constituted to monitor the progress of the technology development missions. These missions will set an example for the development of superior technology through indigenous R & D effort by putting together some of best brains in the academic institutions in a cooperative mode and with the involvement of the Industries. If similar exercises are undertaken by the universities it will have a catalytic effect on University-Industry cooperation for building up relevant and superior technological base.

D. INDUSTRIAL IN-HOUSE R & D:

The survey of R&D activity in India points out that R&D activity in general is nurtured in isolation without significant forward and backward linkages. One welcome feature in the national R & D scenario is the springing up of cooperative research associations in different industry groups such as textiles, plywood, rubber, automobile, electrical and cement. There are, in all 13 cooperative research associations financed jointly by the government and the members comprising of concerned industry. The R & D expenditure incurred by the associations had increased from Rs. 154 million in 1990-91 to Rs. 264 million in 1992-93. This trend needs to be strengthened further.

It is also worthwhile to examine the growth of R & D in industry. The Government has taken several measures towards promoting industrial research in industry itself. The growth of R & D in industry still remains to be inadequate. According to the R & D Statistics for 1992-93, published by the Department of Science & Technology appears that industry as a whole have higher priority for investment on R & D as compared advertising with private sector according more or less equal priority, but less priority than the purchase of new plant and equipment.

The R & D expenditure by Industry, as a percentage of total R & D expenditure is only 21% in India compared to 61% in U.K., 63% in Japan and 72% in U.S.A. The time has come now that the Indian industry should increase their share of contribution towards R & expenditure through either their own R & D units or through supporting research in universities, if they want to survive against global competition.

CONCLUSION:

Globalisation of the Indian economy is inevitable. We may have our own approach to market economy—through 'human face' and 'middle path' to overcome social imperative but it is a foregone conclusion that the Indian economy is getting gradually integrated into the global economy as we cannot live in isolation in the present day context. That being the ca while taking care of social-compulsions and imperatives in the transition period, we have look to the means of building our economic strength if we want to play our own-role effectively in the global economy. For this, we need technological superiority. It is logical, therefore, every possible effort should be made to modernise and strengthen our technological base, obviously through our own indigenous effort, if we want economic survival in the changed global scenario.

THE ENGINEER'S CONTRIBUTION TO SUSTAINABILITY

SUMMARY

'Sustainable development' is a well accepted concept now. It implies a model of development in which both the present and the future are taken into consideration. Natural resources, ecology and economic growth are to be managed in such a manner that it leads to sustainability. In this process three basic tenets are paramount. Firstly, temporal sustainability demands careful maintenance of the delicate balance between productivity parameters and conservation practices. Secondly, environmental sustainability implies development strategies which are eco-friendly, energy efficient and waste minimal and thirdly, economic models should optimise growth subject to ecological, economic, social and cultural constraints which may include pro-poor and gender equity bias. With this perception of sustainable development, the engineer's contribution to sustainability assumes greater significance. The areas having significance to sustainability which offer opportunities for contributions by engineers are many. A few of them are environmental engineering, environmental infrastructure (water supply, sanitation, drainage, solid waste management), pollution control, shelter, urban planning and development, transport, energy, communications, computers and information systems, space technology and remote sensing, ocean development, bio-technology, biomedical engineering, agriculture, irrigation, food processing, industries and engineering constructions. The rapid pace of urbanisation today is the most important phenomenon transforming developing countries, by acting as a catalyst for economic and social change, and that needs to be given greater focus for sustainable human settlements development. To be able to make effective contributions to sustainable development, the engineer himself needs preparedness in terms of relevant education, training and awareness about contemporary innovations leading to professional competence, professional values and ethics, maintaining visibility and showing concern for Total Quality Management (TQM). The universities, engineering institutions, R & D organisations, various Engineering academies and Institutions of engineers and international bodies like the Commonwealth Engineers' Council and others can play an important facilitating role in the engineer's contribution to sustainability, through their state-of-the-art and futuristic approaches and programmes, either formal or non-formal. For this to happen in a rewarding manner, strong linkages among these constituents and with industries are vital.

The author while tracing the engineer's contribution also discusses thrust areas and challenges facing engineers in contributing to sustainable development in this key note address paper.

OVERVIEW

The twentieth century has seen some spectacular changes of social, economic, scientific and political significance. Tremendous developments in science and technology and their application in agriculture, industry, improvement in longevity and quality of life and in many other areas of human activity, have been the land marks of this century. However, these achievements have extracted their price in terms of large scale indiscriminate damage to life support systems.

Till the middle of the present century, upto the end of the Second World War, concern for the issue of environment was only peripheral. Natural resource was considered as something 'infinite' and 'free'. The relevance of the issue of environment was pioneered by engineers thereafter with a number of Environmental Impact Assessments (EIA), which were carried out as isolated exercises without their integration into the development policy. In early 1970's, debate on "environment versus development" was heightened with the "limits to growth" argument, thereafter the development policy undergoing a significant shift towards a "basic needs approach" in early 1980s. The United Nations Conference on Human Environment (UNCHE) also known as Stockholm Conference in 1972 and the subsequent efforts focussed on developing guidelines for appraisal of development decisions also from 'environmental' angle. The setting up of World Commission on Environment and Development by the United Nations and the subsequent elaborate public debates on the subject and publication of the Commission's report 'Our Common Future' in 1987 led to the emergence of sustainable development as a new environmental dimension.

SUSTAINABLE DEVELOPMENT

Sustainable development implies a model of development in which both the present and the future are taken into consideration. Natural resources, ecology and economic growth are to be managed in such a manner that it leads to sustainability. In this process, three basic tenets are paramount. Firstly, temporal sustainability demands careful maintenance of delicate balance between productivity parameters and conservation practices. Secondly, environmental sustainability implies development strategies which are eco-friendly, energy efficient and waste minimal and thirdly, economic development models should optimise growth subject to ecological, economic, social and cultural constraints, which may include pro-poor and gender equity bias as well.

URBANISATION SCENE AND SUSTAINABLE DEVELOPMENT

Today nearly half the world's population lives in cities and by the year 2025 A.D. the quantum reaches to more than two-thirds. The stress of such population growth is overwhelming. Despite growing investments in environmental infrastructure, approximately 380 million urban population in the developing world still do not have adequate sanitation and at least 170 million lack access to a nearby source of safe drinking water. With the world reaching a point at which nearly half of its people are living in cities, it is clear that the goal of achieving a sustainable mode of life on our planet envisaged at Rio cannot be achieved unless the urban environment is sustainable. The great urban centres of the world are the crucibles of our common future. The path of sustainable development is, therefore, inextricably inter-linked with the future of development of our human settlements; we must use the scarce water and land resources efficiently; we must recycle, manage, and dispose of waste materials in a manner which minimizes environmental degradation. Agenda 21, adopted in Rio, set the framework for the current dialogue on sustainable human settlements aspects as an integral part of urban environment.

ENVIRONMENTAL DEGRADATION

Despite development efforts both poverty and environmental degradation in cities continue to increase at alarming rates. The developing countries face formidable obstacles in addressing problems of environmental degradation. The sustainable human settlements approach would need financial resources, effective settlements management and technology inputs. Sustainable human settlements development will require a wide range of new technologies, both for production and urban services which are environment-friendly in nature. Engineer's contribution in providing appropriate new technologies can pave the way in a big manner for a model for sustainable human settlements development. Engineers have to take this challenge as we move into the next century. The technological innovations should succeed in making a better use of human, natural and financial resources to meet human needs with technology being realistic, appropriate, economically viable and ecologically sustainable. It should be replicable with costs low enough and the benefits high enough to make wide spread implementation feasible.

ENGINEER'S ROLE IN SUSTAINABLE DEVELOPMENT

Development per-se, involves interference with nature. A continuous process of engineering and re-engineering is inevitable as the pace of development accelerates and expands to meet growing aspirations and needs. It is in the balancing between the needs of development and the need to ensure sustainability that expertise and experience of the engineer is of crucial importance. The engineer has to juxtapose developmental solutions against sustainability and implement only those solutions as to meet the prescribed standards of sustainability. His role is thus vital. He is in the best position to ensure that the sustainability is adequately catered for while finding developmental solutions.

OCEAN BASED RESOURCES

(A) EXPLOITATION OF MARINE LIVING RESOURCES:

Fish is one of the cheapest sources of protein to mankind. Over-exploitation of fishes along the coastal waters (below 50 mtrs. depth) is causing depletion of resources and as an alternative it needs to capture fish in the deeper areas (beyond 50 mtrs. depth). Designing and fabrication of suitable nets for catching selective species of commercially important fish through modern engineering methods helps in increasing the catches. Development of fuel efficient long-range fishing crafts economise the cost of fishing operation.

(B) HARNESSING OF OCEAN ENERGY:

Development of engineering systems for harnessing wave energy, tidal energy and Ocean Thermal Energy Conversion (OTEC), would make available pollution-free energy in the form of electricity to the coastal population. This reduces the burden of dependence on fossil fuels, which are not environment-friendly.

(C) ENGINEERING FOR ENVIRONMENT:

Deployment of engineeringly designed structures facilitates settlement of corals in the coral reefs. Thereby, the coral reefs are rejuvenated in areas where corals were destroyed in the past. Development of satellite-based monitoring system with the help of development of suitable instruments facilitates monitoring the changes in the distribution of coral reefs and mangroves. The satellite-based technique is faster, less time consuming compared to the conventional survey methods.

IRRIGATION

The technologies that strengthen human society's power to manipulate the hydrology in a beneficial manner are those of dam building for creating storages (large or small); construction of canals and aqueducts enabling even long-distance transfer of water; loss prevention by spread of monomolecular films on the water surfaces to conserve water against the extreme heat in summer; pumping from great depths; irrigation by drip system; reuse of water through repetitive treatment; and purification and obtaining usable waters from normally non-usable quantities such as the highly saline sea water through high-tech processes like osmosis. A society armed with such technologies can utilise the available water resources in a far more beneficial manner and thereby build up a greater degree of confidence in supporting the existing as well as increasing population. This may be difficult to achieve in the case of a technologically less developed society. The water resource engineer is in the center of sustainable development of this Mother Nature's precious gift to mankind i.e., water.

BIO-TECHNOLOGY

Developments in bio-technology, including genetic engineering, in offering solutions to problems of health and disease, agriculture and food production, industry and environment are enormous. The advent of recombinant DNA, hybridoma, plant and tissue culture technologies with innovations in downstream processing to handle large scale production of biological products has ushered in a new bio-technology revolution. Bio-technology has wide application in several sectors of economic relevance for both developing and developed countries. It is generally skill and not capital intensive. It generates employment and at the same time is also capable of miniaturization and automation. It can be applied either in the decentralized rural environment or set up in a modern urban industrial complex. The development and application of bio-technology is location specific and may lead to sustainable use of industrial resources.

SPACE TECHNOLOGY

The space and remote sensing technology is perhaps the most potent tool in the process of achieving sustainable development. Remarkable developments in space technology and its applications during the past few decades have firmly established the immense potential of space to transform the life style of human society as a whole. With this potential, the perceptions of development have undergone significant alterations with space technology providing unique solutions in the areas of communications, meteorology and natural resources. It is rightly said that space activities can be viewed as a technology drive for the entire economy benefitting a wide range of space and non-space related industries. The space programmes comprising, among other things, designing and building of remote sensing and communication satellites and launch vehicles for putting satellites into orbits and design and manufacturing of ground electronic equipment needed for remote sensing, communication, T.V. broadcasting, E-Mail services and meteorological forecasting are the areas in which the engineer has to play an important role. The roles of engineers in the areas of computers, telecommunications and Information Technology (IT) are equally vital.

FOOD PROCESSING ENGINEERING

Fruits and vegetables are the important source of micro nutrients. Due to lack of preservation and processing facilities, especially in developing countries, estimates show that considerable loss of fruits and vegetables take place. Similarly, fishes of low-unit value remain mostly unutilised or under-utilised due to absence of any kind of preservation and processing. Many of the species have great potentialities of being converted into value added by-products which can supplement protein not only to the diet of man but also of fish and prawn. Food processing engineering provides vital means of not only reducing this substantial loss, but also ensuring longer storage and shelf life, uniform availability, higher quality food stuffs and better nutrition.

URBAN SUSTAINABILITY

It is important that a clear understanding of the inter-relationship between urban development and urban environment is developed because lack of this understanding makes "urban sustainability" complicated and difficult. The major areas which are directly linked to ensuring sustainable development where the engineers could make visible impact are discussed as under:

a) WATER SUPPLY, SANITATION AND DRAINAGE.

Depletion of water availability to urban centres has become a serious issue. Sustainability is a patent issue when cities are forced to tap water from increasingly long distances. In view of the limits to the drawl of ground water, the urban planning process should ensure reservation of areas for drainage and *round water recharge accordingly. The overall strategy for sustainable water supply should identify and implement strategies and actions to ensure the continued supply of affordable water for present and future needs, and to reverse the current trends of resource degradation and depletion. Water resources need to be protected through the introduction of sanitary waste disposal facilities. The adopted systems need to be ecologically sound, low-cost with upgradable technologies, and should include urban storm water run-off and drainage programmes, promotion of recycling and reuse of waste water and solid wastes and the control of sources of industrial pollution.

High costs of conventional sewerage treatment systems have prevented most cities in the developing countries from installing them. Recent initiatives in anaerobic treatment process as well as improved approaches in oxidation, pisciculture, aquaculture and sewage farms in treatment and waste water application need to be pursued more widely and consistently. Resource recovery from waste water treatment has to be an important principle in these efforts.

b) SOLID WASTE MANAGEMENT.

Of the various categories of pollutants, municipal solid wastes contribute significantly towards environmental degradation. Industrial solid wastes, which often get mixed with domestic wastes due to inadequate disposal facilities cause toxic effects on human, animal and plant life. The waste problem is especially severe in the rapidly growing informal settlements of the developing world, where population densities and health risks are high, public awareness of the hazards of uncontrolled disposal is low and the consequent need for municipal waste disposal services is greatest. A strategy for waste prevention, minimization and reuse should become the basis for all future solid waste management programmes. Waste minimization can be achieved by modifying industrial processes and changes in the design and use of products.

c) POLLUTION CONTROL.

In several cities in developing countries the general environment—air, water and land—is badly polluted adversely affecting the health of hundreds of millions of people. Appropriate air pollution control technologies need to be developed on the basis of risk assessment and epidemiological research considered as part of the introduction of clean production processes and suitable safe mass transport. Air pollution control capacities emphasising monitoring networks and enforcement programmes should be installed in all major cities. Prevention and control methods are required to reduce indoor air pollution.

Water pollution control efforts should aim at the integrated environmentally sound management of water resources and the safe disposal of liquid and solid wastes. This should include the establishment of protected areas for sources of water supply, the safe disposal of refuse, the control of water associated diseases, the sanitary disposal of excreta and sewage and using appropriate systems to treat waste water in urban and rural areas.

d) SHELTER

Shelter is fundamental to an individual's physical, psychological, social and economic wellbeing. The Global Strategy for Shelter by the Year 2000, adopted by the United Nations General Assembly in 1988, has the goal of providing adequate shelter for all by the end of this century. Developing countries need to adopt national shelter strategies focussed on the use of new and innovative financing mechanisms, such as specific housing schemes. Shelter efforts of poor and vulnerable groups should be supported by facilitating their access to land, financing and building materials, reforming existing codes and regulations, and actively promoting the regularisation and upgrading of informal settlements.

e) CONSTRUCTION INDUSTRY

The construction industry, which provides shelter, infrastructure and employment, is vital to the achievement of national socio-economic development goals. It provides basic infrastructure for all developmental activities. But it can also damage the environment by degrading fragile eco-zones using harmful materials, consuming excessive energy and increasing air pollution. In promoting sustainable construction industry activities, developing countries need to encourage the use of local materials and labour-intensive construction methods to generate employment.

f) Urban Planning and Development

Urban planning techniques require innovative approaches. There is a need to assess the population based on resource planning and resource availability in an urban region. This is different from conventional planning approach which plans for certain pre-determined density, based on which the demand for resources is assessed. Urban land-use planning and promoting the integrated provision of environmental infrastructure—water, sanitation, drainage and solid waste management—in all human settlements is essential for environmental protection, increased productivity, better health and poverty alleviation. In providing land for human settlements and promoting sustainable land-use planning and management policies, there is a need to inventorise land resources and develop urban land resource management plans for meeting the demands of residential, commercial, industrial, open spaces, transport and agriculture, in an integrated manner. Coordination is essential to ensure that the poor are not denied access to serviced land.

g) Transport.

Transport congestion and pollution from vehicles have emerged as two strong manifestations of deteriorating urban environment in developing countries. In view of the inappropriate land use planning policies, the cities in developing countries have long travel distances. While the integration of transport and land use planning as a continuous but long term goal is to be stressed, in the near and medium term, urban environment in the cities of developing countries will depend on how quickly the problems of poor public transport and high pollution are addressed. In recent years, several cities in the developed countries have been able to achieve some improvement in controlling air pollution from vehicles only by a concerted and multi-pronged strategy, which clearly assign roles for the different institutions involved. Such city-based strategies are long overdue for evaluation for replication in the cities of developing countries.

h) ENERGY

At a global level, most of the energy is derived from fossil fuels and is used in urban areas. Transport accounts for close to 30 per cent of global commercial energy consumption and about 60 per cent of the total global consumption of liquid petroleum. In developing countries, rapid motorization and the lack of resources for investment in urban transport, traffic management and infrastructure have combined to create increasing health, noise, congestion and productivity problems. Developing countries are at present faced with the need to increase their energy production to accelerate development and raise the living standards of their population, while reducing energy production costs and energy-related pollution. Science and technology should play a pivotal role in the long-term energy planning. The long-term strategy should aim at sustainable energy supply and demand systems consistent with the overall economic growth and improvements in the quality of life. On the supply side, science and technology should provide the inputs necessary for expanding the renewable energy supply base through cost-effective and environment friendly technologies that will ensure that consuming sectors obtain energy at affordable prices through clean technologies. On the demand side, thrust of science and technology should be towards improvements in the end use efficiencies through cost-effective processes and technologies so that demand can be regulated without compromising on the quality of energy supplies.

TOTAL QUALITY MANAGEMENT (TQM)

Total Quality Management (TQM is a management philosophy that builds customer driven learning or organisations dedicated to total customer delight with continuous improvement in the effectiveness of the organisation and its processes. TQM is a multi-dimensional pursuit of Quality, Effectiveness, Efficiency, Culture and Welfare. It leads to better customer service, economy orientation and meet social needs and professional accountability. Such being the importance of TQM, it should not only form part of the technical education but ample training facilities should be made available for the working engineers to getting exposed to such techniques so as to enable them to equip better to play their role effectively in the economic development.

INTERACTION

For effective contributions to sustainable development, the engineers himself needs preparedness in terms of relevant education, training, awareness about contemporary innovations leading to professional competence, professional values and ethics and maintain visibility. The universities, engineering institutions, R & D organisations, various Engineering academies and Institutions of engineers and international bodies like the Commonwealth Engineers' Council and others can play an important facilitating role in the engineer's contribution to sustainability, through their state-of-the-art and futuristic approaches and programmes, either formal or non-formal. For this to happen in a rewarding manner, strong linkages among these constituents and with industries are vital. To bring about such a meaningful interaction, a Model for University-Industry-National R & D Laboratories-Professional Bodies and Academies Interaction has been formulated and published by the author. The Model identifies areas of interaction between these constituents. Each of these constituents should have a consultancy unit / cell and it would be desirable to have a central coordination mechanism for promoting effective interaction.

CONCLUSION

The engineer's contribution to economic development is well known since ages. The engineer, however, has to have a clear exposure to the modern development concept namely, sustainable development, in its entirety. The changed context naturally necessitates the engineer's preparedness in terms of updating his professional competence and training. In this process, the universities, industries, national R & D organisations and the national and international academies and councils of sciences, engineering and technology have a greater role to play in facilitating the engineer's contribution to sustainable development effectively.

VALUE ORIENTATIN OF EDUCATION

ADDRESS AT THE VALEDICTORY
FUNCTION OF THE SEMINAR
ON VALUE EDUCATION

Shri Kireet Joshiji, Director of the Seminar, Shri Giri, Education Secretary, Prof. Bhuvan Chandel, Member-Secretary, Indian Council of Philosophical Research, distinguished participants and ladies and gentlemen,

It is indeed a great privilege for me to be with you this afternoon to preside over the Valedictory Function of the Seminar on Value Education organised under the auspices of the Indian Council of Philosophical Research. I am grateful to the organisers, especially to Shri Kireet Joshi, for giving me this splendid opportunity.

I have listened with deep interest to the outcome of the Seminar proceedings and also the excellent Valedictory Address delivered by Shri Giri. I am extremely benefitted and enlightened on the subject of value education. I can only express the earnest hope that some of the important recommendations of the Seminar and the observations made by Shri Giri would provide useful inputs for developing an action oriented plan for implementation. I am optimistic that the contribution of the Seminar will be well received.

During the last seven Five Year Plans, there have been several attempts to evolve policies and projects to formulate programmes relating to value orientation of education. Many Commissions and Committees deliberated on this subject and made numerous recommendations. More the Committees and Commissions and their recommendations, it has been observed that in the area of value orientation of education, there is greater difficulty in formulations of programmes and projects. Why so? Value orientation programmes do not involve much expenditure of financial resources but deeper thinking, greater investment of time and planning based on multiple variables. This is not the time to apportion blame. Over the last 45 years or so, since we achieved independence in 1947, hard facts have emerged which have to be reckoned within our future planning and not to be by-passed.

Let us take an overview of the current scenario. Why is our record in this specific area so very bleak? Right from the very beginning our preoccupation with the narrow definition of the terms 'values' and 'secularism', not only narrowed our vision but even blurred it. The term 'secularism' in the Indian Constitution has been presented in various forms. The term actually meant that no discrimination should be practised by the State against any sect on grounds of religion or faith. Further, people belonging to various religious persuasions should be able to enjoy equal freedom in the matter of practising and propagating their religion. The term secularism did not prescribe the inculcation of properly thought out moral end spiritual instructions geared to the cultivation and development of a proper sense of human values— which are universal, in the minds of students and teachers in our educational institutions. Religions may be different, routes may be many but the goal is one—to realise 'one-self'. This was overlooked and no serious attempts were made to observe the common strands. Fortunately, there is a consensus that a well-conceived programme of value orientation of education has no religious bias but is truly secular.

Over the years, there has also been confusion about the definition of values and the conceptual framework of the programme. Various Committees and Commissions, on the basis of their analysis, suggested a large number of instrumental and sub-values. We have been presented with a hierarchy of values which are too numerous to be understood. The NCERT did a good service to identify these sub-values numbering about 84—a baffling number indeed! It should be difficult for any curriculum planner and material writer either to give any rating or any weightage in the absence of any rating and weighing machines. Thanks to various international and national Commissions and Committees, of late a consensus seems to have emerged that there should be a balance between the five facets of human personality, namely, physical, intellectual, emotional, psychic and spiritual. This is a great forward move. The five components of human personality are linked with the five major objectives or ideals of education, namely, skill; knowledge, balance, vision and identity. We have also started realising that moral values, social values, scientific values, aesthetic values, ethical values, democratic values, personal values, religious values, political values, economic values, altruistic values, etc., are only a description of attitudes, behaviour patterns, habits, etc.

If one were to read through the reports of various Commissions and Committees with discerning eyes and in-depth analysis, a beautiful synthesis of five human values, namely, truth, righteousness, peace, love and non-violence, conforming to the five facets of human personality and five ideals of education, as stated earlier, emerges. To my mind it is a beautiful merging based on deep analysis and study of human nature and promotion of human value through education resulting in the blossoming of the human personality. I am glad to mention that this concept of integrating the five-fold facets of human personality with educational ideals and values has been successfully worked out, through intensive pioneering efforts in Sri Sathya Institute of Higher Learning (Deemed University) which was established in 1981—about eleven years back. These pioneering efforts have been commended by leading academicians, scientists and policy planners, at the highest level in our country. We have an operational model before us which is dogma-free and has universal application irrespective of caste, creed, community, region or country.

I am also very happy to know that the Navodaya Vidyalayas, set up by the Central Government, as model institutions throughout the country, with the objective of pursuit of promotion of academic excellence, promotion of national and social integration, cultural development, have also concluded that the five basic human values, namely, truth, righteous conduct, peace, love and non-violence cover all the values which may be classified by experts under various categories.

Though we see a ray of hope and the emergence of consensus about the evolution of dogma-free basic universal values which will be acceptable to everyone, we have many miles to go before we reach the goal. This relates to the implementation of the programme in all its seriousness. We have to reckon with the value system of teachers,—"the hidden curriculum"—who are key to the success of the programme. By and large, they tend to be inspired by the life styles of their superiors, the administrators, public men and the milieu around. Electronic media is yet another area which plays a significant role in the inculcation of values. We have to design, both short and long-term strategies, to convert the vicious circle into a virtuous circle.

I can assure you that concrete recommendations which will emerge from this Seminar will also be considered for incorporation in the Report of the Core Group on Value Orientation of Education appointed by the Planning Commission. The Core Group has a very delicate task to perform—converting platitudes and policy statements into concrete operational programmes. I would like to affirm very strongly that the Teacher—the Guru—is the kingpin, the real foundation on which the edifice of value system can stand. Let us lay this foundation with all our commitment. We, in the Planning Commission, have realised, that a lot of time and effort has gone into various aspects of development of education in terms of infrastructures, constructions, scientific equipments, etc., but not enough has been done in the area of "man-making" and "people building". This is a great task and a challenge. We have to rise to the occasion. The Planning Commission, therefore, strongly felt that the time has come when, as a National Policy and Planning Organisation at the apex level, it should study this aspect of human resources development. For the first time in the history of national planning in India, the Planning Commission felt it very necessary to constitute a Core Group on Value Orientation of Education. As a Member of the Planning Commission, I am the Chairman of this Group. I am sure that the Core Group will bring out concrete and comprehensive recommendations which can be implemented in well-thought-out phases. I do presume that, in the initial years of the formulation of the concrete projects and programmes, covering all stages of education, its phasing both in time and space, the Planning Commission will have an opportunity to promote this major innovative programme—which has great potential for national development—in consultation with appropriate administrative organisations at the national and state levels.

GANDHI AND VALUE EDUCATION

Revered Acharya Tulsi ji, Dr. Ramjee Singh, the Vice-Chancellor, distinguished invitees, members of the Indian Society of Gandhian Studies, ladies and gentlemen,

It is indeed a great honour for me to participate in the XVI Annual Conference of the Indian Society of Gandhian Studies being hosted by the Jain Vishva Bharati Institute, a deemed university, which is one of the Centres of excellence in value education. I am grateful to Acharya Tulsi ji and Dr. Ramjee Singh for providing me this wonderful opportunity of speaking to a galaxy of educationists who are dedicated proponents of value education. I am happy to visit this beautiful village Ladnun which happens to be the birth place of Acharya Tulsi and which has all the requisites of a location for the pursuit of gurukul system of education. I am equally delighted to visit the campus of this great deemed university, Jain Vishva Bharati Institute, which is dedicated to the study of Jainology and Non-violence.

In ancient India Rishi Parampara and Gurukul system of education went hand in hand. It means, to run a Gurukul system we need people of Rishi status. In modern times it is perhaps rare to find such Rishis. However, we have been fortunate to have Mahatma Gandhi, Rabindranath Tagore, Swami Dayanand, Sri Aurobindo, Ramakrishna Param Hamsa, Vivekananda and other great people like Acharya Tulsi. Mahatma Gandhi established Gujarat Vidyapeeth, Swami Dayanand—Gurukul Kangri, Sri Aurobindo—Aurobindo Ashram, Rabindranath Tagore—Shantiniketan and Acharya Tulsi—Jain Vishva Bharati Institute. And we have Ramakrishna Mission. All these institutions have adopted the philosophy of the Gurukul system and are promoting value education. Bhagwan Sri Sathya Sai Baba also established educational institutions running on Gurukul system and pursuing value education. All these efforts are the greatest contributions of modern times to mankind.

There is urgent need for value orientation of education now more than never before. It should become a programme of national importance and urgency. This necessity has arisen in the context of degeneration in moral, social, ethical and national values, both in personal and public life. Personal ethics and moral responsibility towards society declined considerably. Man seems to have completely forgotten his true nature and spirit. Even the relationship between nations seems to be depending on not on humanitarian considerations but on power domination and political expediency. Peaceful coexistence in the world seems to have been threatened. Under the circumstances, the only ray of hope seems to be the pursuit of Gandhian thought and values which are relevant to all the times to come and upholding the human value system through education. In this context, I am happy that the Indian Society of Gandhian Studies has rightly chosen the most relevant themes relating to values namely i) Politics, Religion and Gandhi, ii) Gandhi and Value Education and iii) Gandhian Experiments in non-violence for its XVI Annual Conference. I am obliged and honoured for being invited to be the Chief Speaker at the Panel of Gandhi and Value Education. I have chosen the topic "Value Education—The Need of the Hour" for my talk today.

VALUE EDUCATION—NEED OF THE HOUR

India proved its uniqueness through achieving its freedom by the means of non-violence. Mahatma Gandhi, the Father of the Nation, along with other eminent national leaders and the people, fought against the mighty British using a simple weapon of non-violence and secured independence for the country. It was a glorious reflection on the Indian culture, tradition and philosophy which are deeply rooted in our value system.

Ours is a sovereign, socialist, secular and democratic republic with its Constitution guaranteeing to secure to all its citizens: Justice in social, economic and political spheres; Liberty of thought, expression, belief, faith and worship; Equality of status and opportunity; and to promote among them all Fraternity, assuring the dignity of individual and the unity and integrity of the nation.' These provisions also have their roots in the value system. The integrity of the nation, its rich cultural past and its compositeness, our ethos and human values, equal respect for all citizens irrespective of caste, creed, colour, religion, region and march towards a bright future, were some of the basic considerations which the Constitution makers had in mind while framing the Constitution of India.

What is happening around us today Violence, hatred, mistrust, growing divisive forces, narrow parochialism, separatist tendencies, considerable fall in moral, social, ethical and national values both in personal and public life. Materialistic outlook is manifest in almost every dimension of man's life style and day-to-day living. Materialism has become a major force influencing his conduct and behaviour. It is shaping his character and personality and even determining his life's goal. Human dignity and self-respect founded on good character and integrity are overtaken by arrogance, conceit, hypocrisy and artificial postures. The erosion of character is noticed in social and national life. Personal ethics and moral responsibility towards society have become meaningless where there is dominance of self-interest above everything.

Advancement in science and technology certainly improved the materialistic quality of life of people. But it has also shown the way for destruction. There is a massive build up of deadly weapons in the world which can destroy the world many times over. Peaceful co-existence seems to be difficult. International relations seemed to be devoid of humanitarian considerations. The total scenario in the world, even in the 21st century, in terms of the need for man's balanced frame of mind and the need for good relations between nations for peaceful co-existence, in all probability, may remain the same unless some serious and sincere efforts are made to rectify the situation. The present and the future generations are to be helped to reorient themselves to be imbued with strong commitment to moral, ethical, spiritual and human values if we want to see peaceful world order. This could be achieved by upholding the value system through education.

The serious concern expressed by various high-powered Commissions and Committees set up by the Government since 1947 has been corroborated by the National Educational Policy documents presented to the nation from 1968 onwards, regarding the ineffectiveness of the education structure on the whole to meet the demands of national development. The concern is more pronounced when we are fast moving towards the twenty first century.

How education can promote national unity and Indian culture, integration of the vast continent with various religions and communities and development of basic human values, which is an essential pre-requisite for social and national cohesion? This enquiry has become more relevant in the present day context.

Right type of education could be an important factor in the process of transformation of man. Education should help a person for his total development—physical, intellectual and spiritual. It should help towards disciplined life, self-control, compassionate and humane approach, spontaneous sympathy, regard for all beings and keenness to serve the society. It should enable one not to become self-centred and narrow minded. Education should serve not only to develop one's intellect and skill but also help to broaden one's outlook and make him useful to society and the world at large. True education must humanize a person. The educational system must produce young men and women of character and ability, committed to national service and development. This is possible only through reinforcing the present educational system with value orientation.

The importance and urgency of value education is very well reflected in statements made in the N.P.E. 1986 (with modifications undertaken in 1992), which I quote:

"8.4. The growing concern over the erosion of essential values and an increasing cynicism in society has brought to focus the need for readjustments in the curriculum in order to make education a forceful tool for the cultivation of social and moral values.

8.5. In our culturally plural society, education should foster universal and eternal values, oriented towards the unity and integration of our people. Such value education should help eliminate obscurantism, religious fanaticism, violence, superstition and fatalism.

8.6. Apart from this combative role, value education has a profound positive content, based on our heritage, national and universal goals and perceptions. It should lay primary emphasis on this aspect".

The whole approach to Value Orientation of Education is beautifully summed up by Bhagwan Sri Sathya Sai Baba, Chancellor of Sri Sathya Sai Institute of Higher Learning, Prasanthinilayam. He said: "The human values cannot be learnt by studying books and listening to lectures. These have to be cultivated by constant practice. Promotion of human values must become an integral part of the education process. National Unity and National

Integration have to become a way of life. Students, Teachers and Educational Authorities should shed narrow and parochial loyalties and prepare themselves to serve society and the World. If all the educational institutions jointly strive to instill human values in students and faculty members, India can become an ideal country and be an example to the whole World."

Mahatma Gandhi attached the greatest importance to the inclusion of moral and religious education in the curricula of schools and colleges. According to him the chief goal of education was 'character building'. He said "Put all your knowledge, learning and scholarship in one scale and truth and purity in the other, the latter will, by far, outweigh the other". He desired that the essential principles underlying different religions should be imparted to the students as a part of their academic courses. Such a study would help the younger generation to imbibe Sarva Dharma Samanathwa or equal respect for all religions. This kind of religious tolerance and reverence is needed for establishing true secularism in our country. The Kothari Education Commission has also strongly recommended the introduction of moral, social and spiritual values in all educational 'institutions from primary to the university stages. It would be correct to say that in the absence of proper ethical values and an atmosphere of religious tolerance, it would not be possible to make India a truly secular state in accordance with the spirit of our Constitution.

At a seminar held in Sevagram on Gandhian Values in Education during February, 1970, the following conclusions were drawn:

"The ultimate objective which Gandhiji had in view was the evolution of a non-exploitative, non-violent society conducive to the welfare of all. To this end, it is essential to emphasise three fundamental values in education, viz.,

- dignity of manual labour through the use of work as a part of the educational programme;
- a sense of social awareness and social responsibility through the involvement of students and teachers in meaningful programmes of community service; and
- the promotion of a secular outlook or Sarvadharma Samabhava through an understanding of the fundamental unity of all religions.

Suitable programmes should be developed to realize these values and students should be involved in their planning and implementation". These conclusions are still relevant and worth giving serious consideration.

A lot of time and effort had gone into various aspects of development of education in terms of faculty, buildings, equipment etc., but not enough has been done in the area of 'man-making' and 'people building'. This is a great task and a challenge. The Planning Commission, therefore, strongly felt that the time had come when, as a National policy and planning organisation at the apex level, it should study this aspect of human resources development. For the first time in the history of National planning in India, the Planning Commission felt it necessary to constitute a Core Group on Value Orientation of Education under my chairmanship. The Core Group has since submitted its report. It has been able to present a concrete Plan of Action relating to various levels of educational development, involving inter-departmental collaboration. Teacher has the most important role to play in the value development. The Group is of the view that teacher's personal, professional and social life is the crucial factor in the promotion of values. The most powerful influence of his personality lies in the 'hidden curriculum' of his personality and behaviour and the silent message which his students can and do get through his thinking, discipline of mind and refinement of taste.

The Group has recommended some reforms in the selection procedure of the teachers and a well thought out programme of pre-service training of the newly recruited teachers and in-service orientation programme of the existing teachers with emphasis on value orientation of education through direct, indirect and integrated methods. For this purpose, models of both pre-service teacher education and in-service teacher orientation have been suggested to be taken up by the Academic Staff Colleges of Universities, National Council for Educational Research and Training (N.C.E.R.T.) and Regional Colleges of Education and pace-setting training institutions even at the district level.

As a follow-up of the recommendations of the Core Group, the Ministry of Human Resources Development has constituted a Standing Committee on Value Orientation of Education under my Chairmanship to oversee the implementation of value orientation of education at all levels right from the school to university level in the country. The Standing Committee is working out the detailed blue print for the implementation of value orientation of education at school level, college level, university level and to use the electronic and print media and to involve other organisations like non-governmental organisations or voluntary organisations for promotion of value orientation of education.

Finally, before I conclude, I would like to reiterate what we have said in the Report of the Core Group. "The urgent need for value orientation of education should not be merely a matter of brave declarations. The programme needs patience and careful and comprehensive planning. It needs to be built into our educational system, our media institutions, our cultural organisations, in the teachings of science and humanities, in all kinds of educational, social and political endeavours so that they have cumulative impact on the minds of our children and youth when they are receptive and uncorrupted by cynicism. If we have the necessary determination and firm commitment then 'we shall overcome'."

I am sure that the outcome of this Annual Conference of the Indian Society of Gandhian Studies, with such a galaxy of intellectuals concerned with value education gathered here, will be very valuable and I assure you that the recommendations of the conference will receive utmost attention by the Standing Committee on Value Orientation of Education.

ENGINEERING &
TECHNOLOGY

Inaugural Address At The 33ʳᴅ National Convention Of The Indian Institution Of Industrial Engineering

Mr. President, distinguished delegates, ladies and gentlemen,

It is indeed a great privilege for me to be with you this afternoon to participate in the inaugural session of the 33rd National Convention of the Indian Institution of Industrial Engineering and I would like to express my heart-felt thanks to the organisers for inviting me as the Chief Guest and to inaugurate the Convention. I offer my greetings to all the delegates who have come from various parts of the country to participate in the convention.

This is my first visit to this industrial city of Jamshedpur, which has its picturesque location with the confluence of two rivers—the Kharkai and Subarnarekha. I have great admiration for the city which was an unknown adivasi hamlet, which ultimately grew into the first industrial city in India. I am sure, the credit should go to the great industrial visionary, Jamshetji Nusserwanjee Tata.

I am happy to note that the-Indian Institution of Industrial Engineering is engaged in the propagation and promotion of the Industrial Engineering profession in the country and offering the Graduateship examination which is equivalent to a Bachelors Degree in Industrial Engineering. It is heartening to note that its Members **are** specialised in the areas of Work Study, O & M, Ergonomics, Production Planning and Control, Material Management, Value Engineering, Operational Research, Computer Sciences etc. Such being the Membership of the Institute, it has great potential to play an important role in the economic development of the country.

As you are aware, we are launching the Eighth Five Year Plan in the backdrop of certain strengths in the economy as well as certain concerns which have surfaced over the recent years. The Government has taken new initiatives and bold decisions to reorient and restructure the economy, to meet the challenges of the present economic crisis in the country.

The strength of the economy can be seen in the fact that now almost for a whole decade the economy has grown at the rate of 5.5% which should be considered as a reasonably good step-up over the performance of the previous three decades when the growth averaged at 3.5% per annum. This performance was accompanied with a perceptible rise in growth in the agricultural income, a significant increase in the rate of growth of per capita consumption and a decline in capital output ratio, resulting from better utilisation of capacities and improvement in operational efficiencies. The Sixth and Seventh Plans also paid particular attention to the strengthening and modernisation of infrastructure and provided more incentives to private sector investments.

The weakness of the situation is inherent in the fact that this growth was financed in a manner which was neither envisaged nor healthy for the economy. In spite of the advantage of a decline of the capital output ratio requiring somewhat a lower level of investment than was projected in the Plans, financing of the Plan became very difficult. Even this lower level of capital formation was financed by a much lower than the Envisaged level of domestic savings and a much higher than the envisaged level of foreign savings, which is reflected in the gap in the current account of balance of payments. This gap in the current account added to external debt and debt servicing at a higher pace, raised the share of short term loans resulting in a funding problem and caused a severe depletion of foreign exchange reserves resulting in a crisis.

Internally also financing the public sector plan depended increasingly more on high cost borrowing and deficit financing. There has been a mounting burden of subsidies and interest payments on the non-plan side of the Government budget. The rate of inflation has been at a much higher level getting now into double digits.

In the context of the above scenario, it is imperative to provide for more decentralisation, enlist people's participation in national programmes and schemes, to strive to achieve targets with less financial outlays and to improve the efficiency of the system. Naturally the industrial sector has to play an important role in the present situation through total quality and total productivity. The theme of the Convention "Industrial Engineering in the Management of Total Productivity" is most appropriate and timely. I must congratulate the Indian Institution of Industrial Engineering for choosing such an appropriate theme.

A new philosophy is emerging in the industry. In the past it was believed that it was the system and technology and automated equipment which really made the difference. Others have opined that it is management control, audit and workforce discipline which is very much required. And yet, some have felt that it is really the motivated employee who will bring about the necessary improvements in productivity. And now, there is an emphasis on consumer satisfaction, in having partnerships with suppliers, on pride in workman-ship and Total Quality Management. Undoubtedly effort expended in any one direction or specific area without considering the overall needs, does not bring about the desired results. Productivity Improvement, therefore, has to be an all encompassing effort in all of the above areas and everybody in an organisation has to be aware of it and must participate in bringing about continuous improvement. This requires a change in our work culture; the way we look at things and in our attitude towards work. Here comes the importance of Total Productivity. To this we have to club Total Quality Concept so as to be able to become competitive in the world industrial scene. Therefore, let us work towards "Total Quality and Total Productivity".

In the context of achieving targets with less allocation, achieving total productivity is imperative. According to Peter Drucker, the Management Consultant, "Productivity is the power to expand at nobody's expense, which seems to be relevant. The total productivity management is the arena for engineers, industrialists, managers, planners, politicians, customers, union leaders and the society as a whole. It relates to the global concern for survival and growth.

We must also harness the resources judiciously and efficiently. There are natural resources, ocean resources and mineral resources. Man himself is a precious resource and the development of this resource has facilitated the harnessing of other resources. The human being is like an uncut diamond, to make him a gem, a lot of education and training becomes necessary. "Man" makes the organisation and he plays the most vital role in the attainment of the goals and objectives of an enterprise. It is the "Man" behind the machine who is more important than the machine. It is his morale, motivation, devotion, dedication and development which are important for improvement in performance, productivity and the growth of an enterprise. A research study conducted by the Asian Productivity Organisation shows that Indian industry is becoming more technology-intensive. Blending of human resources and technology to achieve organisational goals therefore becomes a major challenge.

The strategy for promoting quality of work life and productivity should include the following facets:

- Human resource planning including recruitment and selection of people and their utilisation keeping in view the present and future needs of organisations.
- Development of a culture of creativity, innovation and excellence, and upgradation of knowledge and skills through planned training Interventions on a continuous basis.
- Promotion of participative style of management through development Programmes.
- Effective performance appraisal system linked to merit-based reward schemes.
- Career and succession planning.
- Consultative mechanisms for involving people in the change process.
- Two-way organisational communication.

Technical and Management Education is one of the significant components of Human Resource Development spectrum with great potential for adding value to products and national economy for improving the quality of life. The past four decades have been marked by phenomenal expansion of technical education facilities. India has come to have one of the largest systems of technical education in the world. The annual admission capacity of degree and diploma levels is 37,000 and 75,000 respectively. However, serious imbalances and distortions have come about in the growth of technical education. The quantitative expansion has resulted in lowering of the standards. Due to various social pressures, the expansion of higher education exceeds that of economic development. Besides this, there exists a structural imbalance of skill requirement of the business sector and the traditional curriculum by the educational institutes. These factors give rise to problem of unemployment and under-employment. However, the industry should realise that Human Resource Development is a time consuming process and the educational system cannot adapt quickly to new industrial requirements. There are many such issues—such as management and financing of higher education, improving the quality of teachers, distance education, accreditation and grading of institutes, which require analysis at the micro and macro levels.

Industrial Engineering, which started with Industrial Revolution, is the first theory of scientific management by Frederick Winslow Taylor which was applied to bring efficiency at work place by work study. This got further into Taylor's piece rate system. The definition and scope of Industrial Engineering is best contained in A.I.I.E. definition.

The Industrial Engineering profession has undergone transformation and as a Specialist function now it aids to:

i)   Work system design, improvement, installation and maintenance
ii) Diagnosis, analysis and synthesising solution of operational / strategic problems of system nature
iii) Improve and ensure enduring levels of productivity in total sense.

Hence, Industrial Engineer is a designer of both hard and soft system in the economy and that is why this profession can contribute the highest to the Management of Total Productivity.

The contribution of Industrial Engineer in Management of total productivity in manufacturing are well practised in the following areas.

1) Method improvement 2) Work measurement 3) Value Engineering 4) Material utilisation 5) Energy conservation 6) Inventory Management 7) Capacity utilisation 8) Maintenance Management 9) Low Cost automation 10) System improvement.

What the present situation demands is the increased stress in the Agriculture and services sectors which may require some "Bare-foot" Industrial Engineers as the scope for improvement of productivity is enormous. The new Industrial Engineering curriculum must include such stress areas.

The Industrial Engineer, as any other professional, needs updating of knowledge and competence in the present day context of fast changing knowledge. Suitable refresher programmes as well as avenues for upgrading qualifications should be made available. This could be done through regular continuing education programmes, through part time teaching and through distance education mode for those who are away from the universities and engineering colleges' areas. In this context, distance education in engineering and technology can play a vital role.

Industrial Engineers should develop total productivity objectives, supplement them with Productivity Management Plans, develop measurement norms and the controls & monitoring systems.

Industrial Engineer has the knowledge, wisdom, background and will power. What I urge is that such potential of the Industrial Engineers should be utilised to assist the Industries to become active and important partners in the economic development of the country and to occupy a place of pride in the industrial world.

I take pleasure in inaugurating this Convention and wish it a grand success.

REHABILITATION, RENOVATION AND REPAIRS OF STRUCTURES

I am very much delighted to be with you this morning to participate in the inaugural session of the International Conference on "Rehabilitation, Renovation and Repairs of Structures" being organised by the Department of Civil Engineering, Andhra University, which is my Alma mater. I am grateful to the Vice Chancellor, Prof. Gopalakrishna Reddy to have invited me to inaugurate the conference. I left the University College of Engineering, graduating from the Department of Civil Engineering about three decades ago with great aspirations to pursue and shine in the Civil Engineering profession. But destiny led me differently and pushed me into academic administration and now into national planning. I am happy to see that all my teachers who joined at the time of my student days have brought glory to the department and the University through their remarkable achievements and contributions.

Realisation of the need for maintaining, repairing and checking of existing structures is a recent concept. It was only in the last decade or so the planners, engineers and architects started recognising that all structures need regular maintenance to ensure good serviceability. Initially it was applied to bridges and it is now rapidly spreading to other structures like buildings, industrial plants, chimneys, historical monuments, dams, etc.

Rehabilitation is accepted as a viable alternative to the process of demolition and rebuilding. Economic considerations and time constraints have made obligatory to look for rehabilitation and repair of distressed or damaged structures rather than their total replacement or reconstruction.

It is necessary to differentiate between repair which is restoration of damaged structure to its original form and strengthening where the aim is to increase its load carrying capacity.

Broadly speaking the failure of most of the structures occur because of one or a combination of following causes:

i.   Change in traffic pattern or overloading.
ii. Corrosion of re-bars and pre-stressing steel.
iii. Structural overstress due to unforeseen hazards like earthquake / flood etc.
iv. Faulty design and construction practices.
v.   Natural ageing of the material.
vi. Neglect of proper and timely maintenance.

However, the single main cause of the premature deterioration of concrete structure is corrosion of reinforcement and pre-stressing steel. This problem is more magnified in India because of hot and humid coastal environment. In almost all cases of corrosion, chloride attack and carbonation are the chief reasons. In pre-stressed structures the pre-stressing steel is also prone to stress corrosion.

The most common forms of distress observed in concrete structures are:

i.   Flexural and shear cracks.
ii. Spalling of concrete.
iii. Corrosion of steel.
iv. Snapping of prestressing cables.
v.   Dislocation of bearings.
vi. Displacement of decks.
vii. Sinking and tilting of foundations.

Whenever the structure shows signs of damage or distress the following steps need to be taken.

a) Primary investigation followed up by detailed investigation.
b) Diagnosis.
c) Laying out specification for repair.
d) Selection of material.
e) Service preparation.
f) Actual repairs.

g) Periodical maintenance.

h) Maintenance of reports etc., for future repairs.

REPAIR TECHNIQUES:

Today there exist a vast range of repair material and techniques. Some of the common repair measures are:

a) Gunite / Shotcrete.
b) Cast concrete.
c) Pumped grout with preplaced aggregates.
d) Modified cementitious mortar.
d) Epoxy mortar.
e) Epoxy injection.
f) Coatings for rebars and concrete.

SPECIALISED REPAIR TECHNIQUES:

I. EXTERNAL PRESTRESSING:

The concept of external pre-stressing for restoration and strengthening of structures is of comparatively recent origin. This method has been used successfully in many repairs in India. Special attention is to be devoted to the mechanism of transfer of force from the external anchorage to the element being stressed. Protection of external cable from corrosion is of primary importance.

II. EPOXY BONDED PLATES:

Strengthening is usually achieved by adding additional material to the member in question. It is difficult to achieve conformity of structural action between new and original material. Epoxy bonded steel plates have overcome this problem and in combination with crack injection proves to be a very efficient solution for reducing crack widths. Tests have proved that epoxy bonded steel plates with section 8 to 12 mm by 100 to 200 mm exhibit same efficiency for crack control as ribbed bars with equal cross section.

Polymer Impregnation

Polymer impregnation can be carried out to seal the pores in concrete and thereby greatly reduce the permeability of concrete to moisture and aggressive solutions. The method consists in impregnating concrete with a low viscosity monomer which is subsequently polymerised in situ. Monomer system can be injected under pressure through predrilled holes and injection ports either from the top of the slab or the bottom of the slab. Injection ports may be located on a grid of about 200 mm to 300 mm. Monomer system consists of a monomer, a cross linking agent and an initiator. The soffit of the slab should be coated with epoxy to contain the monomer. The addition of cross linking agent which is a bi-functional or poly-functional monomer increases the rigidity of the polymer, its softening point temperature and its resistance to the action of solvents. Where reducing permeability to arrest water seepage is the only criterion, cross linking agent may be omitted. The common method of polymerization techniques used are the thermal catalytic method and the promoted catalytic method. In the thermal catalytic method, the initiator decomposition takes place by the addition of polymerization promoters and no heat is required. In both cases the free radical initiates polymerization.

Thermal catalytic polymerization is a preferred method because of rapid polymerization rates and short processing times. Polymer impregnation has the additional advantage of binding together any weak and crumbling concrete. Durability will also increase due to reduction in permeability.

Conclusion:

Despite advancement of technology, it is not uncommon to find in some structures high levels of deterioration due to lack of maintenance, insufficient protection of the steel, poor quality of concrete and faulty detailing. Fortunately, today we have a number of tools to help us in investigations.

Concrete will remain the most favoured construction material for its beauty and other advantages. Regular maintenance of concrete structures is necessary. Structures should be built in such a way that inspection and maintenance can be carried out without any special efforts.

Rehabilitation, Renovation and Repairs of structures is a difficult task requiring specific qualifications, and therefore make it necessary that such works should only be entrusted to specialists with required experience.

I congratulate the organisers for organising this prestigious International Conference and hope the outcome of the deliberations of the Conference will enrich our knowledge about rehabilitation, renovation and repairs of structures. I take pleasure in inaugurating the Conference and wish it all success.

Boiling, Condensation And Two-Phase Flow Heat Transfer

I am privileged to participate in the Inaugural Session of the International Symposium / Workshop on "Boiling, Condensation and Two Phase Flow Heat Transfer" being organised by the Department of Mechanical Engineering, Andhra University. I am grateful to the Vice-Chancellor, Dr. Gopalakrishna Reddy for inviting me to inaugurate this Symposium. I should congratulate Prof. Sarma for organising such an important Symposium on a topic of relevance to the country's economic development. When I was going through the objectives of the Workshop, I was impressed with the objective "to develop networking amongst the Indian and foreign universities". This attracted my attention as it forms one of the ways to help coping up with the present resources inadequacy situation for higher education. The other day I was delivering the key-note address at the Symposia on "Resources Crunch and Science Education" being organised by the Forum on Science Education at the Indian Science Congress, Jaipur. While talking about the Imperative need for re-oriented approach to science and technology, in the context of resources crunch, I identified four areas which need to be pursued by the universities. They are: optimal utilisation of the available resources, international cooperation, resources mobilisation and establishment of corpus fund. International linkages in science and technology could be a means to: i. assist in the implementation of national programmes; and ii. open up avenues for collaborative interaction in the frontier areas or in those sectors which lead to the acquisition of knowledge not available within the country.

International cooperation will also serve as a tool for sharing of India's experience and expertise in science and technology with other developing countries.

The overall modalities of cooperation should be such that they should ensure the enhancement of self-reliance. Of course we have to keep in view our security considerations and sensitivity of the country.

The modern developments in the fields of the high pressure boilers, nuclear reactors and chemical process equipment are dependent on the accurate knowledge of the boiling, condensation and two-phase flow processes. Economic growth envisages many fold increase in the power output from the power plant and production from the chemical process plants and industrial units which necessitated to predict with certainty the heat transfer characteristics and the limitations of the thermal equipment. Along with the increase in the size of the power plants, an uninterrupted supply of power has become more important to develop the economy of any country. The effective heat transfer in the power generating equipment has been closely related to the availability of power. Due to the limitations and uncertainties in the prediction of heat transfer, the need for a better understanding of the boiling heat transfer and the underlying mechanism of two-phase flow has been one of the main goals in the process of the development of the heat transfer knowledge for many years. Although our present knowledge of boiling phenomena and boiling heat transfer performance is based on the extensive research in this field, there is still a great need for further development and better understanding of these complex phenomena.

Because of their prominence in the design and development of the power plant equipment there has been a constant endeavour all over the world to develop different augmentation techniques involving the processes of boiling, two-phase flow and condensation. The overall objective has always been to decrease capital outlay and to achieve compactness of the equipment. I am glad the present Symposium is covering in detail an important area like the two phase flow, a thorough knowledge of which is vital in the design of the thermal equipment related to high pressure boilers, nuclear power plants and chemical process units.

It is very much relevant to look back, compile and review our knowledge and experience to know the state-of-the-art in the field of study and evolve new design procedures with a comprehensive approach giving priority to the survival and safety of human life. In this regard although certain technologies appear to be very significant options, one should be aware of the implications that may crop up.

The physical phenomena involved in the sub-cooled boiling are of great importance from the practical point of view in the power generating systems with high power densities such as nuclear reactors. A number of problems cannot be solved completely without a full understanding of the mechanisms and physical processes underlying the two phase flow problems.

There has been a worldwide interest in the two phase flow stability problems with large liquid vapour density ratios experiencing phase change due to volumetric heat generation in open and closed systems. In such cases, the highly rigorous mathematical models are not of any relevance and purely empirical approaches cannot be extrapolated with any reliability because of the problems associated with scaling up. I would also like to invite the attention of the participants to the safety aspects, which need to be kept in mind while designing high temperature/ high pressure devices like boilers, specially where the size of the boilers is large or it is used in a nuclear power plant. These units like other process industries can lead to major accidents in the proximity of their locations. Although robotics and remote control techniques are being adopted by the industries, but ultimately, the physical intervention of man in case of disasters cannot be ruled out to suppress the malfunctioning, contamination and proliferation. The researcher and the designer should foresee all types of problems and be prepared with an answer to combat and control the situation.

I am sure the present International Symposium will deal with a detailed study of boiling, condensation and two phase flow phenomena which provides the necessary background for an effective thermal management, the neglect of which often leads to wastage of the energy resources and ineffective use of thermal energy both in power plants and process industries and I hope it will have a useful outcome.

INAUGURAL ADDRESS AT THE NATIONAL WORKSHOP ON "SYSTEM DYNAMICS"

I am highly delighted to participate in the inaugural session of the National Workshop on 'System Dynamics' being organised by the System Dynamics Society of India and the Industrial Engineering Division, Department of Mechanical Engineering, College of Engineering, Andhra University. I am grateful to the organisers, especially to Dr. Divakar Roy, Coordinator of the Workshop, for inviting me to inaugurate the Workshop. It gives me immense pleasure to visit this great industrial city of Visakhapatnam and the prestigious Andhra University once again. It is a matter of pride for me that the Andhra University happens to be my *alma-mater*. I passed out of the University College of Engineering during 1961, having graduated in Civil Engineering. Later on, I took my doctorate in Structural Engineering from the University of Liverpool. However, I have ended up in a sort of 'internal **brain drain**' in the sense that I have drifted from the professional career and took to educational administration, planning and policy formulation. But luckily there is a comforting feature that I am dealing with subjects of Higher and Technical Education, Urban Development, Water Supply and Sanitation in the Planning Commission, which in some ways relate to my educational background. Being an honorary Professor of Civil Engineering in the Department of Civil Engineering of this University, I shall be able to keep alive my academic activities.

I know about the achievements of the Department of Mechanical Engineering, which has a proud tradition and a long standing reputation.

I could recall with a sense of pride the names of teachers from this Department who had so nicely taught us during our first year of B.E. Degree Course.

I am happy to note that the System Dynamics Society of India, established in 1987, promotes the understanding and application of System Dynamics for the benefit of organisations and the society at large. It is heartening to note that the Society brings out an international journal of System Dynamics and also offers in-house training programmes. It is a nice coming together of the Department of Mechanical Engineering and the System Dynamics Society of India in organising this Workshop.

I must congratulate the organisers for thinking of a Workshop on such an important discipline. System Dynamics is a modelling and simulation methodology permitting insight into the dynamic behaviour of complex socio-economic systems. It effectively handles the managerial issues related to economic, industrial, sectoral and environmental systems. It facilitates problem solving through relying on modelling of cause-and-effect relationships by the use of simple diagrammatic tools and user-friendly software. Some of the applications of System Dynamics include corporate planning, production and inventory management, stock market dynamics, transportation policy planning, tourism, manpower planning, rural development, quality planning, environmental impact analysis etc. In System Dynamics, the model is simulated using DYNAMO, DYSMAP or DYMOSIM. The beauty of the System Dynamics lies in its ability to handle the following:

i. to dynamically model. Complex relationships of a large number of variables,
ii. to model a wide variety of real world situations,
iii. to incorporate features of both exploratory and normative approaches,
iv. to consider many related aspects of a problem resulting in a holistic approach,
v. to explicitly model qualitative factors,
vi. to experiment with policy alternatives, and
vii. to generate future scenarios.

Urban Dynamics, World Dynamics and Limits to Growth, published by Jay W. Forrester, are some of the interesting and important contributions in the area of System Dynamics. The scope for System Dynamics seems to be unlimited in the present day complex world situations.

During the 90's, India is becoming progressively more integrated into the global economy. With the advent of the New Industrial Policy and Liberalisation, the Indian industry is exposed to domestic and global competition. Knowledge based industries will be on the increase and the levels of skills required is going to be high. In the changed situation, we need to have a work force having a scientific bent of mind and possess the much needed scientific temper and skill to maintain high quality of productivity at par with world standards. Relevant high quality R & D capability is to be developed. In the regime of New Industrial Policy and liberalisation, the Indian industry has to meet the challenges through modernisation, upgradation of the competence of the work force, utilisation of now management techniques and increased efficiency and productivity while maintaining quality. In the context of 'globalisation', the System Dynamics Approach should play an important role in industries and other sectors of the economy. The senior and middle level executives from industry, government, autonomous organisations, R & D laboratories, academic institutions and NGOs should have proper exposure to System Dynamics and be able to appreciate its role. Towards this end, the present Workshop will be more useful.

Earlier in my speech I referred to the need for development of competent workforce and relevant R & D capability in the changed situation. This responsibility mainly falls on the higher and technical education and R & D laboratories in the country. Let me now briefly refer to the higher and technical education systems and the imperatives they face in the changed economic scenario. The changed economic scenario in the country could be viewed in terms of: (i) resources crunch, (ii) economic reforms with considerable dose of liberalisation (iii) globalisation of Indian economy, and (iv)Indian industry getting exposed to global competition. The changed economic scenario imposes two major imperatives on the system of higher and technical education in the country. Firstly, they have to cope up with the resources inadequacy situation and secondly to respond to the demands of providing competent manpower and R & D capability to the industry in the changed environment. The systems of higher and technical education have to respond to these challenges in the best possible manner. In the present situation, the higher and technical education systems in the country are being put to test.

A High Power Committee was appointed by the Ministry of Human Resource Development, under my Chairmanship, to suggest measures for mobilisation of additional resources for technical education. The High Power Committee made far reaching recommendations. The Committee felt that there is urgent need for institutions and government to make long term resource planning for the development of technical education. The Committee made detailed recommendations on specific actions to be implemented by the Government of India, State Governments, AICTE, industries and the institutions. The need for self-reliance was underscored. It identified 3 major imperatives to improve self-reliance:

a) Economy in expenditure
b) Increasing cost effectiveness of institutions, and
c) Mobilising resources.

Some of the major recommendations of the Committee are :

i.   The Central Government should examine the feasibility of levying an educational **cess** on industries for funding technical education and R & D activities in technical institutions.

ii.   The Government of India may set up an **Educational Development Bank of India (EDBI)** for financing soft loans for establishment of institutions and also to assist students to meet their fee and living requirements.

iii. A **National Loan Scholarship Scheme (NLSS)** may be set up under EDBI to provide soft loans to needy students.

iv.   Wherever necessary, the State Governments may also set up a **State Education Fund,** supplementing the **NLSS,** to give assistance to needy students in the form of loan scholarships at nominal interest rates and easy repayment terms.

v.   The plan allocation for technical education sector, both central and state, should be based and related to the plan outlays in the industrial and service sectors and as a matter of policy, these sectors should have an appropriate share earmarked for technical manpower development and this share be made available to Ministry of Human Resource Development to be used exclusively for the development of technical manpower.

vi. The tuition fees in all government funded and aided institutions in all the states should be revised to a rational level of at least 20% of the annual recurring cost per student.

vii. A corpus fund is to be established in every institution.

The Report contains important recommendations and if these recommendations are implemented, it would go a long way in the development of technical education in the country.

I am sure the participants will get benefited through this National Workshop on System Dynamics. I take great pleasure in inaugurating the Workshop and wish it a grand success.

COMPUTER AIDED ENGINEERING OF PROCESS PLANTS

Dr. Rama Rao, distinguished guests, participants of the Seminar, ladies and gentlemen,

I am highly delighted to be with you this morning to participate in the inaugural session of the Golden Jubilee Seminar on "Computer Aided Engineering of Process Plants", being organised by the Design and Engineering Division of the Indian Institute of Chemical Technology. I am grateful for being invited to inaugurate the seminar. The idea behind organising the Seminar appears to be to bring together the academic institutions, research institutions, software developing institutions and the other industries, to a common forum and to discuss the state of the field of computer applications in process industry. The main areas of interest for the seminar seem to include important aspects like computer applications in design and development, computer graphics, expert systems, maintenance management and safety.

I am happy to note that the Indian Institute of Chemical Technology with its R& D potential is fully geared to meet the requirements of technology development and transfer. With its highly professional and dedicated scientists, excellent laboratory and instrument facilities for research work, pilot plant facilities for scale-up studies and expertise in design and engineering of chemical plants, I have no doubt the Institute is ideally suited to take up such a task, which is the need of the hour. The Institute is known nationally and internationally for its significant contributions, both in basic and applied research in chemical sciences.

Limited resources situation demand that we should optimise the use of the available resources and further generate resources through interaction.

Hyderabad is a place where there are a number of national laboratories situated besides a number of universities. The State universities are starving of funds. They can conveniently share the physical infrastructure facilities like costly equipment available with the national laboratories and also involve the scientists in teaching and research work. I am sure, the heads of these national laboratories will be too glad to interact and allow their facilities to be used by the universities. This kind of interaction I have attempted when I was the Vice-Chancellor of Jawaharlal Nehru Technological University four years ago. I must appreciate Dr. Rama Rao's full cooperation in this regard.

The universities and the national laboratories can think of establishing joint centres, which will facilitate providing better research and other facilities to the university sector. I fully support the view that deemed to be university status may be accorded to selected national laboratories to facilitate offering post graduate programmes in certain special areas of science, engineering and technology.

Establishment of consortia of universities that can work in collaboration with higher institutions of learning such as, IITs, IISc., TIFR, etc., and also some of the national laboratories would enable to utilise their superior resources both human and material and the university system will get benefitted most in the process. We are all living now in an era of change. Momentous changes have taken place right across the globe, which have an impact on the international relations and world trade. Changes have also taken place in India through restructuring of its economy and liberalisation policies. The result is globalization and global competition.

Today technological changes are taking place at greater pace and the world is passing through an exciting stage of technological progress in several fronts. Technology is perhaps the most important resource to any nation. Invention, innovation, investments in risky ventures, adoption of new technologies and new products, etc., are the major processes in wealth creation and making the countries technologically superior. Recognising the importance of a strong Science & Technology base in the national development, the Government of India have formulated policies and created an impressive infrastructure in terms of institutions, skills, R & D facilities and a conducive environment to promote S & T in the country. The S & T allocations from the Central Government in successive five year plans have increased from Rs. 20 crores in the first plan (1951-56) through Rs. 67 crores in the second plan, Rs. 144 crores in the third plan, Rs. 373 crores in the fourth plan, Rs. 1381 crores in the fifth plan, Rs. 3668 crores in the sixth plan to Rs. 8245 crores in the seventh plan. An outlay of Rs. 9338 crores has been made for the eighth five year plan period (1992-97). Taking into account an estimated Rs. 5800 crores as the non-plan expenditure, the total allocation for S & T during the eighth plan period works out to over Rs. 15,000 crores.

Industry is the back bone of developing economies. Indian industry, while practically non-existent at the time of independence, has now grown substantially covering the manufacture of a host of items ranging from common consumer products to hi-tech products, both for domestic needs and for exports. However, the Indian industry is largely based on the inputs it has received in the past by way of foreign investments, technical collaborations, import of industrial machinery, capital goods and other items. The investments in the manufacturing industry alone is estimated to be over Rs. 100000 crores by the end of 1991-92. Industrial production is estimated to be of the order of Rs. 500000 crores during 1992-93. Of this, it is estimated that small scale industries contributed to nearly 45% and the remaining 55% coming from medium and large scale industrial units. Further, it is estimated that nearly 90% of the industrial production is based on technologies imported and / or indigenised and the remaining is based on technologies generated within the country.

A number of major policy changes have been announced by the Government in 1991 towards making India a global player in the world market. The industrial policy changes are aimed at making the Indian industries globally competitive in terms of scales of operations, quality, cost-effectiveness, exports and eco-friendly. The new policies have also facilitated acquisition of technologies from abroad and greater foreign investments. Factors such as pollution control and environment protection, energy efficient and eco-friendly technologies, cost-effectiveness and increased quality standards have become more important.

The Prime Minister, in the first Full Planning Commission meeting held in September, 1991, referred to two important issues. The first one was related to the need for modernising teaching, research and other facilities in engineering institutions especially at I.I.T.s, which are regarded as Centres of excellence. The second stressed the need to adopt futuristic approaches in meeting the emerging challenges in science and technology. He said, "A poor country like India cannot go on changing technology every year. We must adopt futuristic approaches". Recently he also stressed the need for assessing and analysing the technology imports related to foreign investment in India. Planning Commission has promptly initiated the thinking process in these areas and allocated financial outlays for modernisation and technology development.

Technology plays an important role as knowledge-based industries will be on the increase during the 90's and beyond. The process of upgradation or acquiring new technologies can take place in the following manner: (i) Indigenous R & D effort to help the Indian industry; (ii) Technology import by the Indian Industry; and (iii) Technology import related to foreign investment in India.

With regard to the indigenous R & D effort, the Planning Commission initiated Technology Development Missions in a mission mode in eight generic areas, involving the five I.I.T.s and the Indian Institute of Science, Bangalore. The missions involve not only a major research component but also a commitment to technology development through innovation and the subsequent transfer to the Indian industries. Developing, testing and delivery of technology **are** very much a part of the package. A key factor of the missions is the participation by industry from the very beginning and a contribution equal to 25% of the government funding in terms of cash and services or manpower. A National Steering Committee has been constituted under the Chairmanship of the Member, Planning Commission dealing with Higher and Technical Education, for monitoring the progress of the missions. Regional Engineering Colleges are also being encouraged to take up relevant R & D work through thrust area development. They may also look into the R & D needs of the small scale industries sector. The national laboratories and some of the universities are also striving to contribute considerably towards indigenous R & D efforts in the present day changed scenario.

Regarding the technology import by the Indian industry, it is logical to believe that the quality of technology imported may not suffer and only in the process of adoptation they may need assistance from the higher and technical education institutions and the national R&D laboratories. The issue of technology import related to foreign investment in India needs serious attention. It should be carefully studied and assessed so as to know whether the technology brought into the country is of the first rate or of third rate. It is essential to know the correct picture so that we can guard against their inferior quality. A study on this aspect could also provide valuable inputs in the finalisation of our Technology policy.

Reverting to the theme of the present Seminar, I gather that the process Plant Engineering involves a host of stupendous tasks of designs and technical documentation like Production of Piping and Instrumentation

Drawings, Detailed Equipment Drawings, Plot Plans, General Equipment Arrangement Drawings, Instruments and Cabling Drawings, Electrical Machines, Power Distribution and Cabling, Pipe Sizing, Routing, Layouts and Supports and Bill of Material.

Design of equipment and pipe work consumes a large proportion of resources. Out of the total engineering man hours spent on the design of a chemical plant, I understand that the process design consumes 3 to 4 %, the equipment design 10 to 15%, piping design and drafting about 25 to 30% and material control and requisitioning takes about 10% time. Equipment forms about 45% and piping about 25% of the total project cost. This warrants the use of high speed digital computers in order to reduce the time taken for preparation of DE documents. With suitable software, it is possible to check the suitability of materials of construction, abnormal sizes of equipment or other errors like interference and clearances in piping and equipment layouts. The CAD system saves substantial number of man hours required to complete a project with further unquantified benefits gained from elimination of errors.

I am sure the participants will have fruitful discussions, exchange of views, ideas and experiences and the outcome of the Seminar will be all rewarding. I am also happy to note that an exhibition is also being organised during the Seminar making state-of-the-art presentation of software, hardware and services and other associated technologies. I wish the Seminar a grand success.

ENVIRONMENT

ADDRESS AT WORLD ENVIRONMENT DAY CELEBRATIONS

Prof. Priya Ranjan Trivedi, President, World Institution Building Programme and Chancellor, World Environment Conference, Ms. Hema Deepak, Convenor, 1993 World Environment Day Celebrations, distinguished guests, ladies and gentlemen,

I am highly delighted to be with you this evening to participate in the World Environment Day function being organised by the World Institution Building Programme. I am grateful to Ms. Hema Deepak for inviting me to this function as a 'Guest of Honour'. It is only too appropriate that the United Nations Environment Programme (UNEP) headquarters have decided to hold the World Environment Day today with the theme 'Poverty and Environment—Breaking the Vicious Circle'.

Environmental problems arise from diverse causes. These causes may be poverty, ignorance, customs, climate and geographic insufficiency, inadequacy of technology and development. The environmental problems of the developing countries may be attributable to the effects of poverty on one hand and the effects of economic development on the other. Under the conditions of poverty, the environment suffers due to mismanagement in certain areas. For example, grazing, erosion, deforestation, surface water pollution and so on. Other problems arise from the process of development. For example, agricultural growth calls for construction of drainage systems, clearing forests and using fertilisers and chemicals, all of which can cause environmental damage. Similarly, industrial growth leads to the release of pollutants and other diverse effects related to the extraction and processing of raw materials.

It was in 1972 at the United Nations Conference on Human Environment at Stockholm, that a serious thought about a possible poverty-environment nexus was generated. The Brundtland Commission Report in 1987 was of the view that poverty and environmental stress have cause-effect relationships. It was at Rio that the issues of the extent of pollution caused by the rich North and the poorer South were brought into proper focus and the concept of 'one-worldism' with environment equally on everyone's agenda was evolved, paving a way for the establishment of the Commission for Sustainable Development.

The view that poverty of the poor nations is the greatest polluter needs some re-examining. If it is accepted that the threat to sustainability is high level of consumption, then the consumption levels of the rich nations constitutes a major portion of the threat to sustainability. The Report titled:'Consumption Patterns-The Driving Force of Environmental Stress',prepared by Jyoti Parikh and others says that the industrialised countries with 24% of the world's population have a share of global consumption of various commodities extending from 50 to 90%.The consumption of food products by industrialized countries ranges from 48 to 72%.The industrialised countries consume 60% of fertilizers,81% of paper,85% of chemicals,92% of cars and 75% of world's energy. Environmental stress is proportional to these consumption levels. The industrialised world is responsible for 70% of annual emissions of carbon di-oxide and 77% of cumulative carbon di-oxide emissions. Clearly, consumption patterns of the rich are unsustainable because of overuse of non-renewable resources. Nevertheless, consumption patterns of the poor are also to some extent, unsustainable because of bad land use and degradation of the village commons. There appears to be strong evidence that environmental degradation increasingly victimises the poor. The report of the World Health Organisation Commission on Health and Environment titled 'Our Planet, Our Health',prepared for the Earth Summit, inextricably links environment and health. The Report claims that one of the most pressing problems in the world today is ill health and premature death caused by biological and chemical agents in the environment. While respiratory diseases due to air pollution and hazards due to chemical agents are common to both the rich and the poor nations, health problems related to diarroheal, parasitic and mosquito borne diseases originating from water pollution and inadequate sanitation are exclusive to poor nations only. While environmental degradation causes disease, poverty plays a major role in the sustenance of disease. Clean water, sanitation and cleaner energy systems can dramatically improve the health status of the poverty ridden people and contribute to their economic development.

It is appropriate to view environmental degradation as the cause whose effect is increased incidence of poverty. Poverty and environmental degradation is indeed a vicious circle. But the need of the hour is that the collective intellect of the nation should engage itself in devising ways and means to break this vicious circle. The magnitude of the problem is immense but not insurmountable. Fortunately, much work has been done by individual research organisations, the government and the NGOs in environment related issues in India and it should be possible to draw a blue print to break the vicious circle of poverty and environment.

In attempting to break the vicious circle, the crucial issue to be considered is whether there is a dichotomy between development and environment. The real choice is not between development and environment, but between environmentally sensitive and environmentally insensitive terms of development. It is the choice of development strategy alone that can break the poverty-environmental degradation cycle. Our environmental agenda has to be built up on the foundations of this strategy. A symbiotic relationship between ecology and economy has to be evolved.

Population stabilisation should not be a forgotten issue on our environmental agenda. One issue where the Indian delegation had to face some uncomfortable moments at the Rio Summit was the issue of population. Literacy campaign, population education and involvement of NGOs in overcoming the cultural barriers in accepting the small family norm should complement the efforts of population control.

Synchronising eco-regeneration with the ongoing rural development programmes appears to be a logical step towards breaking the vicious circle of poverty and environment. The Eighth Five Year Plan has envisaged a massive hike in the Rural Development outlay. A fresh impetus was given to Jawahar Rozgar Yojana in the 1993-94 Budget. The 73rd Constitution Amendment Act has given Panchayati Raj a Constitutional status. A means for social infrastructure development and a decentralised administrative structure for rural development are now irrevocably put into place.

From an environmental stand point, rural employment programmes can play a key role in improving the natural resource base and increasing overall rural production.

Environmental regeneration demands heavy labour inputs—whether it is reforestation, construction of water harvesting structures or soil conservation.

But as the economic returns are not immediately tangible, impoverished people are likely to neglect these tasks if left to themselves. Rural employment programmes under the aegis of JRY can help villagers solve this problem because they have the capacity to mobilize impoverished labour in order to regenerate the environment. In economic terms, this would be an investment in building up rural natural capital, resulting in water harvesting structures to irrigate farm lands to increase crop production, well stocked forests and grass lands to support dairy development and raw materials like bamboo, grasses, wood etc., for a variety of handicrafts. Rural environment's sustainable employment supporting capacity can thus go up substantially. JRY has the potential to bind employment generation and environmental regeneration in a way that can build India up from its roots. A substantial part of the JRY funds have to be apportioned for environmental regeneration. It is important that people should be allowed to decide their own development priorities. But it is equally important that before the choice of channeling the JRY funds is made by the people, they should be equipped with the knowledge of the symbiotic relationship between environment and sustainable human development. Environmental education must go hand in glove with the ongoing literacy programmes. A scheme should be envisaged which would train villagers living in the different eco-systems of India to understand the dynamics of their individual ecosystems and plan to improve the natural resource base of their villagers. Voluntary organisations should be involved in a big way in such educational programmes. Environmental regeneration should be a people's movement.

Pollution control in urban areas needs a different approach. There should be a strategic shift to clean and green technologies. Sustainable industrial development is not a matter of mere high-tech but of appropriate sci-tech. U.S. Vice-President Al Gore, in his book 'Earth in the Balance' proposes a new scheme called Strategic Environment Initiative (SEI). According to him, the purpose of the SEI will be to phase out older, inappropriate technologies while simultaneously developing and disseminating a new generation of sophisticated and environmentally benign technologies. As reiterated by the Indian Union Minister for Environment, technology to reduce pollution has to be developed and made available on acceptable terms. Left to the market mechanism, the chances of such technology reaching the poorer countries is very remote. An alternative available is to encourage indigenous research effort to be directed at green technologies through a system of incentives and penalties. An appropriate example is that of Madras Refineries Ltd., which, due to severe shortage of water in Madras, is forced to opt for cleaning up of the city's sewerage water along with recycling its own effluents to meet its water needs. It is for the first time in the country that a city's sewerage water has become an economic commodity which otherwise would have been a pollutant.

According to David Pearce, Director of the London Environmental Economics Centre, the only way to get the environment on the economic agenda is to demonstrate that the environment matters to the economy. The issue of forcing the industry and the markets into resource friendly directions through the concept of ecological tax reform is engaging the minds of economists, environmentalists and the government officials in India also. But such models and methodologies have to be our own. While the focus of environmental issues in the affluent nations is for a better quality of life, the environmental problem of the poorer countries is the disappearance of the resource base on which the very survival of millions of people depends. Ecological tax reform is a concept in its infancy in India and needs to be fully developed with utmost caution.

Another area that needs closer examination vis-a-vis environment is that of energy production. The Tata Energy Research Institute's report on Fuel Consumption Trends calls for a clean energy policy to prevent the country from being trapped in an oil intensive development pattern. The assumptions of the report may have been a bit pessimistic but there is no denying the fact that the future energy scenario is grim. If efficiency of energy production and consumption is not stepped up, there are going to be serious environmental implications in both energy producing and energy consuming regions. In a Conference of State Ministers of Non-Conventional Energy Sources, the Prime Minister said that "generating electricity with conventional sources with low or no pollution is now almost impossible. This more than ever before underscores the need for non conventional sources." Compared to the total electricity production of about 70,000 M.W., the share of non conventional sources is now only about 700 M.W. The increased R & D efforts in non conventional sources of energy should be coupled with the National Energy Efficiency drive.

Another area that has a significant bearing on the issue of environment is that of Rural and Urban Sanitation. Inadequate drainage is directly linked to the resurgence of malaria, diarrhoeal diseases and environmental degradation. The Urban Basic Services for the Poor (UBSP), a programme launched in 1990-91, coupled with Environmental Improvement of Urban Slums (EIUS) programme and the NRY, aim to provide physical amenities, low-cost sanitation and environmental improvement of urban slums. This is a unique opportunity for community level micro-planning. Under the UBSP Programme, about 70 lakh beneficiaries are expected to be benefitted by the end of the Eighth Plan with a considerable improvement in urban environment. A Workshop on Drainage held at New Delhi in 1991, has put for certain strategies to encourage and develop community participation in all aspects of drainage and to develop more appropriate technologies for community drainage. People's awareness, NGO's involvement, appropriate legislation and local training are some of the strategies proposed.

The concept of eco-municipalities and green cities has to catch on in India. In the Northern part of the globe, eco-municipalities and green cities are the newest urban dreams. There is thinking in Sweden that conventional cities are ecologically non-sustainable. To survive, cities have to import their food, energy and resources from constantly expanding surrounding areas. In doing this, the cities consume more and more resources and export corresponding amounts of residual products such as air / water pollution and solid waste. This trend needs to be broken. Self-sustaining urban eco-cycles have to be designed to help break the destructive unsustainability of cities and towns. Environment and development need not be at loggerheads with each other. The positive links between efficient income growth and the environment need to be exploited. The key to sustainable growth is not to produce less but to produce differently. Economic development and ecological balance have to be fused together into the same developmental strategy in order to successfully break the vicious circle of poverty and environmental degradation.

I admire the Indian Institute of Ecology and Environment for its commitment to the noble cause of environmental regeneration along with poverty alleviation. And the yeoman services rendered by Dr. Priya Ranjan Trivedi for the cause of environmental awareness in India and abroad need to be richly commended. I have great pleasure in joining you all on the World Environment Day and I wish the function a grand success.

ADDRESS AT THE 1993 WORLD ENVIRONMENT CONGRESS ON GLOBAL ENVIRONMENTAL EDUCATION—VISIONS OF 2001

I am privileged to be associated with you on the occasion of the inaugural function of the 1993 World Environment Congress. The topic 'Global Environmental Education', selected for the Congress is relevant and timely since environmental education is considered critical for promoting sustainable development and for improving the capacity of the people to address themselves on environmental and developmental issues. Providing environmental education to everybody for protecting our planet before entering twenty first century is of utmost necessity. The task of disseminating awareness and knowledge towards respecting our environment and for conserving it is of the highest importance and requires proper and undivided attention on the part of everybody. Environment being the most precious irreplaceable natural resource, its protection has become the greatest international common cause of our times.

"Environment" is a term encompassing various facets of natural and human aspects and the environmental issues are so complex that the issues are embedded in wide matrix. Right across the globe there is a growing concern on the need for preservation of environment which has a direct relationship with sustainable development. Extensive knowledge on the carrying capacity of the eco-systems and the impact of increased population pressure on nature and its ability to support life is required to promote the concept of sustainable development. It was at the Rio Conference that the issues of the extent of pollution caused by the rich North and the poorer South were brought into proper focus and the concept of 'one-worldism' with environment equally on everyone's agenda was evolved.

Environmental problems arise from diverse causes. These causes may be poverty, ignorance, customs, climate and geographic insufficiency, inadequacy of technology and development. The environmental problems of the developing countries may be attributable to the effects of poverty on one hand and the effects of economic development on the other. The threat to sustainability also comes from high levels of consumption of the rich nations. It is said that the industrialised countries with 24% of the world's population have a share of global consumption of various commodities extending from 50% to 90%. The consumption of food products by industrialised countries ranges from 48 to 72%. They consume 60% of fertilisers, 81% of paper, 85% of chemicals, 92% of cars and 75% of world's energy. Environmental stress is proportional to these consumption levels. The industrialised world is responsible for 70% of the annual emissions of carbon di-oxide and 77% of cumulative carbon di-oxide emissions. Clearly, consumption patterns of the rich are unsustainable because of over use of non-renewable resources. Nevertheless, consumption patterns of the poor are also to some extent, unsustainable because of bad land use and degradation of the village commons. While environmental degradation causes diseases, poverty plays a major role in the sustenance of disease. Clean water, sanitation and cleaner energy systems can dramatically improve the health status of the poverty ridden people and contribute to their economic development. Population stabilisation also should be important issue on our environmental agenda. Literacy campaign, population education and involvement of Non Government Organisations in overcoming the cultural barriers in accepting the small family norm should complement the efforts of population control.

Environmental education should attempt to create awareness and concern for environmental issues at the local, national and global context bringing in all the available scientific and traditional knowledge on the dynamics of the natural and socio-economic environment and imparting the same to all sections of the society including professionals, decision makers and Non-Government Organisations. Such an attempt can enlighten the public at large and also support the decision makers to promote ecologically sound socioeconomic development.

The broad areas of human concerns like ecology and environment have started attracting the attention of many educational planners which can broaden the scope of various schools of thought. Environmental education is needed for promoting conservation of natural resources and sustainable development. As a primary task it is absolutely necessary to create adequate awareness. The role of non-government organisations in disseminating environmental concerns have so far been successful. However, there is an urgent need to develop appropriate environmental education materials for promoting conservation of natural resources and sustainable development.

The Government of India has taken up measures to incorporate environmental concerns in the educational system. In this regard the achievement made by National Council of Education Research and Training (NCERT) is noteworthy. At the primary and middle school levels significant improvements have already been made with the introduction of environmental studies as a part of the science learning.

The role of universities, with regard to environment, essentially lies in evolving new teaching and research programmes covering various facets of physical sciences and synthesising these with the socio-economic and cultural environment of the country.

Research programmes in the universities should be formulated in order to attain a better understanding of the carrying capacity of the earth which requires development of new analytical and productive tools. They should also aim at integrating physical, economic and social sciences in a broad frame so that the impact of economic and social behaviour on the environment is fully appreciated. To integrate the available information on all relevant sciences, the universities and the research institutions should interact and collaborate. The universities may take up the task of training scientists, decision makers and Non-Government Organisations to improve their capabilities and create public awareness on environment. Detailed studies are required to have a better understanding of our own resource base and ecological systems and also to monitor them in order to meet our environmental challenges. They must also equip themselves to provide the required information to decision makers and involve them along with teachers and scientists in research programmes.

There should be a strategic shift to clean and green technologies. Sustainable industrial development is not a matter of mere high-tech but also of appropriate sci-tech. We have to phase out older and inappropriate technologies while simultaneously developing and disseminating a new generation of sophisticated and environmentally benign technologies. We have to encourage indigenous research effort to be directed at green technologies through a system of incentives and penalties.

Sustainable development demands technologies which are least polluting, uses natural resources optimally and also recycle wastes. These technologies should be compatible with the socio-economic, cultural, environmental and developmental priorities of our country. There is an urgent need to undertake human resource development and strengthen institutional capacities for research and development and conduct integrated assessment of available technologies and technological needs which suit the objectives and priorities of the country's development. Therefore the need to stimulate research and development within the scientific and technological community is of prime importance.

An area that needs closer examination vis-a-vis environment is that of energy production. There is no denying the fact that the future energy scenario is grim. If the efficiency of energy production and consumption is not stepped up, there are going to be serious environmental implications in both energy producing and energy consuming regions. Increased R & D efforts in non-conventional sources of energy should be coupled with the national efficiency drive. A clear energy policy to prevent the country from being trapped in an oil intensive development pattern is urgently needed.

Mass media should be made effective to incorporate environmental awareness at all levels. It should be capable of covering issues related to population 'explosion, depletion of natural resources, deforestation, loss of bio-diversity, pollution etc. Exposure to environmental issues could educate even the common people and bring-in changes in their attitudes, promote skills and ability to participate as well as solve various problems. A question often asked is to which section of the society environmental education is to be imparted as a priority. At present all sections of the society, the public at large whether in cities or towns, children, teachers, planners, administrators—all need environmental education.

I am happy to note that the World Environment Congress aims at preparing everybody for protecting our Mother Earth before we enter the 21st Century and it will have sub-themes relating to many areas of environmental concern for discussion. I hope a suitable implementation programme will emerge.

I wish the Congress a great success.

Environmental Education In University Curricula

I am very happy to participate in the Inaugural Session of the UGC Sponsored National Symposium and Workshop on Environmental Education in University Curricula being organised by the A.P. State Council for Higher Education in cooperation with the Jawaharlal Nehru Technological University. I am grateful to the A.P. State Council for Higher Education and the J.N.T.U. for inviting me to this inaugural session.

It gives me immense pleasure to participate in this inaugural session being organised in the JNTU Campus and that too, in the very Conference Hall which was inaugurated during my tenure as Vice-Chancellor. When I took over as Vice-Chancellor during 1988, three factors triggered my enthusiasm for preparing the University for achieving excellence: first one relates to the fact that the State of Andhra Pradesh unfortunately missed the opportunity of having an IIT in the past and therefore we need to develop at least this Technological University in the State on par with that of an IIT; and the second factor was that the University emblem bears the inscriptions of a part of a Sloka in the Bhagwad Gita, *"YogahaKarmasu Kousalam"*, one of its interpretations being Excellence in Action", indicating that the motto should be to achieve excellence. Thirdly, the University bears the name of Pandit Jawaharlal Nehru and therefore it should stand up to his expectations. In one of the convocation addresses, Nehru said, "A University stands for Humanism, for Tolerance, for Reason, for Progress, for the Adventure of ideas and for the Search for Truth". To fulfill these objectives it was evident that the university should work towards achieving excellence while responding to the requirements of the changed situations. Thus, ten schools, mostly in emerging areas were established to serve as a nucleus for the University and for achieving excellence. Similarly, some centres were also established in the Constituent Colleges situated at Hyderabad, Anantapur and Kakinada, depending on their strengths. To meet the resources inadequacy situation the philosophy adopted was to have minimum core faculties in each School and involve the experts and scientists from outside for teaching and research. With regard to infrastructure facilities, again, minimum facilities were envisaged in each school complimented by the facilities available in the nearby universities and national laboratories. I am happy to note that one such school "The School for Water Resources and Environment" is doing excellent work and is now organising the present national symposium and workshop on environmental education.

Some of the thrust areas identified in technical education for the Eighth Plan are:

(i) modernisation and upgradation of infrastructure facilities; (ii) quality improvement in technical and management education; (iii) responding to new Industrial Policy and Industry-Institution—R & D Laboratory Interaction; (iv) resource mobilisation. Even before the Eighth Plan started (from 1st April 1992), the university had already initiated steps on the above thrust areas. For example, for resource mobilisation a Bureau for Industrial Consultancy and Research and Development Activities (BICARD) has been established. A Model for university—industry interaction was formulated. The process of modernisation and upgradation of facilities had been initiated with the funding from University Grants Commission and Ministry of Human Resources Development.

Quality of teaching and research has been improved, involving industries and national laboratories, thereby bringing in relevance also. The Jawaharlal Nehru Technological University has a great potential for development.

There are four vital issues which need focussed attention in our country's progress.

They are: (1) population control, (2) eradication of illiteracy (3) environmental protection and maintaining ecological balance and (4) arresting erosion in human values. In all these four important areas, there is greater scope for universities and other educational institutions to play vital roles.

In this context the topic chosen for the symposium and the workshop is quite relevant and timely since environmental education is considered critical for promoting sustainable development and for improving the capacity of the people to address themselves on environmental and developmental issues. Providing environmental education to everybody for protecting our planet before entering 21st Century is of utmost necessity. Environment being the most precious irreplaceable natural resource, its protection has become the greatest international common cause of our time.

"Environment" is a term encompassing various facets of nature and human aspects. The environmental issues are so complex that the issues are embedded in a wide matrix. Right across the globe there is a growing concern on the need for preservation of environment which has a direct relationship with sustainable development. Extensive knowledge on the carrying capacity of the eco-systems and the impact of increased population pressure on nature and its ability to support life is required to promote the concept of sustainable development. It was at the Rio Conference that the issues of the extent of pollution caused by the rich North and the poorer South were brought into proper focus and the concept of 'one-worldism' with environment equally on everyone's agenda was evolved.

Environmental problems arise from diverse causes. These causes may be poverty, ignorance, customs, climate and geographic insufficiency, inadequacy of technology and development. The environmental problems of the developing countries may be attributable to the effects of poverty on one hand and the effects of economic development on the other. The threat to sustainability also comes from high levels of consumption of the rich nations. It is said that the industrialised countries with 24% of the world's population have a share of global consumption of various commodities extending from 50% to 90%. The consumption of food products by industrialised countries ranges from 48 to 72%. They consume 60% of fertilisers, 81% of paper, 85% of chemicals, 92% of cars and 75% of world's energy. Environmental stress is proportional to these consumption levels. The industrialised world is responsible for 70% of the annual emissions of carbon dioxide. Clearly, consumption patterns of the rich are unsustainable because of over use of non-renewable resources. Nevertheless, consumption patterns of the poor are also to some extent, unsustainable because of bad land use and degradation of the village common lands. While environmental degradation causes diseases, poverty plays a major role in the sustenance of disease. Clean water, sanitation and cleaner energy systems can dramatically improve the health status of the poverty ridden people and contribute to their economic development. Population stabilisation also should be an important issue on our environmental agenda. Literacy campaign, population education and involvement of Non-Government Organisations in overcoming the cultural barriers in accepting the small family norm should complement the efforts of population control.

Environmental education should attempt to create awareness and concern for environmental issues at the local, national and global context bringing in all the available scientific and traditional knowledge on the dynamics o the natural and socioeconomic environment and imparting the same to all sections of the society including professionals, decision makers and Non-Government Organisations. Such an attempt can enlighten the public at large and also support the decision makers to promote ecologically sound socioeconomic development.

The broad areas of human concerns like ecology and environment have started attracting the attention of many educational planners which can broaden the scope of various schools of thought. Environmental education is needed for promoting conservation of natural resources and sustainable development. As a primary task it is absolutely necessary to create adequate awareness. The role of non-government organisations in disseminating environmental concerns have so far been successful. However, there is an urgent need to develop appropriate environmental education materials for promoting conservation of natural resources and sustainable development.

The Government of India has taken up measures to incorporate environmental concerns in the educational system. In this regard the achievement made by National Council Educational Research and Training (NCERT) is noteworthy. At the primary and middle school levels significant improvements have already been made with the introduction of environmental studies as a part of the science learning.

The role of universities, with regard to environment essentially lies in evolving new teaching and research programmes covering various facets of physical sciences and these with the socio-economic and cultural environment of the country. Research programmes in the universities should be formulated in order to attain a better understanding of the carrying capacity of the earth which requires development of new analytical and productive tools. They should also aim at integrating physical, economic and social sciences in a broad frame so that the impact of economic and social behaviour on the environment is fully appreciated. To integrate the available information on all relevant sciences, the universities and the research institutions should interact and collaborate. The universities may take up the task of training scientists, decision makers and Non-Government Organisations to improve their capabilities and create public awareness on environment. Detailed studies are required to have a better understanding of our own resource base and ecological systems and also to monitor them in order to meet our environmental challenges. They must also equip themselves to provide the required information to decision makers and involve them along with teachers and scientists in research programmes.

There should be a strategic shift to cleaner and green technologies. Sustainable industrial development is not a matter of mere high-tech but also of appropriate sci-tech. We have to phase out older and inappropriate technologies while simultaneously developing and disseminating a new generation of sophisticated and environmentally benign technologies. We have to encourage indigenous research effort to be directed at green technologies through a system of incentives and penalties. Sustainable development demands technologies which are least polluting, uses natural resources optimally and also recycle wastes. These technologies should he compatible with the socio-economic, cultural, environmental and developmental priorities of our country. There is an urgent need to undertake human resource development and strengthen institutional capacities for research and development and conduct integrated assessment of available technologies and technological needs which suit the objectives and priorities of the country's development. Therefore the need to stimulate research and development within the scientific and technological community is of prime importance.

An area that needs closer examination vis-à-vis environment is that of energy production. There is no denying the fact that the future energy scenario is grim. If the efficiency of energy production and consumption is not stepped up, there are going to be serious environmental implications in both energy producing and energy consuming regions. Increased R & D efforts in non-conventional sources of energy should be coupled with the national efficiency drive. A clear energy policy to prevent the country from being trapped in an oil intensive development pattern is urgently needed.

Mass media should be made effective to incorporate environmental awareness at all levels. It should be capable of covering issues related to population explosion, depletion of natural resources, deforestation, loss of bio-diversity, pollution etc. Exposure to environmental issues could educate even the common people and bring in changes in their attitudes, promote skills and ability to participate as well as solve various problems. A question often asked is to which section of the society environmental education is to be imparted as a priority. At present all sections of the society, the public at large, whether in cities or towns, children, teachers, planners, administrators—all need environmental education.

I congratulate the organisers for their thoughtful idea of organising such an important Symposium followed by a workshop on Environmental Education in University Curricula. I wish the symposium and the workshop a grand success.

SCIENCE

INAUGURAL ADDRESS AT THE 58TH ANNUAL CONFERENCE OF THE INDIAN MATHEMATICAL SOCIETY HELD AT BANARAS HINDU UNIVERSITY, VARANASI

Honourable Chancellor, President of the Indian Mathematical Society, Dean of the Faculty of Science, Members of the Society, distinguished invitees, Ladies and Gentlemen,

I deem it a privilege for having been invited to inaugurate the 58th Annual Conference of the Indian Mathematical Society. I am grateful to Prof. Jha, Vice-Chancellor of B.H.U. and the President of the Mathematical Society for giving me this splendid opportunity. The place and the venue, being Varanasi and Banaras Hindu University respectively, add dignity to this annual conference and I congratulate the organisers for their wonderful selection. Varanasi, a great temple city, is a place most Indians used to visit at least once during their life time. From time immemorial Varanasi has been a lode star, attracting scholars and pilgrims, both oriental and occidental. I am highly delighted to visit this great ancient city, Varanasi. I am equally delighted to visit the campus of this famous Banaras Hindu University, whose beginnings had been so tenderly nurtured by the venerable Pandit Madan Mohan Malaviya who was selfless, loyal, gentle but not weak, determined but not aggressive, a spirit as clear as the mountain air, as described by Dr. Radhakrishnan, that revered teacher, scholar, philosopher, statesman and the second President of India. It is a rare honour too to be associated with a function being held at a place where fifty two years ago,

Dr. Radha Krishnan addressed an august gathering as this, on the occasion of the Silver Jubilee celebrations of this university. Banaras Hindu University was a unique experiment of residential educational culture initiated at a time when there were only five examining universities at Calcutta, Bombay, Madras, Allahabad and Lahore. It symbolises the great Indian culture and tradition. On the shores of the holy river Ganges, this University is a beacon of knowledge attracting avid learners from all over the world. It is heartening to note that this University has a separate faculty of Indian system of medicine, which is now acquiring international importance. Banaras Hindu University is also playing its role in the nation's quest for the advancement of Science and Technology for enriching the quality of life of its people. Today it stands shoulder to shoulder with the other centres of excellence in the immense task of achieving scientific and technological excellence. A galaxy of Mathematicians has gathered here to discuss aspects of development of Mathematics and its application. Mathematics is said to be the queen of all sciences. I would describe it as the life blood of all civilizations. The story of man from his humble beginnings to his advancement into an electronic age is that of progressive development in the realm of Mathematics. There is no science or art that does not involve mathematics at some stage or other. While fine arts like painting, music or poetry involve a simple mathematical rhythm, frontier areas of technology like space satellites or computers use advanced applications of mathematics. Mathematics is universal and essential for progress of life and civilization. No other science is as universal as mathematics is. G.H. Hardy, the eminent number theorist, thought that "Riemann's Zeta Function", which is some kind of ready reckoner formula for the number of prime numbers less than a given number, cannot have any practical applications other than being purely mathematical. But, surprisingly, it found a useful application in measuring the temperature of industrial furnaces. While the tools of mathematics are truly wonderful, the strides of mankind in striving for mathematical excellence are amazing. Game theory and queueing have found a useful application in optimisation of production cycles and achieving better productivity in industries. Operations research has evolved useful techniques in management like the CPM and PERT analysis. Econometrics is now a proven mathematical tool in economic modelling. Crick and Watson's structure of the DNA Molecule, the double helix is a complex problem in geometry. A system of binary numbers has revolutionised the world by ushering in a new age of computers.

The tools of differential and integral calculus have helped engineers to design and construct bridges, tunnels and tall buildings which are the symbols as well as necessities of modern life. Mathematics today has advanced so much that the birth of universe or the origin of life can be explained adequately only in mathematical terms.

In ancient times, India occupied a place of pride among the great civilisations in the sphere of mathematical attainments. Great Indian mathematicians like Aryabhatta, Varahamira, Brahmagupta, Shridara, Mahaviracharya and Bhaskaracharya attained high peaks of mathematical excellence. The discovery of zero, the decimal place value system of notation, generalisation of Algebra, the Sine function, the foundations of indeterminate analysis and many results in astronomy stand to the credit of these great ancient mathematicians. It is with a deep sense of pride and gratitude that we now look upon the pioneering work done by Prof. V. Ramaswamy Aiyer in 1906, in starting the Indian Mathematical Society with a view to secure a place of pride for India in the modern mathematical map. It is with nostalgia that we now remember the hard work done by Prof. Narain, Prof. T.R. Venkataswamy Naidu, Prof. R.N. Apte, Prof. Hanumantha Rao and several others for the progress of the Indian Mathematical Society. It is heartening to note that the journal of the Indian Mathematical Society started in 1909 has won international acclaim. The credit of publishing the early works of the Indian Mathematical prodigy, Srinivasa Ramanujam goes to this journal. The gesture of the society in starting a second journal called 'Mathematics Student' for the benefit of research students and in promoting the cause of higher education in mathematics is greatly appreciated. The Society has also spared no efforts in establishing international linkages for wider dissemination of knowledge and has extended the frontiers of mathematical knowledge beyond India. On this score, the reciprocity arrangements entered into with the American, British and Australian Mathematical Societies are to be highly commended. I have a strong belief that under the able stewardship of the Indian Mathematical Society, India will regain its glory as a great centre of mathematical excellence. Here, a word on **'relevance'**. The Universities and the Institutes of Higher Learning have three main functions to perform in the present day context. They are (i) teaching, (ii) research, and (iii) interaction. Interaction is the third dimension in the pursuit of knowledge in the university system. The interaction could be for two purposes (a) social and (b) economic development. The social purpose involves interaction with the society through extension and community development activities. The interaction for economic development may take the form of providing the competent manpower, appropriate science and technology inputs and offering training programmes for upgrading the competency of the work force.

In all the above three areas of function, a thread of **"relevance"** is to be interwoven in the present day context of changed global and domestic economic. In case of research, we have to blend scholarship with relevance. As far as basic research is concerned it should continue to be pursued freely so that we may not slip back from the 'forefront' status in certain areas. But with regard to other research, we have to make conscious efforts to seek relevance. This approach equally applies to all areas of science.

With these few words, I take pleasure in inaugurating the Annual Conference of the Indian Mathematical Society and wish it a grand success.

Address As Chief Guest On The Occasion Of Science Day Celebrations At The Avinashilingam Institute For Home Science And Higher Education For Women

Dr. (Mrs.) Rajammal Devadas, Vice-Chancellor, Ladies and Gentlemen,

I am happy to have been invited as the Chief Guest for the Science Day celebrations at the Avinashilingam Institute for Home Science and Higher Education for Women, a deemed university. I am grateful to the Vice-Chancellor for giving me this opportunity.

I am indeed very delighted to visit this famous city Coimbatore, which is considered as one of the most important textile centres in the country, comparable only to Bombay and Ahmadabad. Coimbatore has also the distinction of being the most highly industrialised district in Tamil Nadu, in which a large proportion of the population lives by industries, trade and other avocations. The development of textile industry on a large scale is mainly due to the growth of abundant cotton in this district.

It is heartening to note that the Avinashilingam Institute for Home Science and Higher Education for Women is providing for achieving excellence in higher education, research and extension for women in various fields of knowledge and offering opportunities for imbibing the highest ideals of Indian womanhood as propounded by Sri Ramakrishna, Swami Vivekananda, Mahatma Gandhi and other saints together with ethical, social and spiritual values which form the basis of all human development. I have known this Institute even before it became a University, when it was called Avinashilingam College of Home Science, and had visited the college more than once and I am visiting the University for the first time. I admire the commitment of Dr. Rajammal Devadas for Home Science and her contributions in this field. I am sure that under her stewardship, the University is growing from strength to strength to shape itself into a real centre of excellence in home science and higher education for women.

Following the initiative of the National Council for Science and Technology Communication (NCSTC), the Government of India, during 1987, designated February 28th as the National Science Day (NSD). The purpose of celebrating NSD is to remind us of our responsibility towards the potential prospective scientists among our children in terms of their early identification and subsequent nurturing to full fruition. The idea is also to focus attention, on this day, on the responsibility of science and scientists towards society at large in terms of bringing out the required socio-economic changes and vice-versa. Dr. Abdus Salam, the Nobel laureate in his "Notes on Science, Technology and Science Education in the development of the South" in 1989 observed "This globe of ours is inhabited by two distinct species of humans. According to the UNDP count of 1983, one quarter of mankind, some 1.1 billion people are developed. They inhabit 2/5ths of land area of the earth and control 80% of the world's natural resources, while 3.6 billion developing humans—Les Miserables—the mustazeffin (the deprived ones)—live on the remaining 3/5ths of the globe.

What distinguishes one species of human from the other in terms of their status as developed or developing is the ambition, the power, the elan which basically stems from their differing mastery and utilisation of present day science and technology . . . ."

To quote Alfred North Whitehead: "In the conditions of modern life, the rule is absolute: the race which does not value trained intelligence is doomed . . . . Today we maintain ourselves, tomorrow science will have moved over yet one more step and there will be no appeal from the judgement which will be pronounced . . . . on the uneducated". The message is thus quite clear. Creating, mastering, and utilising modern science and technology is very essential for the development of a country in the modern context. Science and technology has no doubt made significant contributions to the overall development of the country. From a very merely agriculture based society in early 40's, India today is rated among the industrialised nations having a sound base of industries, side by side with a highly developed agriculture. Pandit Jawaharlal Nehru assigned to Science and Technology a pivotal role in the national development. The Scientific Policy Resolution (1958) states that: "The key to national prosperity, apart from the spirit of the people, lies, in the modern age, in the effective combination of three factors—technology, raw materials and capital of which the first is perhaps the most important, since the creation and adoption of new scientific techniques can, in fact, make up for a deficiency in natural resources, and reduce the demands on capital". This vivifies the role of Science and Technology in the national development.

The situation arising out of the impact of the present global and national economic scenario and with the emergence of an era of global consciousness resulting in the Indian industry being exposed to global and indigenous competition, brings out the need for a work force having a scientific bent of mind and possessing the much desired temper and skills to maintain high quality and productivity at par with world standards. We have to train men and women of calibre and competency of world standards and provide the needed R & D capability. In addition, the explosion of knowledge in the science and technology sectors require highly talented men and women whose fast grasp of knowledge would enable them to respond to the desired innovations in advancing frontiers of knowledge and know-how. At higher levels, the development of new science and technology is normally expected to be from the university system in addition to the contributions made by the various national laboratories and research organisations. However, the university system does seem to be riddled with certain problems like obsolescence, shortage of teachers, increasing demand for admissions, resources inadequacy, lack of relevance and poor management. These problems are to be tackled with imaginative approaches and reforms in higher and technical education.

The question of improving under graduate science education at the Indian Universities / Colleges was considered in the Planning Commission during 1989 and a Working Group was constituted to suggest ways and means to improve the undergraduate science education. The Working Group suggested a three tier approach to tackle this problem. At the first level, it is suggested that we should organise a programme for highly talented and motivated students to be conducted at some very select institutions. The institutions can be selected by the University Grants Commission in the light of their track record. At the second level, the Working Group suggested to identify two to three colleges per state, roughly 100 colleges in the country. They should be given a liberal financial assistance to improve library, laboratories and other infrastructure and also to recruit qualified and motivated teachers for the purpose of training students at the under graduate level. These colleges should be autonomous colleges or even should enjoy the status of deemed universities. The first two levels will cater to roughly 16% of students undergoing science education at the undergraduate level. The remaining 84% students study in other affiliated colleges and therefore suggested that these colleges be provided with a library of video tapes on various science subjects prepared by eminent teachers and researchers in the subject. These tapes should be addressed to the syllabi of the under graduate courses. In order to coordinate the efforts at the three levels, the Working Group suggested a Coordination Council chaired by the Chairman, University Grants Commission. These recommendations need all serious consideration.

During the recent past there have been significant developments in the field of communication technology. For example, use of satellites for telecast of educational programmes and computers for learning. Harnessing of the power of such 20th century communication revolution for educational purposes is vital for quality improvement in education especially in the areas of Science and Technology. In this context the UGC's 'country wide class room' programme is one of the best examples. The broadcast aims to upgrade, update and enrich the quality of education, while extending its reach. They are attempting to overcome the obsolescence of the syllabus and present the latest advances in all fields, including the newly emerging ones. The programmes seek to arouse the interest of the viewers and broaden their horizons. They would seek to provide new insights, bring in new findings and take students on vicarious tours of places and laboratories they would rarely see. Inter-relatedness of various disciplines and of developmental problems would be highlighted. Motivation, innovation, creativity and analysis are the guiding elements in these programmes. The pleasures of discovery, of exploration and revelation, of hitting on a solution are being highlighted, along with the importance of searching, probing and questioning. Such laudable and innovative programmes should be encouraged and supported by all the concerned as they would help enrich the quality of education not only in Science but also in other disciplines. Academics, Scientists, Engineers and Technologists should increasingly participate in the process of preparing these TV programmes. Radio should also be utilised for selective educational programmes. Non-broadcast mode video educational course material should also be encouraged so that each college especially those who are in the far flung areas can maintain a library of video tapes for the use of their students and teachers. Teacher education is another important component which could be taken up through the UGC countrywide class room programme.

Equal importance should be given to science education at school level. Teaching and learning science have two main aspects: (i) Imparting knowledge so that the student is able to understand several phenomenon in and around the surroundings, and (ii) Inculcation of a scientific temper or method of science as part of life. In science teaching, method of science should be given preference to imparting simple theoretical knowledge of scientific principles so that the children develop a scientific spirit early in their life. Children's imaginative power, logical thinking and liking should be kept in view while' formulating the programmes. In addition to the formal approach to the science education through schools, colleges, universities and other institutions, there is an informal approach to science education as well which is not tied, restricted or limited to any strict institutional framework. In this category of informal science education, the activities and programmes of the National Council or Science and Technology Communication (NCSTC) are noteworthy. Their programmes make use of all media, means and methods which lend themselves to conveying scientific ideas and messages effectively. Bharat Jan Vigyan Jatha (BJVJ) of 1987 received wide acclamation from all quarters. The Bharat Jan Gyan Vigyan Jatha of 1992 envisages science popularisation and literacy related activities and was intended to reach nearly a third of our population.

The National Council of Science Museums (NCSM) is also doing commendable work in popularising Science and Technology among the students in particular and the masses in general, through a wide range of programmes and activities organised by its various science museums / centres. In addition to popularising science and technology, it is supplementing science education in schools and colleges and organising various educational activities to foster a spirit of scientific enquiry and creativity among the students. I am sure the University might have undertaken appropriate activities under the NSD Programmes for the year 1993. On this occasion of the Science Day celebrations, I offer my greetings to all of you and wish greater success in your future NSD celebrations.

RESOURCE CRUNCH AND
SCIENCE EDUCATION

ABSTRACT

Science and Technology are interdependent. Scientific advances help to develop new technologies. At the same time the need for new technologies provide the impetus for new scientific discoveries. Competitiveness in technology would require a high level of scientific capability. As such, talking about science education spills into science research and technology development too.

Soon after independence we wanted to build a strong, modern, dynamic and self-reliant India. In that context, the country had faced the greater challenge of rapidly industrialising the predominantly agricultural economy and in that process, it had to create wide-based infrastructure in higher and technical education institutions, research laboratories and industries covering a very wide spectrum of disciplines and capabilities. The R & D effort in science and technology during the past four decades has brought about greater achievements in various fields. With the advent of the new industrial policy and liberalisation, the Indian industry is exposed to domestic and global competition. During the 90's, the country is progressively becoming more integrated into the global economy. Knowledge-based industries will be on the increase. The levels of skills required are going to be high. In the changed context, we need to have a workforce having a scientific bent of mind and possessing the much desired temper and skill to maintain high quality of productivity at par with world standards. In addition, we have to gear up our R & D efforts commensurately. Another dimension which has added to the changed scenario is the resources crunch situation in the country. In the overall changed scenario, there is thus need for reorientation in our approach towards funding of science and technology on one hand and towards bringing about more relevance in education and research in science and technology on the other. At the same time, upholding of academic, financial and administrative freedom with a reasonable resources support is essential for the system to achieve excellence and to meet the challenges of the new situation.

INTRODUCTION

The level of growth and application of modern science and technology determines the status of a nation as developed or developing. There is a growing concern about the increasing gap between the poor and the rich, the North and the South in the world. It was repeatedly noticed by the U.N. Agencies that more than 80% of the wealth, two-thirds of the metals, and three-fourths of the energy produced the world over, goes to the possession of the industrialised countries, which are termed as developed and make up only 20 per cent of the world population.

It is evident that the distinction between the developed and the developing countries is mainly due to their differing mastery and utilisation of modern science and technology.

Pandit Jawaharlal Nehru, the first Prime Minister and the architect of modern India, assigned to Science and Technology a pivotal role in national development. This has been reflected in the formulation and adoption of the Scientific Policy Resolution of 1958. It recognised science and technology as the key to national prosperity besides cultivating scientific spirit and scientific temper. It envisaged effective combination of technology, raw materials and capital to achieve national prosperity. With scarce capital and critical materials, India has to heavily depend on modern technology to overcome such, limitations. In response to the need for guidance on a wide ranging and complex set of inter-related areas of science and technology, industry, economy and trade, the Technology Policy Statement (TPS) was announced by the Government in 1983. Its main objectives are to develop indigenous technologies and help absorption of the imported ones wherever needed. Now a new Technology Policy is being contemplated in view of the new economic policy and the changed global scenario.

Planning for Science and Technology

India is in a unique position as far as science and technology are concerned. We have to utilise science and technology for solving the basic needs of the people such as food, shelter, clothing, health etc. Our large S & T manpower should take up the tasks of not only contributing to the frontiers of science and technology, but also help to use these tools for modernising our economic and commercial sectors. In addition, there are areas of science and technology of immediate concern to us where we must become world leaders. With this background, our approach to planning should include (a) use of science and technology in planning, and (b) planning for science and technology per se. In planning, conservation and efficiency have big roles to play. We have to combine efficient use of nature as well as human resources to achieve spectacular growth and in this context, science and technology should be applied to maximise conservation and reduce wastage.

Deficiency in the University System

The development of Science and Technology is normally expected to be from the University system. However, the national scenario in Science and Technology education is not so encouraging. There seems to be numerous reasons for this state of affairs. A large number of universities are ill equipped and thus are not able to scale new heights in their achievements. Obsolescence, shortage of teachers, increasing demand for admissions, inadequate resources, lack of relevance and poor management are some of the problems encountered in the science and technology education today. These problems are to be tackled with innovative approaches and reforms in higher and technical education.

Plan Outlays

Plan-wise approved outlays for education, including general, higher and technical education are shown in Table—1, 1A, 1B and 1C. It may be seen that the percentage of technical education out of the total allocation for education varied from 12.88% in Sixth Plan to 14.21% in Eighth Plan. The corresponding figures for higher education varied from 20.89% to 11.20%.

RESEARCH AND DEVELOPMENT

A year after independence, India was able to spend a meagre Rs. 11 million on R&D activity in the Central Government sector. Four decades later, the figure grew to more than Rs. 30,000 million. In the year 1991-92, Rs. 38,273.3 million were spent on R&D by the Central Government. The approximate corresponding figures for the states sector and the private sector are Rs. 3,719.4 million and Rs. 6,314.7 million bringing the total expenditure on R&D in 1991-92 to Rs. 48,307.4 million. A country such as U.S.A. invests upto $150 billion on R& D per year and Japan invests $100 billion per year. India invests about one billion dollars per year towards all efforts in science and technology.

A significant factor is the multiplicity of R&D agencies in the country, leading to a particular agency specialising in a particular type of activity. There is a preponderance of Central Government expenditure on R&D in almost all spheres of activity. It can be seen that Central Government accounted for about 80% of the total national R&D input in 1990-91, of which the major share went into applied research and experimental development.

It is worth examining the growth of R&D in industry. The Government has taken several measures to promote research in industry. By the end of 1990-91, there were 1164 in-house R & D units, in both the public and private sectors, and in the future it is likely to grow to around 1500 by the year 1995. The growth of R& D in industry remains, however, unimpressive.

In-house R&D activity is bound to receive a setback at times of severe resource shortages. Advertising expenditure and expenditure required for purchase of plant and machinery etc., compete with R&D expenditure and, in a profit-oriented environment, take precedence for achieving short-term goals.

R & D activity in general in India is nurtured in isolation, without significant forward and backward linkages. One welcome development, however, in the national R& D scenario is the establishment of cooperative research associations in various industry groups such as textiles, plywood, rubber, automobile, electrical and cement. There are, in all 13 cooperative research associations financed jointly by the government and industry. The R & D expenditure of these associations increased from Rs. 157 million in 1988-89 to Rs. 185 million in 1990-91. This trend needs to be encouraged.

R & D expenditure by industry, as a percentage of total R & D expenditure, is only 21% in India, compared to 61% in U.K., 63% in Japan and 72% in U.S.A. The time has come for Indian industry to increase its contribution to R&D expenditure through either in-house R&D units or through supporting research in universities. This is essential if it is to survive against global competition.

IMPACT OF THE CHANGED ECONOMIC SCENARIO

The result of the impact of the global and national economic scenario is the emergence of an era of global consciousness. The Indian industry is exposed to global and indigenous competitiveness. To meet this challenge the industry requires modernisation, upgradation of the competence of the work force, utilisation of modern management techniques, increased efficiency and productivity and maintain quality. This situation thus requires a work force having a scientific bent of mind and possessing the much desired temper and skills to maintain high quality and productivity at par with the world standards. R & D efforts should also be geared up. The science and technology education and research has therefore to respond to these emerging challenges to train men and women of calibre and competence of world standards and provide the needed R & D capability.

The explosion of knowledge in science and technology sectors requires highly talented men and women whose fast grasp of knowledge could enable them to respond to the desired innovations in advancing the frontiers of knowledge and know how. We have been able to attract the very best, highly talented students to take up higher education in engineering, medicine basic and applied sciences. However, the success in this regard will depend upon our abilities to cope up with the emerging pressures of resources crunch on the one hand and the need for upgradation of the quality of education on the other.

NEED FOR REORIENTATION

Higher and technical education institutions, business and industry and national R & D organisations have vital roles to play in economic development. In the present day global situation, interaction and interdependence are well recognised. The need for interaction, collaboration and networking is more pronounced in the context of the resources crunch situation. The Universities and institutions of higher learning should be able to interact with national laboratories and industrial organisations. Through interaction, their excellence should be shared with others for national development. The time had come that the universities should move towards less dependence on government funding. Indian industry currently being exposed to global competition needs reorientation and support from the universities. It should build up confidence in the capabilities of the universities and support their research and academic programmes. The national R & D laboratories also expected now to generate funds and allow others to share their equipment and expertise.

LINKAGES

Time is ripe now for strong linkages between technical institutions, industries and national R & D laboratories. This linkage will result in (i) sharing and optimising the use of resources, (ii) development of indigenous technology appropriate to our national priorities and resources, (iii) adapting the imported technology wherever needed for preparing the industries to meet global competitiveness, (iv) enriching teaching and research in universities with the backup of practical and field experience, (v) universities and R & D laboratories getting valuable clues for research orientation and (vi) fund generation. The process of interaction will contribute towards excellence, which in turn will contribute towards national development. A model for university, industry and R & D laboratory interaction has been proposed by me and published. The Model is shown elsewhere in this Volume.

COPING UP WITH THE RESOURCES CRUNCH

To cope up with the resources crunch situation the following measures could be taken.

1. Optimal utilisation of the available resources:

a) Within the universities or institutions duplication and wastage should be avoided. Pooling and sharing of costly equipment is desirable.

b) Networking of facilities like computers and libraries could be resorted to locally. For example within a city networking of computers and libraries of all the universities and research organisations could certainly lead towards optimal utilisation of resources. Similarly, national networking could also been resorted to. In this context the University Grants Commission's project on Information and Library Networking (INFLIBNET) is quite relevant.

c) Establishing sound linkages between universities and national research laboratories, would facilitate sharing of facilities, exchange of faculty and experts and undertaking joint academic and research programmes.

d) Establishment of consortia of universities that can work in collaborationwith higher institutions of learning such as TIFR, IISc., IITs, etc., would enable to utilise their superior resources, both human and material.

e) According Deemed-to-be-University status to selected national laboratories to initiate post-graduate programmes in certain special areas of Science, Engineering and Technology.

f) Establishing of joint centres to be run by the national laboratories and theUniversities. It will provide better research and developmental facilities to the university sector.

2. Resources Mobilisation:

As a part of resources mobilisation, establishing strong linkages with industries would go a long way. It would enable the industry to support the research and academic programmes in addition to dedicated financial contributions. The universities can also commercialise their research output, undertake consultancy and training programmes.

3. INTERNATIONAL COOPERATION:

International linkages in science and technology could be a means to assist in the implementation of national programmes, as well as to open up avenues for collaborative interaction in the frontier areas or in those sectors which lead to the acquisition of knowledge not available within the country. The overall modalities of cooperation should be such that they should ensure the enhancement of self-reliance and at the same time, avoid impingement upon considerations of security and sensitivity of the country. International cooperation will also serve as a tool for sharing of India's experience and expertise in science and technology with other developing nations.

4. ESTABLISHMENT OF CORPUS FUND:

For achieving excellence, a university should have academic, financial and administrative autonomy. Considerable academic autonomy is already available. There should be ample financial and administrative autonomy as well. In the present day system of government funding there is rigidity coupled with inadequacy. The inadequate situation is going to be worse in the context of the resources crunch. Financial autonomy is vital for continuation of the institutions as real Centres of excellence. Therefore, the institutions should strive for fund generation and reduce their dependence on government gradually and thus pave the way towards self-reliance. Creation of 'corpus fund' for each university or institution would be an appropriate mechanism to achieve the objective of self-reliance. The corpus will be in the form of an endowment fund. Revenue obtained from such fund can eventually be used to reduce the required support from the Government. The corpus fund could be created with contributions from industry, alumni, charitable trusts etc., as well as from the government. Indian Institutes of Technology, Indian Institute of Science and Indian Institutes of Management have already accepted the concept and they are in the process of creating corpus funds with the support of the government.

CONCLUSION

In the changed economic scenario with pronounced resources inadequacy situation the need for reorientation in the development of science is obvious. To make up for resources inadequacy and to respond to the demands on the system in the changed situation, innovative approaches towards maximising utilisation of the available resources and interaction, collaboration and networking should be sought. In addition, freedom of operation should be provided through autonomy in academic, financial and administrative aspects. Thus, a total and comprehensive approach is needed in the improvement of quality of science education in the present day context of resources crunch situation.

Table-1
PLANWISE APPROVED OUTLAYS

(Rs. in crores)

PLAN	SECTOR	TOTAL EDUCATION	HIGHER EDUCATION	TECHNICAL EDUCATION
1	2	3	4	5
SIXTH (1980-85)	Centre	659.21	288.75	168.00
	States/UTs	1666.81	197.25	131.65
	Total	2326.02	486.00	299.65
			(20.89%)	(12.88 %)
SEVENTH (1985-90)	Centre	1738.64	420.00 *	220.00
	States/UTs	3718.45	541.17	461.79
	Total	5457.09	961.17	681.79
			(17.61%)	(12.49 %)
EIGHTH (1992-97)	Centre	7443.33	700.00 **	824.00
	States/UTs	12156.73	1495.68	1962.38
	Total	19599.73	2195.68	2786.38
			(11.20 %)	14.22 %

*   **Indicates Actual Expenditure**
**   **Indicates Proposed outlay by states/UT/s Governments**
( )   **Figures in brackets are percentages out of the total allocation for education.**
Source: For Education Sector: Annual Plane analysis 1986-87, 1991-92, 1992-93
For S & T: Eighth Plane Document (1992-97)

Table-1A
PLANEWISE TOTAL OUTLAY OF EDUCATION
OUTLAY/ EXPENDITURE HIGHER AND TECHNICAL EDUCATION
FROM FIRST TO EIGHTH YEAR PLAN

(RS.CRORES)

FIVE YEAR PLANS	TOTAL PLANE OUTLAY	TOTAL END OUTLAY	%OF END OUTLAY TO PLAN OUTLAY	OUTLAY HIGHER EDN.	EXP. HIGHER EDN.	OUTLAY TECHNICAL EDN	EXP. TECHNICAL EDN.
1	2	3	4	5	6	7	8
FIRST PLAN (1951-56)	1960	169	8.62	15	14	23	20
SECOND PLAN (1956-61)	4762	277	5.82	47	48	51	49
THIRD PLAN (1961-66)	8577	560	6.53	82	87	142	125
FOURTH PLAN (1969-74)	15779	822	5.21	183	195	106	106
FIFTH PLAN (1974-79)	40097	1285	3.21	292	205	156	107
SIXTH PLAN (1980-85)	97500	2524	2.59	486	537	278	318
SEVENTH PLAN (1985-1990)	180000	6383	3.55	*420	1190	683	1085
EIGHTH PLAN (1992-97)	434100	21217	4.89	1515.55	-	2786.38	-

SOURCE: Planning Commission, Government of India, New Delhi
* Only Central Sector outlay

TABLE- 1B

EIGHTH PLANE OUTLAY FOR MAJOR HEADS OF EDUCATION

S. NO.	MAJOR HEAD	CENTRE	STATES	U.T.S	TOTAL
1.	General Education	6619.00	9607.19	587.16	16813.35
2.	Technical Education	824.00	1804.66	157.72	2786.38
3.	(Total-1and2)	7443.00	11411.85	744.88	19599.73
4.	Art and Culture	385.00	324.76	17.92	727.68
5.	Youth Affairs and Sports	350.00	509.06	30.54	889.60
6.	Grand Total (3-5)	8178.00	12245.67	793.34	21217.01

TABLE-1C

ABSTRACT OF OUTLAY OF EIGHTH FIVE YEAR PLAN (1992-97)

SL. NO.	SUB-HEAD		EIGHTH FIVE YEAR PLANE (1992-97)		
			PROPOSED OUTLAY	OUTLAY RECOMD.BY THE WORKING GROUP	APPROVED OUTLAY
1	2	3	4	6	
1.	Elementary Education	CENTRE	3588.18	2880.00	2880.00
		STATE/UTs	6676.00	8128.98	6056.46*
		TOTAL	10264.18	11008.98	8936.46
2.	Adult Education	CENTRE	1746.82	1519.00	1400.00
		STATE/UTs	497.04	394.44	394.44*
		TOTAL	2243.86	1794.44	1794.44
3.	Secondary Education	CENTRE	2950.59	1519.00	1519.00
		STATE/UTs	3447.97	-	-
		TOTAL	6398.50	-	-
4.	Higher University Education	CENTRE	1100.00	700.00	700.00
		STATE/UTs	1495.00	-	-
		TOTAL	2595.00	-	-
5.	Other Educational Programme	CENTRE	207.01	120.00	120.00
		STATE/UTs	253.49	-	-
		TOTAL	460.50	-	-
6.	General Education (Col. 1 To 5)	CENTRE	9592.54	6619.00	6619.00
		STATE/UTs	12370.78	10194.35	10194.35
		TOTAL	21963.32	16813.35	16813.35
7.	Technical Education	CENTRE	1200.00	824.00	824.00
		STATE/UTs	2465.70	1962.38	1962.38
		TOTAL	3665.70	2786.38	2786.38
8.	Sports And Youth Affairs	CENTRE	1239.27	350.00	350.00
		STATE/UTs	710.41	539.60	539.60
		TOTAL	1949.68	889.60	889.60
9.	Art And Culture	CENTRE	1370.21	385.00	385.00
		STATE/UTs	513.27	342.69	342.69
		TOTAL	1883.48	727.69	727.69
10.	Total Education (Col. 6 To 9)	CENTRE	13402.02	8178.00	8178.00
		STATE/UTs	16060.16	13039.02	13039.02
		TOTAL	29462.18	21217.02	21217.02

* Indicate Earmarked Outlay

ADDRESS AS CHIEF GUEST AT THE VALEDICTORY FUNCTION OF THE NATIONAL CHILDREN'S SCIENCE CONGRESS

I am highly delighted to be with you this morning to participate in the valedictory function of National Children's Science Congress, being organised by the NCSTC network. I am grateful to Dr. Sehgal for inviting me to this valedictory function as the Chief Guest. It gives me great pleasure to see such a vast gathering of young children coming from various parts of the country along with their teachers, to participate in this year's National Children's Science Congress. I have had occasions to attend Indian National Science Congress but I must say that I am happier on this occasion than on those occasions. I would like to offer my congratulations to all the award winners in today's function and the others who could not get the awards need not be disheartened as participation itself should give the greatest satisfaction. The spirit of participation in any event should only matter and not whether one wins or loses. This spirit should be inculcated among the young students.

The NCSTC Network is doing yeoman service towards popularisation of science and technology and promotion of scientific attitudes and temper among the people. I must congratulate the NCSTC Network for striking upon the concept of National Children's Science Congress. The National Children's Science Congress has laudable objectives, which include encouraging children to adopt "learning by doing method" for science, to relate science education with practical real life situations, to replace the existing science practicals in schools / colleges with the real life projects that the children can do and to encourage, to use the whole environment around as a laboratory. In our country today, the teaching of science in schools is beset with inadequacies. Many schools are not having the required equipment in the laboratories and even those who are having these laboratories do not provide practicals related to life situations. The approach and concept adopted in the National Children's Science Congress, using the whole environment as a laboratory, is worth replicating in all the schools in the country.

The focal theme for this year's National Children's Science Congress "Cleaning up India", is most relevant. "Cleaning up India" could relate to our surroundings and also erosion in values, societal evils etc. As children, you may mostly be concerned with the first aspect i.e., cleaning up our surroundings. I am very happy to know that some good reports are presented by some of you. A few minutes ago, I have had occasion to glance through a couple of reports, one on Drinking Water and the other relating to superstitions. I was very much impressed with these reports.

Science and technology have greater roles to play in the national development. You may be surprised to know that 80% of the world's wealth is in the hands of 24% of the world's population, who are known as 'developed', the remaining 76% of the population are termed as 'under-developed' or 'developing'. The distinction between these two categories could be related to their differing mastery in creation and application of science and technology for development. Chacha Nehru assigned a key role to science and technology for our country's development and formulated the Scientific Policy Resolution, 1958. No doubt, science and technology brings in development and prosperity but it has its ill effects also. You being young children should at least try to understand the implications at this stage so that when you grow up and become scientists, you will be in a better position to appreciate and try to guard against the ill effects of science and technology. The ill effects of science and technology may relate to the human destruction and destruction to environment and ecology. I am always reminded of what late Prof. D.S. Kothari used to say about science and technology. He said that our approach to science and technology is leading us towards three D's—destruction, dilution and death. Therefore, something needs to be done so that instead of three D's, we will have three H's—honesty, humility and humaneness. That something which needs to be incorporated is perhaps the 'human approach'. Advancements of science and technology have led us to the creation of nuclear, biological and

SELECTED SPEECHES OF DR. D. SWAMINADHAN

conventional weapons, which will lead to mass destruction of the humanity unless the 'human approach' is highlighted and appreciated.

Destruction of environment has been enormous, leading to pollution of land, water and air. This is causing great hardships to the people and their health. For example, emission of chlorofluorocarbons (CFC) by the refrigerator and air conditioner are affecting the ozone layer which protects the living beings on the earth from the bad effects of sun rays. That is why I advocate for 'human approach' and green 'approach' for science and technology which will lead towards sustainable development. Sustainable development may be defined as "a process of change in which the exploitation of resources, the direction of investments, the orientation of technological development and institutional change are all in harmony and enhance both current and future potential to meet human needs and aspirations".

SELECTED
SPEECHES *of* DR. D. SWAMINADHAN

FORMER MEMBER OF
PLANNING COMMISSION,
GOVERNMENT OF INDIA

SECOND PART

EDITED BY
DR. DEVARAKONDA SWAMINADHAN
2013

DEVELOPMENT STUDIES

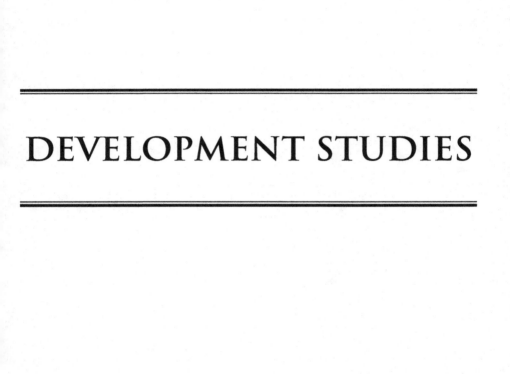

Address At The Expert Group Meeting To Deliberate On Implications Of Economic Reforms For The Urban Sector

Dr. Raja Chelliah, Mr. Menezes, Mr. Reddy, Mr. Basak, Dr. Basu and distinguished participants,

It is a great privilege for me to address the experts and fellow professionals who have assembled here today to deliberate on the subject of "Implications of Economic Reforms in the Urban Sector". This is a subject of national importance and deserves high priority. If we have to make best use of the series of economic reforms initiated by the government to boost the economy, the focus on reforms in the urban sector is imperative. In this context, today's Expert Group meeting is vital and timely. I would like to extend my thanks to Dr. Raja Chelliah and his colleagues in the National Institute of Public Finance and Policy and theconcerned ministerial and departmental colleagues for their ready response in organising this meeting.

It is now well recognised that urbanisation process signifies increasing contribution of urban areas to GDP and in a sense to the aggregate socio-economic development process. At the same time deterioration in the physical environment and quality of life in the urban areas has been evident. Physical and economic infrastructure has hardly kept pace with the demands of increasing population and industrial activities which are located largely in and around urban areas. This is attributable to quite a few factors of which the financial and organisational weakness of urban local bodies and absence of facilitating environment for stepping up investment in infrastructure are probably the most important ones. In pursuance of this, the essence of VIIIth Plan strategy for urban development has been stated as:

"The challenge of reorienting the urbanisation process, thus, lies in overcoming the infrastructural deficiencies and taking the best advantage of economic momentum inherent in urbanisation".

The above strategy has gained significance in the context of recent announcements of the government for further liberalisation in trade, industry, fiscal and monetary policies. In the medium and long term perspective, the aim of this liberalised economic policy is to promote economic growth by achieving higher economic efficiency and integration of the domestic economy with the rest of the world.

If this has to happen, it is evident that demands of physical and economic Infrastructure would go up considerably in near future. The challenge to provide such infrastructure will be felt more in urban areas and that too in and around large cities where most of the expansion of economic activities is likely to take place. The challenge is all the more pronounced because these cities are already facing severe strain on the existing resources and have limited organisational and financial absorptive capacity to respond to the dynamism of economic regeneration.

If we look back and examine the Plan support in terms of financial provision, with regard to urban infrastructure, it would appear rather insignificant. During Seventh Plan, urban development per se accounted for about Rs. 1,800 crores (including State and Central Sector) or about 1% of the total Plan outlay. However, if we include Housing and Urban Water Supply Sector, this will come to a little over Rs. 7,000 crores (about 4%) during the Seventh Plan. During the Eighth Plan, it is likely to be same in proportional terms. Whatever estimates of investment requirement of urban infrastructure we may take, the direct contribution of Plan outlay would remain insignificant. Thus the strategy for financing of urban infrastructure has to go much beyond the conventional plan support. As a part of the Eighth Plan strategy, role of institutional finance has been given due emphasis. As a matter of fact, in a sector like Housing, institutional funding through HUDCO and other agencies is much more than the direct Plan outlay for the sector. It is also expected that in view of the remunerative nature of some of the investment in urban infrastructure and services, internal resources generation and private sector participation would play complementary role. The major consideration is, however, speed and ability with which the urban local bodies can introduce / augment user charges. Another major issue is the envisaged role of directed credit from

Public Financial Institutions for financing Housing and Urban infrastructure because this policy has to fit in with the contemplated reforms in the financial sector.

It is imperative that we create an enabling environment to facilitate such flow of Investment. This enabling process is not merely limited to provision of finance but has to take the totality of institutional, legal and procedural sub-systems operating in the urban environment. Thus liberalisation of macro policies may not be enough. It is also necessary that procedural simplification, de-bureaucratization and removal of legal bottlenecks are introduced simultaneously to create the facilitating environment for enhancing flow of investment in the urban sector. Many of these changes may be required at the level of urban local bodies with supporting legal and procedural provisions by the State Government.

It is equally important that the interests of the urban poor as well as the small towns and less advantaged cities, vulnerable groups are safeguarded while creating this enabling environment. How this is to be done—by way of targeted subsidies, higher budgetary support or direct programmes of poverty alleviation—is a matter of debate. Another point to which I would like to draw the attention of the galaxy of experts assembled here today is the impact of liberalised industrial licensing on growth of metro cities and regional spread of urban development. We need to deliberate whether there is a need for complementary measures for regulatory process so that we do not end up with a concentration of economic growth in areas which cannot be sustained further purely on resource and cost considerations.

I have tried to give you a wide spectrum of concerns and considerations ranging from financing of urban services to removal of legal and procedural bottlenecks and implications of liberalisation of industrial licensing policy. I am sure that at the end of today's meeting, we will gain further insight into some of these issues and probably prepare an outline of followup action plans. I can assure you that Planning Commission would give topmost priority to these concerns because we are convinced that urbanisation process and economic development are inextricably linked.

INAUGURAL ADDRESS AT THE POLICY SEMINAR ON "INTEGRATED HUMAN SETTLEMENT PROGRAMME"

Dr. Vinay Lall, distinguished participants, ladies and gentlemen,

I am highly delighted to participate in the inaugural session of the Policy Seminar on "Integrated Human Settlement Programme" being organised by the Society for Development Studies. I am grateful for being invited to inaugurate the seminar. Organisation of such a Seminar is very timely because India as well as other developing countries are passing through a very critical stage in which the sustainability issue of the development process at large has assumed an unprecedented sense of urgency. While the issue of food security for the growing population with a large base has been at the centre stage in the initial stage of planned development in India, the concerns of sustainability are dictated by the pace and pattern of urbanisation and associated problem of deteriorating environmental quality of human settlement. The challenge of sustainable development is not merely one of conservation of land and water resources but of integrated development of human settlements in a rural-urban continuum. The solution to this challenge lies not merely in the physical and technological domain but involves an integrated approach, including social, economic, environmental and more importantly participatory dimensions of development to human settlement. The subject was clearly recognised in the Rio Declaration on Environment and Development which puts human beings at the centre of concerns for sustainable development. The Human Settlements Chapter of the Agenda 21 of the Rio Conference states "the overall Human Settlement objective is to improve the social, economic and environmental quality of human settlements and the living and working environments of all people, in particular urban and the rural poor". The significance of integrated human settlements has been perhaps most explicitly highlighted in the Draft Statement of Principles and Commitments prepared for the Summit on HABITAT II to be held in 1996 which will be a logical extension of the first ever international conference on Human Resettlements i.e. HABITAT I held in 1976. It is perhaps worth noting the opening remarks of Mr. Boutros Boutros-Ghali, Secretary General of United Nations in the First Substantive Session of the Preparatory Committee of HABITAT II held in April 1994. "The question of human settlements is urgent. There must be no delay. The time for getting organised is over. The time to address substance is here".

I am happy to note that the above broader dimension of human settlements, rather than housing per se has been gaining an increasing recognition both among the planners and practitioners in India. In a sense, the topic of today's Seminar is a definite pointer to this. It will be perhaps worthwhile to recapitulate the previous policies and programmes adopted in our country in this respect and then to think forward of an integrated approach to human settlements with the overall objective of improving the entire environment of all people in a sustainable manner. While I am sure that the galaxy of participants in today's Seminar would deliberate in a detailed manner the various dimensions of this subject of national importance. I would also like to share with you some of my thoughts on the subject.

You will all agree that the National Housing Policy (NHP) of India, as adopted by both Houses of Parliament, can make the most conspicuous contribution towards achieving the global objective of 'adequate shelter for all'. The NHP has also recognised housing as an integral part of human settlements as illustrated in its Statement. "Housing forms an important part of the strategy of the Government for the alleviation of poverty and employment generation and is to be viewed as an integral part of the overall improvement of human settlements and economic development." The VIII Plan has also explicitly incorporated the basic thrust of NHP, evolved various plan schemes within the resource constraints and more importantly brought in the critical role of housing credit in achieving the targets for creation of new housing stock as well as upgradation of existing units in urban and rural areas. There have also been significant efforts in preparing housing action plans at State levels and also dealing with various problems relating to development of land and infrastructure as also legal constraints to supply of land in urban areas. In the technology front, significant efforts have been underway in promoting eco-friendly and local resource based material as also earthquake resistant housing.

In spite of such encouraging developments, it is evident that the goal of adequate shelter for all and more importantly long term sustainability of measures for improving the quality of human settlements at large are not likely to be achieved in near future if we assume the extrapolation of current trends and programmes in housing and allied sectors as valid. There are a few compelling factors (or issues) which need to be examined more critically and a suitable strategy evolved for integrated human settlements. Important of them are:

a) Sustainability of the goal of adequate shelter for all is achievable only through a process of integration of housing programmes with income and employment generation programmes.

b) Concentration of population in large cities with attendant problem of very high investment requirement for providing basic infrastructure and also socio-economic dimensions of absorption of migrants, characterised by low skill and economic status in the city development process, pose the real challenge of integrated development of shelter and infrastructure in an affordable manner.

c) Speculative motives in development / transaction in real estate market which often hinder development of equitable and efficient land and housing market in large cities.

d) Absence of location specific technological and institutional solutions to the development of housing and infrastructure.

e) Lagged response of housing and urban infrastructure sector to the policy of economic liberalisation initiated in our country, particularly formulation of strategies to the financial sector reforms in the absence of which the envisaged flow of credit to the housing sector would not materialise.

f) Absence of appropriate institutional linkages between the formal and informal segments of housing finances system.

g) Weak financial and management base of local government and other development agencies that are expected to play an increasingly important role in the provision of housing and infrastructure in the trail of decentralisation strategy adopted.

I find that the base paper prepared by the Society for Development Studies has addressed some of the critical issues or missing links towards develo ping a strategy for developing integrated human settlements in a sustainable framework. In particular the emphasis on 'composite economic infrastructure' and 'composite credit instruments' outlined in the paper deserve special mention. It will be useful to deliberate on this subject to work towards operational strategies rather than limiting the discussion only to conceptual frame. The Working Group on Housing Development Strategy for North-East Region set up by the Planning commission has also covered new grounds on integrated approach to sustainable shelter programme.

While concluding, I would like to emphasise that the role of government must be clearly understood in this complex task of providing adequate shelter for all and developing a sustainable human settlements strategy. The roles of financial institutions, building industry, NGO / CBOs as also the planning and scientific community should be clearly recognised as complementary in nature. It is however not enough stating the role of the government as a 'facilitator' and it is equally important to identify the stages in which and the instruments through which the government will facilitate the achievement of the overall objective of the integrated human settlements. This, I think, will require a <u>macro level assessment of the situations, scenarios and alternative strategies</u> pertaining to human settlements as well as <u>micro level orientation of the programmes and also the delivery mechanisms</u>. This approach can be successful only when there is participation at all levels i.e. a combination of people-based development efforts at grass root level together with planning and policy inputs from the technologists, planners and decision makers. I would urge upon the participants to discuss during this policy seminar both the macro and micro level issues so that an operationally feasible integrated human settlements strategy in the context of a sound theoretical frame can emerge.

I take pleasure in inaugurating the Seminar and wish it a great success.

ECONOMY

INAUGURAL ADDRESS AT THE NATIONAL SEMINAR ON 'DR. BABASAHEB AMBEDKAR AND HIS IDEAS ON ECONOMIC GROWTH WITH JUSTICE'

Prof. Narayana, distinguished delegates of the Seminar, ladies and gentlemen,

It is a privilege for me to be with you today to inaugurate the National Seminar on 'Dr. Babasaheb Ambedkar and his Ideas on Economic Growth with Justice being organized by the Centre for Rayalaseema Development Studies, Department of Economics, Sri Krishnadevaraya University. I express my heartfelt thanks to the organisers for giving me this opportunity. I am delighted to visit Anantpur once again, as I like this place as one of the most serene and a place of healthy environment. I am sure all the delegates will enjoy their stay at Anantpur.

It is heartening to note that Sri Krishnadevaraya University is celebrating Dr. Babasaheb Ambedkar's Birth Centenary by organising a National Seminar on his Ideas on Economic Growth with Justice. Dr. Ambedkar was a legendary figure of modern times. His works and thoughts could very well be characterised as belonging' to that trend of thought called 'Social Humanism'. Mahatma Gandhi aptly described him as "a man who has carved out for himself a unique position in society", adding further that "Dr. Ambedkar is not the man to allow himself to be forgotten". The Nobel laureate Gunnar Myrdal spoke about Ambedkar as "All over the world—the memory of B. R. Ambedkar will live for ever as a truly great Indian in the generation which laid down the direction of Independent India".

Among the galaxy of thinkers and philosophers of India, Dr. Ambedkar undoubtedly occupies the most important place. His personal bitter experiences, progressive western education, extensive reading and wide mass contacts, provided him the required perspective, theoretical frame, the depth and dimension for understanding and analysing any problem, particularly the social problems of India,

The Constitution of India is a living testimony to the greatness and the vision of Ambedkar. He relentlessly fought for justice, liberty, equality and fraternity for all. The Constitution of India, of which he was the architect, provides to secure to all its citizens:

Justice in social, economic and political spheres; Liberty of thought, expression, belief, faith and worship; Equality of status and of opportunity; and to promote among them all; Fraternity assuring the dignity of the individual and the unity and integrity of the Nation.

Dr. Ambedkar favoured the idea of economic growth with justice from the core of his heart. In his speech in the Constituent Assembly on 25th November, 1949 he gave a warning and I quote—"on 26th January, 1950 we are going to enter into a life of contradictions. Inpolitics, we will have equality and in social and economic life we will have inequality. In politics, we will be recognising the principle of one man one vote and one vote-one value. In our social and economic life, we shall by reason of our social and economic structure, continue to deny the principle of one man one value. How long shall we continue to live thislife of contradictions? How long shall we continue to deny equality in our social and economic life? If we continue to deny it for long, we will do so only by putting our political democracy in peril. We must remove this, contradiction at the earliest possible moment or else those who suffer from inequality will blow up the structure of political democracy which this assembly has so laboriously built up".

It was at his insistence that the Directive Principles were incorporated in the Constitution. These principles were meant to ensure social and economic democracy in addition to political democracy which was secured by the provision of fundamental rights. Dr. Ambedkar said that the word "directive" should be retained in the heading because the intention was that the Constituent Assembly should give certain directions to the future legislature and the future executive as to the manner in which they should exercise their legislative and executive powers. He was of the view that in the exercise of the Directive Principles, the State could enact much for the general welfare of the community which may even contravene the fundamental rights. Thus, these were the obligations imposed by the Constitution upon the various Governments in the country. The main purpose was to provide economic and social justice. To quote him again, "in our judgement, the Directive Principles have a great value for they lay down that our aim is economic democracy. Because we did not want to merely have a Parliamentary form of Government to be instituted through various mechanisms provided in the Constitution, without any direction as to our economic ideal, as to what our social order ought to be, we deliberately included the Directive Principles in our Constitution."

In particular, Dr. Ambedkar vigorously justified the two directive principle of state policy which directed the state to avoid concentration of economic power viz. (i) that the ownership and control of the material resources of the community are so distributed as best to subserve the common good, (ii) that the operation of the economic system does not result in the concentration of wealth and means of production to the common detriment. The Constitution has abolished forced labour and prohibited exploitation of child labour. Property rights are guaranteed. Equal right of work, equal pay for equal work and adequate means of livelihood both to men and women are guaranteed under the state policy.

Thus, Dr. Ambedkar's economic thought had a moral purpose. He studied economic activity from the point of view of its effect on human welfare. He was not concerned with wealth or economic relations as such, but in their relations to man and his choices. What mattered much for him was the distribution of wealth equitably among the common people. To him, the problems of distribution were more important than any other economic problem. He highlighted economic matters when it became expedient in the field of politics.

I must congratulate the organisers to have thought about a seminar on Dr. Babasaheb Ambedkar and his Ideas on Economic Growth with Justice as a part of his Birth Centenary Celebrations, which would really serve as a great tribute to that great Son of India.

I take pleasure in inaugurating the seminar and wish it all success.

ADDRESS AT THE CONFERENCE OF THE INTERNATIONAL FRIENDSHIP SOCIETY OF INDIA, NEW DELHI ON "ECONOMIC GROWTH AND NATIONAL INTEGRATION"

Respected Chairman, Secretary-General, Members of the International Friendship Society of India and friends,

I feel honoured to have the opportunity to address such a gathering as this and share my views with you on "Economic Growth and National Integration" the topic of today's Conference. I thank the organisers for having invited me to this Conference and confer on me the honour.

National integration implies unification and consolidation of a community with the Objective of ensuring maximum well being of largest number of its members. It implies provision of education, better economy, social, political and moral status, provision of equal opportunities, employment and social securities which are basic to civilized life.

All the big countries in the course of time have undergone the process of integration either through socialism or capitalism. Many of the European countries achieved integration through capitalism. On the other hand in many of the Afro-Asian countries socialism became the process of integration. In comparison to Capitalist and Marxist principles of integration, India adopted a unique one. India aims at socio-economic progress. We have adopted a secular, democratic constitution ensuring all sections of people their fundamental rights. Coexistence, tolerance, cooperation and unity are supposed to be fundamentals in National

Integration in India. We have to pay due regard to each caste, class, community, faith and belief.

The problem of integration in the Indian context has three distinct aspects—political, economic and social and I would like to dwell on the economic aspect since this is the topic of the Conference. Economic problem arises out of prevailing economic disparity in the society in terms of higher and lower class and the haves and have-nots. Because of the size of the country, uneven distribution of resources and different levels and rates of development in different parts, certain problems do arise which are mainly concerned with seeking to remove the disparity between the economically well off and poor parts.

Pandit Jawaharlal Nehru, the architect of modern India and the first Prime Minister, embarked on the path of planned economic development. Planning for the economic development in India started in 1951 with the objectives of achieving rapid agricultural and industrial development, expansion of opportunities for gainful employment, progressive reduction of social and economic disparities, removal of poverty and attainment of selfreliance. The Indian Planning, to quote Dr. Manmohan Singh from the Seventh Five Year Plan document "provides a framework of time and space that binds sectors, regions and states together and relates each year's effort to the succeeding years. By strengthening the social and economic fabric of the country as a whole and of the different regions and states, it makes a powerful contribution to the goal of national integration. The Planning process has contributed a great deal to evolve a broad national consensus regarding the basic objectives, strategies and design of our development policies. This has helped to generate broad mass support for national economic policies which has added greatly to the cohesion and stability enjoyed by our polity".

Planning in our country is an instrument for achieving the Nation's basic goals and objectives. The past four decades of planning has brought about creditable growth and development. Our agricultural economy is robust and resilient. We have a large pool of skilled manpower and ample entrepreneurial resources. We have built a diversified industrial structure that will hold us in good stead. Above all, life expectancy which was barely 32 years at the time of independence has gone upto 58 years at present. The Eighth Five Year Plan has been launched in the backdrop of certain strengths in the economy as well as certain concerns which have surfaced at the beginning of the Plan. The context of planning has also undergone a change in view of the emerging trends and also since certain bold initiatives have been taken to reorient and restructure the economy. There are new perspectives about the role of planning and the efficacy of government sponsored actions for development and change.

The focus of the Eighth Five Year Plan is on clear prioritisation of sectors / projects for intensive investment, making available and ensure effective utilisation of resources, creation of social security net and creation of appropriate organisations and delivery system to ensure that the benefits of investment in the social sector reach ultimate beneficiaries. Its emphasis is on building a long-term strategy and sets forth priorities of the nation. It works out sectoral targets and tends to provide promotional stimulus to the economy to grow in the desired direction.

The Plan lays emphasis on human development in all its many facets. It is towards this ultimate goal that employment generation, population control, literacy, education, health, drinking water and provision of adequate food and basic infrastructure are listed as the priorities of the Eighth Plan. Provision of the basic elements which help the development of human capital will remain the primary responsibility of the Government.

The Eighth Plan envisages better performance of the public sector units and higher resource mobilisation both by the Centre and the States. It stresses the essential need to involve people in the process of development. Peoples' initiative and participation is the key element in developmental processes. For the first time a new direction is given to achieve these objectives by creating the right type of institutional infrastructure. An effort is being made to work out the institutional strategies by creating or strengthening the various peoples' institutions at the district, block and village level and also by relating the intended programmes to the needs of the people. The Plan seeks to assign a larger role in formulating and implementing the developmental projects to Panchayats and Nagar Palikas which will be elected by the people. These institutions will be vested with adequate financial resources, technical / managerial inputs. They will be given adequate powers of decision-making. Involvement of voluntary agencies and other peoples' institutions is felt essential for effective and micro-level participatory planning.

The Plan pays special attention to rural employment by creating adequate earning opportunities to the rural poor in the villages itself thus preventing migration to the urban areas. In the process of providing employment, creation of durable productive assets is planned. These assets will enhance productivity and create more job opportunities, leading to sustained development.

The Eighth Plan is a flexible one with scope for change, innovation and adjustment. It envisages raising of large components of resources both by the States and Central Ministries. These are required in some of the sectors like power, transport and communications. The resource gap is sought to be filled in these sectors by private sector investment.

The Plan envisages an average growth rate of 5.6% in GDP. It would be financed mostly from domestic resources. The realisation of the objectives of the Plan calls for an integrated set of micro-economic policies and the utmost financial discipline on the part of all concerned—the Central and State Governments, public and private enterprises and the financial institutions. It also seeks to evolve a consensus and fruitful cooperation among all the "social partners" in development, namely, government, farmers, trade unions, business etc. The Plan is thus a joint endeavour in national development.

Achievement of a high growth rate and sustaining it over the decades will be an important goal of the Eighth Plan. Employment generation and poverty alleviation objectives are ultimately related to growth. However, the growth has to be accompanied with a sharper regional focus of reduced disparity and more dispersed benefits. The backward regions and the weaker sections of the society, if not protected fully, are more likely to be left behind in the natural process of growth. Adequate protection will have to be continued to be provided to the poor and the weaker sections of the society. Adequate food supply, control on inflation, effective working of public distribution system and developmental programmes which generate adequate employment are among the main components of the strategy to take care of the poor.

In conclusion, I would say that economic growth accompanied by development of economically backward regions, reduction in regional disparities and in raising of living standards of the poor and downtrodden through the policies being adopted in the Eighth Five Year Plan will lead to national integration.

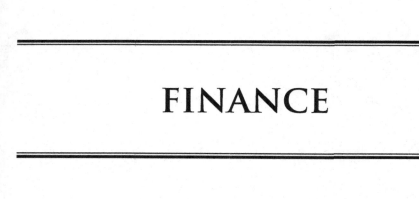

FINANCE

ADDRESS AT NATIONAL MEET TO DISCUSS ISSUES AND GUIDELINES PERTAINING TO THE STATE FINANCE COMMISSIONS HELD IN VIGYAN BHAVAN, NEW DELHI

I am highly delighted to participate in the inaugural session of this National Meet organised to deliberate on various issues pertaining to the State Finance Commissions (SFC) and to deliver the key note address. The very fact that Shri K.C. Pant, Hon'ble Chairman of the 10th National Finance Commission has kindly agreed to inaugurate this meet, gives the right signal for the significance attached to this meeting. I am happy to see such an overwhelming response from the Chairmen and Member-Secretaries of the State Finance Commissions, concerned State Secretaries, officials of the Ministries of Urban Development and Rural Development, various National institutes, particularly the NIPFP, NIUA, Institute of Social Sciences and above all from some eminent experts in the field. We are grateful to you all for responding to the initiative taken by Planning Commission in sponsoring this meeting.

The setting up of SFC is indeed a milestone towards the efficient governance based on the principles of democratic decentralisation. I firmly believe that the Articles 243-I and 243-Y of the 73rd and 74th Constitution Amendments respectively providing for the establishment of SFC in each State, once in five years, symbolise the most significant instrument or tool for achieving the objective of establishing a network of strong local government institutions in both rural and urban areas.

Functional decentralisation matched with adequate financial resources to municipalities and panchayats through both devolution of funds and other resource augmentation measures is the heart of the process of setting up of institutions of Local Self-Government. It pre-supposes that the functional **decentralisation should go hand-in-hand with the financial devolution.**

This in turn highlights the challenge and responsibility of the SFC in recommending (i) principles and quantum of devolution of net proceeds of taxes, duties, tolls and fees leviable by the State to municipalities and panchayats, (ii) determination of taxes, levies, duties, fees etc. to be assigned to these local bodies; and (iii) grant-in-aid to these local bodies from the Consolidated Fund of State. The task before the SFC is all the more complex because there is no precedent nor there is pre-determined divisible pool or uniform base of taxation, levies based on which recommendations can be made. In addition, there are complicating factors like widely varying sizes and financial base of the urban local bodies within a State, extremely inadequate source of revenue of the panchayats and probably also the varying level of service required for different categories of local bodies. In the context of this complex task before the SFC, it would appear that the conformity legislations passed by State Governments can hardly throw any light on the guidelines and tasks to be performed except by way of stating the general terms of reference which in most cases, is replication of the provisions made in the Constitution Amendment Act itself.

It is in this background, I feel, today's meeting is quite crucial because it will give unique opportunity of exchange of views not only among the Chairmen and Members of SFCs but also an opportunity for dialogue with experts and institutions involved in such work either on conceptual front or applied studies. Another important aspect which I would like to emphasise is that in this initial and preparatory stage of SFC, it is important to achieve an element of uniformity in concept and information base. The objective of today's meeting is not to arrive at any set of specific recommendations with regard to principles of devolution or criteria for grant-in-aid which, in any way, have to be State specific, but to have a vivid thinking as to how to respond to this challenging task in the quickest and most efficient manner. I am sure that the deliberations will be directed in the desired direction by the Chairmen of various sessions.

Another important issue which we have been deliberating in the Planning Commission is how to achieve the best coordination between urban and rural systemwhich have got inseparable functional linkage. SFC, which is to oversee the requirements of both urban and local self-governments, will set probably the best example of achieving such coordinating principles and mechanism.

As it is now evident that the setting up of SFC will usher in a new State-local government fiscal relationship which was almost non-existent in the past in any formal manner, a clear understanding of its role and task, conceptual frame for detailed work and above all acceptability of its recommendations by the State Government, are some of the pre-requisites for the next stage of democratic decentralisation to take concrete shape. The three essential functions of SFC would consist of recommendations pertaining to (i) sharing of State revenue from taxes, tolls, fees etc.; (ii) assignment of taxes, tolls, fees etc., to local government; and (iii) criteria for distribution of grant-in-aid. An additional function has been suggested under Article 243-Y (Municipalities) to recommend measures for improving the financial position of municipalities.

It would be useful for the SFC to keep in view some broader conceptual frame and also the basic problems and issues, relating to with the large majority of panchayats and municipalities before detailed plan of work is formulated. While some of the basic issues would be common with those dealt by the National Finance Commission, there are other distinct issues before the SFC. Moreover, unlike the National Finance Commission, the information base readily available with SFC, will be quite poor. I am sure that with such a galaxy of experts and officials participating in this meeting it should be possible to discuss threadbare all the basic issues and operational guidelines. Nevertheless, I would like to place before you some of these issues, which I think, need specific attention. These are:-

a) While the long-term goal of a healthy State-local bodies fiscal relationship should bring about fiscal autonomy to the extent possible through assigning larger number of taxes and other sources of finance, there may be larger dependence in the immediate future on the resource transfer from the State. This may be particularly true in view of extremely weak existing resource base (own sources) of both panchayats and smaller municipalities;

b) Another aspect that needs to be looked into by the SFC is whether a differentiated principle of devolution of finances and assignment of taxes would also be necessary among different categories of municipal bodies and panchayats. In the short-term context, resource raising capability of panchayats may be quite limited. It way also be true for some of the smaller municipalities and nagar panchayats. Accordingly larger reliance may have to be placed, for such local bodies, on grant-in-aid and purpose specific transfer. In case of financially stronger municipal bodies, thrust should be on raising finances from own sources with a greater degree of freedom on the part of the local bodies and also on resource augmentation measures including use of land. At the same time, it should be kept in view that the level and per capita cost of various services is much higher in larger cities, thus requiring larger investment support. The issue of equity will also be an important consideration for SFC. The equity issue has to be dealt with both in terms of balancing the revenue and expenditure of the local government derived from the allocation of specific functions and also the need for greater support for financially weak local government institutions, either urban or rural. While various dimensions of the equity can be studied from the working of the various National Finance Commissions including the 10th National Finance Commission, I feel that the balancing of the twin objectives of efficiency and equity would be more complex in case of SFC. Even lack of basic information like per capita income, level of services, cost norms at district and sub-district level would pose a challenge to the SIC in working out recommendations regarding share of taxes and criteria of grant-in-aid on an objective basis.

c) Traditionally, the regular functions of most of the urban local bodies have been limited to maintenance of various civic services and on the capital side, there has been very limited direct participation of municipalities from its own sources. In case of panchayats, in the recent past there has boon a significant transfer of development functions (Plan expenditure). The operation of Jawahar Rozgar Yojana through panchayats is the most significant example in this regard. This function raises a very basic issue whether the SFC should deal with both Plan and non-Plan or restrict itself to the non-Plan (revenue expenditure).

Realising the importance of the task before the SFC, which should help in achieving the final objective of ushering in a strong local government structure, I would urge the participants to have free and frank discussions on all the basic, conceptual and operational issues of significance. I am indeed happy to see that this initiative in bringing together Chairmen and Members of the State Finance Commissions, other concerned agencies and ministries and the experts on the subject to deliberate on the formidable task of ushering a healthy State-local government fiscal relationship, has come at the most opportune time. We should seize this opportunity not only to clarify the conceptual basis but also to prepare grounds for the working of the SFCs on a systematic and uniform basis. While each SFC has to deal with specific situations and priorities, I strongly underline the need for developing a common information system, and a set of indicators before the details are worked out by each SFC.

I would once again express my gratitude to K.C. Pant, Chairman of the Tenth Finance Commission in agreeing to give the inaugural address and I am sure it will :;et the tone for discussions at this National Meet. I would also like to record my high appreciation for the spontaneous cooperation we have received from the concerned Central Ministries, State Governments and also various National institutions.

I wish for the most interesting and productive outcome in the two days deliberations on this important national subject.

GENERAL

GENERAL

INAUGURAL ADDRESS AT THE RURAL PROJECT OF THAKUR HARI PRASAD INSTITUTE OF RESEARCH AND REHABILITATION FOR THE MENTALLY HANDICAPPED

All over the world, there are millions of fellow citizens with mental handicap. They live in every society of every country. It is a global challenge. According to W.H.O. estimate and other available information, around 2 to 3 per cent of our population are mentally handicapped. It means about 20 million people come under this category. The number may grow with population increase. They suffer for want of adequate services and support. It is compounded due to lack of knowledge and awareness.

Of all the disabilities, the mentally retarded is probably the most handicapped one for they fail to adapt to the setting in which they live. Unlike the physically handicapped, the mentally retarded individuals are unaware and ignorant of their on cognitive condition and hence need special attention from all sides.

In India, the institutional facilities for the mentally handicapped are grossly inadequate. Even out of the existing 200 institutions. 90 per cent cater to the urban per cent areas and the remaining 10 per cent to the rural areas. Paradoxically, 80 per cent of the mentally handicap are from rural areas. This means, 90 per cent of the facilities are catering to the 20 per cent of the disabled in urban areas and only 10 per cent of the facilities are thinly spread to serve the 80 per cent of the mentally handicapped. Therefore, there is every need to set up and extend facilities to the rural areas on priority basis. And, in this context, the efforts by the Government should be supplemented by dedicated, voluntary organisations to tackle this massive human problem.

The Thakur Hari Prasad Institute of Research and Rehabilitation for the Mentally Handicapped is one of the outstanding voluntary organisations in this country which is offering dedicated services to the mentally handicapped through its professionally managed rehabilitation and research programmes. Having etched out a place of pride in voluntary social action in the field of mentally handicapped in urban areas so far, it is now extending its reach to the rural areas through setting up of a Centre at Rajamundry. I must congratulate Shri Thakur Hari Prasad for his yeoman services for the cause of the mentally handicapped and now for establishing this centre at Rajamundry.

The problem of the mentally handicapped is enormous: in the rural areas. Facilities to identify disabilities at an early stage and provide services for early intervention to reduce the disability are very meagre; are almost nil in the rural areas. To compound this problem, we have misconceptions and superstitious beliefs which are becoming major stumbling blocks to the rehabilitation scenario. It is said that the cost of launching a suitable programme for the mentally handicapped is very expensive. In addition, there is scarcity of trained manpower in this area. It is in this context the idea of low cost programme aimed at the large majority of the mentally handicapped is the need of the hour. The programme anticipates the involvement of non-professionals and vast human resources development; the rich, the nonrich, to provide the minimum care. Involving such a vast human resource leads to demystification of the technical know-how of the training of the mentally handicapped in order to take the technique to the door steps of the needy. It results in empowering the parents, the family members and the community with knowledge and know-how of mentally handicapped. This community based programme relies on generating maximum community participation and in making the community ultimately responsible for running the programme so that it becomes self-reliant and a propelling force. I am happy to note that the Centre essentially concentrates on developing a model community based programme with inbuilt research component.

I take this opportunity to congratulate Shri Thakur Hari Prasad for such an innovative approach for solving the problems of the mentally handicapped in rural areas.

I take pleasure in inaugurating the Centre and wish it all success.

Presidential Address On "Life And Message Of Swami Vivekananda"

It is a great privilege for me to be with you this evening at the anniversary day public meeting being organised by the Ramakrishna Mission, New Delhi. The subject for the meeting is "Life and Message of Swami Vivekananda". I am grateful to Swami Gokulanandhaji for inviting me to preside it is heartening to note that in Ramakrishna Mission, founded by Swami Vivekananda, monks and laymen cooperate in various service activities for the poor and in spreading the message of Sri Ramakrishna and Vedanta as interpreted by Swamiji. The Ramakrishna Mission has amply fulfilled the ideals and vision of Swami Vivekananda through its dedicated and selfless services.

Swami Vivekananda lived for thirty nine and a half years of fruitful life (born on 12th January 1863 and died on 14th July 1902). We wish he lived longer so that he could have further guided the humanity towards enlightenment and peaceful co-existence. Swami Vivekananda is not merely a historical figure, not merely a symbol of the past, but a living power working for the good of mankind. His life had been full of message. He was the foremost disciple of Sri Ramakrishna, and a spiritual teacher of the East and the West. He was a patriot saint of modern India combining in himself the fiery national spirit of a patriot and the spirituality of a saint. He made Indians to take pride in their past. He combined in himself the ancient and the modern, the East and the West, the sacred and the secular. In Swami Vivekananda, one could see the synthesis and the harmony of all the human energy and a torch-bearership for harmony of all religions of the world.

Born with a yogic temperament, Swamiji used to practice meditation even from his boyhood. At the threshold of youth he had to pass through a period of spiritual crisis when he was faced with the inner conflict about the existence of God. It was at this time that he first met Sri Ramakrishna, a Prophet of the modern age. This event may be said to symbolise the meeting of the ancient world and the modern world, and the dialogue between the East and the West as Sri Ramakrishna represented the ancient India and Vivekananda represented the modern world.

He extensively travelled all over India. These travels gave him first hand knowledge about the socio-economic condition of the people and the cultural and historic forces present in society. He was deeply moved at the utter poverty and backwardness of the masses. He believed that the degradation of India took place because the life giving principles of Vedanta had not been applied in practical life to solve social and national problems and because of the poor masses had been denied access to these enlightenment principles. Swami Vivekananda saw the necessity of spreading both spiritual knowledge and secular knowledge among the masses. He wanted a mass awakening effect through an intensive educational programme. He was the first great religious leader in India to focus the attention of the people on the plight, of the masses, to formulate and define the philosophy of service, and to organise large scale social service and relief operations in the country.

He strongly believed that the cultural exchange between India and the West in relation to spiritual wealth of India and the western science and technology was vitally necessary for India's socio-economic development as he believed that, the nation's isolation from the world culture at that time was one of the causes of our down fall. He contributed remarkably well in this aspect.

Swami Vivekananda attended the World Parliament of Religion-, held in Chicago in September 1893 and made historical speeches. The spectacular effects of Swamiji's participation and addresses at the Parliament of Religions are: (1) the West realised that India possessed great spiritual wealth which in turn led to the ending of India's cultural isolation; (2) Swamiji's addresses gave Hinduism a sense of unity and identity which it had lacked; (3) it provided a clear understanding of and a strong foundation for harmony of religions; (4) His definition of religion as direct self-realisation and manifestation of man's innate divinity gave western people a totally new concept of religion, as Sister Nivedita had put it; (5) His appearance at the world Parliament of Religions marked the beginning of his life as a world teacher.

One of the great achievements of Swami Vivekananda was meeting the challenges posed by modern science and social thought. He showed that religion too, like science was based on certain universal and eternal truth which could be tested and verified through direct experience. He also showed that both science and religion have the same ultimate goal namely to find the foundational unity of the universe.

Swami Vivekananda attempted to develop a new system of ethics based on the intrinsic purity, freedom, immortality and unity of the self which constituted a very important contribution to moral philosophy. This can bring in a new social order based on love, equality and service if applied in practical life. His principle of harmony of religions and his formulation of universal religion as the sum total of all the existing religions, with each religion accepting the best elements of other religions, assumed great importance as a means of establishing peace and goodwill among the people and nations. India has ha-1., from time immemorial, a strong sense of cultural unity. Swami Vivekananda revealed the true foundations of this culture and thus clearly defined and strengthened the sense of unity of India as a nation.

The new social order which Swami Vivekananda envisaged has got more relevance in the present day context. The present situation around us is quite alarming, because of violence, hatred, mistrust, growing divisive forces, narrow parochialism, separatist tendencies, considerable fall in moral, social, ethical and national values both in personal and public life. Materialistic outlook is manifest in almost every dimension of man's life style and day-to-day living. Materialism has become a major force influencing his conduct and behaviour. It is shaping his character and personality and even determining his life's goal. Human dignity and self-respect founded on good character and integrity are overtaken by arrogance, conceit, hypocrisy and artificial postures. The erosion of character is noticed in social and national life. Personal ethics and moral responsibility towards society have become meaningless where there is dominance of self-interest above everything.

Advancement in science and technology certainly improved the materialistic quality of life of people. But it has also shown the way for destruction. There is a massive build up of deadly weapons in the world which can destroy the world many times over. Peaceful coexistence seems to be difficult. International relations seemed to be based not on humanitarian considerations but on power domination and political expediency. The total scenario in the world, even in the 21st, century, in terms of the need for man's balanced frame of mind and the need for good relations between nations for peaceful co-existence, in all probability, may remain the same unless some serious and sincere efforts are made to rectify the situation. The present and the future generations are to be helped to reorient themselves to be imbued with strong commitment to moral, ethical, spiritual and human values if we want to see peaceful world order. This could be achieved by upholding the value system through education and through realising the new social order advocated by Swami Vivekananda.

Mahatma Gandhi attached the greatest importance to the inclusion of moral and religious education in the curricula of schools and colleges. According to him the chief goal of education was "character building". He said "Put all your knowledge, learning and scholarship in one scale and truth and purity in the other, the latter will, by far, outweigh the other". He desired that the essential principles underlying different religions should be imparted to the students as a part of their academic courses. Such a study would help the younger generation to imbibe Sarva Dharma Samanathwa or equal respect for all religions. This kind of religious tolerance and reverence is needed for establishing true secularism in our country. Swami Vivekananda' principle of harmony of religion, could also lead to this. It would be correct to say that in the absence of proper ethical values and an atmosphere of religious tolerance, it would not be possible to make India a truly secular state in accordance with the spirit, of our Constitution.

The need for launching a programme of value orientation of education has assumed great urgency in the above context. Realising this urgent need for implementation of this important programme, the Planning Commission, as the highest policy and planning organisation in the country, appointed a Core Group on Value Orientation of Education. The Core Group submitted its report which contains, concrete plan of action for implementation of the value orientation of education at all levels from school level to the university level. Based on the recommendations of the Core Group a Standing Committee on Value Orientation of Education has been constituted by the Ministry of Human Resource—Development under my chairmanship. I feel that in addition to the deliberations of the Standing Committee, we need valuable suggestions from expert and organisations like the Ramakrishna Mission who are practitioners of value orientation of education in the country so that we will have sound programmes formulated and implemented. We are looking forward for fruitful interaction with Ramakrishna Mission in the area of value orientation of education.

Speech As A Special Guest Of Honour At The 15TH India— NRI World Convention

Dear Friends,

It gives me immense pleasure to address this India—NRI World Convention. I am grateful for being invited to address this august gathering. I take this opportunity to highlight India's policies and perspectives on foreign investment under the New Economic Policy regime.

Until recently, India's policy towards foreign investment was somewhat conservative. This was in keeping with her overall economic policy framework, which emphasised inward-oriented, import-substituting industrialisation strategy. Development experience across the globe suggested that under such a policy regime, a liberal foreign investment policy did not necessarily benefit the host country. More often than not, in a highly protected economy, a freer foreign investment policy helped foreign investors to exploit the sheltered domestic market without necessarily leading to technological upgradation and modernisation of the host country. It was, therefore, natural that India followed an extremely selective policy towards foreign investment and made technology transfer almost a precondition for foreign equity participation.

Judged by the then prevailing consensus on development economics across the World, the inward-oriented development strategy was considered appropriate especially for a large country like India with a sizeable domestic market. It is not just coincidence that almost all development economists including most Western experts did endorse the Indian Model of development as the most ideal one for a less developed country with a large domestic market. The strategy and the policy framework did yield considerable positive results in the three decades following Independence. Key achievements—of the strategy were the development of a highly diversified industrial structure, rapid growth in agriculture, self-sufficiency in food and above all a substantial reduction in poverty. Judged by any standards, these were no mean achievements.

In retrospect, the development strategy that India followed worked reasonably well until about the early 1970s. However, starting with the break-down of the Brettonwoods system and the two oil shocks in the 1970s, the international economic environment underwent almost continuous changes in the subsequent decade. Coinciding with these developments, the Indian industrial sector which until about the early 1970s compared favourably with the rest of the World started flagging in terms of technology and competitiveness.

By about the mid-1970s, the technological gap between domestic industry and the international economy started widening thus posing constraints on rapid progress. Therefore, ever since the late 1970s it was increasingly realised that many of the State controls and regulations on economic activities have outlived their utility and were in fact hampering rather than helping growth and development. By around the same time, a number of official committees had further confirmed these early apprehensions. Prompted by these emerging events, the Government has been attempting to move the policy regime towards greater outward orientation and openness since the early 1980s. The New Economic Policy initiated in July, 1991 is in a way a continuation of these early efforts. However, the policy changes initiated this time have been bolder and swifter than the earlier attempts at cautious opening up.

With the recent policy reforms, our perception of the role of foreign investment in the industrialisation of the country has undergone a sea change. Our apprehensions of the foreign investors exploiting domestic industry have now become a thing of the past. We now welcome foreign investment, both direct and portfolio, in-virtually all sectors of the economy. I do not intend to enlist the details of the various policy changes initiated over the last two years. I am sure most of you are already well informed of these changes. Suffice it to mention at this stage that we now view foreign investors especially NRIs and persons of Indian origin as partners in India's development. I am convinced, as are the people of India, that India's future is inextricably linked to your active participation in our efforts at rebuilding

India. I am sure, you will endeavour to build an economically strong India in the same manner you have struggled to preserve the Indian identity and promote Indian culture in the alien lands.

I am happy to note that you have already responded very positively to our initiatives at domestic deregulation and external opening up. In the last three years since August 1991, approvals of foreign direct investment in the form of equity have been of the order of about $5 billion. Though the actual inflow has been relatively small at about $ 1.5 billion, it is significant that much of it is accounted for by NRI investment. The amount of NRI investment in India may not be as impressive as that of expatriate Chinese investment in China, but I am sure that this is only a beginning and hope to see much larger inflows in the years to come. Perhaps, some misconceptions about India stand in the way of much larger inflows of NRI investment. I take this opportunity to clear some of these doubts and apprehensions that you may have.

First of all, I like to take this opportunity to reassure you that the reform process initiated over the years is almost as irreversible as time. It can only move forward. Our plan of action on the policy front detailed in the Eighth Plan document should remove any residual fears that you may have on the reversibility of economic reforms. As the Plan document articulates, in the next few years, India would substantially reduce barriers to trade, both tariff and non-tariff, deregulate the domestic economy, reform and strengthen the financial sector and allow much larger role for private sector in managing the affairs of the economy. The Government's role would basically be focussed on providing internationally comparable infrastructure, development of human resources and strengthening of institutions required for the efficient functioning of a market economy.

Secondly, I would like to assure you that your investment in India is as safe as anywhere in the world. India has never defaulted in repayment or repatriation of capital or on the payment of interest and dividend. Foreign financial institutions would testify to India's credibility on this score.

It is not an accident that foreign corporate investors are not waiting for the international credit rating agencies to revise India's rating before investing in India. If you scan the Indian financial newspapers, you will find daily announcements of one foreign company or the other coming in with investment proposals. Even the Moody's has lately revised India's credit rating upwards. Standard & Poor should do the same any time now.

Thirdly, a major concern of foreign investors & NRIs intending to come to India is the prospect of facing bureaucratic procedures and delays in getting investment proposals approved and obtaining various clearances. With deregulation of economic activity many of these problems have been eliminated. Foreign investment proposals through the automatic approval route are cleared within two weeks. Proposals which are not covered by the automatic route are cleared by the Foreign Investment Promotion Board generally within a month; in exceptional cases it may take a maximum of forty-five days. For obtaining various clearances, a single-window facility is available in many States in the country. However, there may be scope for further streamlining the procedures. I can assure you that the Government of India would be very receptive to your suggestions on approval procedures.

Fourthly, India offers a highly profitable industrial environment. A recent study conducted by the ICICI based on 565 companies assisted by it for which audited results for 1993-94 are available, suggests that the corporate sector has done very well in terms of profitability, notwithstanding the industrial recession. Half-yearly results of most companies during 1994-95 show that the same upward trend continues. I do hear concerns about India's corporate tax rate being somewhat higher than that in some of the other developing countries. The Indian Government is aware of this concern. We are in the process of reforming the country's tax system. As you are aware, some of the recommendations of the Chelliah Committee have already been implemented. A reduction of the corporate tax rate to internationally comparable level is a part of the Government's tax reform programme in the next few years.

Fifthly, possibilities of political instability have been mentioned in certain quarters as a barrier to sustained flow of foreign, including NRI, investment. In this context, I need only to point out that India has been and continues to be the largest and perhaps the most vibrant democracy in the World. Political parties may come and go as has happened earlier. But the democratic institutions and traditions which have been so assiduously built and nurtured over the years have withstood the test of time. In a system such as ours, different views on important issues are but natural. There is, however, no logical conclusion that these imply instability of purpose. The broad agenda on policies is always formulated on the basis of nationwide debate and consensus. Nothing else can perhaps better ensure continuity of policies and programmes than such a consensual approach.

Sixthly, prospective investors in India sometimes seem to be apprehensive about the infrastructural facilities in the country. The Government recognises the critical importance of infrastructure inputs like power, transportation and telecommunications for attracting foreign investment. The Eighth Plan Document has emphasised that energy, transport and communication which have traditionally been in the public sector would be opened up to the private sector investment. The goals of the energy sector envisage elimination of power shortages in different parts of the country, achievement of a minimum hydel share of 40% in the total installed capacity, adoption of a conservation approach towards use of petroleum products without compromising on the needs of growth, stepping up the levels of output of coal and lignite and promotion of cost-effective technologies for the development of nonconventional energy resources. In the transport sector, the goals include strengthening of the road network, entry of private sector in road transport, stepping up the pace of electrification of railways and creation of adequate air cargo and shipping capacity. A beginning has already been made for setting up a few power projects in the private sector. The plans to privatise various telecommunication services are also in advanced stages of implementation.

The Government has also initiated important schemes to develop industrial infrastructure facilities in selected centres in the country. One such scheme relates to setting up of industrial parks for export production. We are looking forward to foreign investment in these industrial parks in order to create infrastructure of international standards. I am sure these efforts would enable India to upgrade its infrastructure capabilities in a big way. The Government is aware that foreign investment especially NRI investment can provide a critical supplement to resources and technology in all the infrastructure sectors. NRI investors have a tremendous opportunity to invest in these sectors and profit from it.

I hope that these clarifications will dispel some of the apprehensions and concerns of the NRIs and other investors in India. For those who are still hesitant, I would like to mention some of the more positive aspects of investing in India. Take for example, the vast domestic market and the opportunities it presents.

India is the third largest economy in Asia and the twelfth largest in the world in terms of the size of GDP. In addition, India has a high savings rate, a well-developed financial sector, abundant raw materials, and above all relatively inexpensive but highly trained manpower. Today there is a middle and higher income class of over 250 million people with an increasing appetite for consumer goods and up-market services and an emerging rural market of over 400 million people. Both these groups have immense and increasing purchasing power. It is estimated that about 10% of India's national income is spent on durable consumer goods. This means that at present the size of the durable consumer goods market alone is of the order of $25 billion annually. What is more important, the future growth potential of this market is tremendous. There are not many other countries which can offer such opportunities for growth and prosperity.

In terms of manpower, India has a large reserve of over 20 million scientificallyqualified and technically skilled work force, the third largest in the world. Although our literacy rate is still around 50 per cent, our 400 million literates constitute more than the combined population of USA and Japan. We have a network of technical and management institutes of the highest standards for the development of human resource. In addition, India has a large pool of highly educated entrepreneurs. Complementing these, we have a large labour force with one of the lowest unit costs of labour and consequently one of the cheapest manufacturing bases in the world. It is some of these positive features of India that attracted many multinationals including companies such as Unilever, GEC, ICI, Glaxo, Nestle, Matsushita etc. even in the old regime of highly inward-oriented economic policies. At present there are approximately 300 foreign joint ventures in the country. Recently, Ford, IBM, General Motors, Kellogs, Peugot, Mitachi, BMW, Motorola, Alcatel, Alsthom & Castrol etc. have signed agreements and more are expected as India liberalises. Not many developing countries possess a stock market as developed as India's. With over 6,500 companies listed on more than 20 stock exchanges and an investor base of 20 million plus and which is growing, the Indian stock market provides an increasingly attractive conduit for investment. The Indian Stock market now operates within a system of laws and regulations designed to provide investor safety and liquidity through clearly articulated ground rules. Three statutes govern the stock market operations. The Companies Act deals with issue, allotment and transfer of securities and various aspects relating to company management. The Securities Contracts (Regulations) Act deals with the procedure for recognition of Stock Exchanges, their management and their powers to make rules, bylaws and provisions relating to listing of securities. The Securities and Exchange Board of India (SEBI) has replaced the erstwhile Controller of Capital Issues through an Act of Parliament in 1992. Following this enactment, pricing of primary issues which were earlier administered by the Government has been freed.

The ambit of stock market operations has been further widened with the setting up of Over the Counter Exchange of India (OTCEI) & the National Stock Exchange (NSE). OTCEI is a national, automated screen-based market catering to small companies and companies assisted by venture capitalists who intend to raise finance from the market in a cost-effective manner. OTCEI is also an institution which is meant to provide a convenient, efficient and transparent avenue for investors at large. A larger screen based NSE has already started dealing in debt instruments at Bombay. Trading in equity is scheduled to start from next month. With NSE becoming operational, accessibility to market information will become easier and transactions more transparent than in the existing ring-oriented exchanges will become possible.

All in all, with the economic reforms of recent years, the old distinctions between productions for the domestic market and for exports, between purchase of domestic and foreign goods, between domestic and foreign companies and between domestic and foreign capital are fast vanishing. India is truly becoming an integral part of the global economy. I think this is the right time for you to join in this process of India's globalisation. I hope you too would feel the same. Before I conclude, I take this opportunity to extend to you a hearty welcome to India. I am sure you will find for yourself the sort of economic environment that we have created and the new opportunities that are awaiting.

Once again, I would like to express my gratitude to the organisers of this historical convention for inviting me to speak.

SPEECH DELIVERED AT THE TYAGARAJA ARADHANA FESTIVAL ORGANISED BY SREE SHANMUKHANANDA SANGEETHA SABHA, DELHI

Endaro Mahanubhavulu! Andariki Vandanamulu!

From time immemorial, music in our country has been cultivated as an effective accessory of religious and spiritual pursuit. Its role as a 'sadhana' for 'bhakti' has been exemplified by the lives and practices of bhaktas and men of self-realisation. Saint Tyagaraja was the foremost composer of Carnatic music in the seminal form of Kritis or Kirtanas blending with religious devotion. Tyagaraja was born in May, 1767 at Tiruvarur, a great centre of Siva worship and music. It is said that Tyagaraja was named after the presiding deity 'Tyagaraja' of Tiruvarur.

A kriti of Tyagaraja is always sung only to the Prince of Ayodhya, who was the incarnate Lord, the complete Avtar, the Supreme Being. Each kriti is a recordation of all the nine rasas and bhakti the ultimate rasa. Rama Bhakti and Rama Nama were in the very blood of Tyagaraja and that Rama and Rama Nama formed his heirloom, was mentioned by Tyagaraja in a number of his songs. He pays obeisance to different deities and sages in the songs set in the appropriate ragas.

Saint Tyagaraja's compositions numbering about six hundred embody in the fullest measure the unity of music, spiritual fervour and splendourous poetic utterance. One of the group of five long compositions called the Pancharatnas, the one in Sri Raga 'Endaro Mahanubhavulu' is said to have been composed when the Kerala musician Shatkala Govinda Marar called on Tyagaraja. The song, a natural expression of respect, is an omnibus obeisance paid to all the blessed souls, sages, devotees and scholars and experts in the arts.

While Rama remained his 'favourite deity' (Ishtadevata), Tyagaraja was free from sectarian feelings. Tyagaraja sang of Siva or Vishnu in different manifestations and of Devi and Kumara with the same fervour and in the same terms as he used in his addresses and appeals to Rama. This religious liberalism, if we can say so, is a heritage coming down from the henotheism of the Rigveda and flows as a natural outcome of the Upanishadic doctrine of the One Supreme Impersonal Brahman taking man; personal forms for blessing the seekers. Apart from demonstrating this urbanity of worship by these songs on different forms of Divinity, Tyagaraja expressly states that his devotion and adoration of Rama was free from any invidious distinctions as to the superiority of one faith over the other i.e., mata-bheda. He condemns those who waste their time in disputation about the different faiths.

Several songs of Sri Tyagaraja are completely in Sanskrit and in his two plays Naukacharitram and Prahlada Bhakt Vijayam, he has composed a few Sanskrit slokas too. All hi Telugu songs are replete with Sanskrit expressions. If one is to discourse on Bhakti, as performers of Harikatha do, there area better handy and apt texts than these songs of Tyagaraja. In fact, the use of Tyagaraja Kritis in such contexts, as the Harikatha affords, brings out their dual excellence, the meaning and the music and the further excellence in several cases of the mutual appropriateness of the two.

According to the tradition to which he belonged, Saint Tyagaraja entered in his last days the Fourth Ashrama of Sanyasa and later attained Mahasamadhi on 6th January, 1847.The celebration in honour of this day, the 'Aradhana' as it is called in the case of Sanyasins, is a great occasion for musicians and lovers of music to gather at the spot of his internment on the banks of the Kaveri at Tiruvayyaru to pay their tributes to that great poet-composer Tyagaraja who made a long lasting contribution to Telugu literature, Carnatic music and Indian culture.

I am happy that Sree Shanmukhananda Sangeetha Sabha, New Delhi is organising the Tyagaraja Aradhana Festival for the last four days. Today Radha Venkatachalam and Madurai T.N. Seshagopalan are offering their music concerts, which is a befitting tribute to that great Saint Tyagaraja. I would like to offer my felicitations to all the artists on this occasion. I would also like to take this opportunity to thank the organisers for providing me this wonderful opportunity.

INTEGRATION OF THE AGED INTO THE DEVELOPMENT PROCESS IN INDIA

INTRODUCTION

The term aged, elderly or senior citizens which is used to describe a section of human population, usually refers to a particular group of persons who have either reached a certain chronological age or have involuntarily withdrawn from employment or business. As such there exists no precise definition of the aged. However, based on a combination of age and incapacity to work criteria, the aged may be regarded as those who are in the age group of 60+ and or have retired from employment or disengaged from business after having had their innings. Traditionally, the aged enjoyed place of honour and respect in the family and community and were treated as repositories of experience, skill and wisdom. With the breaking up of joint family system, changes in the family size from large to small, the individual and secular trends are appearing in Indian society also. As a result, the aged as a group, have become socially vulnerable and need intimate attention of the society.

The aging of population is a world wide but recent phenomenon. The advancement in physical and medical sciences, economic development, rapid expansion of public health services alongwith social welfare and social security measures have resulted in increase of life expectancy. It has brought about a demographic transition leading to sharp increase in the population of the aged. This phenomenon was first experienced in the more developed countries and is now being witnessed in the developing countries also. This increased aged population should be viewed as a resource and its potential could be exploited for economicdevelopment of the nation.

GROWTH OF AGED POPULATION

In tune with the trends obtaining world over, the population of the aged in India has also been increasing at a faster rate during the last four and a half decades. The population of the aged, recorded as 20.19 million in the 1951 census, has escalated to 54.68 million in 1991 and is projected to increase further to 75.70 million by 2001. The decadel growth of 10.47 million between 1971 and 1981 and that of 11.51 million between 1981 and 1991 census is highly significant both in terms of numbers and rate of growth. The projected decadal growth for 1990s of 21.01 million and rate of growth of 38.42 percent will further aggravate the scenario of the population of the aged. The following table presents the growth of population of aged in India.

Table 1 Population of Person 60+ (India)

(Population in millions)

Year	No. of persons	%age to population	Decadal increase in population60+	
			No	Decadal rate of growth(%)
1951	20.190	5.66		
1961	24.712	5.63	4.522	22.40
1971	32.700	5.97	7.988	32.32
1981	43.172(a)	6.49	10.472	32.02
1991	54.685(b)	6.54	11.513	26.67
2001	75.696(b)	7.63	21.011	38.42

(a) Excluding Assam
(b) Projected

SOME INTERESTING FACTS

The National Sample Survey Organisation's (NSSO) survey of 42nd round, published in 1989, presented some interesting facts about the aged population in India which may be Seen in the following table.

Table (2) Facts About Aged

(In Percent)

	Rural	Urban
Persons in lakhs	394.51	87.35
Sex Ratio (No. of females per1000 males)	675	697
Economically independent	34.02	28.94
Living alone	7.99	5.94
Willing to move to the home for the aged	19.10	17.60
Having Chronic disease	45.00	44.80
Physically immobile	5.40	5.50
Gainfully employed	40.55	26.76

According to the NSSO, out of 482 lakhs elderly citizens (1989), 395 lakh were in rural areas and 87 lakh in urban centres. While about 41 percent of them were found to be working in rural India, only 27 percent of them were working in urban India indicating large section of the aged remaining unemployed and therefore dependent on others. The survey showed that 12 percent of aged males and a little over one percent of the aged females were living alone in rural India whereas about 10 percent and a little less than one percent of aged males and females respectively, were living alone in urban India. The survey also revealed that 44 to 47 aged males per 1000, reported physical immobility as against 67 to 68 aged females per 1000 and that the proportion of the aged persons with chronic diseases varied between 443 to 455 per 1000 at the national level. The tragic status of the aged is revealed by the fact that about 37 percent of the aged were willing to move to old age homes.

TRENDS

It would transpire from the above analysis that a significant feature of the Indian demographic scene of the post independence era has been the continuous increase in the number of the aged as also their proportion to the total population. This trend is likely to continue. The situation analysis of various aspects affecting the aged both in rural and urban areas also indicates their none too happy life in the declining years.

PROBLEMS OF THE AGED

The aged are by no means a homogenous group. Their needs and problems vary according to their age, family background, health, economic status, living environment etc. Those of the elderly who have all along been poor and whose families continue to be poor, constitute the most vulnerable section of the aged population. The women among them are in a worse condition than men. Similarly those in rural areas are worse off than those in urban areas. Further the needs and problems of the elderly also differ from those of other sections needing social services. While the children and women need physical protection, development inputs and social welfare measures, the aged suffer from multiple problems of economic, social and physiological nature. The loss of income and employment creates economic problems. Failing health and sickness, nutritional deficiencies and poor housing facilities affect their physiological and economic condition. The physio-social and environmental problems arise out of feelings of neglect, unwantedness, loneliness etc. Figure 1 summarises the problems of the aged.

AGED AS A RESOURCE

With the development of social services and a greater thrust on human resource development, the children, youth and women became the participants and targets of the development process. The aged continue to be neglected and are the recipients of only welfare services. The aged should not be viewed only as a problem but also as a precious resource which should be harnessed for promoting the economic and social development of the community. Considering the importance of the elderly in the Indian society and their past contributions, the family, community, government and the elderly themselves, should organise and plan services for the elderly.

An overwhelming majority of India's working force is engaged in the unorganised sector. Agriculture, small scale trade, commerce, handicrafts, road transportation and life long vocations like lawyers, doctors, chartered accountants and further down the ladder washermen, cobblers, potters and so on, all offer scope for continuing useful activity well into the later years, indicating absence of the concept of retirement in the unorganised sector. However, those serving in the organised sector, have to retire at a specific age irrespective of their health status and capacity to continue working. Retirement leads to inactivity and lack of involvement. The aged naturally feel cut down in size and cease to be economically productive. The aged and retired people, unless they are working, have plenty of free time which is utilized in odd jobs connected with household work and looking after children.

The most precious asset the aged possess is their vast reservoir of accumulated experience so long as their health and mental faculties do not deteriorate. They can make valuable contributions towards development and welfare of community. In fact, the skills and time of the aged is part of national asset which should not be allowed to remain dormant but utilised in the national development process.

While thinking about utilization of the expertise and energies of the elderly in the nation building endeavour, a distinction has to be made between the capable and needy aged. The retired elderly in the age group of 58-70 years and who are in sound physical and mental health, essentially form the target group whose skills and time could possibly be utilized. The aged among this group who are ready or could be motivated to give their expertise and experience and time, according to Pannu, may be called as `effective elderly'. It is necessary to devise ways and means to create an environment conducive for the optimal harnessing of energies and expertise of these effective elderly and use them as a resource for betterment of the society.

INTEGRATION OF THE AGED INTO THE DEVELOPMENT PROCESS

In order to integrate the aged into the development process, a **SENIOR CITIZENS MOVEMENT** needs to be started in an organised manner. The starting point could be the establishment of voluntary organisations of the aged in the form of their associations at the local level and apex bodies at the

SELECTED SPEECHES OF DR. D. SWAMINADHAN

city, district, state and national levels. Presently, there are a few associations of the aged in some cities, but no apex level organisation even at the city level. There is little coordination among the activities of associations of the aged even in the same city. In rural areas, there are hardly any voluntary organisations which can focus on the aged. There is need for building up of proper organisational base of effective elderly's movement. The existing organisations of the aged viz. Association of Senior Citizens, the Citizenship Development Society and Help Age India could jointly promote an apex national level organisation for starting Senior Citizens' movement and encourage local, city, region, state and national level organisations of the effective elderly with the objective of integrating them with the national development process. A systematic identification of effective elderlies in each locality with specialised skills and experience and with a sense of dedication and organising them may constitute the first step in this direction.

The aged, utilizing advantage of their rich and varied experience should take lead in organising themselves into groups through which they can participate in the nation building activities. Many among the elderly have provided leadership in the past. There is much that voluntary effort can do to motivate the untapped resources of the aged. Through their organisation, the aged could demonstrate what they could contribute towards the development and welfare of the community and what the community should do for them by highlighting the needs and problems and potentials of the aged. Some of the areas where the organisation of the elderlies could contribute meaningfully are specified below:

EDUCATION:

The National Literacy Mission has launched an ambitious programme of achieving functional literacy for all sections of the population. It has already achieved dramatic results in some parts of the country. The elderly, as individuals, in groups or their organisations can meaningfully involve themselves in attainment of this desirable objective of total literacy.

SOCIAL WELFARE:

The welfare schemes for children in need of care and protection, destitute women, handicapped and the aged etc. are being implemented by voluntary organisations. The elderly can play an effective role in providing linkage between the homes being run for these vulnerable sections and the neighbourhood. The senior citizens can identify persons in the local community to sponsor / adopt children from children homes. They can also help in assisting and organising street children. Similarly, running of old age homes, welfare of handicapped and destitute women, etc. are other areas of social welfare which could benefit from skills and energies of the elderly. The senior citizen could also assist in drug abuse prevention. They can identify drug addicts, counsel them and bring them round to counselling / de-addiction centres and create awareness in this regard.

HEALTH

The elderly could be involved in provision of medical services, particular in health and nutrition education. It is well known that primary health centres are under staffed, as the doctors and para-medical workers fight shy of rural assignments. The retired staff from semi urban areas could be very meaningfully re-employed in rural areas. They can also be helpful in taking up health education programmes such as advocating of immunisation of children and expectant mothers, nutrition and diet, sanitation etc. In some of the south East Asian countries, particularly in Thailand, organised groups of senior citizens are inducted as village health communicators and village health volunteers. They have proved highly effective in improving people's knowledge, attitudes and practices relating to primary health care and in implementation of health care programmes. In Thailand, Old Peoples Clubs are successfully demonstrating the value of complementary primary health care programmes.

RURAL DEVELOPMENT

The Council for Advancement of Peoples Action and Rural Technology (CAPART) helps the NGOs in the field of rural development. Installation of pumps, construction of low cost housing and sanitary latrines in rural areas are some of the activities which can be undertaken by the retired people particularly the technical personnel.

OTHER SERVICES

The service of pensioners like doctors, engineers, agriculturists and social scientists can be utilised for provision of medical service, agriculture extension work etc. The organisation of the aged could also organise common services like payment of electricity, water and telephone bills, shopping by elderly, taking patients to hospitals, old age homes, day care centres etc., for those who are too old to do these things for themselves. They could maintain liaison with civic and welfare authorities.

NATIONAL SENIOR CITIZENS SERVICE

In order to promote the utilisation of the skills, time and energy of the aged, a concerted effort has to be made. Mr. Pannu has suggested constitution of a National Senior Citizen Service (NSCS), which will provide opportunities for involvement of the effective elderlies from organised sector. The NSCS should be a decentralised areas-wise and discipline-wise services requiring pragmatic application. In this regard, a number of steps are required to be taken by the Central and State Governments which include:

(i) Identification of the problems and needs of the country which are capable of being addressed by the senior citizens
(ii) a separate Directorate could be established for utilisation of the skills of elderly in the Ministry of HRD to (a) quantify the number of effective elderly by discipline and area who could be included in the NSCS, (b) coordinate various plans of different Ministries, (c) create State-wise directorates to support and coordinate with the NGOs, social workers and retired personnel who wish to devote time for the cause of nation, (d) develop net-working of NGOs and promote new NGOs for the under developed regions.

The NSCS need not be a drain on national exchequer. It should consider various means of income generation and be self supporting by way of peoples' contribution and voluntary action with no monetary benefits. In essence, it really involves identification of national growth and development goals, assessment of national needs, their priorities and policy formulation for induction of senior citizens in the voluntary sector and in exercises of decentralised planning.

Conclusion

In view of the increase in the population of the aged and mounting expenditure on their welfare, it is all the more necessary that the aged involve themselves in voluntary services for the development of the nation. It would be in the interest of the aged themselves to involve them in a voluntary service mode to fill their time gainfully and arrest writing off of their skills, capacities and experience.

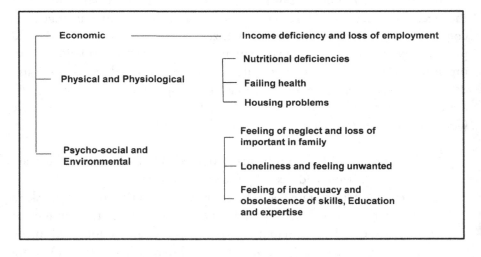

Fig: 1: Specific problems faced by the Aging

REFERENCES:

1. Dr. Paul Chaudhry D.1992. *Aging and the Aged*: Inter India Publications, New Delhi.
2. Maj. Gen. R. S. Pannu (Retd.).1994. *Utilisation of Skills and Time of the Aged:* Research and Development Journal, Helpage India, Vol. I No.1, Oct. 1994.
3. Mr. Pankaj Kumar Mandal.1995. *The Neglect of the Elderly:* The Economic Times: Oct 26, 1995.
4. George A. Attig and Krasae Chanawongse.1989. *Elderly People As Health Promoters*: World Health Forum, Vol.10, 1989.
5. Ms Gayatri Ramachandran.1995. *Help Them Age With Grace:* Saturday Times (Times of India Supplement) Oct. 28, 1995.
6. Yogendra Singh.1994. *Changing Trends in Indian Families and Adjustment of the Aged:* Research & Development Journal, Help Age India, Vol I, No.1, Oct., 1994.
7. Mr. Harish Chandra.1985. *Welfare of the Aged:* The Hindustan Time, Nov.20, 1985.
8. Mr. Harish Chandra.1986. *Retired? Do not Despair*: The Hindustan Times, April 1, 1986.
9. Vandana Majumda.1985. *End of the Road*: Sunday Magazine, Oct.6, 1985.

PLANNING

INAUGURAL AT THE
SEMINAR ON 'PLANNING IN
NINETIES AND BEYOND'

Shri Ramakrishnayya, President of today's function. Shri B. P. R. Vittal, participants of the Seminar, ladies and gentlemen,

It is indeed a great privilege for me to be with you this morning to inaugurate the Seminar on 'Planning in Nineties and Beyond' being organised by the Prakasam Institute of Development Studies as a part of the celebration of "Two Decades of Prakasam Institute of Development Studies". I am thankful to the organisers, for giving me this splendid opportunity.

The Planning process in India started in early 50s. Independent India wanted to build a modern, strong, dynamic and self-reliant nation which could stand abreast with the developed world. Pandit Jawaharlal Nehru, our first Prime Minister embarked on the path of planned economic development. Growth, modernisation, self-reliance and Social justice are the basic objectives governing Indian planning. India proved that democratic planning is not only desirable but feasible as well.

The process of planning developed with the successive five year plans and techniques of planning got refined. The initial plans were mainly a statement of objectives. The plan proper was a bill of expenditure on projects. The information base to link the deployment of resources with income generation at the macro-economic level was limited. Over time the techniques. For balancing the requirement of financial resources against their expected generation were evolved. Such balances were established also at the level of principal commodities—food, coal, electricity etc. The system of material and financial balances evolved during the Third and Fourth Five

Year Plans helped in planning for capacities in industrial and infrastructural sectors and in taking investment decisions. Later more comprehensive and economy-wide models, which could consider all sectors of economy, such as the input-output model, were introduced. This helped establishment of inter-sectoral consistency in plan projections. More recently, these models helped in linking sectoral investments with the sectoral targets.

The past four decades of planning has brought about creditable growth and development. Our agricultural economy is robust and resilient. We have a large pool of skilled manpower and ample entrepreneurial resources. We have built a diversified industrial structure that will hold us in good stead. There have been great achievements in the fields like Computers, Nuclear Power Plants. Oceanography, Space, Genetic Engineering and Biotechnology. Above all, life expectancy which was barely 32 years at the time of independence has gone up to 60 at the present.

As you are aware, we are launching the Eighth Five Year Plan in the backdrop of certain strengths in the economy as well as certain concerns which have surfaced over the recent years. The context of planning has also undergone a change in view of the emerging trends and also since certain bold initiatives have now been taken to reorient and restructure the economy. There are new perspectives about the role of planning and the efficacy of government sponsored actions for development and change.

The strength of the economy can be seen in the fact that now almost for a whole decade the economy has grown at the rate of 5.5% which should be considered as a reasonably good step-up over the performance of the previous three decades when the growth averaged at 3.5% per annum. This performance was accompanied with a perceptible rise in growth in the agricultural income, a significant increase in the rate of growth of per capita consumption and a decline in capital output ratio, resulting from better utilisation of capacities and improvement in operational efficiencies. The Sixth and Seventh Plans also paid particular attention to the strengthening and modernisation of infrastructure and provided more incentives to private sector investments.

The weakness of the situation is inherent in the fact that this growth was financed in a manner which was neither envisaged nor healthy for the economy. In spite of the advantage of a decline of the capital output ratio requiring somewhat a lower level of investment than was projected in the Plans, financing of the Plan became very difficult. Even this lower level of capital formation was financed by a much lower than the envisaged level of domestic savings and a much higher than the envisaged level of foreign savings, which is reflected in the gap in the current account of balance of payments. This gap in the current account added to external debt and debt servicing at a higher pace, raised the share of short term loans resulting in a funding problem and caused a severe depletion of foreign exchange reserves resulting in a crisis.

Internally also financing the public sector plan depended increasingly more on high cost borrowing and deficit financing. There has been a mounting burden of subsidies and interest payments on the non-plan side of the Government budget. The rate of inflation has been at a much higher level getting now into double digits.

In the recent past, a series of policy measures to revitalize the economy have been initiated. These include correction of fiscal imbalances, a downward adjustment of the external value of the rupee, the enlargement and liberalization of replenishment licensing system, the new industrial policy and various other development measures. These policies are expected to make a significant impact on fiscal health, export growth, prices and private initiative in industrial development.

In spite of the adverse economic situation, one cannot overlook the imperative of keeping up the pace of growth in order to generate adequate employment, alleviate poverty and meet the most essential needs. This calls for a reorientation in our approach to planning. The imperatives of growth in the face of the challenges outlined above demand an innovative approach to development which is based on a re-examination and reorientation of the role of the government, harnessing the latent energies of the people through people's involvement in the process of nation building, creating an environment which encourages and builds up people's initiatives rather than their dependence on the government and which sets free the forces of growth and modernisation. In addition, we have to strive to achieve targets with less financial outlays and to improve the efficiency of the system. The State has to play more of a facilitating role and has to concentrate on protecting the interests of the poor and the underprivileged.

The planners should work on building a long-term strategic vision of the future and decide on the priorities of the Nation. They should try to concentrate on anticipating future trends and evolve integrative strategies for achieving highest level of development of the country in keeping with the competitive international standards.

The role of the Planning Commission in this context will be Indicative. The endeavour will be to develop the Core Sector through allocation of funds, ensure growth of economy through policy package and give greater responsibility to the States for the development of social sector.

The Planning Commission will play an integrative role and help in the development of a holistic approach to the policy formulation in critical areas like Energy, Human Resources Development, Backward Areas Development, Management of Balance of Payment etc. Planning Commission will play a mediatory and facilitating role for managing the change smoothly and creating a culture of high productivity and efficiency in the Government.

In addition to the Resource Allocation Role, in the present environment of severe resource constraint, Planning Commission will also concern itself with the resource mobilisation for development as well as with the efficient utilisation of the funds.

The key to efficient utilisation of resources lies in the creation of appropriate selfmanaged organisations at all levels. In this area, Planning Commission will play Systems Change Role and provide internal consultancy for developing better systems. In order to multiply the gains of experience, Planning Commission will play an Information Dissemination Role also.

The approach to the Eighth Plan will have four-fold focus:

i. Clear prioritisation of sectors / projects for intensive investment in order to facilitate operationalisation and implementation of the policy initiatives taken in the areas of fiscal trade and industrial sectors and human development.

ii. Making available the resources for these priority sectors and to ensure effective utilisation of these resources.

iii. Creation of a social security net through employment generation, improved health care and provision of extensive education facilities throughout the country; and

iv. Creation of appropriate organisations and delivery systems to ensure that the benefits of investment in the social sectors reach the intended beneficiaries. While formulating the Plan we must ensure that:

   a) People's initiative and participation is made a key element in the process of development;

   b) We must plan for alleviation of poverty with emphasis on
      i) Population Control
      ii) Employment generation, and

iii) Provision of minimum needs of health care, literacy, drinking water, rural roads and rural energy.

For the Eighth Five Year Plan the following objectives will have the priority:

I.   For Economic Development
   (a) Energy
   (b) Transport
   (c) Communications

II. For Human Development
   (a) Employment Generation
   (b) Population Control
   (c) Literacy
   (d) Health including drinking water
   (e) Rural Electrification

III. For Agricultural Development
   (a) Irrigation, including intensive use of watershed management concept in rain-fed / drought-prone areas.
   (b) Export promotion of agricultural products.
   (c) Diversification of agriculture to horticulture and pesiculture, water management and wasteland development.

Our strategies to achieve these objectives will be:

I.   Resource Allocation to priority areas through
   (a) Central Plan Assistance
   (b) Resource mobilisation by the States
   (c) Private Sector participation
   (d) Raising resources through multilateral / bilateral funding and other fiscal instruments like bonds etc.

II. Human development through allocation of resources by creation of appropriate single window village / block / district level self-managing organisations.

We will also like to create a National grid of existing NGOs who are doing goon work in the field by recognising, encouraging and supporting the work being done by them. A network of trained and motivated experts / individuals who are willing to work in rural areas in honorary capacity will be set up.

A system of incentives / dis-incentives for achievement/ non-achievement of the agreed targets will be worked out.

Momentous changes are taking place in the world. The end of cold war, the transformations in Eastern Europe and the Soviet Union and the imminent emergence of a common market in Western Europe are events of truly historic significance. These changes will have a profound impact on both the structure of international relations and the world economy. Simultaneously, most developing countries have embarked on bold measures of reform in restructuring their economies and opening up to forces of competition, both domestic and foreign. The wave of economic reforms that is sweeping the developing world and the hitherto centrally planned economies has important implications for India in the 90's and perhaps, beyond.

I must congratulate the Prakasam Institute of Development Studies for organising this seminar at an appropriate time and I am sure that the outcome of the seminar will be valuable for the planners and the academicians and the others concerned. I take pleasure in inaugurating the seminar and wish it all success.

ANDHRA BANK ENDOWMENT LECTURE INDIA'S PLANNING IN NINETIES

Distinguished Vice-Chancellor Prof. Gopalakrishna Reddy, Head of the Department of Commerce and Management Studies Dr. Panduranga Rao, faculty members, students, invitees, ladies and gentlemen,

I consider it as a privilege for having been invited by the Andhra University to deliver the Andhra Bank Endowment. Lecture for this year in the Department of Commerce and Management Studies. I express my grateful thanks to the Vice-Chancellor, the Head and Faculty of the Department of Commerce and Management Studies and the Andhra Bank authorities for giving me this splendid opportunity. When Dr. Panduranga Rao and some of his fellow faculty members, during their visit to Delhi sometime during 1991, invited me to deliver the endowment lecture, I readily accepted, partly with a selfish motive of gaining an opportunity to visit this great University, which is my almamater. Subsequently, invitation for the endowment lecture was also extended by the former Vice-Chancellor, Prof. K. V. Ramana and graciously renewed by the present Vice-Chancellor, Prof. Gopalakrishna Reddy. I am personally grateful to them.

I am happy to note that the Andhra Bank has instituted an endowment lecture in the University. To my mind this is one of the finest examples of University and banking sector interaction. Only the other day, I have delivered an endowment lecture at Sri Venkateswara University on "Imperatives of University—Industry—R & D Organisation Interaction for National Development" and presented a model for effective interaction between those sectors. Interaction and interdependence are well recognised approaches in the present dayworld. The universities and various sectors of the economy should have effective interaction which will not only benefit mutually but also contribute towards national development. One should therefore encourage and appreciate the kind of interaction Andhra Bank and the Andhra University are having at present, the scope of which could be widened further.

Initially the topic suggested for the lecture was "Indian Economy—Challenges and Prospects". However, keeping in view the fact that I am not an expert in Economics, I decided to talk on "India's Planning in Nineties", as I may be justified and feel relatively more comfortable by virtue of my association with Planning Commission.

Independent India wanted to build a modern, strong, dynamic and self-reliant nation which could stand abreast with the developed countries. Pandit Jawaharlal Nehru, the architect of modern India and the first Prime Minister, embarked on the path of planned economic development. The Planning process in India thus started in early 50's. Growth, modernisation, self-reliance and social justice are the basic objectives governing Indian planning.

The Indian Planning, to quote Dr. Manmohan Singh from the Seventh Five Year Plan document ".... provides a framework of time and space that binds sectors, regions and States together and relates each year's effort to the succeeding years. By strengthening the social and economic fabric of the country as a whole and of the different regions and States, it makes a powerful contribution to the goal of national integration. The planning process has contributed a great deal to evolving a broad national consensus regarding the basic objectives, strategies and design of our development policies. This has helped to generate broad mass support for national economic policies which has added greatly to the cohesion and stability enjoyed by our polity."

Planning in our country is an instrument for achieving the nation's basic goals and objectives. The process of planning developed with the successive five year plans and techniques of planning got refined. The initial plans were mainly a statement of objectives. The plan proper was a bill of expenditure on projects. The information base to link the deployment of resources with income generation at the macro-economic level was limited. Over time the techniques for balancing the requirement of financial resources against their expected generation were evolved. Such balances were established also at the level of principal commodities—food, coal, electricity etc. The system of material and financial balances evolved during the Third and Fourth Five

Year Plans helped in planning for capacities in industrial and infrastructural sectors and in taking investment decisions. Later more comprehensive and economy-wide models, which could consider all sectors of economy, such as the input-output model, were introduced. This helped establishment of inter-sectoral consistency in plan projections. Until recently, these models helped in linking sectoral investments with the sectoral targets.

The past four decades of planning has brought about creditable growth and development. Our agricultural economy is robust and resilient. We have a large pool of skilled manpower and ample entrepreneurial resources. We have built a diversified industrial structure that will hold us in good stead. There have been great achievements in the fields like Computers, Nuclear Power Plants, Oceanography, Space, Genetic Engineering, Biotechnology and Agriculture. Above all, life expectancy which was barely 32 years at the time of independence has gone up to 58 years at the present.

Momentous changes are taking place across the world. The end of cold war, the transformations in Eastern Europe and the disintegration of the Soviet Union and the imminent emergence of a common market in Western Europe are events of truly historic significance. These changes will have a profound impact on both the structure of international relations and the world economy. Simultaneously, most developing countries have embarked on bold measures of reform in restructuring their economies and opening up to forces of competition, both domestic and foreign. The wave of economic reforms that is sweeping the developing world and the hitherto centrally planned economies has important implications for India in the 90's.

We are launching the Eighth Five Year Plan in the backdrop of certain strengths in the economy as well as certain concerns which have surfaced over the recent years. The context of planning has also undergone a change in view of the emerging trends and also since certain bold initiatives have now been taken to reorient and restructure the economy. There are new perspectives about the role of planning and the efficacy of government sponsored actions for development and change.

The strength of the economy can be seen in the fact that now almost for a whole decade the economy has grown at the rate of 5.5% which should be considered as a reasonably good step-up over the performance of the previous three decades when the growth averaged at 3.5% per annum. This performance was accompanied with a perceptible rise in growth in the agricultural income, a significant increase in the rate of growth of per capita consumption and a decline in capital output ratio, resulting from better utilisation of capacities and improvement in operational efficiencies. The

Sixth and Seventh Plans also paid particular attention to the strengthening and modernisation of infrastructure and provided more incentives to private sector investments.

The weakness of the situation is inherent in the fact that this growth was financed in a manner which was neither envisaged nor healthy for the economy. In spite of the advantage of a decline of the capital output ratio requiring somewhat a lower level of investment than was projected in the Plans, financing of the Plan became very difficult.

Even this lower level of capital formation was financed by a much lower than the envisaged level of domestic savings and a much higher than the envisaged level of foreign savings, which is reflected in the gap in the current account of balance of payments. This gap in the current account added to external debt and debt servicing at a higher pace, raised the share of short term loans resulting in a funding problem and caused a severe depletion of foreign exchange reserves resulting in a crisis.

Internally also financing the public sector plan depended increasingly more on high cost borrowing and deficit financing. There has been a mounting burden of subsidies and interest payments on the non-plan side of the Government budget. The rate of inflation has been at a much higher level getting now into double digits.

In the recent past, a series of policy measures to revitalize the economy have been initiated. These include correction of fiscal imbalances, a downward adjustment of the external value of the rupee, the enlargement and liberalization of replenishment licensing system, the new industrial and trade policies and various other development measures. These policies are expected to make a significant impact on fiscal health, export growth, and private initiative in industrial development. In line with the present thinking in economic policies, the priorities and processes of planning are also undergoing change.

In spite of the adverse economic situation in the country, one cannot overlook the imperative of keeping up the pace of growth in order to generate adequate employment, alleviate poverty and meet the most essential needs. This calls for a reorientation in our approach to planning. The imperatives of growth in the face of the challenges outlined above demand an innovative approach to development which is based on a re-examination andreorientation of the role of the government, harnessing the latent energies of the people through people's involvement in the process of nation building, creating an environment which encourages and builds up people's initiatives rather than their dependence on the government and which sets free the forces of growth and modernisation. In addition, we have to strive to achieve targets with less financial outlays through improved efficiency and productivity. The State has to play more of a facilitating role and has to concentrate on protecting the interests of the poor and the under-privileged.

The planning process should focus on building a long-term strategic vision of the future and decide on the priorities of the Nation. It should try to concentrate on anticipating future trends and evolve integrative strategies for achieving highest level of development of the country in keeping with the competitive international standards.

We are moving towards a system of Indicative—Planning. Indicative Planning is a way to promote rapid and orderly economic growth without coercion or bureaucracy, a way to reconcile the economic planning with decentralised decision making, private enterprise, democracy and efficiency. It provides direction for the growth of the economy by spelling out clear goals and providing help in reaching them. Indicative planning concentrates on orienting, regularising and accelerating development.

The role of the Planning Commission will now be Indicative. The endeavour will be to develop the Core Sector through allocation of funds, ensure growth of economy through policy package and give greater responsibility to the States for the development of social sector.

The Planning Commission will play an integrative role and help in the development of a holistic approach to the policy formulation in critical areas like Energy, Human Resource Development, Backward Areas Development, Management of Balance of Payment etc. It will play a mediatory and facilitating role for managing the change smoothly and creating a culture of high productivity and efficiency in the Government.

The key to efficient utilisation of resources lies in the creation of appropriate selfmanaged organisations at all levels. In this area, Planning Commission will play a Systems Change Role and provide internal consultancy for developing better systems. In order to multiply the gains of experience, Planning Commission will play an Information Dissemination Role also.

The Approach to the Eighth Plan will have four-fold focus:

i)   Clear prioritisation of sectors / projects for intensive investment in order to facilitate operationalisation and implementation of the policy initiatives taken in the areas of fiscal trade and industrial sectors and human development.

ii) Making available the resources for these priority sectors and to ensure effective utilisation of these resources.

iii) Creation of a social security net through employment generation, improved health care and provision of extensive education facilities throughout the country; and

iv) Creation of appropriate organisations and delivery systems to ensure that the benefits of investment in the social sectors reach the intended beneficiaries.

While formulating the Plan the following will be kept in view:

a) People's initiative and participation is made a key element in the process of development;

b) Plan for alleviation of poverty should have emphasis on
   i) Population Control
   ii) Employment generation, and
   iii) Provision of minimum needs of health care, literacy, drinking water, rural roads and rural energy.

For the Eighth Five Year Plan the following objectives will have the priority:

I. For Economic Development
   (a) Energy
   (b) Transport
   (c) Communications

II. For Human Development
   (a) Employment Generation
   (b) Population Control
   (c) Literacy
   (d) Health including drinking water
   (e) Rural Electrification

III. For Agricultural Development
   (a) Irrigation, including intensive use of watershed management concept in rainfed / drought-prone areas.
   (b) Export promotion of agricultural products.
   (c) Diversification of agriculture to horticulture and pesiculture, water management and wasteland development.

Strategies to achieve these objectives will be:

I. Resource Allocation to priority areas through:
    (a) Central Plan Assistance
    (b) Resource mobilisation by the States
    (c) Private Sector participation
    (d) Raising resources through multilateral / bilateral funding and other fiscal instruments like bonds etc.

II. Human development through allocation of resources by creation of appropriate single window village / block/ district level self-managing organisations.

The impact of our planning process is diluted due to two factors viz. (i) Population growth and (ii) Illiteracy. India is the second most populous country in the world. According to the 1991 Census of India, the population is 844 million. The population is expected to cross the one billion mark by the year 2000. Such an increase of population will have *very* serious social, economic and environmental consequences, undermining the progress made in development. A mass movement in Population Control can alone improve the situation.

The total literacy rate is 52. 11 % with literacy rate for males being 63.86% and that of females being 39.42%. Thus, there is still a large chunk of illiterates in the country. Development and literacy are inter-linked and a high rate of illiteracy is certainly a drag on the nation's growth and development. Literacy is not only an important factor in personnel development but also to realise the fruits of development process of a nation to the desired extent. In India the number of illiterates is going up in absolute terms due to increase in population. Population increase is outpacing our efforts at making the people literate. If we do not tackle the problem of illiteracy on a war footing, we will end up in having about 52% of the world's illiterates in India by the turn of the century. Such an enormous problem could only be tackled through, again, a mass movement with a spirit which could only be paralleled to that prevailed during the Independence movement. Eradication of illiteracy and population control are the biggest challenges to the India's Planning in 90's.

RURAL DEVELOPMENT

ADDRESS AT THE FOURTH NATIONAL WORKSHOP ON INTEGRATED RURAL ENERGY PROGRAMME IN EIGHTH PLAN

It is a great pleasure for me to be with you this evening at the Valedictory function of the Fourth National Workshop on Integrated Rural Energy Programme in Eighth Plan, being organised by the Planning Commission and the Government of Andhra Pradesh. I would like to offer my heartfelt thanks to the organisers for giving me this opportunity to deliver the Valedictory Address. I should congratulate the organisers for organising such an important Workshop at an appropriate time like this when we are finalising the Eighth Five Year Plan.

Free India wanted to develop into a modern, strong, vibrant and self-reliant nation so that it would be standing abreast of the developed nations of the world. Pandit Jawaharlal Nehru, the first Prime Minister and the architect of modern India, chose the path of planned economic development for the country during 1950s. Growth, modernisation, self-reliance and social justice are the basic objectives of the Indian planning.

During the past four decades of Indian planning, the country has achieved creditable growth and de velopment. Our agricultural economy is robust and resilient. We have a large pool of skilled manpower and ample entrepreneurial resources. We have built a diversified industrial structure that will hold us in good stead. There have been great achievements in the fields like Computers, Nuclear power plants, Oceanography, Space, Genetic

Engineering, Biotechnology and Agriculture, Energy Sector has its own share of achievements.

Dr. Abdus Salaam, a Nobel laureate, categorised the people of the world into two categories viz., the developed and the developing. Nearly one quarter of the world's population, inhabiting $2/5^{ths}$ of the land area control 80 per cent of the world's natural resources and they are termed as 'developed'. The remaining three quarters of the humanity, inhabiting $3/5^{ths}$ of the globe are termed as 'developing'. What distinguishes one category from the other is their differing mastery and utilisation of present day science and technology. Hence developing nations should pay more attention to create, master and utilise modern science and technology. Countries with predominant rural component should apply modern science and technology more in rural development activities. India falls into this category.

India being a country with 70 per cent of the population living in its villages, unless its efforts towards development have an impact on the rural sector, it cannot achieve real growth and development. Therefore, enough attention should be paid towards the programmes and schemes meant for rural development. In this context, Rural Energy Programme assumes greater significance as it has its inputs to all other sectors related to rural development. Careful planning with proper science and technology inputs should be the watchword in rural energy systems development.

The quality of life of the people, especially in rural areas, reflects the fruits of development and growth. Energy is one of the ingredients towards growth and development and relates to the level of the quality of the lives of the rural people. Even though impressive progress has been made on energy supply programmes and technologies including those for rural electrification and farm mechanisation, the spread of benefits among rural people has not been even. Rural areas continue to be starved of energy, because of both poor availability of commercial energy and also continued poor affordability of the rural people. In the above context, the Planning Commission took the initiative in designing and developing the Integrated Rural Energy Programme and is helping its implementation in coordination with the state governments and union territories, as a regular plan programme during the Seventh Plan period. The major focus of the programme has been to prepare and implement micro-level integrated rural energy plans, and projects with the 'Block' as the unit of planning, incorporating the diverse sources of energy, commercial and non-commercial and preference for locally available resources, to meet energy requirements for different income groups and their end-uses for agriculture and rural development. This programme envisages not only the provision of energy for meeting basic needs of the rural people, but also aims at generating local employment and promoting income generating activities, while at the same time attempting to maintain the ecological balance and preventing the environmental degradation of the rural areas. To facilitate this process, the necessary infrastructure at national, state, district and block levels for planning, implementation, training and R & D work, has been created under this programme during the Seventh Plan. The results of the studies, project reports and the experience in the planning and implementation in the field and subsequent follow-up action on this programme have given the required feed back on the need for reorienting and modifying the design and contents of the IREP programme in the Eighth Plan.

Taking into account the global economic scenario and the economic crisis in the country and the subsequent remedial measures taken by the Government through its policy initiatives to restructure and revitalise the economy, there are certain imperatives emerging in the approach to the Eighth Plan. They include—re-examination and re-orientation of the role of the government, harnessing the latent energies of the people through people's involvement in the process of nation building, creating an environment which encourages and builds up people's initiatives rather than their dependence on the government. The State has to play more of a facilitating role and has to concentrate in protecting the interests of the poor and the under-privileged. Some of the above concerned imperatives should reflect in the IREP programme during the Eighth Plan.

The areas that call for increased emphasis in IREP programme include improving linkages with agricultural and rural development sectors and increased attention to environmental problems and people's participation. Keeping in view the energy requirements in the immediate future, the IREP programme could play a significant role in enhancing agricultural production and thereby creating scope for employment generation while preventing environmental degradation. Similarly the IREP programme can become a powerful means for promoting rural industries and thus accelerate the process of decentralised development. The linkages would be possible only if IREP programme becomes a major peoples' programme in Eighth Plan, and for this purpose the intimate involvement of the proposed beneficiaries at all stages in the preparation and implementation of this programme has to be organised in the Eighth Plan.

India has been the pioneer in the field of renewable energy research and the first family size bio-gas plant was made in India in early 30's—and the first practical solar cooker was made in early 50's. Presently more than 25 research institutions, universities and IITs are engaged in basic and applied type of research in renewable energy. More than 110 private and public undertaking industries are involved in the fabrication and installation of various renewable energy devices. The Government of India has established a full fledged Department of Non-Conventional Energy Sources (DNES) where primary aim has been coordinating, funding and demonstration of activities in the field of renewable energy sources. Short term and the long term courses are offered to students in the field of renewable energy in a few Indian universities and IITs.

In rural India, the energy is normally derived from fuel wood, kerosene, agro-waste, animal dung and in some villages from electricity. The energy requirements are going to increase every year since the population is increasing and also the standard of living is improving even in rural India. Due to the heavy load on fuel wood the forests are disappearing very fast, resulting in land slides, soil erosion etc. Apart from this, burning of fossil fuels like coal, fuel wood, agro-wastes etc. has resulted in pollution of environment. The new and renewable sources of energy like solar energy, bibenergy etc. can supplement the energy requirements. The solar energy can be used for water heating, space heating, space cooling, cooking of food etc. The improved wood burning stoves which are now common in the country can help in reducing the consumption of fuel wood and also the pollution to the atmosphere. The use of gobar gas for cooking and lighting applications is quite well known in the rural areas of the country. All these energy sources thus help in conserving commercial sources of energy and meet the environmental condition.

While the concept of the integrated approach for rural energy seems to be elegant an unexceptionable, the problems really are in implementing this deceptively simple concept. A large number of departments and agencies are involved in the supply of energy to rural areas. These include electricity, fuel wood, new and renewable sources of energy, coal among others. The user Departments are Agriculture. Rural Development, Village and Small Industries, Department of Social Welfare, Women and Child Development and some others.

The various programmes of agriculture and rural development need some form of energy inputs. In some cases, like agriculture production activities, these inputs have to be provided for in a planned and specified time; for example electricity for irrigation or diesel for diesel pumps sets. In other cases various possibilities of energy supply are available. Cooking can be done by wood or kerosene or cow dung or by using bio-gas, solar cookers and even electricity. The choice of these different options is left to individuals depending on preferences and also at affordability.

In order to improve the energy efficiency, we need upgraded version of technology not only for utilising more efficiently the conventional sources of energy but also tapping the abundant other sources of energy. IREP Programme has, therefore, to coordinate not only energy demand with supply and for this purpose work out the linkages between end-use and supply options but also to provide linkages between technology development efforts in the laboratories and transfer them to the land.

Technology development and its utilisation should be the center piece of the IREP Programme, for which emphasis should be given in the Eighth Plan. For this purpose, we have to provide mechanisms for coordination with the R & D work going on in various universities as well as professional institutions of engineering and sciences, with the work being done in the Central and State Government energy agencies and their linkages with the field IREP projects. In the above context and in the context of the general resources crunch, there is greater need to forge strong linkages for interaction between universities, industries, R & D organisations and various sectors of the economy, which will result in : (i) pooling, sharing and optimising the use of resources, (ii) development of indigenous technology appropriate to our national priorities and resources, (iii) enriching teaching and research in universities with practical and field experience, and (iv) universities and R & D laboratories getting valuable clues for research orientation. The process of interaction will not only lead to mutual benefit of the partners but also contribute to national development.

For bringing out greater interaction between university, industry and R & D organisations, a 'Model for University-Industry-R & D Organisation Symbiosis' has been suggested by me. There should be specific cells / units in the universities, R & D laboratories and industry to act as contact points and for coordination. At the national level it is desirable to create a National Cell to promote and coordinate the linkages between the various sectors of the economy, university industry and organisations. I am sure the outcome of the Workshop will be fruitful arc offer valuable inputs towards the formulation of broad directions for the IREP programme during the Eighth Plan.

Address At Three-Day National Seminar On Rural Sanitation

Access to sanitation is not simply a technical issue, but also a crucial component of social and economic development. Sanitation should be viewed in its composite sense involving the waste disposal system, water supply, sewerage, prevention of environmental pollution and to keep clean, healthy and productive. Excreta disposal remains the main component of Sanitation. Human excreta is associated with more than fifty diseases and it causes nearly 80% sickness. Statistics indicate that intestinal diseases like Diarrhoea, Cholera, Dysentery, Typhoid etc. claim 5 million lives every year, while 50 million suffer from these diseases resulting in tremendous loss of human days and productivity. Adopting proper waste disposal system through inexpensive methods, entire sanitation situation of the country can be improved and these diseases can be brought under control.

The rural sanitation has been over years primarily an individual's initiative. Naturally, due to a very low level of income and life-style and land-use, the use of modern sanitation was negligible. However, the increasing population-density and health-hazards brought it in the purview of plan efforts only in the recent past. It got fairly good recognition only during the Seventh Plan, when not only the "Centrally Sponsored Rural Sanitation Programme" was initiated, but also this was included in the 'Minimum Needs Programme' and the 'Revised Twenty Point Programme'. Under the Centrally Sponsored Rural Sanitation Programme, against the originally approved Seventh Plan outlay of only Rs. 4 crores, the actual allocation provided during the operational years of the Plan was as high as Rs. 70.65 crores. In spite of all these efforts, the programme, however, could not pick up mainly due to poor response from the beneficiaries as well as the implementing agencies and the State Governments, because the 'felt-need' could not be generated adequately. As against the increased allocation of Rs. 70.65 crores for the Centrally Sponsored Rural Sanitation Programme, only about Rs. 16 crores could be utilised during the Plan period. In the State Sector MNP also, the expenditure was only about Rs 49 crores against an outlay of Rs 96.75 crores. And the result was that plan efforts could not make any significant dent on the programme. The physical scenario has been very much disappointing. As low as 0.5% of rural population was having access to sanitary latrines at the beginning of the preceding decade, which has now risen to only about 2.7%? If we compare this with safe drinking water facility, the imbalance can clearly be noticed. Where only about 31% of rural people had access to safe water at the beginning of the last decade, the coverage now has increased to about 78%. On the financial front also, the picture about water supply is very bright. As against the originally approved Seventh Plan outlay of Rs.1202 crores under the central sector and Rs. 2253 crores under the State Sector, the utilisation was as high as Rs. 1899 crores and Rs. 2571 crores respectively. In short, it could be said that while the Water Supply received a very high priority during the recent past, the sanitation could not even get a modest beginning. The purpose of comparison is not that the Water Supply programme needs to be decelerated, but to highlight the imbalance between the two vital human needs, which are complementary to each other in achieving the goal of protecting their health and improving the efficiency. It is to be clearly understood, that without basic sanitation, full benefit of safe drinking water cannot be achieved.

Before gearing up the rural sanitation programme, one must now analyse the reasons of its not picking up in the past. It is felt that the programme was highly target oriented with no aspect of sustained motivation or IEC (Information, Education and Communication) component. Implementation merely for target achievement in spite of lack of real demand resulted in non-use of constructed latrines. In some cases 100% subsidy provided under the programme to economically weaker sections resulted in lack of beneficiary's involvement. More over, the funds were thinly spread all over the country without focussing on the areas where the demand existed.

Taking lessons from the past, the following approaches would have to be adopted in order to make the programme a success:

- Decentralisation of the programme with full involvement of NGOs and people's participation, particularly the women, at all stages of the programme such as planning, project formulation, execution etc., is essential.

- Generation of 'felt-need' and motivation by awareness campaign through mass media and effective communication is needed. Indifference towards insanitation is a perpetual problem in the rural society. There is, therefore, a need to create more awareness about one's hygiene. Here, the NGOs and the community leaders can play a vital role by providing self-less service.

- We should adopt simple yet appropriate low-cost technology followed by sound construction practices for wider usage. The UNICEF and other agencies like Sulabh International have already developed several low cost designs to suit various geological and climatic conditions as well as needs and habits of the people of various regions. The most commonly used are single-pit or twinpit pour—flush latrines.

- The programme may have to mainly depend on people's contribution with less subsidy. Studies have shown that the people properly motivated and provided with the technology, can themselves launch the programme without much subsidy. Even people below the poverty line, if well motivated, may be prepared to install the latrines, provided the low-cost economic model is available to them.

It is estimated that about Rs. 30,000 crores would be required, if the entire rural population is to be provided with the facility of sanitary latrines. Keeping in view the severe resource-constraint as well as the other competing demands, it would not be possible for the State and Central Governments to provide such a huge amount in one or two Five Year Plans. The outlay during the Eighth Plan for the Rural Sanitation Programme is about Rs. 675 crores which is even more than ten times of the expenditure during the Seventh Plan. Of this Rs. 380 crores are in the Central sector and balance Rs. 295 crores in the State sector. But this can benefit only about 19 million population as per the existing pattern of financing, which is mainly subsidy oriented. This will only marginally raise the cumulative population coverage at the end of the Plan i.e. from the present 2.7% to 5%. The Eighth Plan, therefore, suggests restructuring of the programme based on the lessons learnt from the good work done in certain places in Gujarat, Tamil Nadu, West Bengal, Bihar, Uttar Pradesh, Andhra Pradesh, Rajasthan, Madhya Pradesh and Maharashtra. It also suggests to adopt the concept of "Total

Environmental Sanitation", which includes a package of services consisting of personal hygiene, food-hygiene, cattle waste disposal, waste water disposal etc. rather than mere construction of sanitary latrines. It would also be necessary to integrate this programme with other Rural Development Programmes and have linkages with water availability, primary health-care, women's welfare, immunisation etc., all linked to cleanliness as a basic human need.

For the success of the Rural Sanitation Programme on a longer term basis, the following suggestions are made:—

- A national drive is to be given to the programme. Increasingly more private initiatives through motivation be targeted;
- It should be implemented through local body / village panchayat with full involvement of beneficiaries in a decentralised fashion;
- Women being the main beneficiaries of the programme, their special needs and privacy be given due attention and they are provided a dignified role within the community;
- Non-governmental organisations are to be fully involved in the various aspects of implementation;
- The programme may be restructured removing all the short—comings and incorporating the new approaches, based on the lessons learnt from the good work done in certain places;
- The organisational set-up also needs to be strengthened and restructured to suit the requirement of the programme;
- 'Whole-village' as well as 'Integrated' approaches and 'Total Sanitation' concept are to be adopted;
- Selection of villages is to be made carefully and only those villages be chosen where people are well motivated.
- In the project approach, linkages with ICDS (Integrated Child Development Scheme), DWCRA (Development of Women and Children in Rural Areas) and TRYSEM (Training of Rural Youth for Self-Employment) should be given top most priority;
- The savings of any other sectors of the rural development may preferably be diverted to Rural Sanitation.
- With these words, I conclude and hope that the outcome of this seminar would greatly benefit the programme of Rural Sanitation in the coming years.

"Planning For Rural Development"-A.B.Shetty Memorial Endowment Lecture, Mangalore University, Mangalore

Professor Savadatti, Vice-Chancellor, distinguished invitees, members of the faculty, students, ladies and gentlemen,

It is indeed a great honour for me for having been invited to deliver the A.B. Shetty Memorial Endowment Lecture of the Mangalore University. I thank the Vice-Chancellor for giving me this opportunity. I am happy to note that this lecture is instituted in the memory of late Shri A.B. Shetty, who, though by religion a Hindu, had a broad minded approach to all human problems and barriers of caste, religion, riches and poverty never came in the way of his dealings with people. Perhaps, because of such a noble approach, he endeared himself to all sections of society and emerged as an undisputed leader of South Kanara. His noble and humane approach is even more relevant in the present day context of the need for communal harmony and unity.

I am equally delighted to visit the campus of this great Mangalore University. The location with its abundant sea and rich forests provide the natural environment for research and the heritage of its educational traditions provide adequate motivation and strength for the University. The V.K.R.V. Rao Commission had perhaps rightly hoped that this University would be a 'University with a difference'. The University system in the country can make positive contributions to society through establishing close and vital links with it. I am happy to note that this University-Society interaction is one of the distinguishing features of the Mangalore University and as a part of its Decennial Year celebrations it has started a Village Adoption Programme and adopted the villages of Konaje Handal Panchayat in which the University is located. This impressed me most and even influenced me in selecting the topic "Planning for Rural Development" for the Endowment lecture. Dealing of such a topic needs wide coverage relating inputs from many sectors of development in the rural context and I will try to do justice to the extent possible within the time constraints of an endowment lecture like this.

THE PLANNING PROCESS:

Planning has been one of the pillars of our policies since Independence and our present strengths derive from its achievements. Pandit Jawaharlal Nehru, the architect of modern India and the first Prime Minister, embarked on the path of planned economic development for the country. Growth, modernisation, self-reliance and social justice have been the basic objectives governing Indian planning.

Momentous changes have taken place right across the world and in India in the recent past. The international political and economic order is being restructured everyday, and as the twentieth century draws to a close, many of its distinguished philosophies and features have also been swept away. To quote our present Prime Minister, "In this turbulent world, our policies must also deal with changing realities. Our basic policies have stood us in a very good stead and now provide us the opportunity to respond with flexibility to the new situations so that we can work uninterruptedly towards our basic aim of providing a rich and just life for our people".

In the present changed economic scenario, it would be conducive for development if State intervention is withdrawn in certain sectors opening them up to market mechanism. But certain social sectors would still need state intervention through planning. Planning is thus essentially for macro economic management, for taking care of the poor and the downtrodden, who are mostly outside the market system and have little asset endowment. The challenge of today is to effectively dovetail the market mechanism and planning so that they are complimentary to each other. The success of development programmes can be multiplied manifold if the people are wholeheartedly involved in their implementation. The implementation strategy for the Eighth Plan, therefore, relies on building and strengthening people's institutions and making people active participants. The role of the Government will be to create opportunities for the process of people's involvement in developmental activities.

RURAL DEVELOPMENT:

Rural development is a wide concept encompassing all aspects of improvement in the quality of life of the rural people and the rural areas. It implies both economic betterment of people as well as greater social transformation. Increased participation of people in the rural development process, decentralisation of planning, better enforcement of land reforms and greater access to credit inputs go a long way in providing the rural people with better prospects for economic development. Improvements in health, education, drinking water, energy supply, sanitation and housing coupled with attitudinal changes also facilitate their social development. Alleviation of rural poverty has been one of the primary objectives of planned development in India. Rural poverty is inextricably linked with low rural productivity and unemployment, including under-employment. Hence it is imperative to improve productivity and increase employment in rural areas.

The Eighth Five Year Plan envisages integration of Poverty alleviation programmes, Area development programmes and the Sectoral schemes. It is necessary to prepare a District plan, taking into account the physical, fiscal and human resource endowments of the area, the needs of the people and the resources available from different schemes. Viable activities in different sectors can be identified and necessary infrastructure as well as forward and backward linkages ensured. The social aspect of development, including education, health and access to safe drinking water can also be dovetailed with the plan for economic development. Such an integrated programme can be taken up at least in one district in each State on a pilot basis.

As envisaged in the Eighth Plan, to reach ultimately the goal of full employment by the turn of the century, we will have to concentrate on creating job opportunities, particularly in the rural areas. In view of the substantial step-up in the Central Plan outlay of Rural Development to Rs. 30,000 crores in the Eighth Plan, Rural development programmes will have to be revamped in order to become more effective and more productive.

RURAL POVERTY ALLEVIATION PROGRAMMES:

Due to their differing socio-economic background, the poor are not a homogenous group. There are considerable variations in the incidence of poverty of various sections of the poor. Employability, risk bearing capacity, credit worthiness, access to poverty alleviation programmes, enterprise etc. are likely to vary from one person to another. The investment needed to help the poor to cross the poverty line through self employment or wage employment thus varies considerably.

It has been estimated that of the households below the poverty line, about 20% consist of small farmers, 25% marginal farmers, 40% landless agricultural labourers, 7.5% rural artisans and 7.5% others. The agricultural labourers and marginal farmers belonging to the Scheduled Castes and Scheduled Tribes constitute one of the poorest sections of the population. It has also been observed that there has been a decline in the share of self employment and the share of permanent labourers in the total agricultural labour force. A large mass of the poor are reduced to the status of landless labour struggling to survive on casual labour. It is expected that the share of casual labour in the total labour force will increase in the coming years, which means the problems of the poorest groups consisting of casual and Scheduled Castes and Scheduled Tribes labourers are likely to be more serious.

Poverty is a result of multi-dimensional deprivation of the poor. The terms "anti poverty programmes" or "poverty alleviation programmes" will, therefore, cover a wide range of programmes that aim at reduction of poverty in some way or the other. Some major schemes which have been initiated for the enhancement of incomes and improvement in the levels of living of rural poor in India, as a part of the poverty alleviation package are the Minimum Needs Programme (MNP), Small Farmers Development Agency (SFDA), Marginal Farmers Agricultural Labourers Development Agency (MFAL), Integrated Rural Development Programme (IRDP), National Rural Employment Programme (NREP) and Rural Landless Employment Guarantee Programme (RLEGP) and later the Jawahar Rozgar Yojana (JRY). Government intervention for rural development and poverty alleviation can be summarised to include a package of the following measures:

(a) Measures designed to stimulate growth in the economy;
(b) Sectoral programmes to develop sectors like agriculture, animal husbandry, horticulture, pisciculture, sericulture etc;

(c) The Minimum Needs Programme to improve access to basic social services like drinking water, health, education and literacy, housing, nutrition, rural roads, rural electrification, etc;

(d) Area Development: Schemes for special intervention in the backward areas like the Desert Development Programme (DDP), the Drought Prone Area Programme (DPAP), and the Hill Area Development Programme (HADP);

(e) Special employment programmes like the IRDP and JRY to supplement employment opportunities;

(f) Special measures for the welfare of the Scheduled Castes, Scheduled Tribes, women, children and other disadvantaged groups, as well as social security measures such as old age pension and insurance.

INTEGRATED RURAL DEVELOPMENT PROGRAMME (IRDP):

In the mid-seventies along with wage employment and special area development programmes, a self employment programme was introduced, known as Integrated Rural Development Programme (IRDP). IRDP is a programme which calls for detailed micro-level planning. The starting point is the survey for identifying families with an annual income less than the poverty line. Priority is given to the poorest of the poor for assistance under the programme. The identified families are consulted about their preference for income generating activities. A plan is prepared of activities for such families in the Block showing the activity selected, type of assistance required, nature of support services required and other relevant details.

IRDP is implemented through District Rural Development Agencies (DRDAs) specially set up in each rural district in the country for the implementation of rural development programmes. The State Level Coordination Committee (SLCC) monitors the programme at the State Government level. The Ministry of Rural Development, Government of India, is responsible for release of central share of funds, overall guidance, policy making, monitoring and evaluation of the programme at the National level.

The IRDP has many positive features. Its major achievement has been in providing the poor, an access to institutional credit. Although only about 3% of the resources of the banks are utilised for IRDP, the fact that 40 million poor families have been provided some assistance by the banks is a significant achievement in itself. Nearly 90% of the assisted families felt that they had benefited from the IRDP, 97% of the assisted families felt that the assets were in keeping with their needs and aspirations; 90% of the assisted families felt that family employment had increased as a result of IRDP assistance and about 88% reported that as a result of assistance under IRDP their family income had increased. About 77% felt that their consumption levels had increased. About 64% felt that their overall status in the village society had been elevated as a consequence of assistance under IRDP.

During the Eighth Five Year Plan it is proposed to assist 18 million families under IRDP. The Plan provision for this will be approximately Rs. 3350 crores. Preparation of credit plan for each family, its proper dovetailing with the block plan, substantial increase in per family investment and better provision of backward and forward linkages will be the main thrust areas.

MINIMUM NEEDS PROGRAMME:

The Minimum Needs Programme (MNP) was introduced in the Fifth Plan with the objective of providing the rural population, particularly rural poor access to certain items of social consumption which form an integral part of the basic needs. Initially there were 8 components under the MNP— elementary education, rural health, rural water supply, rural roads, rural electrification, rural housing, environmental improvement of urban slums and nutrition. During the Sixth Plan, adult education was added. In the Seventh Plan, the list was further expanded with three more components namely, rural domestic energy, rural sanitation and public distribution system. These components form part of the programmes of individual sectors and the allocation for these are part of the sectoral allocations. The planning and implementation of these programmes should be integrated with other ongoing rural development programmes at a decentralised level with the district as the unit of planning. In addition, some provision could be made for basic village amenities as an integral part of the MNP with a certain amount of 'untied' funds allocated to the local level bodies for the implementation and maintenance of these energies. These can include street lighting, primary school buildings, community centres, hand pumps, fish ponds, social forestry, bio-gas etc. The list can be an exhaustive one with the flexibility of spending funds left to the discretion of the village level organisation.

Appropriate Technology for Rural Development:

The fruits of science and technology are to be taken to the door steps of villagers if our intention is to improve the quality of their life. Therefore, appropriate technology should be developed and transferred for rural development. Appropriate technology should be one which can be applied at low-cost, which uses mainly local material and skill, which meets a recognised local need and which fits closely with local situations and aspirations for development. The technology should be simple, economically sound, need-based, employment generating, capital saving, based on minimum use of non-local resources, relevant to mass consumption, relevant to local consumption, complementary to large scale industry, socially relevant and self-reliant. The thrust for development of appropriate technology may be in the areas of energy, agriculture, low-cost transport, low-cost housing, drinking water supply, animal husbandry and human muscle power. A number of appropriate technologies have been developed and are being in the process of transfer. The laboratories of C.S.I.R., I.C.A.R., and I.I.T.s and Engineering colleges are working in the area of appropriate technologies. Still a lot more needs to be done. The universities and engineering institutions should play an important role in the development and application of appropriate technologies. They can explore the possibilities of setting up centres for rural development. As envisaged in the National Policy on Education, setting up of Rural Universities should be pursued. Community Polytechnics are doing a satisfactory job in rural development. More number of Community Polytechnics should be set up. Close collaboration between different organisations engaged in rural development and universities and technical institutions is needed for achieving better results.

Supply of Improved Tool-Kits to Rural Artisans:

The problem of migration from rural areas to urban areas arises mostly due to unemployment situation in the rural areas. This situation could be improved if the skills of the rural artisans are upgraded and modern tools are made available to them so that they can have better self-employment opportunities. In pursuance of Prime Minister's announcement in his

Independence Day Address 1991 regarding supply of modern tools to the rural artisans, Ministry of Rural Development finalised the scheme of supplying of Improved Tool-Kits to rural artisans, after a series of discussions with the concerned Ministries, State Governments and consultations with the experts in the field. It is expected that rural artisans will be able to enhance the quality of the product, increase the production and their income and will be in a position to lead a better quality of life with the use of modern tools. The programme of supply of modern tool-kits for rural artisans is under implementation in the entire country. All traditional rural artisans living below the poverty-line except weavers, tailors, needle workers and bidi workers are covered under this programme. This programme is implemented as a part of IRDP. At the district level DRDA is the nodal agency. Under this programme, any suitable improved hand tool is to be provided. Prototypes of modern tools in pottery, carpentry, black-smithy, leather work, wood craft, metal craft, and lacquer ware have been developed by National Small Industries Corporation, Regional Design & Technical Development Centres and other Organisations. If the State Governments feel that better alternatives of modern tools suitable to local conditions are available in their State they are free to choose those models. It is proposed to cover a total of five lakhs to rural artisans under the scheme during the Eighth Five Year Plan.

TRAINING OF RURAL YOUTH FOR SELF EMPLOYMENT (TRYSEM):

The Scheme of Training of Rural Youth for Self Employment (TRYSEM) started on 15th August, 1979, aims at providing basic technical and managerial skills to rural youth from families below the poverty line to enable them to take up self-employment in the broad fields of agriculture and allied sectors namely industries, services and business activities. This objective was subsequently enlarged to include taking up of wage employment also by trained youth. TRYSEM plays an important role in facilitating diversification of activities taken up under IRDP. Diversification away from the primary sector to secondary and tertiary sectors requires acquisition or upgradation of skills relevant to industries and business enterprises. TRYSEM seeks to impart new skills and upgrade existing skills of beneficiaries who are by and large attuned only to stagnant levels of agricultural or artisan skills. Training is imparted both through formal training institutions including industrial and servicing units, commercial and business establishments etc. and non-institutionalised mode like master craftsmen. After the successful completion of the training, the trained rural youth can avail of subsidy and institutional credit under IRDP for acquisition of income generating assets. It is expected that the formalities for such assistance 'would be completed during the training period itself. A major problem faced under TRYSEM is the absence of infrastructural support and backward and forward linkages when the trained youth go for self-employment. This has to come largely from the sectoral agencies in the form of development of appropriate technology, production and supply of good quality assets, provision of other inputs, services and marketing facilities.

DEVELOPMENT OF WOMEN AND CHILDREN IN RURAL AREAS (DWCRA):

The programme of Development of Women & Children in Rural Areas (DWCRA) was introduced in 1982 as part of the IRDP. There are 241 districts in which the programme is being implemented with UNICEF assistance as on 30.3.1992. Fifty districts are proposed to be added in each year during the Eighth Five Year Plan. It is expected that all the districts will be covered by the Eighth Plan. DWCRA sub-programme has a strategy different from IRDP in that instead of the family being the focus, groups of poor women are assisted through a package.

The mission of DWCRA programme is to improve the status of poor women in the rural areas. The main strategy being adopted is to improve access of poor women to employment, skills training, credit and other support services. It is expected that the target group would also be the focus of convergence of other services like welfare, health, nutrition and education. DWCRA has provision for child care also. The groups which have been successful are the result of proper planning, proper selection of activities, training support, proper raw material supply, marketing linkages and regular follow up.

DWCRA is a programme with certain inherent strengths. It provides for formation of groups of women with an accent on income generation. These groups are provided easier access to credit, training and other inputs. These groups also function as pressure groups and help their members to transcend social and gender barriers through improving the economic base of women.

The key to uplifting the status of women lies in increasing the employment opportunities and the income in the hand of poor women in rural areas. During the Eighth Five Year Plan period, it is envisaged that all the districts in the country will be covered by DWCRA programme.

RURAL EMPLOYMENT:

In the field of rural employment, the process of planning had generally proceeded on the assumption that economic growth by itself will result in increased employment opportunities and that accelerated rate of economic growth will be able to meet the employment requirements of growing labour force. The results achieved, however, did not validate this assumption. This led to increasing efforts for taking up schemes for providing additional employment opportunities. Special schemes of employment generation were, therefore, taken up from time to time in the country.

The National Rural Employment Programme (NREP), which was launched in October, 1980, based on the experience in implementing the employment schemes like Rural Manpower Programme, Crash Scheme for Rural Employment, Pilot Intensive Rural Employment Programme and Food for Work Programme became a regular part of the Sixth Five Year Plan from April, 1981. The programme was implemented as a Centrally Sponsored Programme on 50:50 sharing basis between the Centre and the States. During the mid-term appraisal of the Sixth Five Year Plan, it was realised that the hard core of rural poor was not getting full benefit under NREP. A new scheme known as Rural Landless Employment Guarantee Programme (RLEGP) was introduced from 15th August, 1983. The experience of implementation of NREP / RLEGP over the years made it necessary to reconsider the whole issue and it was later decided that these two programmes should be merged into one single rural employment programme to be known as Jawahar Rozgar Yojana (JRY). The objectives of the Jawahar Rozgar Yojana, launched with effect from 1.4.1989 are: generation of additional gainful employment for the unemployed and underemployed persons both men and women in the rural areas; creation of sustained employment by strengthening rural economic infrastructure; creating community and social assets; creating assets in favour of rural poor for their direct and continuing benefits; positive impact on wage levels and overall Improvement in the quality of life in the rural areas.

People below the poverty line constitute the target group under the JRY. Preference is given to the members of Scheduled Castes and Scheduled Tribes for employment. 30% of the employment opportunities under the Yojana are required to be earmarked for women. All rural works which result in creation of durable productive community assets can be taken up under the Yojana. Important physical assets including water harvesting structures, drinking water wells and ponds, school buildings, rural roads have been constructed under JRY all over the country.

Indira Awaas Yojana (IAY), a Centrally Sponsored Scheme, was launched during 1985-86 as a sub-scheme of Rural Landless Employment Guarantee Programme (RLEGP) and continued as a part of Jawahar Rozgar Yojana (JRY). The objective of the IAY is to provide houses to the members of Scheduled Castes / Scheduled Tribes and freed bonded labourers below the poverty line, free of cost. 6% of the resources at the national level are earmarked for IAY and are distributed amongst the States in accordance to the proportion of poor among Scheduled Castes, Scheduled Tribes and freed bonded labourers out of the total rural population belonging to this particular group. The houses under IAY, as far as practicable, should be built on micro habitat approach or in a cluster, so as to facilitate the development of infrastructure such as internal roads, drains, drinking water supply etc., and other common facilities. Care should also be taken to see that the houses under IAY are located close to the village and not far away so as to ensure safety and security; nearness of work place and social communication.

With the substantial step up in the outlay for Rural Development in the Eighth Five Year Plan to Rs. 30,000 crores, the resources for the JRY will also be stepped up to about Rs. 18,400 crores in the Central Plan. In addition, the State share of about Rs. 4,600 crores will become available for JRY. Under the JRY, the Annual Plan outlay has so far been of the order of Rs. 2625 crores in recent years, consisting of Central Budget outlay of Rs. 2100 crores and the State Plan provision of Rs. 525 crores. With these resources, it had been possible to generate wage employment opportunities of about 900 million man days per year. It should be the objective to create a minimum of 1000 million man days each year in the Eighth Five Year Plan. This will be in the form of supplementary employment. The various components of JRY such as Million Wells Scheme (MWS), Indira Awaas Yojana (IAY), construction of school buildings etc., would also continue with appropriate streamlining. These will serve to create rural infrastructure and assets in favour of the rural poor. Separate schemes will also be formulated for regions having out-migration of labour. Innovative projects can also be drawn up for meeting specific objectives. The success of an employment programme of the magnitude of the JRY depends largely on its efficient implementation in the field. It is necessary that the existing monitoring, inspection, audit and vigilance arrangements at the State level are strengthened to ensure proper utilisation of funds allotted to JRY.

SMALL FARMERS AGRI-BUSINESS CONSORTIUM (SFAC):

The Finance Minister, in his Budget Speech 1992-93, had stated "special attention needs to be paid to supporting innovative ideas for generating incomes and employment in rural areas through support to various types of agri business. As an experimental measure, Government proposes to set up a Small Farmers' Agri Business Consortium as an autonomous corporate entity funded by the Reserve Bank of India, NABARD and IDBI. The Consortium will function on the principles of economic efficiency, environmental soundness and social equity".

The basis for the programme components and the contents of the projects to be taken up by the SFAC is based on a document prepared by International Commission on Food and Peace under the Chairmanship of Dr. M.S. Swaminadhan entitled "Prosperity 2000". The rationale for the programme is based on large untapped potential for agriculture development in the country. An accelerated agricultural development could form the strategy for eradication of unemployment and poverty in the rural areas and increase agro based exports. The programmes represent a major reorientation in the agriculture development process focussing on selected crops and agro based industries with largest technical, economic, market and employment potential. The programmes are expected to:

(i) Utilise proven technologies.
(ii) Create a large number of new jobs for unskilled labour.
(iii) Tap huge market potential both domestic and exports.
(iv) Generate high value added products and profits to primary Producers.

The main programme areas identified are:

(i) Horticulture including both area expansion, establishment of processing plants and improve marketing of horticulture produce.

(ii) Aquaculture—Development of 50,000 ha. of intensive fish farms to raise fish production to 4.5 million tonnes and providing income generation through intensive fish farming and increasing the employment opportunities.

(iii) Sericulture—Doubling mulberry silk production through integrated model silk village clusters.

(iv) Improve cotton productivity and production to facilitate exports and providing raw materials for additional handlooms and textile units.

(v) Sugar—Increase the area and productivity of sugarcane both for meeting the internal consumption as well as exports.

(vi) Foodgrains—Concentrate on improving production and production of rice and wheat through additional area being brought under irrigation and enhancing productivity through spread of improved technologies.

(vii) Oilseeds—Increase the area under irrigated oilseeds as well as improving the yields.

(viii) Wasteland reclamation for forestry and fodder.

(ix) Dairy and Poultry development.

The Planning Commission had initiated the exercise for working out the modalities for the establishment of Consortium. It was decided that this should be set up by associating financial institutions, private sector industrial units, Central and State Government representatives, National Dairy Development Board, National Horticulture Board and other agro-inputs, Central public sector undertakings, research institutions and progressive farmers, in the form of a registered society. It is contemplated that a similar set up at district / project levels to be set up. 12-15 districts have been identified where the work is to be initiated as pilot projects. It has also been envisaged that there will be a Policy Planning Advisory Council at the apex level at the centre, to provide necessary direction and government support. The Chairman of the Advisory Council will constitute the Governing Board of the Society at the national level.

RURAL WATER SUPPLY:

The subject of drinking water supply in the rural areas is the responsibility of the States. A National Water Supply and Sanitation Programme was introduced in Social Welfare Sector in the year 1954. The States gradually built up the Public Health Engineering Departments (PHEDs) to attend to the problems of water supply and sanitation. In spite of these efforts, it was observed during mid-sixties that Rural Water Supply Schemes were implemented only in the easily accessible villages neglecting the hard core rural areas. The Central Government, therefore, requested the States to identify such villages as Problem Villages (PVs) so that efforts could be directed towards tackling clearly identified problem villages. Government of India provided assistance to the States to establish Special Investigation Divisions in the Fourth Five Year Plan to carry out identification of problem villages.

Taking into account the magnitude of the problem and in order to accelerate the pace of coverage of Problem Villages, the Government of India introduced the Accelerated Rural Water Supply Programme (ARWSP) in 1972-73 to assist the States and Union Territories with 100 per cent grants-in-aid to implement the schemes in such villages. But with the introduction of Minimum Needs Programme (MNP) during the Fifth Five Year Plan from 1974-75 it was withdrawn. The programme was however reintroduced in 1977-78 when the progress of supply of safe drinking water to identified problem villages was not found to be as per expectations.

In the year 1977 the United Nations Water Conference, perhaps for the first time, separated the issue of drinking water and sanitation from other water issues. It suggested and adopted the Decade approach and adopted programmes with realistic standards of quality and quantity to provide water for urban and rural areas. The Conference recommended that each country should develop national plans and programmes for water supply and sanitation giving priority to the segments of the population in greatest need. India was a signatory to the resolution seeking to achieve the targets by 1991. The Water Decade programme was accordingly launched on 1st April, 1981 in India with a view to achieving definite targets of coverage of population by 31st March, 1991. Till the beginning of the Sixth Plan, the pace of coverage was rather modest at about 94,000 problem villages., During Sixth Plan itself 1.92 lakh problem villages were covered leaving a balance of 1.62 lakh problem villages (including spill over and newly identified villages) at the beginning of the Seventh Plan. Achievements during the Seventh Plan were also equally marked covering about 1.53 lakhs villages. With the stepping down in the coverage in the last 2 Annual Plans which was primarily because of more remote and difficult villages being covered during these years. At the beginning of the Eighth Plan, only about 3000 villages were left uncovered. In August, 1985, the subject of Rural Water Supply and Sanitation was transferred from the Ministry of Urban Development to the Department of Rural Development, with the objective of securing faster implementation of the programmes and their integration with other rural development programmes. The National Drinking Water Mission was launched as one of the five societal Missions in the year 1986. The Mission has since been renamed as Rajiv Gandhi National Drinking Water Mission. Government of India continues to give highest priority to rural water supply through the activities of the Mission and ARWSP. It also forms part of the State funded MNP and point No. 7 of the 20 Point Programme, 1986. Problems in the provision of drinking water have also been identified and treated as Sub-Missions to benefit from integrated scientific and technological approaches. These are: guinea worm eradication; control of flurosis; removal of excess iron; control of brackishness; scientific source finding, conservation of water, recharging of aquifers and water quality surveillance. In addition, emphasis has also been placed on the following aspects Improvement of traditional methods; purification of water; improvement of material and design; improvement of maintenance methods; establishment of management information systems and procedures; community involvement through panchayats and voluntary agencies and awareness campaigns.

The following objectives have been visualised for the Eighth Five Year Plan:

i)   Highest priority to be given to ensure that the remaining about 3000 'No—Source' hard-core problem villages in some states are provided with sustainable and stipulated supply of drinking water by March, 1993;

ii) Equally important would be to ensure that all the partially covered villages having a supply level of less than 40 liters per capita per day (lpcd) numbering about 1.5 lakh including hamlets, are fully covered with safe drinking water facilities by the end of the Eighth Plan on sustainable basis;

iii) Ensure that SC / ST population and other poor / weaker sections are covered fully on a priority basis;

iv) The stipulated norms of supply would be 40 lpcd of safe drinking water within a walking distance of 1.6 kms or elevation difference of 100 metres in hilly areas, to be relaxed as per field conditions applicable to arid, semi-arid and hilly areas. At least one hand-pump / spotsource for every 250 persons to be provided. Additional 30 lpcd in DDP / DPAP areas for cattle to be provided; v) Achieve zero incidence of Guinea worm disease by 1993 and total eradication by 199.5, besides progressively finding solutions for other bacteriological and. chemical problems like excess fluorides, salinity and iron in water sources; The implementation of the programmes is monitored both at the State Government and Central levels in the Ministry of Rural Development and Ministry of Programme Implementation. The monitoring covers the following aspects: Coverage of 'No Source' problem villages to partial coverage or full coverage; villages already partially covered to full coverage; population benefited separately in general category, SCs and ST; physical and financial progress of Mini Missions and Sub-Missions; implementation of ARWSP schemes; externally funded projects; operation and maintenance of schemes.

RURAL SANITATION:

Rural Sanitation is an essential requisite for reaching the country's commitment to attain Health for All by the year 2000. Sanitation has to be treated as a package of facilities and services and not to be identified merely with the construction of sanitary latrines alone. The major components of sanitation are handling of drinking water, disposal of waste water, disposal of human excreta, garbage disposal, home sanitation and food hygiene, personal hygiene and sanitation in the community.

Sanitation is primarily the responsibility of the States as it is a subject in the State list and the Government of India has been providing necessary support and assistance to the States. In the year 1954, Sanitation Programme was introduced in the health sector in the Plans. In 1986, it was included as Point No. 8 of 20-Point Programme. Rural Sanitation was also included as part of the State Sector Minimum Needs Programme (MNP) from 1987-88. Rural Sanitation programme was launched in 1986 under NREP, RLEGP and Indira Awaas Yojana. The Central Rural Sanitation Programme was also introduced in 1986. During the period from 1986-87 to 1991-92, with a total investment of about Rs. 318 crores under all the programmes, it was possible to construct 22.67 lakh household latrines benefitting rural population of about 2.73%. The main reasons for slow progress and low coverage are: absence of demand or felt need; very low priority accorded to sanitation; low community participation; absence of user involvement; inadequate emphasis on information education and communication; insufficient financial resources, lack of coordination among implementing agencies, lack of inadequate infrastructure, institutional mechanism and sectoral planning and shortage of trained manpower. The objectives for the Eighth Plan are:

i) Achieve coverage of about 5 per cent of rural population (cumulative) with their full involvement with sanitation facilities by the end of Eighth Plan. Information, Education and Communication (IEC) should be an integral part of rural sanitation programme. In this context, it is desirable to adopt a concept of 'total environmental sanitation' and provide guidelines to the rural population in regard to proper environmental sanitation practices, including disposal of refuse, garbage and waste water through the mechanism of local village leaders and community organisations and construct biogas plants adjacent to the sanitary complexes; ii) Convert all existing dry latrines into low-cost sanitary latrines. For effective implementation, the Rural Sanitation programme should be restructured providing for the following elements:

(a) All activities under this programme will be undertaken through local body / village panchayat and with beneficiary participation;
(b) Wherever feasible, NGOs will be involved in the implementation of the programme;
(c) Women will be actively associated with the implementation of the programme;
(d) Some contribution should be solicited from the beneficiaries, at least in the form of physical labour, in order to engender among them the realisation that the assets created belong to the local community.

Rural Housing:

Housing is one of the basic requirements for human survival and is a necessity for socio-economic development. Housing encourages economic activity, generates employment opportunities and creates a basis for healthy and hygienic social life. The need for improved housing is most acutely felt amongst the rural poor who, as a result of their inability to generate the needed resources, are forced to live in conditions of squalor. The present state of shelter and quality of the human environment in rural areas is an extension of the problems of high population growth, increased rural impoverishment and unemployment, the differential priorities accorded to industrial and urban growth, low levels of access to social services and linkages like education, health and communication, marginalization of women and under privileged classes and an alarming deterioration in the quality of the physical environment.

As per 1981 Census, total housing stock in the rural areas was 77.4 million dwelling units with a housing gap of million dwelling units. It has been estimated by the National Building Organisation (NBO) that, as on 1.3.1991, the housing shortage in rural areas was of the order of 20.6 million units. In addition to these, two million new units are needed each year for the increased population.

The rural houses are mostly kutcha and only a small portion can be categorised as Semi-pucca / pucca. The predominant material for construction of roofs and walls in rural houses continues to be bio-mass, mud etc. The percentage of walls built with mud, an unburnt brick etc. was as high as 57% and those with bio-mass materials was 13% as per 1981 census data. Similarly, bio-mass material, bamboo, mud etc. constituted 46% of the composition of roofing material for rural areas.

In rural areas, 44.38% of households were one-room units and 28.87% reportedly two-room units, thus accounting in all for about 73% of the total housing stock in 1981 census. The one-room dwelling units had an average population 4.61 per room, against 2.84 of two-room units. Whereas the one-room dwelling units sheltered 36.66% of the total rural population, the two room dwelling units sheltered 29.38% of the rural population. The National Housing Policy recognises that rural housing is qualitatively different from urban housing in that the housing activity in rural areas is not so much based on cash economy and depends much more on land rights and access to resources. The strategy for rural housing will be based on: Support to varying needs of shelter including new construction, additions and upgradations; providing assistance by way of dissemination of appropriate technology and delivery system for 'promoting self-help housing; assuring land and tenure rights by enactment of enabling laws for conferment of homestead rights; prevention of alienation of homesteads on tribal land; avoiding unnecessary displacement or de-housing of rural settlements due to development projects; and where unavoidable, ensuring proper rehabilition of the households, with full community involvement, according to the national income in this regard; rehabilitation of households affected by natural calamities in terms of assistance for reconstruction and access to services, within the national scheme of calamity relief; preserving the customary and traditional rights of access to housing resources based on forest materials and common village resources; promoting the maximum use of indigenous materials and construction techniques with due regard to geoclimatic variations in different regions; the coordinated provision of water supply, sanitation, roads, and other basic infrastructure services to existing and new habitations besides employment opportunities which will also help to reduce the migration to urban areas; the establishment of a suitable institutional structure including strengthening of existing organisations at state, district and local level, with responsibilities for the implementation, supervision and monitoring of rural housing schemes and with the full involvement of beneficiaries, voluntary agencies and village panchayats; giving special attention to the needs of the poorest segments of Scheduled Castes, Scheduled Tribes and other disadvantaged persons.

The development of house sites and the upgradation of rural housing will be linked to activities under the Integrated Rural Development Programme, Jawahar Rozgar Yojana and other programmes for the creation of rural assets and employment. The rural communities languish in the near total absence of Housing Finance Institutions. The Apex Cooperative Housing Societies and their primary institutions have also not touched even the fringe of the housing and infrastructure problems of rural settlements. Housing in rural areas is mainly by the private efforts. This is evident from the 44th round of NSS, which shows that only 5.18% of total finance for rural housing comes from formal agencies. Bulk of the resources for rural 'housing comes from savings (42.57%), borrowing from friends and relatives (9.36%) and other resources (22.03%). Housing finance from the banking sector is meagre. According to the existing RBI guidelines, only 1.5% of the incremental deposits are allocable for housing. This generates only Rs. 100-150 crores of resources for housing. The rural areas get hardly anything out of this. There is no separate organisation in most of the States for looking after the housing needs of the rural areas. At the State level itself, there is no nodal department dealing with rural housing and different aspects are dealt with by a multiplicity of departments. The access of the rural poor to traditional housing materials like bamboo, reeds, thatch, grass etc. has been adversely affected because of the dwindling production, limitations placed on their availability and transportation under various enactments and their monetisation. Measures, therefore, will have to be devised to tackle the problems by ensuring increased production of such products; modifying the enactments to remove the obstacles in the path of easy accessibility of such materials; and operating a balanced price policy so that the housing needs get preference and due share, besides ensuring the availability of material at affordable rates to the rural poor.

The problem of rural housing should not be viewed in terms of finance and resources alone. The construction of new housing stock and upgradation of unserviceable kuccha houses will only materialise if homestead rights are conferred on rural poor, basic conditions are created in making available appropriate building materials, access to bio-mass and natural resources and upgradation of the traditional skills of the local artisans involved in the shelter construction and improvement. Further, State and the public agencies should mount programmes for provision of infrastructure facilities with full involvement of the rural community which will set the pace for housing programmes and improvement of settlements.

RURAL HEALTH:

The National Health Policy (1983) reiterated India's commitment to attain "Health for All" (HFA) by 2000 A.D.". Primary health care has been accepted as the main instrument for achieving this goal. Accordingly, a vast network of institutions at primary, secondary and tertiary levels has been established. Control of communicable diseases through national programmes and development of trained health manpower have received special attention. It is towards human development that health and population control are listed as two of the priority objectives of the Eighth Plan. The Health for All (HFA) paradigm must take into account not only high risk vulnerable groups, that is mothers and children but also focus sharply on the underprivileged segments within the vulnerable groups. Within the HFA strategy "Health for underprivileged" will be promoted consciously and consistently. This can only be done through emphasising the community based systems reflected in our planning of infrastructure, with about 30,000 population as the basic unit for primary health care. Development and strengthening of rural infrastructure through a three-tier system of Sub-centres, Primary Health Centres (PHCs) and Community Health Centres (CHCs) for delivery of health and family welfare services to the rural community was continued during the Seventh Plan. But lack of buildings, shortage of manpower and inadequate provision of drugs supplies and equipments constituted major impediments to full operationalisation of these units. The approach and strategy for rural health during the Eighth Plan will include consolidation and operationalisation rather than major expansion, of the work of sub-centres, PHCs and CHCs so that their performance is optimised.

EDUCATION:

It is universally acknowledged that the goal of Plan efforts is human development, of which human resources development is a necessary prerequisite. Education is a catalytic factor which leads to human resource development, comprising of better health and nutrition, improved socio-economic opportunities and more congenial and beneficial environment for all. There is greater evidence now that high literacy rates, especially, high female literacy rates, are associated with low rates of population growth, infant mortality and maternal mortality besides a higher rate of life expectancy. Realisation of the goals of universalisation of elementary education and eradication of illiteracy are paramount if the fruits of development have to reach all sections of society effectively. Although the country has not so far achieved the goal of Universalisation of Elementary Education (UEE) and Eradication of Adult Illiteracy (EAI), the 1991 Census results reveal a literacy rate of over 52%, with a higher rate of growth for female literacy. This is highly encouraging and the country can hope to achieve the broader goal of "Education for All" (EFA) by 2000 A.D.

RURAL ENERGY

A major constraint in improving the living conditions in rural areas is the nonavailability of energy for meeting subsistence and production needs. Rural areas are often the worst affected by the present all round scarcity of commercial energy including petroleum products and electricity. Even basic energy needs for the rural population are not being met because of widespread scarcity of commercial energy. Non-commercial energy consisting of firewood, cow dung and agricultural waste continue to provide from 80 to 90 per cent of the total energy consumed in the rural areas for the subsistence activities of cooking and heating. Energy needs for production purpose in rural areas including agricultural requirements are made mainly from draught animals and human labour, both of which are most inefficiently utilised. Fiscal and administrative measures as well as controls on energy distribution have so far made little impact in the rural areas while commercial forms of energy such as electricity, kerosene and diesel oil are now making inroads into the rural areas, their consumption is still largely confined to the more affluent households. Though kerosene is used by many lowincome rural households for lighting, the majority of the rural households cannot afford to utilise commercial fuels for other end uses due to their low purchasing power. The pattern of supply and consumption of energy in rural areas needs to be studied in order to provide sustainable and affordable supply of energy sources for meeting the growing energy needs of the rural population. The locally available renewable energy sources based on the nonconventional technologies will have to play an increasingly important role in meeting the rural energy needs. The Integrated Rural Energy Planning Programme (IREP) which was taken up as a planned scheme in the Seventh Plan has been a major effort in this direction for planning for energy for rural development, taking into account the concerns for equity and social justice.

This programme has now sufficient experience in micro-level energy planning for meeting subsistence and production needs. But the extension and intensification of the programme has to be carried out by effective linkage of the programme and its implementation, with the State and District planning set up on the one hand and with the agricultural and rural development programmes on the other hand. The IREP in the Eighth Plan has also to ensure sustainability of energy supply to the rural areas in view of the growing gap between energy demand and supply and the grave damage that is being done to the eco-system because of steady depletion of the biomass cover. The environmental aspect has, therefore, to be suitably incorporated in the micro and macro level rural energy planning framework.

DEVELOPMENT ADMINISTRATION:

During the Seventh Plan the various rural development programmes were planned and implemented by a single agency at the district level called District Rural Development Agency (DRDA). A Committee set up to review the existing administrative arrangements for rural development reemphasised the need for decentralised planning at district level and below. It was envisaged that planning and implementation of sectoral activities would be decentralised and integrated into a unified activity with a horizontal coordination at the district level. Similarly, at the block level too an integrated area plan is imperative, based on the availability of local skills and resources.

Panchayati Raj institutions are in existence in almost all States and Union Territories but with considerable variations in their structure, mode of election etc. They suffer from inadequate resources, both financial and technical. To revitalise the panchayats a Constitutional Amendment Bill has been recently approved by the Parliament.

VOLUNTARY ACTION:

Recognising the important role of voluntary agencies in accelerating the process of social and economic development, the Seventh Plan placed a great deal of emphasis on people's participation and the voluntary action in rural development. The role of voluntary agencies has been defined as providing a basis for innovation with new approaches towards integrated development, ensuring feedback regarding impact of various programmes and securing the involvement of local communities, particularly those below the poverty line. The need for a cadre of trained animators / enumerators and social organisers were recognised and a massive programme for training the identified persons was prepared with the help of established voluntary organisations. At the Central level the Council for Advancement of People's Action and Rural Technology (CAPART) is the agency for providing and assisting voluntary action in the area of rural development.

It has been realised that the key to efficient utilisation of resources lies in the creation of appropriate self-managed organisations at all levels. In this area, Planning Commission will play a systems change role and provide internal consultancy for developing better systems. The Approach to the Eighth Five Year Plan has focussed on creation of appropriate organisations and delivery systems to ensure that the benefits of investment in the social sectors reach the intended beneficiaries. People's initiative and participation is made a key element in the process of development. Towards this end, the Planning Commission had appointed a Task Force on Self-Managed Institutions for Integrated Development. A Voluntary Action Coordination Cell has been established to take follow up action on the recommendations of the Task Force. A scheme for launching the experiment of micro-level participatory planning in the Eighth Plan has been formulated.

DROUGHT PRONE AREAS PROGRAMME (DPAP):

Drought has been a recurring feature of Indian agriculture. Long term counter measures in the form of dry farming projects in the Second Five Year Plan and the Rural Works Programme in the Fourth Five Year Plan culminated in the launching of the Drought Prone Areas Programme (DPAP) in 1973.

The objective of drought proofing is sought to be achieved by integrated planning and development of drought prone areas on watershed basis for conservation, development and harnessing of land, water and other natural resources including rainfall. Resources of other similar programmes of the Centre and the State Governments should be pooled at the district level for this purpose. At present, DPAP is being implemented in 615 blocks of 92 districts in 13 States and the drought prone areas are spread over 5.53 lakh square kilometers. Three core sectors namely land development and moisture conservation, water resources development and afforestation and pasture development which taken together are capable of restoring the ecological balance of an area have been identified. Sectoral weightages in terms of percentage of expenditure in each core sector have been fixed and accordingly 75% of programme allocation is earmarked for these sectors. Tentative allocation for the Eighth Five Year Plan is Rs. 500 crores.

DESERT DEVELOPMENT PROGRAMME (DDP):

On the basis of the recommendations of the National Commission on Agriculture (1974), the Desert Development Programme (DDP) was started, in 1977-78. The objective of controlling desertification is sought to be achieved through integrated planning and development of desert areas on watershed / index catchment basis for conservation of natural resources including rainfall with special emphasis on sand dune stabilisation and shelter belt plantation. Resources of other similar programmes should be pooled at the district level for this purpose. At present the programme covers 131 blocks in 21 districts of 5 States of which Rajasthan, Gujarat and Haryana have hot desert areas and Jammu & Kashmir and Himachal

491

Pradesh have cold desert areas. The hot desert areas cover about 2.6 lakh sq. kms and cold desert about 1.26 lakh sq. km Three core sectors, namely, land shaping and development, water resources development, afforestation and pasture development have been identified and 75% of the programme allocation is earmarked for implementation of core sector activities. The thrust is on afforestation and pasture development for which 40% of the total allocation is earmarked. The DDP is wholly funded by the Centre and allocation is made on the basis of the extent and severity of desertic conditions. Tentative allocation for Eighth Five Year Plan is Rs. 500 crores. For adoption of new technologies and innovative activities developed by various Research institutions and NGOs and for active participation of local community, it is proposed to entrust one watershed project in each of DPAP and DDP States for complete planning and development to a Research Organisation or a NGO.

HILL AREAS DEVELOPMENT PROGRAMME (HADP):

The basic objective of the Hill Areas Development Programme (HADP) has been socio-economic development of the hills and the people living there in harmony with ecological development. The programmes implemented under the HADP have, therefore, aimed at promoting the basic life support systems with sustainable use of the natural resources of the area covered by the programme.

The crucial environmental problems of the hills are deforestation and soil erosion, both leading to the drying up of water sources, flash floods and decline in the yield of food and cash crops, fodder, fuel and other minor forest produce. Poverty in the hills is directly related to shortages of materials for basic subsistence, specially where, under the traditional land and water management systems, the capacity of land to support the population has already been exceeded.

In many hill areas, intensive livestock pressures along with indiscriminate felling of trees for commercial purposes have already led to loss of soil and rapid depletion and destruction of forest cover. Besides, water retention capacity and productivity of land have been adversely affected. These factors have impaired the ecology significantly and also resulted in deterioration in the economic condition for the hill people. Traditional agricultural practices, especially shifting cultivation have also contributed to destruction of forests and soil erosion. Seemingly harmless activity as prolonged grazing by livestock, especially goats and sheep, have further exposed many hill areas to serious ecological degradation. Development activities like construction of buildings, roads, dams, large and medium industries and mining etc., have aggravated environmental problems. Consequently, perennial sources of water springs and small streams have dried up in many areas. The major challenge, therefore, is to devise suitable location-specific solutions so as to reverse the process and ensure sustainable development of the growing population and ecology of the hill areas.

The approach and the strategy of the HADP has evolved over time. The programmesimplemented during the Fifth Plan period were mainly beneficiary oriented. While the emphasis shifted to eco-development in the Sixth Plan, the general tenor of the HADP remained substantially the same as that of the normal State Plan following the same sectoral approach. The Seventh Plan laid particular emphasis on the development of ecology and environment as summed up in three phrases, namely, eco-restoration, eco-preservation and eco-development. It aimed at evolving plans and programmes to take care of socio-economic growth, development of infrastructure and promotion of ecology of the areas covered by the HADP.

During the Eighth Plan, attention will have to be focussed on modernising the agricultural practices and small scale industries at household, cottage and village levels. To achieve this, involvement of the people would be of paramount importance. Actual basic needs of the people have to be met through improved management of their land and water resources.

DEVELOPMENT OF WASTELANDS:

Consequent upon the creation of the Department of Wastelands Development, the National Wastelands Development Board (NWDB) has been reconstituted with the mandate to develop wastelands in non-forest areas for their sustainable use. Though the subject of wastelands falls within the domain of State Government, the problems of land upgradation as well as land utilisation do not recognise State boundaries. The urgency of putting the large resource of wastelands to sustainable use to meet the increasing demand for biomass is a national challenge. Entrusted with the task of development of non-forest wastelands which has not received adequate attention for a variety of reasons, the NWDB is expected to play the role of an effective facilitating agency.

For effective implementation of the programme, the State Governments / Union Territories may undertake the following, which formed part of the agenda for discussion at the Chief Ministers' Conference on Rural Development held in October, 1992 at Delhi: Identify and notify nodal departments and nodal officers for facilitating easy interaction amongst the agencies and institutions concerned with development of wastelands;

Evolve appropriate policy measures and institutional mechanism for promoting / facilitating the development of wastelands by mobilising public participation / involvement and participation of non-government organisations, corporate bodies, etc.

Give priority attention to the development of wastelands and make adequate provisions in their Five Year Plans and the Annual Plans; Consider giving indicative annual physical target for development of wastelands and monitoring progress at regular intervals; Advise / guide the Department of Wastelands Development, from time to time, in regard to issues on which intervention / support of Government of India and its agencies is required to facilitate the development of wastelands.

BANKING FOR RURAL DEVELOPMENT:

Rural Credit is one of the most crucial inputs in all rural development programmes. The objective of the Government has been that of progressive institutionalisation of credit for rural development programmes. There has been a phenomenal expansion of public sector bank branches in rural areas. At the end of March, 1992, as against 41996 total bank branches of the public sector banks, 20535 branches are in rural areas. The proportion of rural branches in the total branch network is 48.9 per cent. The amount of credit channelised into rural areas stands at 44581 crores in March, 1992.

After the concept of social responsibility is introduced, government has stipulated that a certain quantum of credit be earmarked for the weaker sections. The stipulations as they stand now are (i) 40% of the total loans and advances should be in the priority sector comprising of credit to small and marginal farmers, weaker sections, SC & STs; (ii) 18% of total bank lending should be towards agriculture; (iii) A special scheme of DIR advances (differential interest rate) at 4% interest is targeted for the upliftment of the poorest of the poor. Government has stipulated that one per cent of total advances should be towards DIR loans. Rural credit is organised in different tiers. At the base, we have the primary agricultural cooperative credit societies. At the District level, federations of primary agricultural cooperative credit societies called the Cooperative Central Banks (sometimes also termed as District Cooperative Banks) are functioning. The State Cooperative Banks, which form the apex of cooperative banking structure, lend financial support to the District Cooperative Banks. The long-term credit needs in the rural areas are taken care of by the Primary and State Land Development Banks. RRBs (Regional Rural Banks) function in the rural areas as the rural adjuncts of the scheduled commercial banks. In 1990-91, there were 196 RRBs with 14555 branches with a deposit base of 4737 crores and advances of 3599 crores. In addition, the scheduled commercial banks also have a network of rural branches extending credit facilities for a plethora of rural activities. NABARD (National Bank for Agricultural and Rural Development) is established in July, 1982 as an apex organisation to oversee the distribution of rural credit. It is organically linked to the RBI and also acts as the refinancing institution for rural based activities like agriculture, village industries, handicrafts, etc. With a view to rationalise and avoid duplication of effort, a new strategy for rural lending called the service area approach was started in 1988. Under this approach, each branch of the semi-urban / rural areas would be assigned a specific area of 10 to 25 villages within which they will operate adopting a plan approach to harmonise the effort of banks in the task of rural development and to avoid diffusion of efforts over wide areas. To promote rural industries, a new bank called SIDBI (Small Industries Development Bank of India) is established on the lines of the IDBI. To consolidate the achievements of RRBs and to achieve economies of scale, a merger of RRBs into an apex rural bank which would be called NRBI (National Rural Bank of India) is being proposed.

LAND REFORMS AND LAND RECORDS:

Land reforms have been on the national agenda of rural reconstruction for a long time since independence. In a rural society where land is the most relevant source of living for a large section of the people and the rights of land confer socio-economic status and dignity, the importance of land reforms and land records needs more emphasis. The major objectives of land reforms consist of reordering agrarian relations to achieve an egalitarian social structure; elimination of exploitation in land relations; realizing the age-old goal of land to the tiller; enlarging the land-base of rural poor;

increasing agricultural productivity and production; and infusing equality in local institutions. The major components of the strategy of land reforms have been the abolition of intermediary tenures; tenancy reforms; ceiling on ownership of agricultural holdings; consolidation of holding; distribution of Government wastelands including Bhoodan land; modernisation and updating of land records system; conferment of ownership rights on homeless persons; special measures for protection of lands of Scheduled Castes and Tribes; improving the access of land to women and safeguarding of common property resources. Closely linked with land reforms is the issue of land records. Apart from the importance of land records from the point of view of land revenue, the land records are to be looked upon as a means for ensuring social justice in rural areas, crucial documents for the effective implementation of land reform measures particularly for identification of surplus lands and tenancy; identification and demarcation of Government lands and village common lands; and constituting the data base for implementation of rural development and agricultural programmes. The absence of correct land records has often been responsible for many land disputes to the disadvantage of the poor. The modernisation of the land records system and making them more accessible and relevant to rural people is, therefore, a matter of considerable importance.

The land ceiling drive has been hampered by an inadequate and inaccurate record base. There should be effort for both short term and long term improvement in the record base, making full use of modern technology. It has been found that cases remain pending too long for disposal before revenue courts. There should be a time bound disposal of cases by the revenue courts. There should be a dovetailing of the benefits under IRDP, JRY and agriculture programmes to the ceiling surplus land allottees for a quick take off beyond the poverty line. Post allotment support should form a deliberate strategy of the anti-poverty programmes. Distribution of Government Wastelands and Bhoodan lands has been one of the important strategies of land reforms; but this has perhaps not received the attention that had been due to it. There is approximately 12.95 million hectares of waste land in the country. It has been the accepted policy that waste land at the disposal of the Government should be distributed amongst the eligible rural poor. It is necessary that the criteria governing the distribution of ceiling surplus land should also apply to the distribution of wasteland.

CONCLUSION:

Gandhiji said 'The Soul of India lives in Villages'. Nearly three-fourths of our population lives in rural areas. As such, we cannot boast of development in the country unless the fruits of development reach the rural poor. Hence rural development assumes greater importance. Rural development should aim at both economic betterment as well as social transformation while giving due consideration to the resources crunch situation in the country. This calls for an integrated approach for rural development, with the active participation of the people themselves, their institutions at all levels, voluntary agencies and non-governmental organisations. In this national endeavour of utmost importance, the universities, colleges and other institutions have their own legitimate role to play. A thread of social relevance should be interwoven into their teaching, research and interaction activities. The interaction could be both for social purpose, which may be called as extension activity and for economic development purpose as well. In addition to the development of appropriate technology, the potential of the youth and the faculty should be utilised for extension activities. They should adopt nearby villages and help them in literacy, population, education, health and nutrition, family welfare programmes etc. The University community should play an active role in the national rejuvenation with focus on rural development.

URBAN DEVELOPMENT

EIGHTH FIVE YEAR PLAN SCENARIOS WITH SPECIFIC REFERENCE TO URBAN AND REGIONAL DEVELOPMENT

Shri Suri, President, distinguished participants of the Workshop, ladies and gentlemen,

I consider it an honour to be with you this afternoon to inaugurate the Technical Workshop on "Eighth Five Year Plan Scenarios" with specific reference to Urban and Regional Development, being organised by the Institute of Town Planners, India. I would like to express-my thanks to the organisers for giving me this opportunity. I offer my greetings to all the participants of the Workshop who have come from various parts of the country. I am happy to note that the Institute of Town Planners, India, which was established in 1951 to foster professional activities, education, training and research related to urban and regional planning in' the country, have more than 1200 Urban and Regional Planners as its Members. The country needs talented manpower in the field of urban and regional planning. However, only a few institutions and universities are offering under-graduate and postgraduate courses, training programmes and taking up research activities. We have to encourage more universities to offer courses in urban and regional planning. When I was the Vice-Chancellor of the Jawaharlal Nehru Technological University, Hyderabad, until eight months ago, a School of Planning and Architecture was established to achieve excellence in teaching, research and consultancy in the field of urban and regional planning and architecture. The School is offering a course in

Master in Urban and Regional Planning. I must congratulate the Institute of Town Planners, India for their yeoman service in the field of urban and regional development in the country.

During the last four decades, while the total population of India has more than doubled, the urban population has nearly grown four times—from 62.44 million in 1951 to 217.20 million in 1991. The urban population is expected to reach 326 million by 2001 A.D. when the total population will be around 1000 million with about 33 per cent of our population living in towns and cities. The 1991 population census has indicated that India's urban population of 217.20 million is spread over 3969 urban agglomerations and towns of various sizes. An analysis of the growth pattern shows that the structure of urbanization has been changing significantly towards larger cities. The share of cities with population of one lakh size and above has increased from 60 per cent in 1981 to 65 per cent in 1991 and is expected to be 70 per cent by 2001 A.D. The population of 23 cities has crossed one million mark.

The urban sector in India is playing an increasingly dominant role in national economic development. During the period 1970-71 and 1985-86, the share of urban areas in the country's National Domestic Product (NDP) has increased from 37 to 55 per cent. Another significant contribution of urban sector is the absorption of a high proportion of incremental labour force. During the last ten years preceding 1987-88, the growth rate of employment in the urban areas averaged around 4 per cent per annum while the employment growth rate in the rural areas dropped to less than 1 per cent. There is thus a clear indication that the urban areas will absorb the future larger increments to the labour force.

A review of urban policy framework in an historical perspective indicates that until the Sixth Plan (1980-85), urban policies were mainly concerned with questions like city size; housing, slum clearance, improvement and upgrading; preparation of Master Plans and Municipal civic administration. The Seventh Plan marks the beginning by explicitly recognising the problems of urban poor linked with creation of employment opportunities. The urban planning practices are also now accepting the existence of informal sector activities. This is in sharp contrast to the position in the Sixties and early Seventies when the Master Plans prepared for fast growing urban centres almost entirely ignored the informal sector activities. The planning process is also now beginning to recognise that urban policies can also directly contribute to goals such as poverty reduction, unemployment and underemployment.

The haphazard growth, increasing congestion in large cities, high degree of pollution, existence of slums, high land prices and deteriorating urban services are some of the facets associated with present urbanisation and in particular, the continuing growth of large cities. We must recognise that it will be difficult for our rural areas to generate adequate employment to support the growing population in a manner that poverty is not increased. Twenty years ago, about 55 per cent of Gross Domestic Product (GDP) was being created by and was supporting 70 per cent of labour force in agriculture. Today a similar 65 to 70 per cent of the labour force is creating less than 35 per cent as the contribution by agriculture to GDP. The other 30 to 35 per cent of the non-agriculture labour force is, therefore, producing the other 65 per cent of the GDP. The large portion of this non-agriculture sector's contribution is coming from urban areas. In the interest of keeping rural-urban disparities to minimum and also to provide more productive urban activities, among a larger proportion of people, the thrust would have to be on rapid expansion of non-agricultural activities and employment assisted by the promotion of skills at all sizes of urban centres.

Increasing pressure on the land-man ratio in the agriculture sector would continue to swell the number of rural unemployed and forcing them to migrate to urban centres in search of employment. The paucity of employment opportunities in small towns is forcing people to migrate to large cities and hence urban to urban migration is no less significant than rural to urban migration. The large cities are growing or have already grown beyond their sustainable capacity with pressures of overstrained infrastructure facilities, while small towns are decaying. It is, therefore, imperative that small towns are developed to correct this imbalance and to direct the future course of urbanisation to take place in an orderly and balanced manner.

Urbanisation can play a forceful catalytic role to achieve the objective of overalleconomic development of the country through the process of spatial planning of the rural and urban areas in an integrated manner. The development of small towns assumes great importance in this context also. In addition to checking the migration of rural labour containing thereby the size of large cities, the development of small towns would engineer a momentum of overall economic growth of the entire region located within the gravitational influence of a particular town. It is now widely recognised that, because of the existence of close inter-dependence between small towns and the adjoining rural areas for demand and supply of goods and services, economic activities in these areas generate numerous developmental forces which could be harnessed through a network of backward and forward linkages for the mutual benefit of both set of areas.

The issue of provision of urban infrastructure and service and deteriorating urban Environment and quality of life all point to the fact that gap between the demand and supply of services is widening over the years. In several instances, infrastructure and services have deteriorated as a result of increasing pressure of population. There is overwhelming evidence that access of the poor to the basic services is wide spread and increasing. Studies have indicated that access of large segment of a population to, drinking water, sanitation, education and basic health services are shrinking.

The key aim of planning for urban development should be adequate infrastructural support at the State or Regional or local levels. The provision of services and infrastructure remove constraints on the growth of economy. It is important to time the investments in urban services and shelter to coincide with the investments in various sectors of economy.

Fast growth of urban population, spread of the urban areas and spurt in commercial and industrial activities have led to urban transport problems like severe traffic congestion, slowing down of vehicular movement, longer journey hours, increased costs of travel etc. Urban transport is an important service sector and plays a crucial role in the development of the urban economy and the time has come to take immediate stock of the urban transport scenario. Traffic engineering and regulations, widening of roads, interlinking of transport with land use planning, integration of the services provided by various modes of transport, all these need urgent attention. It may be necessary to introduce a multi-modal mass rapid transit system in the super-metros, and for this purpose evolve a suitable technical and financial package. It is also desirable to take advance action to define, segregate and set apart, the alignments for future transport corridors as a part of the plan for the development of each urban entity. This will guide land use planning and facilitate introduction of appropriate transport services, at a later stage, along such dedicated alignments.

In major metropolitan cities, the time has come when planning for future growth must avoid any segmented approach. Infrastructure like transport, telecommunications, energy supply, developed land and basic services like drinking water, sanitation, sewerage, etc., and education and health facilities must be provided for in an integrated manner, while drawing up a perspective plan for the growth of the city. To facilitate the diffusion of activities in metropolitan cities over much wider areas, an overall plan should be prepared inclusive of the contiguous cohesive areas of the metropolitan cities. The plan should be flexible and promote an orderly and environmentally sound development pattern for the future metropolitan growth.

Attention needs to be focussed on not only the growing challenges of urbanisation but on the relationship between urban and rural development. The rapid transformation in the country's urban scenario must be taken into, account and provided for, in order that urban growth assists the process of healthy socio-economic development of the country as a whole. While doing so, it will be necessary to take note of the prevailing dichotomy in rural and urban development and evolve a much needed mechanism for bringing about rural-urban coherence in the management of growth.

Rural development goals cannot be achieved in isolation; it will need to draw sustenance from urban strengths. Economic growth with social equity requires both accelerated agricultural development as well as expansion of urban industry and commerce. The ties between the urban and the rural economy are crucial for promoting wide spread development because the major markets for agricultural surpluses are in urban centres; modernisation of agriculture creates surplus rural labour who seek employment in towns; and many of the functional inputs that satisfy rural basic needs, both physical and social, are distributed from urban basis. Urban and rural development have, therefore, to go hand in hand, considering that what is characterised as urban includes a whole hierarchy of settlements from the metropolis through medium and small towns to the "rural-urban interface" of small towns and rural growth centres.

Two aspects will have to be kept in mind while providing for such synthesis of sectoral and spatial planning:

(a) Spatial development plans would need to be prepared keeping in perspective the 'growth centres concept'. This will provide a framework for identification of growth centres and lower order centres from major towns to central villages where investments can be attracted depending upon the infrastructure available and their potential.

(b) The spatial development plans would provide for:
   i) Selective concentration of activities / facilities at nodal locations with a view to facilitating absorption of potential migrants and sustaining rural-urban continuum.
   ii) Selective channelisation of labour intensive activities.

The scheme of Integrated Development of Small and Medium Towns needs to be so implemented as to emphasise the fostering of the rural-urban inter-dependence and functional relationships. Special emphasis needs also to be given to the strengthening of the economic base of the towns with a view to integrating the sectoral and spatial plans in each given region.

These are certain goals at the national-regional levels which need to be given focus during the Eighth Five Year Plan. The present urban pattern, its form, composition and distribution is such that, unless positive public interventions are made, the present differential and disparities cannot be mitigated. Looking at the perspective, it is imperative to provide for the essential spatial dimensions in our national planning exercise; as the planned development of the human settlements should be one of the key components.

HOUSING

Housing is not only a basic human need but also stimulates economic activity, employment, generates household savings and provides the plinth for the achievement of the crucial objectives in terms of health, education and general wellbeing. Shelter and development are thus supportive of each other. There is a welfare aspect of housing which relates to the quality of dwelling, conforming to socially accepted norms of construction, living space, essential amenities etc.

Despite considerable investment and efforts over successive plan periods, the housing problem continues to be daunting. The housing crisis manifests itself in many ways: growth of slums and unauthorized colonies, overcrowding and deficient services, increasing homelessness, speculation and profiteering in land, and houses and decreasing quality of life. Given the relentless growth of population and urbanisation and the difficult economic environment, the housing problem will further worsen unless concerted measures are taken to ameliorate the living conditions of a vast majority of vulnerable sections of the society both in rural and urban areas. The endeavour of the planning activity should be to accomplish the goal of shelter for all.

The overall magnitude of the housing problem confronting the country, viewed over a span of 20 years from 1981 to 2001, is estimated to be 23.3 million dwelling units in terms of backlog and 63.8 million new dwelling units comprising of 32.6 million in rural areas and the balance 31.2 million in urban areas to meet incremental housing needs.

The Government has been working on the formulation of a National Housing Policy.

The Ministry of Urban Development prepared a draft National Housing Policy document which was widely circulated and discussed. The draft is under finalisation. The thrust of the draft policy is the crucial role of Government to create an enabling environment, to remove constraints to housing activity of various sections of the population, to promote a substantial increase in the supply of housing and basic services, to support upgradation of the housing stock and to stimulate rental housing. The State would address specifically the needs of the houseless, poorer households, SC / ST, women and other vulnerable groups.

Serviced land, housing finance, availability of building materials, and trained construction personnel alongwith appropriate and enabling legal environment as well as institutional framework are essential for increasing the tempo of housing activity.

House construction is largely a matter of private initiative. People build houses using their own financial savings supplemented by loans from public and private institutions, banks or the Government. But the individual initiative needs support. The role of the State is that of an enabler, facilitator and promoter of critical infrastructure for housing activity. This responsibility include creation of mechanisms for enabling savings for future house construction, setting up of the necessary financial apparatus to facilitate grant of loans at reasonable rate of interest, undertaking the acquisition and development of land and ensuring equity in the making available of serviced land for house building purposes. Thereafter, it is really private initiative which comes into play.

The role of housing as a basic input which enhances the productive potential of the human being has been recognised. Housing, however, needs to be looked at in the larger frame-work of human settlements with integrated provision of infrastructure, employment opportunities, services and transport to promote community growth. The long term objective is the provision of "Shelter for All". Given the competing demands on available resources, however, the achievement of this goal will inevitably need to be spread over a reasonable span of time. The provision of sites, affordable shelter and basic services, for all sections of the people will need to be followed up with the housing units, so provided, being progressively improved, in stages, utilising the combined resources of individuals, the community and the Government.

The topic for the Workshop "Eighth Five Year Plan Scenarios" with specific reference to Urban and Regional Development is quite timely as it comes at a time when the Eighth Plan is being finalised. I am sure the outcome of the Workshop will be a valuable input for the Eighth Five Year Plan for Urban Development and Housing. I take pleasure in inaugurating the Workshop and wish it all success.

ADDRESS AT THE NATIONAL MEET ON "HOUSING NEEDS, FINANCE, LEGISLATION, AND POLICY"

I consider it as a privilege to associate myself with the inaugural session of the National Meet on "Housing Needs, Finance, Legislation and Policy" being organised by the Socio-Economic Research Foundation and express my gratitude to the organisers for inviting me to preside over the inaugural session. This National Meet is being organised at a time when we are finalising the Eighth Five Year Plan, which is to commence from April, 1992. I am sure, the outcome of the Meet will offer valuable inputs into the Eighth Plan document on Housing. Utilising this opportunity, I would like to share with this august gathering some of my thoughts on the various aspects of Housing.

HOUSING NEEDS

Housing is not only a basic human need but also stimulates economic activity, employment, generate household savings and provides the plinth for the achievement of the crucial objectives in terms of health, education and general wellbeing. There is a welfare aspect of housing which relates to the quality of dwelling, conforming to socially accepted norms of construction, living space, essential amenities etc.

Despite considerable investment and efforts over successive plan periods, the housing problem continues to be daunting. The housing crisis manifests itself in many ways: growth of slums and unauthorized colonies,

509

overcrowding and deficient services, increasing homelessness, speculation and profiteering in land and houses and decreasing quality of life. Given the relentless growth of population and urbanisation and the difficult economic environment, the housing problem will further worsen unless concerted measures are taken to ameliorate the living conditions of a vast majority of vulnerable sections of the society both in rural and urban areas. The endeavour of the planning activity should be to accomplish the goal of shelter for all.

The overall magnitude of the housing problem confronting the country, viewed over a span of 20 years from 1981 to 2001, is estimated to be 23.3 million dwelling units in terms of backlog and 63.8 million new dwelling units comprising of 32.6 million in rural areas and the balance 31.2 million in urban areas to meet incremental housing needs.

Taking into account demographic and other factors, the housing needs in terms of physical requirement for the Eighth Plan period separately for rural and urban areas for reducing the backlog and meeting the new requirements were estimated by the Working Group on Housing for the Eighth Plan as under :-

	(in millions for five years) (1990-95)		
	Rural	Urban	Total
Backlog (mostly upgradation, repair and renewal)	4.07	1.75	5.82
New Housing Stock	8.15	7.80	15.95
	12.22	9.55	21.77

The shortage in terms of backlog relates the Kaccha and semi-pucca houses needing upgradation.

To tackle the serious dimensions of the housing problem confronting the country, there is a need to step up the investments in the housing sector and urban infrastructure and increasing it at a steady pace thereafter so that there can be a hope for significant change in the housing situation.

HOUSING FINANCE

As per the 1991 Census, the total population of the country is 844.32 million. The expected population by the turn of the century may be around 1000 million. The level of urban population has increased from 23.24% in 1981 to 25.72% in 1991 and is expected to be around 32 to 33% in 2001. There is, therefore, a need for higher percentage of investment in housing. During the last two decades the share of housing sector in national income has been around 3 to 4%. The gross capital formation in construction of residential buildings as a percentage of the total gross domestic capital formation has been about 12% during the Seventh Plan. The percentage of housing investment to total investment in the economy was 34% in the First Five Year Plan and it has gradually declined to 9% during the Seventh Plan.

The lack of financial resources is a crucial constraint to the housing activity. The financial need for housing cannot be made solely by the Government budgetary support and there is need to:-

i) Step up flow of funds from financial institutions to the housing sector;

ii) Increase the level of contribution of the commercial banks to the housing sector;

iii) Increase the level of contribution from financial institutions like L.I.C., G.I.C., P.P.F., etc., and

iv) Industrial Sector should also make investment in housing sector for industrial workers.

Institutional Financing Intermediation has not played a major role in the resource mobilisation efforts for most households for housing. The bulk of the population is still unable to get access to the formal financing institutions. The requirements of housing finance for individuals, groups and institutions comprise new construction, shelter upgradation, land development and infrastructure and finances for cooperatives and private developers. This critical need is met substantially from informal sources and only to a limited extent from formal system.

Housing deserves higher priority for diversion of institutional resources because this is a sector which has immense employment generation potential. According to an estimate, investment of Rs. 1 crore in residential building construction can provide direct employment of 565 man-years and indirect employment of 904 man-years at 1983-84 price level. In view of larger investment requirements, the National Housing Bank, HUDCO, and HDFC type of financial institutions have to play a significant role. Given various constraints on public resources, the role of public sector has to be essentially of 'enabler to help overcome various obstacles including access to credit, developed land, upgradation and new constructions. However, some programmes in public sector would have to address the housing needs of absolutely homeless, disadvantaged groups, Scheduled Castes and Scheduled Tribes, economically weaker sections and other groups in the acute need of assistance. Priority has to be given to identifying the shelterless and devising strategies to house them in a time-bound manner. Innovative methods in mobilising the profits from commercial construction activities, particularly in larger cities, need to be explored. Differential land pricing as to cross-subsidise for housing the urban poor should be adopted in determining the price of the developed land. Another source of revenue could be mopping up of surplus by eliminating private profiteering in land in and around areas of urban centres which arise mainly on account of investments in infrastructure by the State. Another appropriate fiscal means which need to be initiated is recovery of the cost of investment in urban infrastructure and services.

The problem of rural housing should not be viewed in terms of finance and resources alone. The construction of new housing stock and upgradation of unserviceable kuccha houses will only materialise if homestead rights are conferred on rural poor, basic conditions are created in making available appropriate building materials, access to bio-mass and natural resources and upgradation of the traditional skills of the local artisans involved in the shelter construction and improvement. Further, State and the public agencies should mount programmes for provision of infrastructure facilities with full involvement of the rural community which will set the pace for housing programmes and improvement of settlements.

LEGISLATION

There are many legal impediments in the existing laws and regulations constraining access to shelter for poorer households in urban and rural areas. In this context, the following are the more important requirements.

(a) The amendments to be effected in the Land Acquisition Act and the need to introduce procedures for negotiated compensation with a view to speeding up the process of acquisition of land.

(b) Section 20 and 21 of the Urban Land (Ceiling and Regulation) Act, which allow discretionary exemptions, need to be amended.

(c) The Rent Control Act, which was introduced in the pre-independence period, has over time, proved to be counter productive. While regulation to protect the rights of tenants is desirable, the Act, as presently enforced to be a severe disincentive to investment in housing for rental purposes. Rent control legislation should, therefore, be suitably amended to encourage investment in housing.

(d) It will also be-necessary to make suitable changes in the Transfer of Property Act by making changes in land tenurial systems to ensure conferment of tenurial rights on the landless for house-sites. New legislation will be required for regulating the activity of builders and developers and protecting the interest of the consumers.

HOUSING POLICY

The Government has been working on the formulation of a National Housing Policy.

The Ministry of Urban Development prepared a draft National Housing Policy document which was widely circulated and discussed. The thrust of the draft policy is the crucial role of Government to create an enabling environment, to remove constraints to housing activity of various sections of the population, to promote a substantial increase in the supply of housing and basic services, to support upgradation of the housing stock and to stimulate rental housing. The State would address specifically the needs of the houseless, poorer households, SC / ST, women and other vulnerable groups.

Housing has to be considered in the larger context of human settlements. The planning of urban and rural development, location of economic activities and provision of infrastructure and services and transport need to be comprehended in integration with provision of housing. Thus, housing and development are supportive to each other. The investment plan for housing should identify areas of State effort in the form of direct intervention for priority groups, and through the promotion of housing activity of the households, cooperatives and organised sector in a variety of ways. Specifically the involvement of voluntary agencies in rehabilitating slums and disaster affected houses is to be encouraged. The role NGOs in selected areas of policy and planning can be crucial. Similarly, the cooperative societies can contribute significantly to the housing needs of not only the middle income households but also to the low income households by providing suitable support.

The bulk of the housing in the country is constructed by the people themselves. They do supplement their on resource with loans from private or government financial institutions, banks etc. But the initiative, the standards and specifications, and the responsibility are private in character. Government also constructs houses but in terms of investment, this amounted to only about one-tenth of private effort during the Seventh Plan. A major proportion of all housing activity specially in the rural areas is based on biomass resources, and is almost entirely outside the monetised economy. What this means is that it is the people who can and do build the bulk of the housing units themselves. What they cannot do is to obtain land, assemble it in large sizes and arrange the basic infrastructure of water supply, sanitation, roads, lighting etc. Public sector should,' therefore, desist from trying to build houses by itself; its role is to create an environment which enables the full potential and resources of the people to be fully utilised and remove constraints coming in the way. This calls for a major reorientation of the role of public agencies, in the manner outlined below:

(A) ROLE OF GOVERNMENT

It would move towards land and infrastructure development, creation of an enabling environment and removal of constraints to housing activity. The role of the State is to be seen as an enabler, facilitator and promoter of critical infrastructure for housing activity.

(B) HOUSING, AND DEVELOPMENT AGENCIES

Housing agencies and area development authorities in the public sector should act more as promoter and facilitators of housing. They play an increasing role in:

i) Development and supply of serviced land;
ii) Distribution of building materials and components at reasonable rates;
iii) Provision of technical and advisory services;
iv) Development and extension of appropriate construction technology; and
v) Assisting people in various ways to take up construction and upgradation of houses.

(C) NATIONAL COOPERATIVE HOUSING FEDERATION

At the national level, the National Cooperative Housing Federation of India (NCHF) should continue promoting, developing and coordinating the activities of housing cooperatives throughout the country.

CONCLUSION

The role of housing as a basic input which enhances the productive potential of the human being has been recognised. Housing, however, needs to be looked at in the larger frame-work of human settlements with integrated provision of infrastructure, employment opportunities, services and transport to promote community growth. The long term objective is the provision of "Shelter for All". Given the competing demands on available resources, however, the achievement of this goal will inevitably need to be spread over a reasonable span of time.

ADDRESS AT THE 13TH MEETING OF THE N.C.R. PLANNING BOARD

I am happy to be present in the 13th Meeting of the NCR Planning Board and participate in its deliberations. The concept of planning and development of the National Capital Region has been there for a long time, though a statutory organisation along with a statutory plan became a reality only recently. It is a good augury that the participating States and the Union Territory of Delhi have fully subscribed to the philosophy contained in the NCR Plan and its implementation can now be taken up in right earnest. The concept of partnership, which has been suggested by the NCR Plan, is a laudable concept, and it should be possible for the concerned Central Ministries to channelise at least a part of their investments for the planned development of the NCR in the context of containing the growth of the National Capital within manageable limits.

The Planning Commission is at present engaged in the process of finalisation of the Eighth Plan and we shall try to ensure a positive response from the various sectoral departments in support of the proposals contained in the NCR Plan. Decentralisation of activities from the National Capital and development of the identified priority towns would be possible only if proper infrastructure at regional level is provided. This would include improvement of transport, both rail and road, provision of telecommunications, and making the required amount of power available to bridge the demand-supply gap.

The provision of a regional rail bypass would not only help bypass through-traffic away from the congested Delhi railway corridor, but would also provide a big fillip to the development of the identified priority towns in the NCR Plan. It should be possible for the Ministry of Railways, who has agreed on the need for the bypass to make a start in this direction during the Eighth Plan itself. The ways and means for this could be discussed while finalising their Eighth Plan allocations. Similarly, the other rail proposals need also to be looked into. Inland Container Depot under construction at Tughlakabad should be seen only in the limited perspective of relieving congestion at the existing ICD at Pragati Maidan. The location of a full fledged ICD, as suggested by the NCR Planning Board outside Delhi Metropolitan Area, at Palwal or some other suitable location with an expressway junction is very important and should be the long term objective. The depot at Tuglakhabad should be viewed only as an interim arrangement.

The Ministry of Surface Transport has agreed to meet the requirements of improving the National Highways but it is important that they participate in the programme for constructions of expressways also as this would help relieve congestion on Delhi roads. With expressways, traffic which need not come into Delhi can bypass it without suffering delay. Expressway could be a self-sustaining investment with levy of toll and it should not be a problem for the Ministry of Surface Transport to support this proposal. I would urge the Ministries concerned with Transport to actively participate in the process of decongesting metropolitan Delhi.

Power is again a very crucial requirement. It is obvious that if the requirement of power of the proposed urban development centres can be-met, this would go a long way in meeting the objectives of the NCR Plan. The Planning Commission would take a serious look at this while finalising the Eighth Plan allocations of the Ministry of Energy.

As already stated by me, the Commission is presently engaged in the process of finalising the Eighth Plan provisions for the Central Ministries. A firm picture would emerge only after these have been finalised during the course of the next few months.

MANAGING OUR METROPOLISES:
NEW DIRECTIONS FOR 21ST CENTURY

Prof. Raori, Prof. Misra, distinguished participants, invitees, ladies and gentlemen,

I am highly delighted for having been invited to inaugurate the National Symposium on "Managing our Metropolises: New Directions for 21st Century", which is being organized by the School of Planning and Architecture. I am grateful to Prof. Misra for inviting me to inaugurate this Symposium. I would consider that organising such a Symposium on Metropolises is quite timely and I should congratulate the School of Planning and Architecture for this. I find from the programme that the Symposium will deliberate on all major issues relating to the planning and management of the metro cities. The Symposium could not have been organised at a more appropriate place than the School of Planning and Architecture. It is heartening to note that the School, from a modest beginning in 1941, has broadened its horizon by introducing new thoughts and research areas in planning and architecture. The co-sponsors of this Symposium viz., Delhi Development Authority, Indian Institute of Public Administration, Institute of Town Planners, Municipal Corporation of Delhi, National Institute of Urban Affairs, Operations Research Group and Town and Country Planning Organisation also deserve praise in supporting a timely endeavour of this kind.

Rapid growth of urban population is a distinctive feature of the economic development process in the developing countries. A brief look at the population statistics will reveal the magnitude of this challenge in India. While the population of India grew from 238.4 million in 1901 to 844.3 million in 1991, the urban population grew from a mere 25.8 million in

518

1901 to a phenomenal 217.1 million in 1991. While the decadal growth rate of population in 1991 stood at 23.56%-, the decadal urban growth rate stood at 36.19%. The Ratio of urban population to the total population was merely 10.84 in 1901, whereas it grew to 25.72 in 1991.

While the macro level statistics indicate a trend of rapid urbanisation, the statistics pertaining to the metropolitan cities will not fail to draw our attention to the impending problems of congestion in the metropolitan areas if we do not find the ways and means for better management of our metropolises. According to 1991 Census, the population of Bombay was 12.57 million with a decadal growth rate of 33.43 per cent. Calcutta competes with Bombay in absolute numbers at 10.92 million, but has a lower decadal growth rate of 18.73%. Delhi, finishing third in absolute numbers at 8.38 million has an alarming decadal growth rate of 46.18%, while Madras at 5.36 millions has a decadal growth rate of 24.99%. Hyderabad with a population of 4.28 million has the highest decadal growth rate of 67.03%. While there were only thirteen cities with a million plus population in 1981, the number shot up to twenty three cities in 1991. This trend of high urban growth rate should give us ample reason to focus our undivided attention and energies on the emerging problems of managing our metropolises.

A new dimension has been added by the possible impact of the economic liberalisation process on urban growth. The economic liberalisation process envisages a strategic shift from import substitution to export led growth. Major steps have been initiated to attract foreign direct investment. The expected inflow of international capital creates a demand for a number of urban services. The encouragement given to private sector initiative may give rise to a fresh impetus to industrial activity. Factors like the fiscal and financial sector reforms, the changes in policy and procedures aimed at stepping up economic growth and integration of the Indian economy with the global markets have important implications for the urban sector where most of the new investments are expected to flow. The need for new directions in the management of our metropolises are thus needed not only to facilitate and strengthen economic development but also to support and streamline the process of India's urban transition.

Fresh thinking is needed on urban land reforms. The new economic activities on account of the liberalisation of the economy and the associated population increase will place a great strain on land availability. The existing policies on land holding, transfers of land and high taxes on such transfers result in under reporting of land prices and leads to the creation of a black market which in itself fuels up the upward spiraling of land prices. It has also to be examined if the large tracts of urban land belonging to public bodies like ports, railways, jails etc., can be leased out for commercial activities which would also augment the resources of such public bodies.

Deficits in infrastructure in terms of housing, water supply and sanitation, power, transport and communications have to be met as expeditiously as possible. The Plan support in terms of financial provision, with regard to urban infrastructure however, seems to be insignificant. During Seventh Plan, urban development per se accounted for about Rs. 1,800 crores (including State and Central Sector) or about 1% of the total Plan outlay. However, if we include Housing and Urban Water Supply Sector, this will come to a little over Rs. 7,000 crores (about 4%) during the Seventh Plan. During the Eighth Plan, it is likely to be same in proportional terms. Therefore, the strategy for financing of urban infrastructure has to go much beyond the conventional plan support. As a part of the Eighth Plan strategy for Urban Development, the role of institutional finance has been given greater emphasis.

The urban housing shortage, according to the National Buildings Organisation's data, is 10.4 million houses in 1991 and is expected to increase up to 15.5 million houses by the year 2001. In this context, augmented flow of institutional finance to housing sector assumes great importance. The National Housing Bank, the Life Insurance Corporation and the housing finance subsidiaries of the scheduled commercial banks are playing a significant role in housing finance. However, more incentives have to be planned to encourage the flow of resources into housing finance to create an enabling environment for housing activity as envisaged by the National Housing Policy. The core strategy of the Eighth Plan includes— associating private developers in fringe area development, promotion of low cost building materials and cost effective technologies, and promotion of self help housing as well as shelter upgradation. Public sector bodies like the HUDCO are to play their role as facilitators and enablers.

In the area of water supply and sanitation, the objective of the Eighth Plan is to achieve 100% coverage of safe drinking water facilities in urban areas by the turn of the century. A major policy initiative with reference to water supply is to consider and manage water as a commodity. The billing and collection mechanism has to be strengthened to enhance resource availability to achieve self sustainability.

As regards sanitation, it is envisaged to achieve a coverage of 80% during the Eighth Plan. One of the objectives of the Eighth Plan is to evolve and create a scientific and effective mechanism for collection, transportation and disposal of solid waste and in the process convert as much of the bio degradable material as possible into organic manure. It is desirable that the municipal bodies should bifurcate the water supply and sanitation budget from the general budget. Future projects in urban water supply and sanitation should increasingly rely on institutional finance with stress on cost recovery from users.

Metropolitan transportation is a major problem that should engage our immediate attention. While it may be true that the process of urban agglomeration itself is a phenomenon made possible by the transportation revolution heralded by the advent of the automobile, but the rapid proliferation of automobile population with its attendant problems of congestion and pollution, tends to be a negative factor for urbanisation.

Improvement in the quality of roads, introduction of computer based traffic management systems, construction of flyovers etc., will go a long way in mitigating the problems of metropolitan transportation. An alternative model is the adoption of Mass Rapid Transportation System which is highly capital intensive. Engineering and technological solutions to the metropolitan transportation problem seems to look at only the supply side of the transportation. A viable solution to the problem may lie in attacking the demand side. The normal traffic pattern of any metropolitan area consists of traffic originating on the city periphery and flowing towards the Central area. A reverse peak flow of traffic occurs during the evening, originating in the Central business area towards the city periphery. If this rhythm can be altered by dispersing the activities of the central areas towards the periphery, a new set of nuclei can emerge creating different traffic rhythm. This may, to a great extent, help solve the problems of congestion and pollution. The creation of New Bombay to decongest Greater Bombay is a positive attempt of solving the metropolitan transportation problem from the demand point of view rather than the supply point of view.

The National Capital Region (NCR) Plan is an attempt at development of satellite towns to decongest Delhi. The NCR Plan consists of preferential development of priority towns around the Delhi Metropolitan Area (DMA). A system of integrated transportation is planned for these regions. It is envisaged that the transportation network would lead rather than follow development. The essence of the NCR concept is to diminish the centrality of Delhi, by interconnecting the maximum traffic attracting and traffic generating urban modes in the region surrounding Delhi. A complementary component of the NCR Plan, incidentally studied by the School of Planning and Architecture, is the concept of counter-magnet areas. The counter-magnet areas would be located outside the NCR and sufficiently away from Delhi. They act as the future interceptors of migratory flows and they also act as regional growth centres to achieve a balanced pattern of urbanisation. This kind of holistic approach has to be encouraged for better management of our other metropolises.

Communication is another vital infrastructure input in urban development in general as well as metropolitan management in particular. The demand for telecom services in the metropolises has already far outstripped the supply. The impact of economic liberalization and the consequent possibility of a sharp rise in trade and commerce may put an additional strain on the telecom services. In fact, availability, accessibility, connectivity and reliability of telecom services are a pre-requisite for inflow of capital. As we move towards the twenty first century, the demand for cellular telephones, electronic networks, voice mail services etc., will increase.

Urban agglomeration is also energy intensive. The share of industry and transport stood at 50.4% and 24.5% respectively out of the total energy consumption in 1990—Higher population densities in metropolitan areas mean a higher demand for movement of goods and passenger transport. Vertical growth of a city by increase in the number of highrise buildings would mean increasing vertical transportation against gravity which is more energy intensive. All this put a greater strain on our fossil fuel resources. The increasing rates of fossil fuel consumption will put the world supply of fossil fuels on a dwindling curve. Thus the future management of metropolitan areas should take into account (i) the need for conservation of our fossil fuel resources, and (ii) the need for establishing viable technologies in non-conventional energy sources. Urban architecture should direct itself at designing energy efficient buildings by taking advantage of natural lighting, cooling and heating.

We cannot ignore the environmental concerns that have surfaced in the recent years in our metropolitan areas. Pollution free air for breathing is a primary requisite. The Pollution Control Act has to be implemented in true spirit and stringent punishment should be meted out to the violators / offenders. Better environmental standards can be achieved if the statutory measures are supplemented by environmental education. Environmental improvement of urban slums is constantly engaging the attention of the planners. During the Eighth Plan, the scope of Environmental Improvement of Urban Slums (EIUS) is widened to include NRY Programme and the Urban Basic Services for the Poor (UBSP) programme.

The Integrated Development of Small and Medium Towns (IDSMT) scheme to reduce the push-pull a factor of migration of rural people to the metropolitan areas was drawn up during 1979-80. Until March 31, 1991, a total of 457 towns had been covered under the scheme. The scheme had broadly achieved its objectives but it did not have the desired impact on the hinterland. The Eighth Plan envisaged a fresh approach to the IDSMT Programme, dovetailing the activities under the various employment generation programmes into the supportive infrastructure development programme with a view to (i) generating employment opportunities to reduce the rural-urban and urban-urban migration, (ii) developing growth centres for the betterment of rural hinterland adopting a regional approach, and (iii) providing infrastructural facilities to support the various employment generation activities.

Another important issue in managing the metropolises is the strengthening of urban health care services. When a large population is packed in a small geographical area, any possibility of an epidemic breaking out will have frightening consequences. One of the strategies of the Indian Council of Medical Research (ICMR) and other academic institutions during the Eighth Plan is the development of a centre for Epidemiological intelligence. Such centres need to be developed in all the metropolises with cross linkages. Optimisation of resource utilisation in Medicare, interaction with R & D organisations with a view to constantly bring into application the research findings are other major thrust areas during the Eighth Plan.

CONCLUSION:

When 50% of India's GDP is being produced in urban areas which contain only about 25% of the total population, it is fair to conclude that productivity of urban areas is very high. As a logical corollary, it is not wrong to assume that future development activities get located in cities. Wisdom requires that a nation should be prepared for the eventuality of urban explosion to contain its ill effects at the minimum and to enhance the positive effects to the maximum. The present National Symposium on "Managing our Metropolises: New Directions for 21st Century", is a right step in the right direction at the right time. I once again congratulate the organisers for thinking ahead of times, which is a hallmark of true planning, in organising this Symposium. The deliberations of this symposium are of major consequence not only to India but to all the developing countries of the world. I take pleasure in inaugurating this Seminar and wish it a grand success.

GLOBALISATION OF INDIAN ECONOMY—ROLE OF MATERIALS MANAGEMENT

Shri Bharadwaj, distinguished delegates, invitees, ladies and gentlemen,

I am highly delighted for having been invited to inaugurate the NCR Convention on "Globalisation of Indian Economy—Role of Materials Management" being organised by the Indian Institute of Materials Management in commemoration of Materials Management Day. Materials Management is a very important and responsible function in any organisation, big or small. It is heartening to note that the Indian Institute of Materials Management with 29 branches and 18 chapters spread throughout the country is serving the cause of professionalisation of this important managerial function. The institute is also rendering yeoman service through dissemination of latest information on Materials Management through organisation of seminars, conventions and through publication of their bimonthly journal, "The Materials Manager". I am glad that the institute is also serving the cause of management education by conducting a graduate diploma course in Materials Management and a post-graduate diploma in Materials Management by correspondence. The present convention on the theme "Globalisation of Indian Economy—Role of Materials Management" has come up at a time when the Indian economy is on the threshold of globalisation. I congratulate the IIMM for coming up with such a relevant theme at an appropriate time when the world of business, trade and industry have finally found their new axis of rotation—globalisation.

While a brave new world is emerging all around us, our response to the global change process is equally spectacular. The nations which would anticipate change, exploit change and create competitive change have emerged as leaders in the world economy. Not to be left behind, the rate at which the Indian economy has freed itself from the stifling forces of inertia, to poise itself for a steady trot on the highway of growth, has few parallels in contemporary history. It was only nearly two years ago that we had put our first steps forward towards a structural reform process. The New Industrial Policy Resolution of 1991, which abolished the institution of licensing, is a land mark in our irreversible process of liberalisation of the economy. Further, a permanent seal on the process of liberalisation is put by the full convertibility of the rupee on the external trade account. To integrate our economy into the global economy, and to make our manufactures more competitive in the global markets, major duty reductions on many items of manufactures were also announced.

The recent amendments to the Export-Import Policy were made with a view to further liberalise the Exim Policy in a bid to boost exports. The major thrust of the trade policy reforms, the financial and the fiscal sector reforms are to create a facilitating atmosphere for the Indian industry to compete effectively in global markets. The policy of liberalisation also envisages a quantum jump in foreign direct investment. As the reform process consolidates itself, more foreign capital can be expected to enter the country. Globalisation of Indian economy is a challenge as well as an opportunity.

If we analyse the global technological scenario, the major technological shift, as we enter the twenty first century, is that the logic of the mass production mechanism has been superseded by the logic of innovation. And that logic in turn demands new organisational and management practices. If the opportunities offered by the new trends of globalisation have to be capitalised, it is not sufficient if we merely react to change. Indian industry and organisations need to develop pro-active responses to change. Identifying the drivers of change, assessing forces of resistance to change and building change scenarios should be the organisational responses in a change-prone business climate.

In the ever shifting winds of organisational change, three things have to remain unchanged. They are: (i) cost competitiveness, (ii) quality consciousness, and (iii) delivery performance. Materials management plays a pivotal role in all the three aspects. To commit an organisation to the ideals of quality, cost effectiveness and promptness in delivery schedules in the atmosphere of global interaction, the ethos of materials management in India should undergo a sea change.

It is not only the sales that contribute to profits, but the Materials Wing of an organisation can be a profit centre. The purchase function of an organisation controls a major chunk of the organisation's finances. A major portion of the fixed capital is in plant and machinery and a substantial portion of the working capital is in raw materials, spare parts and other supplies. All these items would have entered the organisation through purchase function only.

It is not incorrect to assume that about 50 to 60% of the cost of production in manufacturing industries would be the material cost. Then, the profitability of the company largely depends upon purchase efficiency. In organisations of average material intensity, it is worked out that the benefit of reducing 5% material cost by effective materials management is the same as increasing the sales by about 30%. Added to this, reducing the internal and external lead times can further reduce the cost of carrying the inventory and directly contribute to profitability.

In the days of severe international competition, it is highly essential that every purchase-rupee is effectively spent so that the final product price is competitive without erosion in profit margins.

Materials management hitherto was only performing the job of purchasing. In thecontext of globalisation of the economy, the scope of materials management has to be widened. Materials Management Wing has now to be involved in almost all the operations of an organisation right from product design stage. Strategic sourcing of a critical item or a part may sometimes obviate the need for developing an auxiliary manufacturing capability which may sometimes prove costlier. The—time and energy saved can be used more productively while the final product works out to be more cost effective.

In the days when time is the scarcest resource, materials management can save a lot of time to the organisation through intelligent demand forecast after a study of the production process and market movement. Thus purchase function should not be a passive activity of acting after an indent is placed but should actively involve in production and marketing functions to gather internal and external intelligence.

Often, the Materials Management wing of an organisation is the only window to the outside world. It is the initial point of contact between the organisation and an outside agency. Materials Management can be an effective source of information for the organisation. The various types of information can be (i) general market intelligence, (ii) supply sources, their strengths and weakness, (iii) price movements, tariffs, taxes, transportation routing, availability and rates, and (iv) product information and new product development.

Globalisation implies quick shifts in markets, wide price fluctuations, and high rate of product development. Materials management should be able to service the organisation with an integrated management information system of which the materials information system would only be a sub-system.

Producing for global markets holds the challenges of quality, reliability, timely delivery and cost effectiveness. For this, consolidation of raw material sources is a prerequisite. Every new vendor takes a considerable quantum of time to go through the learning curve and the time would just be not available. The new role of materials management would be to identify vendors, cultivating them, working with them, associating them in the production process and forming strategic alliances where necessary.

The new challenge of globalisation is the constant need to maintain a competitive advantage by effective management of time. Companies which make decisions faster develop new products earlier and convert customer orders into deliveries sooner have a unique value in the markets they service, a value that can translate into faster growth and higher profits.

The faster the information and material flow through an organisation, the faster it can respond to customer orders or adjust to changes in market demand and competitive conditions. Materials management has to play a leading role in achieving this fast cycle capability. Selecting, training and bringing in suppliers early on into the design process cuts the product development cycle drastically.

Internal lead time can almost be reduced to nil if a computerised system of processing the indents and placing the orders is practised. Even customer orders can be quickly turned to deliveries by networking the factory scheduling system with the sales / dealer networks. Materials management has to reorganise around customers and their needs. Therefore, it is not surprising that in Du-pont production engineers now visit customers to learn customers' needs first hand which usually is considered to be the job of the Sales Department.

Adopting the concept of Just in Time (JIT) may prove valuable in materials management. The philosophy of Just in Time (JIT) concept is that a part or an item has to be procured only when it is necessary and in exact quantities which are currently required. JIT is the ultimate ideal of material management which implies zero inventory level. The need for inventory arises only because of the internal and external lead times. Achieving zero internal lead time is a matter of automation of the information flow process. The real challenge of materials management is to reduce the external lead time to zero. This can be made possible if the materials management wing cultivates vendors who can deliver materials within hours of placing the order. The logistics of JIT have to be worked out by materials management and the vendor organisations. Relocating the vendor's warehousing in the premises of purchasing organisation and blanket order systems are some of the ways of achieving JIT levels. Deep cooperative and synergic relations have to be developed with the vendors to confirm to JIT standards.

Globalisation of business is contributing to increasing transnationalisation of organisations. The job of materials management is going to become correspondingly more difficult to that extent. In the near future, it is likely that production facilities, due to cheaper labour markets, are increasingly going to be located in the developing countries. Organisations are going to function from many countries with independent manufacturing capabilities or a single product may be assembled nearer the market location but parts manufactured in a dozen other countries. Whatever may be the finer variations, this scenario is likely to prove difficult to materials management.

Already, world over, the centralised purchase system is giving way to global purchasing through commodity management teams, the members of which are dispersed in various countries. In 1989, Xerox Corporation of USA had devised and formed a multinational organisation called Central Logistics and Asset Management (CLAM) and four multifunctional, product-focussed teams to integrate the supply chain across geographic boundaries. The aim of CLAM was to reduce excess inventory and inventory related costs by linking customer orders more closely with production. The commodity management teams should include members from purchasing, engineering, finance and quality assurance so that, as a group, they have the necessary expertise to identify world class supplies.

Producing for international markets adds an extra dimension of commitment to total quality. The biggest non-tariff barrier for entry of our goods in international markets is the problem relating to quality. The philosophy of quality circles should permeate the core of the Indian manufacturing activity. The emergence of ISO 9000 in the international industrial scenario is a challenge to Indian industry. Materials management should be committed to Total Quality Management (TQM) and any parts or spares not conforming to international standards should be rejected outright. Materials management should observe extra vigilance in weeding out any sub-quality material flowing into the system.

The new challenges thrown up by globalisation are yet new opportunities that are opened up to make our mark on the international industrial scene. Globalisation implies adoption of and adaptation to new technologies. The added stress on right quality, quantity, time, source and price, the emerging need for effective internal and international interfacing, the new complexities introduced by materials planning in a globalised market scenario throws up an urgent need for executive training / retraining, research and studies in the Materials Management area. In this context, I congratulate the Indian Institute of Materials Management for setting up a National Research and Study Centre at Calcutta.

This Convention on 'Globalisation of Indian Economy—Role of Materials Management' has come up at the right time to create a positive awareness among the intellectuals in the industry, business and government regarding the new challenges of Materials Management in the process of globalisation of the Indian economy. I once again congratulate the IIMM for selecting such an inspiring theme and take pleasure in inaugurating the Convention and wish it all success.

ADDRESS AT THE ALL INDIA MEETING ON STATE URBAN DEVELOPMENT STRATEGY IN VIGYAN BHAVAN, NEW DELHI

I am highly delighted to participate in the inaugural session of the all India Meeting on State Urban Development Strategy being attended by the State Government representatives, Secretaries and other officials of the Ministry of Urban Development, Ministry of Finance, Planning Commission, HUDCO and some of the most eminent experts on urban development. Let me extend a warm welcome to all of you. A cohesive national urban policy is a long felt need and it is now more pronounced in the present day context of rapid urban growth and the changed economic scenario in the country. Realising this need Planning Commission has taken the initiative in organising meetings and discussions on the subject of 'Urban Policy'. This meeting is second in the series and the first one was held in the month of March on 'Implications of Economic Liberalisation for Urban Sector'. I am sure that the outcome of the previous meeting and today's deliberations will provide the needed base for evolving such a national urban policy.

Let me take this opportunity to share with you some of the ideas on which we have been deliberating upon in the Planning Commission and also in the Ministry with regard to future urbanisation trends and problems and the strategies to respond to them. National Urban Policy cannot be developed in isolation and any attempt at development of national policy has to be based on a scientific and realistic appraisal of the trends and issues of the urban development at State and regional levels. This is borne out by the varying pattern and level of urbanisation among different states, the underlying economic forces, natural endowments and institutional factors shaping such urban development patterns. For example, among major States, Maharashtra with 38.7% of population classified as urban has highest level of urbanisation while Himachal Pradesh has only 8.7% of its population residing in urban areas. The relationship between level of urbanisation and rate of growth of population has also not been uniform and varies significantly during the last two decades. For example, States with low level of urbanisation and also lower than national average per capita income like Bihar, Madhya Pradesh, Orissa, Rajasthan, Uttar Pradesh, grew at a significantly higher rate than the average during 1971-81 but this trend is not so conspicuous in the decade 1981-91. There was a significant decline in the growth of urban population for Bihar and Orissa. Among the more developed urbanised States, Maharashtra maintained higher rate than the average growth. Tamil Nadu, Karnataka and West Bengal registered significant decline. Urban growth in Kerala during 1981-91 was most pronounced with highest decadal growth which is perhaps intrinsic to the character of urbanisation in the state. At the other extreme are the low densities and scattered settlements in North Eastern States which may call for a different strategy.

The average rate of urbanisation also declined significantly during 1981-91 (36.2%) compared to the earlier decade of 1971-81 (46.1%). This implies reduced rural-urban migration, though absolute addition to urban population was higher than in the last decade. The other distinctive trend in the urbanisation pattern is increasing concentration of population in Class I towns, the increase being from 60% in 1981 to 65% in 1991. Even accounting for the area adjustment, Class I towns have grown faster than the rest. The most revealing feature of the recent urbanisation trend is the increase in the number of metropolitan cities from 12 in 1981 to 23 in 1991 accounting for over 32% of the total urban population of 217 million residing in about 3600 urban centres. Interestingly, however, the growth of what can be called Mega cities has been significantly lower, particularly for Calcutta and Madras.

The above trends of urbanisation are not of mere demographic significance, they represent largely the outcome of interaction between economic development and urban development. It is to be clearly recognised that viewing urban development in isolation from the overall process of economic development will lead to a wrong strategy. As the

National Commission on Urbanisation in Volume II of its Report stressed "Urbanisation strategy should be part of a bigger strategy of generating economic growth and not one of doling out some residual funds for urban housing etc . . ." This has also been the thrust of the VIII Plan. In the Plan, we have emphasised on the macro strategy for urban development to take due cognizance of rural-urban linkages, relationship between industrial location and other employment generating activities to urban development and more importantly the need for integration of spatial and economic dimension of planning. It is thus desirable not to view the urban sector as being delimited by the activities of your Ministry or department but as an integral part and supportive of the economic development. This is why a well directed strategy for investment in urban infrastructure and institutional arrangements to respond to it becomes crucial in deciding the development policy of not only the urban sector but the States' overall development.

The need for urban development strategy has been accentuated in the context of the recent economic reforms initiated in the field of trade, industry and fiscal policy. As the basic objectives of such economic reforms is to promote productive efficiency and economic growth and as much of the expansion / new economic activities is expected to take place in and around urban areas, enhanced and qualitatively satisfactory provision of urban infrastructure, both economic and physical, will be a pre-condition for the success of the new economic policy. This will call for reforms in the urban sector both of short and long term significance. Such reforms should have the following focus:

(a) Creating 'enabling' conditions to enhance the flow of investment in critical urban infrastructure contributory to growth of economic activities as well as overall improvement to quality of life of the urban dwellers.
(b) Initiate a process of deregulation, simplification and removal of unsustainable Norms and rules to facilitate the process of development of urban infrastructure including housing.

I am appreciative of the fact that there are a large number of macro issues and externalities which cannot be taken care of in the existing set up with limited role of state housing and urban development agencies or urban local bodies. This will call for policy interventions at the national level and much higher degree of coordination among various sectors and departments within the State Govt. Hence I would urge that while preparing

State Development Strategy paper, not limit yourself to—a few selected schemes of the State Government and the Centre but draw up a larger canvas of urban scene and its concerns and consequent macro strategy. It will be necessary to bring in this effort of interactive role of various sectoral policies and programmes and draw up a scheme of prioritisation of public investment among competing demands which have direct bearing on urban development. In this direction, I find some merit in adopting the approach of National Commission on Urbanisation in identifying list of towns showing a higher economic potential identified as GEM (Generator of Economic Momentum) area or any other set of criteria to be chosen by the State Governments which can link the economic potential with the investment frame. This may require reprioritisation of the programmes of various departments which would facilitate realisation of the economic potential of the identified towns and cities. In case of some of the States like West Bengal and Maharashtra where the role of Metro cities is preponderant both in demographic and economic sense, it is necessary to spell out the States' approach to development of metro region vis-à-vis rest of the state. Perhaps a combined strategy of tackling serious infrastructural deficiencies of Metro cities with inducement to growth and promoting intermediate urban centres is worth exploring. Above all, it is essential to keep in view that any strategy we propose has to be sustainable. Our recent concerns for deterioration in environmental quality in large cities need to be translated into definite plans of action.

I am sure that the State Urban Development Strategy Papers prepared by most of the States have addressed some of these macro issues and also identified areas for policy interventions. As this kind of effort is being taken up in an organised manner for the first time and requirements of preparing such a comprehensive strategy go much beyond the existing domain of the functional responsibility of the State Urban Development and Municipal Affairs departments, I think it would be appropriate to proceed in a phased manner. That is why Planning Commission has asked the States to prepare initially an Interim paper which will form the basis of our discussion today. Exchange of ideas among the participating States will not only improve the next version of the urban development strategy paper but also help to work towards National Urban Policy and provide a better operational framework for future investment programmes.

At the end, I would urge upon you to keep in view some of the important issues of operational significance. For example, I feel that strengthening the finance of the urban local bodies through both structural improvement and better management is an immediate task. The provision in the Nagar Palika Bill for setting up of State Municipal Finance Commission to decide on the devolution of revenues raising powers to the urban local bodies should be utilised for this purpose. Similarly, removal of legal and procedural bottlenecks so as to develop an efficient and expanded land market particularly in metro and large cities is another important challenge. Significant efforts have been initiated by the Ministry of Urban Development in respect of removing legal bottlenecks but these measures should be expedited. There is need to rethink on some of the, rigidities in our Master plans, building bye-laws and development rules which inhibit efficient land use and generation of land based resources. Here again, provisions in the Nagar Palika Bill in the form of the district and metropolitan Planning committee need to be taken advantage of. It is also important to keep in view that in the present environment of economic liberalisation, dependence on budgetary support will have to be reduced to the extent possible. Exploring opportunities of privatisation as well as public private combines and expanded role of institutional finance for investment in urban infrastructure would have to be given added importance. However, in the process of this economic liberalisation and emerging investment strategy, the basic objective of the urban local bodies to provide basic services like water supply and sanitation and ensuring access of urban poor to these services should not be lost sight of. This is where I think a careful planning and programming at the State level, which takes best advantage of the existing programmes, large parts of which are addressed to the urban poor and also smaller urban centres, is a pre-requisite for responding to the challenges of urbanisation.

I feel that the present decade provides greatest challenge to the urban planners both because of the inadequate attention paid towards its problems in the past and also because of the realisation that higher economic growth in this decade and beyond will be critically dependent on our success in evolving scientific and realistic approach to urban development at State and National level. I am sure that all of us would work together to respond to this challenge. I wish you for a successful all India meeting on this vital subject of urban development strategy.

PROBLEMS & PROSPECTS OF INDUSTRIAL DEVELOPMENT IN THE NATIONAL CAPITAL REGION

Dr. Bansi Dhar, Senior Vice-President, FICCI, Shri R.N. Singh, President, Bhiwadi Manufacturers Association, Shri H.R. Sharma, Vice-President, Bhiwadi Manufacturers Association, distinguished guests, ladies and gentlemen,

I am delighted to participate in the inaugural session of the Conference on 'Problems and Prospects of Industrial Development in the National Capital Region' being organised by FICCI at Bhiwadi. The choice of the venue of the Conference is an ideal one. It is heartening to note that Bhiwadi industrial area which was a tiny village has now attained the status of 'pride of Rajasthan', with a host of industrial activities. Bhiwadi is a priority town of the NCR Plan. With a present investment of Rs. 400 crores, and providing direct employment to about 30000 workers, Bhiwadi has certainly earned an unrivalled eminence and a strategical importance in the overall NCR picture. I congratulate the Bhiwadi Manufacturers Association for achieving this distinction in a very short span of time.

It is a good augury that at the right juncture, the FICCI has come up with a stimulating theme, 'Problems and Prospects of Industrial Development in the NationalCapital Region'. I congratulate the FICCI for selecting such a relevant and inspiring theme for the Conference.

The concept of the National Capital Region is an idea that has arisen out of the serious concern for the unprecedented growth of Delhi and the belief that its planned growth is possible only in a regional context. Delhi, which had recorded a population of 6.22 million in 1981 has grown to 9.37

million in 1991, with a decadal growth rate of 46%. The NCR Plan—2001 assigns the ultimate population to be restricted to 11 million by 2001 in Delhi and assigns a population of 8.9 million to the DMA towns and the eight priority towns. Delhi at the current point in its demographic history is reeling under heavy population pressure. It is a known fact that every civic amenity including water, power, transport, housing and sanitation has come under severe pressure due to unprecedented immigration. But the concentration of economic activity, leading to a rapid increase of population in the capital city is a world wide phenomenon and India is no exception to it. The ultimate consequences of unbridled urban sprawl and the attendant risk of urban blight and decay can be escaped from switching over from a mono-nodal development pattern to a poly-nodal one. Herein lies the strength of the NCR concept.

The NCR Plan—2001 is a bold and unique initiative of inter-state and inter regional cooperation in a federal frame work. It is a joint venture of partnership for progress through an integrated planning for the balanced regional development of a whole region cutting through state boundaries.

During the Eighth Five Year Plan, an allocation of Rs. 200 Crores has been made to the NCR Planning Board. This is a significant step-up as compared to the Seventh Plan allocation of Rs. 65 Crores. It is envisaged that this allocation alongwith certain internal resources generated by the NCR Planning Board would be utilised as seed money to raise additional resources through a judicious mix of public and private sector investment. Plans are afoot to float a captive financial institution called National Capital Region Development Finance Corporation Limited (NCRDFC). This Corporation may invite equity support from participating states, Delhi Union Territory and other financial institutions such as HUDCO, UTI, NHB, LIC and GIC. The necessary amendment to the NCR Planning Board Act of 1985 has to be made for the creation of NCRDFC as its subsidiary.

An immense amount of planning expertise has gone into the NCR Plan. A host of studies have been conducted to validate the concept and to ensure the success of the Plan. Migration studies in the context of NCR Plan, informal sector in the NCR, land use analysis based on landsat imagery, promotion of employment generation in NCR towns are some of the studies undertaken, which I mention here to substantiate the scientific approach towards the implementation of the NCR Plan. Added to this, the pattern of land use is proposed to be continually monitored using high resolution remote sensing data. The NCR Plan is high on the agenda of the Central Government and the participating state governments. The plan proposals of the Ministries of Urban Development, Surface Transport, Power, Telecommunications and Railways will have a special NCR component. Efforts are being made to dovetail the Delhi Master Plan into the NCR Plan—2001. In addition, the participating state governments— Uttar Pradesh, Rajasthan and Haryana, are drawing up subregional plans under the aegis of NCR Plan—2001. The projects and proposals relating to development of infrastructure in the NCR are constantly engaging the attention of planners. The amount of sustained interest and attention generated by the NCR Plan is immensely satisfying. This should be the basic reason for a high degree of optimism regarding the prospects of industrial development in the National Capital Region.

Proximity to big markets is one of the guiding principles of industrial location. NCR is going to be one of the huge markets in the country. The economic activity generated to service such a huge market would surely be unprecedented. Keeping in view the rural hinterland surrounding the priority towns and the needs of the multitude of city dwellers, food processing industries are likely to flourish in the DMA priority towns alongwith engineering, electronics, electrical and other service industries. A study has been undertaken to identify the core economic activity of each of the DMA towns and the priority towns of the NCR. The industrial development would initially be induced around the core economic activities with concrete linkages developed between them and other economic activities. Thus, there is a potential for textile industry at Meerut, electrical / electronic and engineering industry at NOIDA, food products, metals and chemicals at Ghaziabad, service industries, wholesale trade and commerce at Hapur, agricultural machinery at Bulandshahar, ceramics at Khurja, containerisation at Palwal, fuel oils, building materials and informal sector in Rewari-Dharuhera-Bhiwadi complex, fruits and vegetable processing at Kundli etc.

The pattern of industrialisation of NCR is likely to undergo a sea change in the post liberalisation scenario. With an increased role for the private sector and with the likely participation of the private sector in infrastructure industries like power and transport, a quickened pace of industrialisation is to be expected. With the curbs on foreign equity participation removed there could be direct foreign investment in the NCR region. As the policy package of the NCR Plan is aimed at containing the growth of Delhi within manageable limits and inducing the growth in the priority towns, the best location for industries would be outside Delhi in the NCR region given the incentives vis-à-vis the package of disincentives and regulations against location in Delhi.

There is no denying the fact that the prospects of industrial development of the NCR would be directly proportional to the infrastructure made available. The infrastructural needs would be in terms of power, transport, communications, housing, water supply and sanitation. To meet the cost of infrastructural development, the NCR Planning Board's proposed Eighth Plan outlay comprises of Rs. 1327 crore in the Central sector for expressways, national highways, railways and telecommunications in NCR towns and counter magnet towns. An outlay of Rs. 1513 Crores in the state sector is envisaged for land acquisition and development of sub-regional centres, upgradation of regional roads and infrastructure upgradation. This figure of Rs. 1513 Crores is inclusive of Rs. 397 Crores for power transmission and distribution and Rs. 100 Crore for counter magnet areas. One way of financing these investment proposals could be through the proposed National Capital Region Development Finance Corporation Limited (NCRDFC).

The NCR Plan is grand in conception and needs a high degree of technical and nontechnical coordination among the multifarious agencies involved in its implementation. On completion, it could be a nucleus of economic development. It is not unnatural for a plan of such proportions to have certain teething troubles. In the course of execution of the plan, problems need to be identified and solutions are to be sought. Some of the problems are already identified and efforts are being made to arrive at appropriate solutions. A lower tax structure in Delhi Union territory vis-à-vis the surrounding states is said to be one of the factors for concentration of economic activity in Delhi. Rationalisation of the Sales Tax structure in Delhi is under consideration and this magnetic effect is likely to be appropriately dealt with.

Lack of proper transmission and distribution facilities is identified as the main bottleneck for likely power shortages in the NCR. The decision of the government to open up the power sector for private initiative is likely to attract private investment in this area to augment the power needs.

An area which is being newly urbanised is likely to have a shortage of higher order social facilities like educational / medical / engineering institutions, universities, hospitals, sports complexes and other recreational facilities. While the government is sensitive to such felt needs and strives to provide for such facilities within the existing resource constraints, this is also an area of opportunity for responsible private sector participation.

As the implementation of the NCR Plan progresses, the experience gained by the government and the industry is likely to throw up new issues which may require further dialogue and deliberations. I am also hopeful that the deliberations of this Conference would enlighten us about the problems and prospects of industrial development of the National Capital Region. This is an area of utmost importance to all of us in the interest of balanced regional development. I have great pleasure in inaugurating the Conference and I wish it a great success.

FORMULATION AND FINANCING OF URBAN WATER SUPPLY PROJECTS

It is a great privilege for me to inaugurate the Training Programme on "Formulation and Financing of Urban Water Supply Projects" sponsored by the Ministry of Urban Development and being organised by IIPA. I do feel that this training programme is timely and relevant. In the Planning Commission we have been deliberating on the challenges posed by high rate of urbanisation along with the characteristic feature of concentration of urban population in a few large cities. For example, 23 'Metro' cities alone account for more than $1/3^{rd}$ of total urban population inhabited by about 3700 towns and cities. What is intriguing is that while these large cities account for the major share of income generation in the economy, corresponding financial resource base of the urban Government has not improved resulting in inadequate investment in urban infrastructure. The contribution of the State and Central Government in the process has been rather limited, in view of resources constraint and other competing demands, with the inevitable widening gap between demands for supply of urban services. This gap is perhaps more evident in case of water supply and sanitation than in any other urban infrastructure. This is both because of lumpy and capital intensive nature of investment in the water supply and sewerage and the high technical and financial management requirement for proper maintenance of this system.

Within this perspective, I feel that the theme of these training programmes should address to the basic issues of project implementation and financial management of water supply and sewerage system. I am sure that in the course of this training programme the experts will provide you an opportunity to get into details of various issues involved. I would like to share some of the broader dimensions of the problem of this sector with you.

The service levels in several cities and towns are far below the desired norms, particularly in small towns. The coverage of urban population by protected water supply is estimated to be around 85% at the beginning of the 8th Plan. What is however, more important to note is the inadequacy of water supply both in quantitative and qualitative terms for majority of towns. This inadequacy is both due to lack of investment in augmenting water supply system and in management of system as it exists.

Efforts made in the successive plans have tried to improve the urban water supply system but the gap is still too large. It is expected that the VIII Plan strategies and programmes would make an important dent on the urban water supply system. Two main objectives visualised in the VIII Plan are:

i) To extend safe drinking water facilities to the remaining urban population, so as to achieve the goal of about 94% coverage of population by the end of Eighth Plan and 100% by the turn of the century with the stipulated norms and standards, and

ii) In view of the poor financial base and low coverage with water supply facilities in small towns, particularly those having population less than 20,000, it has been felt necessary to evolve and implement cost-effective special schemes of drinking water supply with some financial support from Centre on a matching basis under a Centrally Sponsored Scheme.

With these objectives in sight the strategies laid down in the VIII Plan give greater thrust to the management of water in exactly the same way as any other resource. This will call for providing local bodies, which are mainly responsible for operation and maintenance, with necessary freedom to raise appropriate user charges to strengthen their financial base. Encouragement to the involvement of private sector in construction and maintenance of water supply system is another important strategy. Above all, better financial management of Water Supply system is a prerequisite for sustenance of the assets created.

I feel that, in the context of above strategy of the VIII Plan, strengthening local bodies through both structural improvement and better management is an immediate task. The provision in the Nagar Palika Bill for setting up of State Municipal Finance Commission to decide on the devolution of revenue-raising powers to the urban local bodies should be utilised for this purpose. It is also important to keep in view that in the present environment of economic liberalisation, dependence on budgetary support will have to be reduced to the extent possible. Exploring opportunities of privatisation as well as public-private combines and expanded role of institutional finance for investment in urban water supply and sanitation would have to be given added importance. However, in the process of economic liberalisation and emerging investment strategy, the basic objective of the urban local bodies to provide basic services like water supply and sanitation and ensuring access of urban poor to these services should not be lost sight of. This is where I think a careful planning and programming at the State level, which takes best advantage of the existing programmes, large parts of which are addressed to the urban poor and also smaller urban centres, is a prerequisite for responding to the challenges of urbanisation.

I would further like to add that majority of metropolitan and mega cities are presently drawing water from very distant places, as all the nearby water sources have either been fully tapped or tied up for various other beneficial uses. Due to this, the cost of transmission, treatment and distribution of drinking water is becoming higher and higher. The National Water Policy of India announced in 1987, has accorded top priority to drinking water supply in allocation of water sources. Irrigation and multipurpose projects should invariably include drinking water component wherever there is no alternative source of drinking water. It is, therefore, necessary to make long term planning of water resources management for a period of 30 to 40 years ahead keeping in view the supply and demand.

Over-exploitation of ground water may result in deterioration of ground water quality and increase in cost of pumping and treatment which necessitates imposition of Ground-water Legislation for effective regulation and control of both surface and ground-water extraction.

The indiscriminate discharge of untreated sewage and industrial effluent into natural water bodies have resulted in deterioration of the quality of surface as well as ground-water day by day. As such, the drinking water supply sources of cities and towns are getting polluted resulting in the increase in cost of treatment. Concerted efforts therefore need be made to treat the municipal as well as industrial effluents to the desired standards before their disposal. The Environmental Protection Act, 1986 has to be implemented effectively by the Government of India and State

Governments. Efforts need be made for re-use and re-cycling of Municipal waste water and industrial effluents for non-domestic purposes.

Keeping the above scenario in view, I strongly feel that there is necessity to have proper planning and implementation of schemes by adopting technically sound, appropriate, affordable and sustainable technologies in water supply and sanitation sector. Implementation of schemes may be done on modular approach, keeping in view proper time frame. Systems should be adopted which involve low maintenance-cost and are amenable to higher efficiency. In a developing country like ours, it is very essential to adopt cost-effective and sustainable technology in urban water supply and sanitation systems. Greater efficiency can be achieved if the overheads in execution are reduced and proper design criteria are adopted. There is, therefore, an urgent need for Human Resources Development by way of proper training for improving the management capabilities and upgradation of skills.

With this perspective, the 2 weeks training programme which has been sponsored by CPHEEO of the Ministry of Urban Development and being organised by Indian Institute of Public Administration will be an important contribution. I congratulate the organisers in this regard. I now take pleasure in inaugurating the training programme and wish it all success.

SUBSIDY ISSUES IN URBAN SECTOR

It gives me great pleasure to be with you this morning to inaugurate the High Level Policy Seminar on Subsidy Issues in Urban Sector, which is being organised by the Society for Development Studies. I am grateful to Shri Baveja for giving me this opportunity. It is indeed encouraging to note the initiative taken by the Society for Development Studies to organize this important Policy Seminar. The subject is extremely timely and relevant in the context of current Macro-economic environment in the country which aims at increasing the over-all economic efficiency of various sectors through a market-determined system. The issue of subsidy is all the more important in case of a developing country like India which needs to achieve the objective of economic efficiency together with that of equity in the context of large incidence of poverty. The fact that this Seminar tries to focus on the issues specifically related to Urban Sector rather than much talked about issues in more pre-dominant productive sectors like Agriculture and Industry, as well as Exports, has brought in added significance to the subject you are going to discuss today.

I am aware that both measurement and impact assessment of subsidies in urban sector as a whole as well as among its Sub-sectors are complex and involve inter-sectoral dimensions, but I think there is a need for making a beginning in this direction with a clearcut conceptual frame. It is indeed a privilege to inaugurate today's policy seminar which aims at making maiden attempts at understanding this complex subject and evolving over-time, the conceptual frame and strategy for dealing with the various dimensions of subsidy in the urban sector.

I must thank Shri G.C. Baveja and his colleagues and also the learned participants for contributing to this innovative venture. I am sure that in course of the Seminar you will discuss the various facets and refinements in the concept and measurement of subsidy and also pin point some of the important areas of changes or interventions required in the Government Policy and Actions. I would like to restrict my address to the contextual frame in which the subject should be discussed and also more important areas in which the professional contribution of planners and economists would be more significant in the immediate future.

In the first place, it needs to be clearly recognised that Urbanisation is a process which is irreversible and it is supportive of economic development in general. Projections made by the recent ESCAP report on Urbanisation in Asia and Pacific region indicate that most of the countries are in transition from being predominantly rural to predominantly urban. The projection is that the region as a whole would be urbanised to the extent of about 55% of its total population by the year 2020. So far as India is concerned, however, we are likely to be at the lower end with about 40% of population being classified as Urban by the year 2020 as against 25.7% in 1991. In the context of contribution of the urban sector to the national product it would be much larger than that of population. Even by the year 1991, the contribution of urban sector to national product level is expected to be around 55% with only 25.7% population being urbanised.

Given this over-all trend of urbanisation, the dimensions which make the issue of subsidies relevant, requiring a comprehensive treatment of all its complexities, are:

(i) Increasing gap between the demand for Urban services and infra-structure and the provision of the same caused by inadequate flow of investment to the sector, both from public and private sources, and weak financial base of deliverers and users of such services and infra-structure,

(ii) Increasing concentration of population in Mega cities and large cities with attendant exponential increase in the per-capita cost (both capital and operational) of providing basic infra structure like Water Supply, Sewerage, Transport, without any concomitant increase in the pricing of services and revenue generation capacities on the part of Urban local bodies,

(iii) Large incidence of Urban poverty which, though declining in relative terms, the absolute number of urban poor still remain staggering. Various estimates of Urban poverty indicate that the proportion of urban poor range between 20% to 40% (or between 42 and 86 million in the year 1991), and (iv) Existence of various forms of subsidies to the urban sector at various levels of Government, mostly by way of ad-hoc response to the needs of the sector rather than as a systematic effort to tackle the balancing issue of economic efficiency and meeting the basic needs of the urban poor.

The features of Indian urbanisation process that I described above make it abundantly clear that there is a need to consider the issue of subsidy as an integral part of the broader issue of economic efficiency and equity. The question is not one of taking an extreme stand on eliminating the subsidies of all types or one of taking the other extreme view that the subsidy should be need-based irrespective of the cost it imposes on the resource allocation efficiency and distortions in the operation of market. I think there are three central issues on which we should deliberate and evolve a clear cut conceptual frame work and perhaps, make a beginning to evolve an appropriate strategy. They are:

a) Inter-sectoral issues of magnitude and effectiveness of subsidies,
b) Intra sectoral issue (i.e. within the urban sector) of the measurement and impact of the subsidies of various forms.
c) esigning desirable and more efficient form of subsidy which, on the one hand, does not distort the market system and, on the other hand, achieves the objective of appropriately targeting of subsidies to those groups who need to be protected in the process of structural adjustment and at the same time help to contribute to the enhancement of the productivity of the sector as a whole.

I am aware that at this seminar you will not be able to spend much time on intersectoral issue which has to be dealt with in a rather broader context of macro economic dimensions of the development process at large in the country, and therefore, you may focus your deliberations more on the other issues. I think you can get into fruitful deliberations if you analyse the urban housing—a sub-sector in which the issues of subsidies have been dealt with at length for a decade or more and there is a wealth of statistical information available in this respect.

The basic rationale for giving subsidy to housing in India stems from the fact that the requirement of new stock creation for the economically weaker sections (urban poor) is estimated at about 3.35 million units which will require a minimum investment in housing of about 9050 crores during the Eighth Plan period. In addition, there are requirements of upgradation, which are mostly limited to EWS category, estimated at 1.75 million units requiring an investment of Rs. 1130 crores. Any computation of affordability of this group, which is defined to include urban households with income upto Rs. 1250 per month, would indicate that they would not be in a position to afford fully loan financed house at market rates of interest. A set of alternative strategies which have been evolved and tried out in this respect are:

a) Providing interest subsidy on housing loans through HUDCO, State Housing and other Development authorities.
b) Providing free or subsidised serviced plots, and
c) Providing direct construction assistance of capital nature particularly among the slum and low income house-holds.

The main argument against such subsidies, particularly on first two counts, has been that benefits have gone most to the unintended groups in the sense that EWS categories benefited through such subsidy scheme have transferred their land or house to the higher income groups or there has been a diversion of such subsidies to other purposes. The two major questions that you may need to deliberate are:

a) In terms of realisation of intended benefits, whether interest subsidy or capital subsidy is more effective and if so, under what circumstances.
b) Whether such subsidies are sustainable in the long run both in terms of resources available and the limited impact it may have on the over-all income upgradation of the poor.

In addition to the above two central issues, I think you should take into account various other forms of subsidies which are often enjoyed not by the urban poor but by the organised sector employees, the producers of different building materials, construction industry and private builders. The Standing Committee on Housing Finance set up by the Planning Commission has recently brought out some evidence of large subsidies going to the organised sector employees in the form of concessional interest on house loans. Similarly the fiscal concessions enjoyed by the individuals constructing a house and building industry need to be looked into and proper recommendations made to the Government. I think you should also consider another important strategy to help housing sector, which may do away with some of the distortions associated with the interest or capital subsidy directly given to beneficiaries. This strategy relates to the alternative by way of supporting the delivery system; technology extension and provision of basic infrastructure. As you are aware this has been given a thrust in the Eighth Plan by way of support programmes for the Building Centres, Building Promotion and Technology Promotion Council etc., but I feel a lot more remains to be done.

With regard to Urban Infra-structure and services other than Housing, there has been no well directed and consistent policy of subsidy. However, if one looks at various estimates of investment requirements as well as operational and maintenance requirements of infrastructure, I think the magnitude of investment and subsidy involved may be larger (than that of Urban Housing) and there is a need for a conscious attempt to evolve a policy. In general, the support from the Central Government either on capital account or revenue account for the provision of urban infrastructure has been limited and most of the financial support comes from State Governments (including externally aided projects), urban local bodies as well as public sector undertakings. The major form of subsidy has been, by way of underpricing of various services which reflects a wide difference between the average price charged to the consumer and the cost of production and maintenance. The most pertinent example is that of Water Supply and Sewerage System. Revenue earned on Water Supply account (even if collection is assumed at 100% efficiency) will, in most cities, meet hardly 50% of the 0 & M cost. If we take the incremental capital cost of new projects of Water Supply and Sewerage System, the capital recovery will only be a fraction. However, in case of some of the World Bank aided and institutionally funded projects, there has been a conscious attempt to recover major part of the cost through cross subsidy both among different income groups of users and different users of water (domestic and industrial).

The over-all argument, however, appears to be that the current form and magnitude of subsidy, forming a major part of the cost of production and maintenance of Water Supply and Sewerage System is not sustainable in the long run. There have been in practice other forms of subsidy in the area of urban infrastructure, though of limited magnitude. For example, charging lower than the market interest in case of loans under plan head from LIC and similarly lower interest rates for small towns in case of infra structure loans from HUDCO have been in practice. The other form of hidden subsidy has been in the nature of under pricing or inappropriate pricing of land and other infrastructure in various Private and Public Township development projects. I strongly feel that one needs to go beyond these general impressions or conclusions. There should be both Macro level study as well as Micro level studies for various sub-sectors of infrastructure which will enable us to understand the problems and measurement of subsidy in a more concrete manner. The question is not one of establishing or eliminating need to subsidise provision of various infrastructure sectors and services but, one of establishing the more desirable form and institutional mechanism for providing such subsidies so that they can be precisely targeted and sustained in the long run. In the context of economic liberalisation process which should lead to growth of both domestic and foreign industrial, commercial and trading enterprises, much of which will be located in or around urban areas, the over-all issue of financial investment in urban infrastructure has to be tackled in an objective manner and within that the issue of subsidy has to be tackled. Before concluding, I would like to emphasize on the fact that issues of subsidy is neither exclusively economic nor a social one but, it involves a delicate balancing of economic and social dimensions of development in an appropriate institutional manner.

I would like to once again congratulate the Society for Development Studies and Shri Baveja for organising this timely Seminar. I take pleasure in inaugurating the Seminar and wish it a very fruitful outcome.

INDIA'S URBANISATION

During the last four decades, while the total population of India has more than doubled, the urban population has nearly grown four times—from 62.44 million in 1951 to 217.20 million in 1991. The urban population is expected to reach 326 million by 2001 A.D. when the total population will be around 1000 million with about 33 per cent of our population living in towns and cities. The 1991 population census has indicated that India's urban population of 217.20 million is spread over 3969 urban agglomerations and towns of various sizes. The share of cities with population of one lakh size and above has increased from 60 per cent in 1981 to 65 per cent in 1991 and is expected to be 70 per cent by 2001 A.D. The population of 23 cities has crossed one million mark. An analysis of the growth pattern shows that the structure of urbanisation has been changing significantly towards larger cities.

Urbanisation can play a forceful catalytic role to achieve the objective of overall economic development of the country through the process of spatial planning of the rural and urban areas in an integrated, manner. The development of small towns also assumes great importance in this context. In addition to checking the migration of rural labour containing thereby the size of large cities, the development of small towns would engineer a momentum of overall economic growth of the entire region located within the gravitational influence of a particular town. It is now widely recognised that, because of the existence of close interdependence between small towns and the adjoining rural areas for demand and supply of goods and services, economic activities in these areas generate numerous developmental forces which could be harnessed through a network of backward and forward linkages for the mutual benefit of both set of areas.

The key aim of planning for urban development should be adequate infrastructuralsupport at the State or Regional or local levels. The provision of services and infrastructure remove constraints on the growth of economy. It is important to time the investments in urban services and shelter to coincide with the investments in various sectors of economy.

Fast growth of urban population, spread of the urban areas and spurt in commercial and industrial activities have led to urban transport problems like severe traffic congestion, slowing down of vehicular movement, longer journey hours, increased costs of travel etc. Urban transport is an important service sector and plays a crucial role in the development of the urban economy and the time has come to take immediate stock of the urban transport scenario. Traffic engineering and regulations, widening of roads, interlinking of transport with land use planning, integration of the services provided by various modes of transport, all these need urgent attention. It may be necessary to introduce a multi-modal mass rapid transit system in the super-metros, and for this purpose evolve a suitable technical and financial package. It is also desirable to take advance action to define, segregate and set apart, the alignments for future transport corridors as a part of the plan for the development of each urban entity. This will guide land use planning and facilitate introduction of appropriate transport services, at a later stage, along such dedicated alignments.

In major metropolitan cities, the time has come when planning for future growth must avoid any segmented approach. Infrastructure like transport, telecommunications, energy supply, developed land and basic services like drinking water, sanitation, sewerage, etc., and education and health facilities must be provided for in an integrated manner, while drawing up a perspective plan for the growth of the city. To facilitate the diffusion of activities in metropolitan cities over much wider areas, an overall plan should be prepared inclusive of the contiguous cohesive areas of the metropolitan cities. The plan should be flexible and promote an orderly and environmentally sound development pattern for the future metropolitan growth.

Attention needs to be focussed on not only the growing challenges of urbanisation but on the relationship between urban and rural development. The rapid transformation in the country's urban scenario must be taken into account and provided for, in order that urban growth assists the process of healthy socio-economic development of the country as a whole. While doing so, it will be necessary to take note of the prevailing dichotomy in rural and urban development and evolve a much needed mechanism for bringing about rural-urban coherence in the management of growth.

Rural development goals cannot be achieved in isolation; it will need to draw sustenance from urban strengths. Economic growth with social equity requires both accelerated agricultural development as well as expansion of urban industry and commerce. The ties between the urban and the rural economy are crucial for promoting wide spread development because the major markets for agricultural surpluses are in urban centres; modernisation of agriculture creates surplus rural labour who seek employment in towns; and many of the functional inputs that satisfy rural basic needs, both physical and social, are distributed from urban basis. Urban and rural development have, therefore, to go hand in hand, considering that what is characterised as urban includes a whole hierarchy of settlements from the metropolis through medium and small towns to the "rural-urban inter face" of small towns and rural growth centres.

HOUSING NEEDS AND POPULATION

1. The overall magnitude of the housing problem confronting the country, viewed over a span of 20 years from 1981 to 2001, is estimated to be 23.3 million dwelling units in terms of backlog and 63.8 million new dwelling units comprising of 32.6 million in rural areas and the balance 31.2 million in urban areas to meet incremental housing needs.

2. Despite considerable investment and efforts over successive plan periods, the housing problem continues to be daunting. The housing crisis manifests itself in many ways: growth of slums and unauthorised colonies, overcrowding and deficient services, increasing homelessness, speculation and profiteering in land and houses and decreasing quality of life. Given the relentless growth of population and urbanisation and the difficult economic environment, the housing problem will further worsen unless concerted measures are taken to ameliorate the living conditions of a vast majority of vulnerable sections of the society both in rural and urban areas. The endeavour of the planning activity should be to accomplish the goal of shelter for all.

3. To tackle the serious dimensions of the housing problem confronting the country, there is a need to step up the investments

in the housing sector and urban infrastructure and increasing it at a steady pace thereafter so that there can be a hope for significant change in the housing situation.

4. The lack of financial resources is a crucial constraint to the housing activity. The financial need for housing cannot be made solely by the Government budgetary support and there is need to:

   i) Step up flow of funds from financial institutions to the housing sector;

   ii) Increase the level of contribution of the commercial banks to the housing sector;

   iii) Increase the level of contribution from financial institutions like L.I.C., G.I.C., P.P.F., etc., and

   iv) Industrial sector should also make investment in housing sector for industrial workers.

5. The problem of rural housing should not be viewed in terms of finance and resources alone. The construction of new housing stock and upgradation of unserviceable kuccha houses will only materialise if homestead rights are conferred on rural poor, basic conditions are created in making available appropriate building materials, access to bio-mass and natural resources and upgradation of the traditional skills of the local artisans involved in the shelter construction and improvement. Further, State and the public agencies should mount programmes for provision of infrastructure facilities with full involvement of the rural community which will set the pace for housing programmes and improvement of settlements.

6. The Government has been working on the formulation of a National Housing Policy. The Ministry of Urban Development prepared a draft National Housing Policy document which was widely circulated and discussed. The thrust of the draft policy is the crucial role of Government to create an enabling environment, to remove constraints to housing activity of various sections of the population, to promote a substantial increase in the supply of housing and basic services, to support upgradation of the housing stock and to stimulate rental housing. The State would address specifically the needs of the houseless, poorer households, SC/ST, women and other vulnerable groups.

7. Housing has to be considered in the larger context of human settlements. The planning of urban and rural development,

location of economic activities and provision of infrastructure and services and transport need to be comprehended in integration with provision of housing. Thus, housing and development are supportive to each other. The investment" plan for housing should identify areas of State effort in the form of direct intervention for priority groups, and through the promotion of housing activity of the households, cooperatives and organised sector in a variety of ways. Specifically the involvement of voluntary agencies in rehabilitating slums and disaster affected houses is to be encouraged. The role of NGOs in selected areas of policy and planning can be crucial. Similarly, the cooperative societies can contribute significantly to the housing needs of not only the middle income households but also to the low income households by providing suitable support.

8. The role of housing as a basic input which enhances the productive potential of the human being has been recognised. Housing, however, needs to be looked at in the larger framework of human settlements with integrated provision of infrastructure, employment opportunities, services and transport to promote community growth. The long term objective is the provision of "Shelter for All". Given the competing demands on available resources, however, the achievement of this goal will inevitably need to be spread over a reasonable span of time.

STATE URBAN DEVELOPMENT STRATEGY AND HOUSING DEVELOPMENT PROGRAMMES

Hon'ble Minister for Urban Development, Mrs. Sheila Kaul, Dr. J.P. Singh, Secretary, Ministry of Urban Development, my colleagues in the Commission, officials in the Ministry of Urban Development and other Central Ministries, State Secretaries, invited experts, ladies and gentlemen,

It gives me, great pleasure to participate in this inaugural session of the meeting organised jointly by the Planning Commission and Ministry of Urban Development to discuss State Urban Development Strategy and the Housing Development Programmes. It is heartening to see the overwhelming response to this meeting. I distinctly recall the first meeting held on the 'State Urban Development Strategy and Policy', a year ago at Delhi, where there was a similar response. Looking at the level of participation in today's meeting and more importantly the amount of work put in by the State Governments in shaping this innovative but difficult exercise, I share a sense of pride and optimism with you all. The readiness with which the Hon'ble Minister for Urban Development, Mrs. Sheila Karl and Dr. J.P. Singh, Secretary have responded to our request for a joint venture in organising this all—India Meeting is indeed encouraging. I am sure that this effort will be carried forward further with the help of Ministry of Urban Development and State Governments not only in providing inputs to framing National Urban Perspective and Policy but also in shaping future investment strategies and programmes in the urban sector. The need for such participative efforts and national level deliberations has become all the more necessary in the context of two landmark happenings which are likely to influence significantly the future urban scene in India. These are (a) passage of State legislation / ordinance to effect the principles embodied in the 74th Constitutional Amendment and (b) carrying forward the process of economic reforms to the urban sector as a necessary condition for achieving the goals of higher economic, efficiency and growth, Let me now share with you some of my views which partly relate to what I said in my last year's address and partly reflect new directions in the approach to urban development, In my last year's address I emphasised on four main themes or premises, namely (a) development of National Urban Policy and Perspective has to be based on scientific and realistic appraisal of the trends art issues en urban development at state and regional levels; (b) it is not desirable to view the urban sector as being limited by the activities or programmes of the Central or State Ministries of Urban development. It is more appropriate to view urban development in inter-sectoral framework with cognizance of rural-urban linkages, relationship between industrial locations and other employment generating activities to urban development and thus to frame State Urban Development Strategy in relation to overall development of the State; (c) in the context of the contributory and critical role of urban infrastructure in furthering the gains from the process of economic liberalisation, the strategy should consist in creating enabling conditions to enhance flow of investment in the urban sector through removal of controls and regulations as well as unsustainable norms while maintaining **a framework of planning and regulation to avoid undesirable trends** in land use and environment deterioration; and (d) strengthening the finances and institutional capacity of the urban local bodies through both structural improvement and better management.

A quick review of interim papers on State Urban Development Strategy prepared by some of the States presents an impression that they have responded to all the issues which were raised last year, though with varying coverage and depth. I think the objective of today's meeting should not be to review the strengths and limitations of various papers which in any way can be done at official levels. Emphasis; should be more on what insights we can gain from such useful exercises in framing our future strategies for urban development and also raise issues of larger significance across States and regions for a national debate. I also feel that some of the aspects and findings can be utilised for a short-term purpose of improvement in the approach or content of the existing urban development programme car facilitating the process of reforms in the urban local bodies initiated through the passage of the 74th Constitutional Amendment. I would like the Ministry to link this exercise with the Mid-term Appraisal of the 8th Plain programmes which is high on our agenda during the next couple of months.

Having made the above general observations on the significance of this exercise and the broad premises on which future work on State Urban Development Strategy should be based; now I would turn to some of the specific aspects requiring more careful assessment leading to development of specific strategies. Among the list of priorities, I think that **macro perspective on relationship between economic development and urbanisation** is a very vital input to the future urban policy, both at the national and State level. I am happy to see from some of the State Reports very extensive references to these dimensions, in particular the effort in co-relating the new industrial location policy, which is based on the principle of deregulation and delicensing, with the pattern of urbanisation in the State as attempted by Maharashtra, Gujarat, Tamil Nadu and other States. This is a very important contribution to our thought process. Some of the State strategies have also specifically pointed the need for dispersal of industries and other economic activities and consequently achieving the goal of balanced regional development. However, I feel that the stated goals need to be viewed in relation to the effectiveness of instruments that are available with us. We have to recognize on the cant hand the inexorability of market forces and, on the other, provide direction and instruments to avoid expected accentuation of external diseconomies in the developed regions and cities. These diseconomies have mare often than not affected more adversely the disadvantaged group, say the urban poor. This dimension of **trade,-off between economies of agglomeration and diseconomies of concentration** is particularly important for Mega and Metro cities / regions in India, some of which are expected to play a key role in economic development in the face of globalisation of Indian economy. Another important dimension we emphasised in last year's meeting was the need for adopting an approach of convergence of various sectoral programmes having bearing on development of towns and cities including those undertaken through institutional funding and private sector. While I am happy to note that most of the State Reports have recognised the need for viewing urban development programmes in an inter-sectoral frame, there is perhaps limited attempt to develop a convergence approach. I feel that this convergence approach can be successful only when we adopt the principle of coordination at policy level as also at programme level. I would urge the Ministry of Urban Development to develop the modalities of operationalising this approach with necessary help from Planning Commission.

With regard to the deliberations on the financing mechanism for urban infrastructure which is becoming increasingly capital-intensive with long gestation period, I feel that the challenge in this regard is more than any problem in urban sector. The existing efforts are far too inadequate to meet the challenge of providing basic infrastructure and services caused by increasing level of urbanisation and more importantly concentration in large cities is a greater problem facing urban India. There has been a clear recognition of this problem in most of the State reports. Most of the State Governments have also worked out the investment requirements particularly for prioritised small and medium towns and a few have also offered some innovative methods of raising additional financial resources. My apprehension is that often this exercise has been, in the nature of identifying list of requirements with expected high levels of financial requirements. What is perhaps more important is to work out more feasible methods of financing which are based on the principle of sound financial discipline arid beneficiary participation with the government's support being provided in the nature of catalytic investment and supporting programmes for the economically weaker sections in evaluating alternative financing mechanism, it may be important to consider institutional options at national, State or even metropolitan an level. Some of the States have already proposed set lip specialised urban infrastructure Corporations and also there is an increasing participation in investment in urban infrastructure from financial institutions and private investment companies. The demand for such investment would grow further with the process of economic liberalisation and it is thus high time that we work out, more viable institutional options together with various measures for strengthening municipal finances through both rationalisation of existing revenue resources and devolution of tax raising powers from the State to Municipal bodies. In this respect, would urge you to keep in view remarkable provision made in the 74th Constitution Amendment by way of a State Finance Commission, This is a subject by itself. You would be happy to note that efforts in Planning Commission has also initiated limited efforts direction, by way of sponsoring through National Institute of Public Finance and Policy a study on the Municipal finance and framing guidelines for State Finance Commission. I understand that Ministry of Urban Development has also initiated significant efforts in this direction. I suggest we should form a small working group to deliberate further on this subject so that this unique opportunity of strengthening Municipal finance through the mechanism of State Finance Commission is fully utilised. In this respect, I would like you to refer to the 1994 World

Development Report of the World Bank which deals with some basic issues on financing and management of infrastructure, including drinking water supply and sanitation. This report, apart from stressing on management of infrastructure like a business with direct participation of users and other stake-holders, makes a good case for better maintenance. It is aptly argued that the success of the development of infrastructure is measured by the quality of service it provides.

With regard to coordination of urban sector policy and programmes at State level, more attention needs to be given. This is particularly so in view of our growing realization that the strategies and policy for urban sector cannot be developed without proper assessment of inter-sectoral linkages and also spatial inter-dependence. I am not sure whether this can be achieved merely by way of setting up of State Urban Development Agencies or by way of setting up Coordination Committee under Chief Secretary or ever a Minister. This perhaps requires integration from below Vv., from municipal level to district and district to state. I am not aware of any studied option In the State Reports (or otherwise) in this direction. There are however, very useful references in the State reports to the coordination and that role could be played by the District Planning Committee which is a statutory unit under the 74th Constitution Amendment. It may be perhaps appropriate to constitute a separate technical group with supporting exercises to develop appropriate modalities for achieving coordination and **inter facing with sectoral plans and also between city / district Plans with State plans.**

I am sure, in course of your deliberations today and tomorrow, you will not limit yourself only to the above issues but also dwell on other aspects as well and., perhaps, suggest more specific action plans. I would urge that while the State Urban Development exercises should be fruitfully extended to its next phase by way of including uncovered issues and more detailed assessment of some critical issues raised, it is equally important to concentrate on a few topics for further deliberations. The follow-up can be done both by way of detailed exercise by State Governments and by setting up special working group at national level. The next stage of work in State Urban Development Strategy should enable us to arrive at a national consensus **on the institutional and financing alternatives** for aiding the process of urban development and also **reorientation in the planning mechanism in the context of focus on decentralisation.** Some of these outputs could be specific to the States and some others would form a part of input to National Urban Policy and Perspective.

I am certain that this Joint venture through pooling together efforts of the Planning Commission, Ministry of Urban Development, State Governments as well as various and representatives of Financial and other institutions, could go a long way in responding to the challenges for the growing urban sector which have remained largely unresolved in the past. I am sure that Hon'ble Minister, Mrs. Sheila Kaul will provide necessary guidance and support to this effort. I wish the meeting a grand success.

HYDERABAD MASTER PLAN 2011

Honourable Chief Minister of Andhra Pradesh, Honourable Minister for Municipal Administration and Urban Development, Government of Andhra Pradesh, Shri Kodanda Reddy, Chairman, H.U.D.A., Shri R.P. Agarwal, Vice-Chairman, H.U.D.A., distinguished invitees, ladies and gentlemen,

It is indeed a great pleasure for me to participate in the Inaugural Session of the Workshop on "Hyderabad Master Plan 2011". I am grateful for being invited to the inaugural session and to deliver the key-note address. Rapid growth of urban population is a distinctive feature of the economic development process in the developing countries. A brief look at the population statistics will reveal the magnitude of this challenge in India. While the population of India grew from 238.4 million in 1901 to 844.3 million in 1991, the urban population grew from a mere 25.8 million in 1901 to a phenomenal 217.1 million in 1991. While the decadal growth rate of population in 1991 stood at 23.56%, the decadal urban growth rate stood at 36.19%. The ratio of urban population to the total population was merely 10.84 in 1901, whereas it grew to 25.72 in 1991. This trend of high urban growth rate brings out the imperative need to focus our undivided attention and energies in the emerging problems of managing our metropolises. A new dimension has been added by the possible impact of the economic liberalization process on urban growth. The economic liberalisation process envisages a strategic shift from import substitution to export led growth. Major steps have been initiated to attract foreign direct investment. The expected inflow of international capital creates a demand for a number of urban services. The encouragement given to private sector initiative may give rise to a fresh impetus to industrial activity. Factors like the fiscal and financial sector reforms, the changes in policy and procedures aimed at stepping up economic growth and integration of the Indian economy with the global markets have important implications for the urban sector where most of the new investments are expected to flow. The need for new directions in the management of our metropolises are thus needed not only to facilitate and strengthen economic development but also to support and streamline the process of India's urban transition.

Fresh thinking is needed on urban land reforms. Deficits in infrastructure in terms of housing, water supply and sanitation, power, transport and communication have to be met as expeditiously as possible. We cannot also ignore the environmental concerns that have surfaced in the recent years in our metropolitan areas. Another important issue in managing the metropolises is the strengthening of urban health care services. Wisdom requires that a nation should be prepared for the eventuality of high rate of urban growth, to contain its ill effects at the minimum and to enhance the positive effects to the maximum.

In the above context of the urban scenario and the imperative need to manage our metropolises in an innovative and effective manner, the idea of a Master Plan for Hyderabad for 2011 assumes greater significance. I congratulate the State Government of Andhra Pradesh and Hyderabad Urban Development Authority (HUDA) in particular in organising this workshop on Hyderabad Master Plan 2011 which is most appropriate and timely. The two important events which have heightened the significance of this workshop are the challenges posed by the highest decadal population growth rate of Hyderabad Urban Agglomeration compared to other large metro-cities in the country and the passage of 74th Constitutional Amendment with accent on decentralisation. The earlier Master Plan for Hyderabad which was brought into force in 1980 requires a revision not in a routine sense of changes in land use or population projection but in a structural sense, with a comprehensive view of the regional system as a whole incorporating physical, economic, social and institutional aspects. Moreover, some of the important programmes initiated by the Government in recent years namely the Mega City project, the World Bank aided Hyderabad and Secunderabad Water Supply and Sewerage system, Mass Rail Transit project, have given a new orientation and pace to the development activities in the city and the region.

I have gone through the status papers of the draft Master Plan prepared by HUDA and a quick appraisal of the Master Plan gives me the impression that it has in general fulfilled the requirements of a comprehensive Master Plan. The most important feature of this plan is the manner in which it has treated the basic issue of very high growth rate of population in the urban agglomeration with attendant problems of concentration and inadequate provision of infrastructure. The other important dimension, though discussed briefly, relates to the legal and financial aspects of the plan which are often missed out in land use dominated concept of Master Plan. In general, I share the thinking of HUDA and State Govt. that the Master Plan for a growing metro region should be essentially viewed in a regional context and integrate tie spatial and economic development. This has been also stated as one of the strategies in the VIII Plan.

Within the overall concept and focus of the Master Plan for Hyderabad, I would like to share with you some of my ideas which may perhaps help not only the deliberations during the two day workshop but also in shaping the future work plan of HUDA in revision and implementation of the 2011 Master Plan.

The four areas which, I believe deserve further debate and reconsideration could be briefly stated as follows:

a) Desirability and feasibility of containing the growth of population of HyderabadDevelopment Area (HDA) to 75 lakhs by 2011 as against the alternative projection of 113 lakhs based on 1981-91 growth rates;

b) Assessment of the expected impact of the Mega City project at assumed level of investment and the need for stepping up and synchronisation of investment in areas outside Hyderabad Urban agglomeration which are not covered by the MEGA City project;

c) Desirability of the concept of the State Capital Region and the modality of implementation of this concept; and

d) Functional and statutory integration of the regional plan of Hyderabad with the individual City / Town Plan and the District Plan within the H.D.A.

There may be definitely equally important issues areas for debate which I leave them to the Technical Groups to resolve. Within the limited understanding of the complexities of Metropolitan regional system of Hyderabad, I would venture to give some of my views on the issues stated above.

The present population of Hyderabad Development Area (including cantonment area) at 45 lakhs accounts for 25% of the urban population of the State. Assuming past trends to continue, the projected population of H.D.A. is estimated at 113 lakhs in 2011 which will account for less than 24% of State's projected total urban population of 486 lakhs. The envisaged or desired level of 75 lakhs for HDA, which will be only 15.5% of the State's projected urban population, appears some what impractical in the context of experiences in other cities in India and even in other countries. I suggest having a relook at the projected population of HDA. It may not be a wise planning to have some sense of complacency with lower population projection which, in turn, will require lower level of investment in infrastructure. At the same time, it is recognised that the past trends should not continue unabated for the next two or three decades and some kind of strategic choice is to be made regarding the spreading out of urban growth in a wider regional system. This is where preparation of State Urban Development Strategy becomes necessary in providing a backdrop and a strategic choice for either metropolitan regional planning or for planning of individual urban centres. I am happy to note that the State of Andhra Pradesh has already prepared a State Urban Development Strategy Report and submitted to the Planning Commission. Based on such reports from some other states also, an All-India Meeting sponsored jointly by Planning Commission and Ministry of Urban Development, Government of India was held at Delhi recently. I do feel that further improvement could be done by the State Government on the State Urban Development Strategy so that a coordinated view of HDA's regional plan and State plan could be taken. This brings me to the concept of State Capital Region and countermagnates. As a long term concept, State Capital Region is a worthwhile one to pursue. I, however, would like one to be cautious about the operationalisation of this concept in the immediate future. I feel that what is most important is a proper investment and development regulations plan within the con fines of the present HDA and this will be a crucial precondition for arresting further concentration within the Hyderabad-Secunderabad city core. As pointed out in the Status Paper, the area of HDA is larger than all other metropolitan regions including Bombay, Calcutta and Bangalore. Mere geographical extension of a planning area without establishing proper economic and functional linkages may not serve the purpose. At this stage, it may be a more useful idea to intensify the development inputs in a regulated frame in the adjoining 9 Municipalities as well as in the rural fringes and smaller towns. Development of counter magnates like Karimnagar, Warangal and Kurnool can be explored and the required transportation and communication linkages established before operationalisation of the concept of State Capital Region.

This leads me on to the other allied issues on the Mega City Scheme, particularly an assessment of the possible concern that this might aggravate concentration of population in the city core. However, if one goes by the essential logic of this scheme and also the fact that very large size of developable area exist in 9 Municipalities as well as in the fringe smaller towns and rural areas within HDA, one need not draw such a conclusion. It should be made clear that Mega City Scheme is intended to cover the entire urban agglomeration (not merely the Municipal Corporation area) and if necessary extendable to urbanisable fringe areas. More importantly, this scheme will be an important step in institutional and financial innovation towards a self sustaining nature of financing of urban infrastructure. This should also be revealed from the fact that unlike most of the Centrally Sponsored Schemes, the Mega City Scheme implies 50% or larger reliance on **institutional finance and private investment.** Similarly, impact of Light Rail Transport Scheme (LRTS) needs to be assessed in a regional context.

In carrying out this exercise, and also linking with the investment plan for the development of the entire HDA, I feel that HUDA should take note of the following important issues:

i.   Detailed assessment of the hierarchical, functional and economic linkages among Hyderabad City, Municipalities, fringe urban areas and rural settlements and also counter magnates;

ii. An assessment of the Industrial Location Policy and employment distribution in different centres within HDA and also in counter magnate areas; and

iii. Need for a larger investment (both in rural and urban programmes) in areas outside the Hyderabad-Secunderabad city core and strengthening of the urban and rural local bodies particularly in terms of financial resources.

While some of these aspects have been referred in the draft Master Plan, I feel that specific studies need to be carried out to cover these issues in greater depth so as to lead to a more objective and feasible regional development strategy as well as investment policy. What needs to be clearly spelt out in the Master Plan for HDA is the relationship between and interface with the urban and rural local governments within HDA and the HUDA. The institutionalization of Metropolitan Planning Committee, which is an important provision in the 74th Constitutional Amendment, also needs to be looked into. While there is some reference to this aspect in the draft document but I feel that a more elaborate treatment of the subject is necessary. I do believe that the institutional and legal aspects of urban development are as much important as financial and physical aspects of urban development. I am sure that HUDA, with the help of this Workshop, will identify the missing links, if any, in the Master Plan and will establish innovative planning approach and mechanism which even other regions and States can follow.

I am happy to see such a good response in terms of participation to this Workshop. I am sure the deliberations will provide valuable inputs for firming up the Master Plan 2011 for Hyderabad. I wish the Workshop a grand success.

CAPACITY BUILDING FOR THE URBAN ENVIRONMENT PROJECT

I am happy to be present at the inaugural of the National Forum represented by civic leaders, representatives of governmental agencies and local authorities, experts on environmental management from academic and research institutions, representatives of nongovernmental and private sector organisations. Convening of this National Forum on capacity building for the urban environmental management by Human Settlement Management Institute of HUDCO, is most timely in view of urban environmental concerns now being increasingly felt. I am grateful for having been invited to deliver the keynote address. The Forum offers a unique opportunity to various actors concerned with urban development to discuss capacity building strategies for urban environment management. I understand that the National Forum will consider "capacity building strategies for urban environment", as evolved by a group of experts in their deliberations, preceding to the National Forum, based on ten case studies of "best practices" of urban environment management and finalise it for wider dissemination.

Urbanisation and economic development have often been considered anti-thetical to urban environment. It is now being recognised that cities are the dynamic centres of economic growth and development and produce more than their proportional share of GNP. Urban cities offer significant economies of scale in the provision of housing and infrastructure services and creation of job opportunities, by increasing their participation in economic development. While cities do face serious environmental problems, but well managed urban centres can make significant contributions to the health and welfare of their citizens. It is therefore

567

important to explore the city's role in environment and focus on strategies for improving the urban environmental management.

The urbanisation process is inevitable and irreversible. Like several other developing countries, India is experiencing rapid urbanisation in recent decades. In the first four decades of this century, the proportion of urban population was less than 14 per cent. Since then the level of urbanisation has steadily increased from 17.29 per cent (62 million) in 1951 to 25.72 per cent (217 million) in 1991. India's urban population of 217 million is the fourth largest in the world. By the year 2001, urban population is expected to increase to over 300 million persons, adding during the decade 1991-2001 approximately 85-100 million persons.

The volume and pace of urbanisation in India is characterised by its contribution to degradation of urban environment. The process itself consumes increasingly greater amount of environmental resources such as land, water etc. Cities are also experiencing urban poverty with over-crowded living conditions, inadequate housing, infrastructure and services—all contributing to increasing deterioration in urban environment. Pollution of air, land and water resources are the major negative manifestations of urbanisation. Untreated domestic sewage and toxic industrial wastes affects the health of the population of cities and surrounding rural areas. Water pollution in cities has caused health hazards.

Apart from natural growth, the rural-urban and intra-urban migrations have been the causative factors for the rapid growth of urban population. This trend has been more pronounced in the bigger cities where majority of the migrants are unable to have affordable helter and find employment mostly in the informal sector. This has resulted in proliferation of slums and slum like conditions in cities. Low-lying lands, river beds, unstable slopes, *nalahs,* unserviced areas at the periphery of cities have become the habitat of the urban poor. With urban expansion during the last few decades, poverty is increasingly becoming an urban problem.

The massive shift of population from rural and smaller urban centres to bigger cities has created complex physical and socio-economic problems. The bigger cities are suffering from traffic congestion, ambient air pollution, solid and hazardous wastes and municipal affluent. The existing deficits of infrastructure, services and housing are mounting. From an environmental point of view, the cities are being perceived as a net consumer of natural resources and exporters of wastes.

Transport congestion and pollution from vehicles have emerged as two strong manifestations of deteriorating urban environment particularly in the metropolitan cities. The major source of air pollution in cities, other than industrial towns, is the automobile exhaust gases. Air samples monitored by Central Pollution Control Board and National Environmental Engineering Research Institute show that in almost all big cities, the pollution level is very close to the maximum permissible limits and in some cases above them.

The conventional approach to examine urban environmental issues is to look into them in terms of water, sanitation, solid waste, land etc. Such sectoral categories unfortunately do not focus adequately the critical social, economic and institutional factors. Also, there is a need to view the urban environmental problems on a spatial scale. Taking an example of water supply and sanitation, its inadequacy is a problem both at the household and at the work place level. At the community level, lack of sanitation leads to water and soil being affected by excreta. At the city level the excreta carried by surface drains may affect water courses at its out fall. At the regional level, the consolidated effect of poor sanitation may lead to a substantial ecological damage. An understanding of the spatial dimensions to properly assess the environmental damage can therefore lead to the most appropriate form of interventions to address environmental problems.

A realisation of the need for integration of socio-economic, spatial, infrastructure, transportation, environment, investment and management aspects in planning process is being increasingly felt. This calls for devising a mechanism for integration at the local level where the policies and various programmes converge for implementation. Therefore, the role of local government is of critical importance.

In June 1992 the United Nations Conference on Development and the Environment, also called the "Earth Summit", took place in Rio. This conference adopted an action programme—Agenda 21, which deals with a wide spectrum of environmental issues. Agenda 21 requires action by national governments as well as by local authorities. In particular, local authorities are required to develop a "Local Agenda 21". It is incumbent upon each local authority to respond to the challenge of producing a local Agenda 21. Essentially, this means that environmental aspects should form an integral part of the decision making process at the local authority level and they should demonstrate awareness of good environmental practice.

Sustainable development requires action to prevent depletion or degradation of environmental assets so that resource and ecological base for human 'activities may be sustained. A new dimension to the concept is the requirement that environmental as well as economic resources should be adequate to meet the present and future needs. This new dimension recognises poverty, resource depletion and resource consumption nexus as contributing to environmental degradation. A sustainable development approach is, therefore, urgently needed in the management of urban environment—an approach that ensures the contribution of cities to national economic development while protecting the urban poor from consequences of environmental deterioration. This implies that the local authorities should consider how their policies and actions affect various kinds of environmental assets and how, in the long term, it can be avoided. Meeting basic needs (minimum standards of drinking water, solid waste management, drainage, sanitation and shelter)—an important component for sustainable urban development, recognises the growing importance of urban poverty. This requires combining development and environmental concerns into a single consistent strategy to address the issues of urban poverty.

A particularly important area where local authorities can contribute to sustainable development relates to land use planning. They need to be aware of the long term and cumulative effect of various decisions on the land use pattern of cities thereby achieving the goals set out in Agenda 21 for healthy and satisfying environment. Basic infrastructure and services such as water, sanitation, garbage disposal, health care, drains, etc., cannot be adequately provided to poorer groups without effective local institutions Outside agencies can only bring knowledge, expertise, capital and advice. But they cannot solve most of the environmental problems at the local level without effective local institutions. There may be potential for private sector enterprises to provide some necessary improvements in infrastructure and services, but a strong competent and representative local government is needed to address *such* problems. Local authorities are particularly better placed to facilitate and encourage active community participation in decision making, which is the corner stone 'of Agenda 21. To achieve this objective, there is a need to develop a partnership between local authorities, other levels of government and community based and private sector organisations. *Such* a partnership will enable local authorities to have a significant impact on national programmes, priorities and, resource allocations by providing a local perspective.

The 74th Constitution Amendment Act, 1992 is the boldest initiative in the process of devolution of power to the people. The Amendment Act has accorded a constitutional status to municipal governments for initiating a process of democratic decentralisation empowering the people at grass root level to participate in the decision making processes.

The Amendment Act incorporates numerous innovations relating to municipalisation, reservation of seats for SC, ST and women in municipalities at various levels, and powers, authority and responsibilities. New provisions have been made regarding the distribution of revenues between the State and the Municipalities. Provisions have also been made for the appointment of a State Finance Commission. In matters relating to planning, new features have been incorporated in the Constitution Amendment Act, such as setting up of a Committee for District Planning and a Committee for Metropolitan Planning. The functions assigned to municipalities are mentioned in the Twelfth Schedule. It lists 18 functions of which urban forestry, protection of the environment and promotion of ecological aspects has been included as one of the functions.

New channels of support must also be found from NGOs and CBOs. There are many examples which reflect the fact that NGOs are among the most active and well organised to identify the critical links between environmental issues and poverty. Such new channels, for instance, can support community level initiatives. Equally significant is the need for partnerships among local actors, including local authorities, NGOs, CBOs and private firms. Local initiatives require an enabling environment. Experience has shown that residents of slums and squatter settlement are better able to meet their own basic needs when their efforts are facilitated by an enabling policy environment.

A cross-sectoral approach, institutional partnerships and grass-roots participation are thus the keys to sustainable urban environment management. Utilising this integrated strategy, sustainable urban development is an attainable goal within the towns and cities in the country.

Management of cities requires careful identification of priorities, resources to meet them. Each city must develop and implement an action programme, based on careful evaluation of its own problems and resources. This is important because most of the cities cannot receive substantial amount of resources from higher levels of government and the resources are to be generated by the cities themselves. It is therefore, desirable that a better use is made of existing resources including increasing the capacity of the city and local governments to tackle both short and long term environmental problems. There are many institutions dealing with the problem of environmental management. However, such institutions are independent environmental agencies. It is now being recognised that such organisations, are not able to perform effectively without proper coordination and public involvement. It is only when local citizens and their leaders become involve that real enforcement of environmental policies and achievement of environmental goals becomes possible. Therefore, involvement of local leadership is one of the key components of the environmental strategies.

Establishing urban environmental priorities should be another step. Experience ha shown that such priorities can vary from city to city and even from one community to another However, the objective of environmental priority setting is one of the potential activities to achieve the reduction of environmental risk at the least possible cost. Development and environmental experts often regard environmental protection and economic development as opposite to each other. Though the importance of clean air, water and other natural resources as vital inputs in sustainable development is recognised, in the long run it can be seen that economic development requires an investment in the environment as well. For setting local priorities for mitigating environmental conditions and planning for future growth, local initiatives are called for. In addition, increasing public awareness and participation for protection of urban environment requires full awareness of the causes and consequences of environmental neglect.

The lack of effective enforcement machinery is often experienced. In spite of the importance of increasing awareness and involvement of public, many organisations dealing with environmental issues isolate themselves without involving the stake holders in their decision making processes.

Creating suitable mechanisms for educating and involving the public can also lead to increased participation of local governments in environmental management. The creation of linkages amongst various levels of government can lead to a more active role for local authorities in decision making and better implementation of environmental agenda at the local level. Capacity Building to improve the institutional framework and arrangements for urban environmental management should interalia, include the following attributes:

- Decentralisation of decision making processes so as to make it become more people oriented, dynamic, and effective.
- Strengthening the role of local governments in order to enable than to develop their own environmental management strategies with the involvement of NGOs, CBOs, private, formal and informal enterprises.
- Participation of various actors through assigning more responsibilities to communities, NGOs and partnerships between them and local authorities.

- Facilitating and supporting the local authorities in formulating and implementing environmental strategies. This would require provision of legal, financial and institutional instruments for effectuation.
- Need for a National framework for urban environmental planning and management which should serve as a reference and context for local planning and management.
- Enhancing the total institutional capacity of the city by developing the capabilities of community leaders, professionals working in local authorities, private sector through training programmes.

There is also a need to create increased awareness of urban environment amongst the general public through local media like TV, radio, newspapers etc. The formulation of environmental policies and programmes and for capacity building, an inventory of successful local experiences related to the conservation of the environment should be prepared. These cases should be documented, evaluated and disseminated. Recognition of innovative initiatives of the actors and stake-holders and the capacity to coordinate activities among institutions will be a positive factor for success.

We look forward to the outcome of this National Forum. We are at the threshold of initiating preparation of the Ninth Five Year Plan (1997-2002) for the country. The recommendations made in this Forum would indeed provide significant inputs in understanding the problems of urban environmental management and sustainable urban development. The Planning Commission would be happy to consider the recommendations through its various Working Groups and Steering Committees already set up for the formulation of the Ninth Plan.

TRIBAL DEVELOPMENT

TRIBAL DEVELOPMENT IN INDIA AND RECOGNITION OF FOREST RIGHTS ACT—2006

I. TRIBAL DEVELOPMENT IN INDIA

PREAMBLE

The Scheduled Tribes population of the country, as per 2001 Census, is 8.43 crore, constituting about 8.2% of the total population of the country. More than half of the Scheduled Tribes population is concentrated in 6 States viz. Madhya Pradesh, Chattisgarh, Maharashtra, Orissa, Jharhand and Gujarat. Tribal communities live in about 15% of the total geographical area of the country.

Article 366(25) of the Constitution of India refers to Scheduled Tribes as those communities, who are scheduled in accordance with the Article 342 of the Constitution. The list of Scheduled Tribes is State/ UT specific and a community declared as a Scheduled Tribe in a State need not be so in another State.

The essential characteristics, first laid down by the Lokur Committee, for a community to be identified as Scheduled Tribes are:

i). primitive traits,
ii). distinctive culture,
iii). shyness of contact with the community at large,
iv). geographical isolation and
v). backwardness—social and economic

Tribal groups, as such are not homogenous and different communities are at different stages of social, economic and educational development. Some communities have adopted mainstream way of life. But at the other end of spectrum, there are certain Scheduled Tribes, 75 in number, known as Primitive Tribal Groups (PTGs), who are characterized by:

1. a pre-agriculture level of technology,
2. a stagnant or declining population
3. extremely low literacy, and
4. a subsistence level of economy

Except Punjab, Haryana, Chandigarh, Delhi and Puducherry, Scheduled Tribes have been scheduled in all States and UTs. In UTs of Laksdweep and Dadra & Nagar Haveli and States of Mizoram, Nagaland, Meghalaya and Arunachal Pradesh, Scheduled Tribes are in majority. In all there are about 700 Scheduled Tribes notified under Article 342 of the Constitution of India. Many tribes are present in more than one State. The largest number of tribes, numbering 62, is scheduled in the State of Orissa. The main concentration of tribal population is in Central India and in the North-Eastern States.

In so far as Scheduled Tribes are concerned, in almost all developmental parameters they lag behind. Tribal Areas are characterized by poor infrastructure and poorer services leading to slower growth.

CONSTITUTIONAL SAFEGUARDS

The constitution has devoted more than 20 articles on the redressal and upliftment of the underprivileged following the policy of positive discrimination and affirmative action, particularly with reference to the Scheduled Tribes. Recognising the special needs of STs, the Constitution of India made certain special safeguards to protect these communities from all the possible exploitation and thus ensure social justice. While Article 14 confers equal rights and opportunities to all, Article 15 prohibits discrimination against any citizen on the grounds of sex, religion, race, caste etc; Article 15 (4) enjoins upon the State to make special provisions for the advancement of any socially and educationally backward classes; Article 16 (4) empowers the State to make provisions for reservation in appointments or posts in favour of any backward class of citizens, which in the opinion of the State, is not adequately represented in the services under the State; Article 46 enjoins upon the State to promote with special care the educational and economic interests of the weaker sections of the people and, in particular, the STs and promises to protect them from social injustice and all forms of exploitation. Further, while Article 275 (1) promises grant-in-aid for promoting the welfare of STs and for raising the level of administration of the Scheduled Areas, Articles 330, 332 and 335 stipulate reservation of seats for STs in the Lok Sabha and in the State Legislative Assemblies and in services. Finally, the Constitution also empowers the State to appoint a Commission to investigate the conditions of the socially and educationally backward classes (Article 340) and to specify those Tribes or Tribal Communities deemed to be as STs (Article 342).

The Fifth Schedule to the Constitution lays down certain prescriptions about the Scheduled Areas as well as the Scheduled Tribes in States other than Assam, Meghalaya, Tripura and Mizoram by ensuring submission of Annual Reports by the Governors to the President of India regarding the Administration of the Scheduled Areas and setting up of Tribal Advisory Councils to advise on matters pertaining to the welfare and advancement of the STs (Article 244(1)). Likewise, the Sixth Schedule to the Constitution also refers to the administration of Tribal Areas in the states of Assam, Meghalaya, Tripura and Mizoram by designating certain tribal areas as Autonomous Districts and Autonomous Regions and also by constituting District Councils and Regional Councils (Article 244(2)). To ensure effective participation of the tribals in the process of planning and decision-making, the 73rd and 74th Amendments of the Constitution are extended to the Scheduled Areas through the Panchayats (Extension to the Scheduled Areas) Act, 1996.

DEVELOPMENT PLANS

High priority to the welfare and development of STs has been given right from the beginning of the first five-year plan. The First Five Year Plan (1951-56) clearly laid down the principle stating that 'the general development programmes should be so designed to cater adequately to the backward classes and special provisions should be used for securing additional and more intensified development for STs'. Unfortunately, the same could not take place. The Second Plan (1956-61), which laid emphasis on economic development, gave a special focus on reducing economic inequalities in the society. Further, development programmes for STs have been planned for, based on respect and understanding of their culture and traditions and with an appreciation of their social, psychological and economic problems. In fact, the same was planned in tune with 'Panchasheel'—the philosophy of tribal development as enunciated by the first Prime Minister of the Country, Pandit Jawaharlal Nehru. An important landmark during the Second Plan was the opening of 43 Special Multi-purpose Tribal Blocks, later termed as Tribal Development Blocks (TDBs). The Third Plan (1961-66) continued with the very same principle of advocating reduction in inequalities through various policies and programmes to provide equality of opportunity to STs. The Fourth Plan (1969-74) proclaimed that the 'basic goal was to realise a rapid increase in the standard of living of the people through measures which also promote 'equality and social justice'. An important step in this direction was setting up of six pilot projects in Andhra Pradesh, Bihar, Madhya Pradesh and Orissa in 1971-72 with a separate Tribal Development Agency for each project. The Fifth Plan (1974-78) marked a shift in approach as reflected in the launching of the Tribal Sub-Plan (TSP) for the direct benefit of the development of tribals. The Tribal Sub-Plan has a two pronged strategy, namely i) promotion of development activities to raise the level of living standards of Scheduled Tribes and ii) protection of their interest through legal and administrative support. The TSP stipulated that funds of the centre and the states should be quantified on the population proportion basis with budgetary mechanisms to ensure accountability, non-divertability and utilisation for the welfare and development of STs.

The Sixth Plan (1980-85) sought to ensure a higher degree of devolution of funds so that at least 50 per cent of tribal families could be provided assistance to cross the poverty line. In the Seventh Plan (1985-90), there was substantial increase in the flow of funds for the development of STs resulting in the expansion of infrastructural facilities and enlargement of coverage. Emphasis was laid on the educational development of STs. For the economic development of STs, two national-level institutions were set up viz. (i) Tribal Cooperative Marketing Development Federation (TRIFED) in 1987 as an apex body for State Tribal Development Cooperative Corporations, and (ii) National Scheduled Castes and Scheduled Tribes Finance and Development Corporation (NSFDC) in 1989. The former was assigned to provide remunerative prices for the forest and agriculture produce of tribal, while the latter was intended to provide credit support for employment generation.

NG SPEECHES OF Dr. D. SWAMINADHAN

In the Eighth Plan (1992-97), efforts were intensified to bridge the gap between the levels of development of STs and the other sections of the society. The Plan not only emphasized elimination of exploitation, but also paid attention to the special problems of suppression of rights, land alienation, non-payment of minimum wages and restrictions on the right to collect minor forest produce etc. However, attention on priority basis, was continued to be paid on the socio-economic upliftment of STs.

The Ninth Plan (1997-2002) aimed to empower STs by creating an enabling environment conducive for them to exercise their rights freely, enjoy their privileges and lead a life of self-confidence and dignity, on par with the rest of society. This process essentially encompassed three vital components, viz. i) Social Empowerment; ii) Economic Empowerment; and iii) Social justice. To this effect, while ST-related line Ministries/ Departments implemented general development policies and programmes, the nodal Ministry of Tribal Affairs implemented certain ST-specific innovative programmes.

The Tenth Plan approach to the tribal development focused on tackling the unresolved issues and problems on a time bound basis, besides providing adequate space and opportunity for the tribals to empower themselves with the strength of their own potentials.

The Eleventh Plan will attempt a paradigm shift with respect to the overall empowerment of the tribals keeping the issues related to the governance at the centre. The operational imperatives of the Vth Schedule, TSP 1976, PESA 1996, RFRA 2006; the desirability of a tribal-centric, tribal participative and tribal-managed development process, and the need for a conscious departure from dependence on a largely under effective official delivery system will be kept in view during this shift.

STRENGTHENING TRIBAL DEVELOPMENT

1. (a) In formulating programmes under Tribal Sub-Plan (TSP) the concept of planning from below may be followed. This involves ensuring actual participation of the beneficiaries.
   (b) A separate budget mechanism for TSP may be adopted.
   (c) The quantification for Tribal sub-plan should be at least in proportion to the tribal population covered under TSP.

2. The 73rd Amendment Act should be implemented in its true spirit in all the states having Scheduled Areas. The Gram Sabhas should be given the right to decision making on all resources within their villages.

3. (a) The tribals are exploited by vested interests, moneylenders, landlords, shopkeepers, contractors and government officials. This is also recognised by the Fifth schedule to the constitution and it lists measures for regulating the money lenders activities in the scheduled areas. Most of the TSP States have enacted legislation in this regard. These provisions should be strictly implemented.

   (b) National ST Finance and Development Corporation and State level Finance and Development Corporations have been set up to provide lending facilities to tribals. However, coverage of ST families by these corporations has been grossly inadequate.

   (c) The working of the National and State level ST Finance and Development Corporation may have to be evaluated and measures undertaken so as to make these corporations perform better and thereby the tribals get benefited to a great extent.

4. Financial allocation to tribal welfare should be increased from the present low levels of allocation. The budget allocations under Plan and Non-Plan reflects the priority or lack of priority of the state in any sector. The poor flow of funds to tribal development, especially health and education are indicators of the lack of political will to allocate adequate funds to the tribal areas. Finances should be allocated not only to maintenance of police, army and for purchase of weapons but also for primary infrastructure and social security needs of the tribals.

5. A national debate on Scheduled Areas with involvement of tribal communities, scientists, academicians, NGO's and other civil society groups may be initiated. The Contemporary times may likely to witness many tribal movements, protests and campaigns as a result of conflicting interest groups like tribals, industries, government and consumers lobbying for stakes over the resources in these areas. There has to be some intense retrospection on the long term vision for the Scheduled areas over tribal rights, public sector and private sector issues, utilization of forest wealth, development projects, etc.

NATIONAL COMMON MINIMUM PROGRAMME (NCMP) RELATING TO SCHEDULED TRIBES

1. NCMP STATEMENT

a) The UPA will urge the states to make legislation for conferring ownership rights in respect of minor forest produce, including tendu patta, on all those people from the weaker sections who work in the forests.

b) Eviction of tribal communities and other forest-dwelling communities from forest areas will be discontinued. Cooperation of these communities will be sought for protecting forests and for undertaking social afforestation.

c) The UPA administration will take all measures to reconcile the objectives of economic growth and environmental conservation, particularly as far as tribal communities dependent on forests are concerned.

d) The rights of tribal communities over mineral resources, water sources, etc as laid down by law will be fully safeguarded.

2. NCMP STATEMENT

Landless families will be endowed with land through implementation of land ceiling and land redistribution legislation. No reversal of ceilings legislation will be permitted.

3. NCMP STATEMENT

The UPA Government will launch a comprehensive national programme for minor irrigation of all lands owned by dalits and adivasis.

4. NCMP STATEMENT

The UPA is concerned with the growth of extremist violence and other forms of terrorist activity in different states. This is not merely a law-and-order problem, but a far deeper socio-economic issue which will be addressed more meaningfully than has been the case so far.

5. NCMP STATEMENT

a) The UPA government will immediately review the overall strategy and programmes for the development of tribal areas to plug loopholes and to work out more viable livelihood strategies.

b) In addition, more effective systems of relief and rehabilitation will be put in place for tribal and other groups displaced by development projects. Tribal people alienated from land will be rehabilitated.

The National Advisory Council on the implementation of the NCMP has been reviewing the progress of implementation of the NCMP which, inter-alia, includes tribal development and welfare.

MONITORING AND EVALUATION

Monitoring and Evaluation is needed to make the programmes and schemes effective to achieve the desired results. In respect of sectoral programmes and schemes of tribal development, policy planning, monitoring, evaluation as also their coordination is the responsibility of the concerned Central Government Ministries, State Governments and Union Territory Administrations and therefore these Ministries and Government departments should put in place effective mechanisms for this purpose. This is in addition to the one adopted by the Ministry of Tribal Affairs. Greater attention may also has to be paid to concurrent monitoring and evaluation through existing field functionaries on the principles of checks and balances.

The National Advisory Council has made following recommendations regarding Effective Monitoring:

"The Ministry of Tribal Affairs and the Planning Commission should set up an effective mechanism to monitor the basic problems of the tribals that have still remained unresolved, such as land alienation, indebtedness, lack of proper rehabilitation after involuntary displacement, ineffective implementation of the Panchayats (Extension to the Scheduled Areas) Act, 1996, adversely affecting the tribals' access to forests (for meeting their basic subsistence needs) and poor programme delivery".

II. ECOGNITION OF FOREST RIGHTS ACT—2006

"The Scheduled Tribes and other Traditional forest dwellers (Recognition of Forest Rights) Act, 2006 is a piece of land mark legislation in independent India that seeks to provide rights over land in their occupation to forest-dwelling Scheduled Tribes and other traditional forest-dwellers who have been residing there for generations but those rights could not be recorded"

-Dr. Manomhan Singh,
Prime Minister of India

INTRODUCTION

It became necessary to address the long standing insecurity of tenurial and access rights of forest dwelling Scheduled Tribes and other traditional forest dwellers including those who were forced to relocate their dwelling due to State development interventions.

Also the forest rights on ancestral lands and their habitat were not adequately recognized in the consolidation of State forests during the colonial period as well as in independent India resulting in historical injustice to the forest dwelling Scheduled Tribes and other traditional forest dwellers who are integral to the very survival and sustainability of the forest ecosystem;

To fulfill the above objectives the Indian Parliament enacted The Scheduled Tribes and other Traditional forest dwellers (Recognition of Forest Rights) Act, 2006. The Act extends to the hole of India except the State of Jammu and Kashmir.

This is an Act to recognize and vest the forest rights and occupation in forest land in forest dwelling Scheduled Tribes and other traditional forest dwellers who have been residing in such forests for generations but whose rights could not be recorded; to provide for a framework for recording the forest rights so vested and the nature of evidence required for such recognition and vesting in respect of forest land.

The recognized rights of the forest dwelling Scheduled Tribes and other traditional forest dwellers include the responsibilities and authority for sustainable use, conservation of biodiversity and maintenance of ecological balance and thereby strengthening the conservation regime of the forests while ensuring livelihood and food security of the forest dwelling Scheduled Tribes and other traditional forest dwellers.

SALIENT FEATURES OF THE FOREST RIGHTS ACT-2006

1. The Act recognises and vests the forest rights and occupation in forest land in forest dwelling Scheduled Tribes and other traditional forest dwellers who have been residing in such forests for generations but whose rights could not be recorded. This would undo the historical injustice done to the forest dwelling Scheduled Tribes.

2. The Act provides for recognition of forest rights of other traditional forest dwellers provided they have for at least three generations prior to 13.12.2005 primarily resided in and have depended on the forest or forest land for bonafide livelihood needs. A "generation" for this purpose would mean a period comprising of 25 years.

3. The cut off date for recognition and vesting of forest rights under the Act will be 13.12.2005.

4. The Act provides for the ceiling of occupation of forest land for purposes of recognition of forest rights to the area under actual occupation and in no case exceeding an area of four hectares.

5. The Act provides for conferring rights in the National Parks and Sanctuaries also, renamed as 'critical wildlife habitat' on regular basis.

6. The Act provides for the right to hold and live in the forestland under the individual or common occupation for habitation or for self-cultivation for livelihood by a member or members of a forest dwelling Scheduled Tribe or other traditional forest dwellers.

7. The Act recognises the right of ownership access to collect, use, and dispose of minor forest produce which has been traditionally collected within or outside village boundaries. The Act has defined the term "minor forest produce" to include all non-timber forest produce of plant origin, including bamboo, brush wood, stumps, cane, tussar, cocoons, honey, wax, lac, tendu or kendu leaves, medicinal plants and herbs, roots, tubers and the like.

8. The Act recognises the right to in situ rehabilitation including alternative land in cases where the Scheduled Tribes and other

traditional forest dwellers have been illegally evicted or displaced from forest land of any description without receiving their legal entitlement to rehabilitation prior to 13.12.2005.

9. The Act provides for the forest right relating to Government providing for diversion of forest land for the purpose of schools, hospitals, anganwadis, drinking water supply and water pipelines, roads, electric and telecommunication lines, etc.

10. The rights conferred under the Act shall be heritable but not alienable or transferable and shall be registered jointly in the name of both the spouses in the case of married persons and in the name of the single head, in the case of a household headed by a single person and in the absence of a direct heir, the heritable right shall pass on to the next of kin.

11. The Act provides that no member of a forest dwelling Scheduled Tribe or other traditional forest dwellers shall be evicted or removed from forest land under his occupation till the recognition and verification procedure is completed.

12. As per the Act, the Gram Sabha has been designated as the competent authority for initiating the process of determining the nature and extent of individual or community forest rights or both that may be given to the forest dwelling Scheduled Tribes and other traditional forest dwellers.

CRITICAL WILDLIFE HABITAT

"Critical wildlife habitats" are notified within existing national parks and sanctuaries for the purpose of keeping them inviolate. Once notified, these cannot be diverted for any other purpose. The term "inviolate" could include areas with no human use to areas with small-scale human activities that are compatible with conservation. The location and extent of CWHs need to be determined through sound scientific criteria.

The Act also specify that in such areas, relocation of people can take place only if it is established that co-existence between human communities and wildlife is not possible, and if the communities give their informed consent. For the first time in the conservation history of India, forcible displacement of people has been made illegal.

This provision is creating a lot of confusion. Some communities fear mass displacement, others consider it a potential ally in protecting forests;

some conservation groups are excited by the prospect it offers, others predict that it will weaken an already beleaguered protected area network.

The CWH process is going to be troublesome given the poor state of preparedness among the bureaucracy and the civil society in most part of the Country. However, everyone should use this historic opportunity to sort out issues and move towards building long term public support integrating conservation, livelihoods and democracy.

METHODOLOGY OF IMPLEMENTATION

At the operational level the Act required State Governments to Constitute committees in order to process the claims of tribal and forest dwelling committees as well as the cases that may arise out of them, leading to judicious distribution of land Rights. The State Governments should ensure quite publicity to the provisions of the act and the setup, at the earliest, monitoring committees at the State and District Levels and also at the lower levels so that the wok could commence at the earliest.

NON-GOVERNMENTAL ORGANISATIONS (NGOs)

THE ROLE OF VOLUNTARY AGENCIES IN IMPLEMENTING THE CBR APPROACH FOR MENTALLY HANDICAPPED AND MENTALLY ILL

I am happy to participate in the inaugural session of the National Seminar on 'The Role of Voluntary Agencies in implementing the CBR Approach for Mentally Handicapped and Mentally Ill being organised by the Thakur Hari Prasad Institute of Research and Rehabilitation for the Mentally Handicapped. I am grateful to Dr. Thakur Hari Prasad for inviting me to inaugurate the Seminar. I must appreciate the yeomen services rendered by Dr. Thakur Hari Prasad to the mentally handicapped through his Institute and his dedicated efforts outside.

Widespread incidence of the disabled persons in the country is one of the main concerns of India's welfare planning. The incidence of disability can be reduced through timely intervention. During the Eighth Plan, under the welfare programmes for the physically handicapped, priority is given to the prevention and early detection of impairments of disability, while taking advantage of the latest advances in technology in prevention, early detection and rehabilitation. Stress is laid on educating the family and the community on the active role they can play in preventing disability, reducing disabling impact on an individual and promoting development of the disabled person. Therapeutic and fitment services will be expanded to enable the disabled to become mobile and self reliant as far as possible. Since education and training plays a vital role in the socioeconomic rehabilitation of the handicapped, these should be paid due attention.

Voluntary organisations, which have played a pioneering role in the past in developing welfare services for the handicapped, will be assisted in their activities to provide services to the handicapped. Assistance is also being provided for organising rural camps for sensitisation, early detection, timely intervention and appropriate referral follow-up of handicapped cases. Financial support to voluntary organisations working in the field of spastics, mentally handicapped and rehabilitation of leprosy cured patients is expanded. Attempts are being made for a more even distribution of services for the handicapped, both between states and within a state, during the eighth plan period.

All over the world there are millions of fellow citizens with mental handicap. They live in every society of every country. It is a global challenge. According to World Health Organisation's (WHO) estimate and other available information, around 2 to 3 per cent of our population are mentally handicapped which means about 20 million people come under this category. They suffer for want of adequate services and support. It is further compounded due to lack of knowledge and awareness.

In our country the institutional facilities for the mentally handicapped are grossly inadequate. Even out of the existing two hundred and odd institutions, 90 per cent cater to the urban areas and the remaining 10 per cent to the rural areas. Ironically, 80 per cent of the mentally handicapped are from rural areas. This means 90 per cent of the facilities are catering to the 20 per cent of the disabled in urban areas and only 10 per cent of the facilities are thinly spread to serve the 80 per cent of the mentally handicapped. Therefore there is every need to set up and extend the facilities to the rural areas on priority basis. In this context the efforts made by the government should be supplemented by dedicated voluntary organisations to tackle this problem. The Thakur Hari Prasad Institute of Research and Rehabilitation for the Mentally Handicapped is to be complimented for its laudable effort in extending its reach to the rural areas through setting up of a Centre at Rajamundry, Andhra Pradesh.

It needs no mention that the problem of the mentally handicapped is enormous in the rural areas. Facilities to identify disabilities at an early stage and to provide services for early intervention to reduce the disability are indeed very meagre. Added to this, we have misconceptions and superstitious beliefs which are becoming major stumbling blocks to the rehabilitation scenario. Cost of launching a suitable programme for the mentally handicapped is very expensive. In addition, there is scarcity of trained manpower in this area. It is in this context the idea of low cost programme adopting the CBR approach for mentally handicapped and mentally ill is the need of the hour. I believe the programme anticipates the involvement of non-professionals and vast human resource—the rich and the non-rich, to provide the minimum care. Involving such a vast human resource leads to demystification of the technical know-how of the training of the mentally handicapped in order to take the technique to the door steps of the needy. It results in empowering the parents, the family members and the community with knowledge and know how of the mental handicap. The basic philosophy behind a good programme should be that the promoter should not be the controller. The promoter should facilitate formation of the programme, help successful initial implementation and then withdraw from the scene of action after the objectives have been achieved to a large extent. It is heartening to note that this approach is adopted in this community based programme which relates to generating maximum community participation and in making the community ultimately responsible for running the programme so that it becomes self-reliant and a propelling force.

The Non-Governmental Organisations (NGOs) work and live closely with the people and their ethos and culture are closely interlinked with the ground level realities. Through years of association they are able to pursue and internalise the felt needs, preferences and interest of the people better than others. With this attitude and perceptions, the NGO's can play a major role in designing and implementing the CBR approach for mentally handicapped and mentally ill. One of the major tasks for the NGO's should be how to build up community level structures and organisations to help the mentally handicapped. If the NGO's succeed in making these grass root level structures and organisations fully participative, they would have succeeded in ensuring community participation to a large extent. Having accomplished this important objective the NGO's should withdraw from the scene of action and continue to play the role of a catalytic agent from outside. I am sure the outcome of the Seminar will provide us with valuable clues and ideas for evolving strategies for the involvement of the voluntary organisations in implementing the CBR approach for the mentally handicapped and mentally ill. I take pleasure in inaugurating the Seminar and wish it a grand success.

PEACE, SECURITY AND DEVELOPMENT: ROLE OF N.G.Os

Peace, Security and Development are inter related. Without peace and security development is hampered.

Individuals need **peace**. Groups of people need peace. Nations need peace. The world needs peace. Peace, security and stability are essential for progress and development. Peace and progress is the ultimate object of the human endeavour. Apart from the individual's peace it has a different connotation in the National and Global context.

In the national context, **peace** is a state of existence without communal disharmony, conflicts arising out of caste, creed, colour, race, gender discrimination, region, religion, ethnicity, inequality of status and opportunity, 'rich and poor' difference, disparity in regional development, human rights violation and not disturbing the 'unity in diversity' status and the harmony with nature.

In the global context, **peace** signifies the state of 'No War' status, defence deterrent, absence of intolerable economic dominance by some countries, no expansionist intensions, good neighbourly relations, respect for freedom, no ideological overtones, absence of religious fundamentalism, terrorism, human rights violations, discrimination and ecological imbalance.

Defence relates to protection against external aggression. 'Security' may mainly relate to internal state of affairs regarding protection against threats and acts disturbing peace in the society and safety of individuals, organizations, institutions in the country against communal violence, terrorism, extremism and militancy etc.

India proved its uniqueness through achieving its freedom by the means of nonviolence. Mahatma Gandhi, the Father of the Nation, alongwith other eminent national leaders and the people, fought against the mighty British using a simple weapon of nonviolence and secured independence for the country. It was a glorious reflection on the Indian culture, tradition and philosophy which are deeply rooted in our value system. Ours is a sovereign, socialist, secular and democratic republic with its Constitution guaranteeing to secure to all its citizens: **Justice** in social, economic and political spheres; **Liberty** of thought, expression, belief, faith and worship; **Equality** of status and opportunity; and to promote among them all **Fraternity,** assuring the dignity of individual and the unity and integrity of the nation. These provisions also have their roots in the value system. The integrity of the nation, its rich cultural past and its compositeness, our ethos and human values, equal respect for all citizens irrespective of caste, creed, colour, religion, region and march towards a bright future, were some of the basic considerations which the Constitution makers had in mind while framing the Constitution of India.

India is a multi-religious, multi-cultural, multi-ethnic and multi-lingual society. Unity and Diversity has been our strength. Hinduism, Buddhism, Christianity, Islam, Sikhism and Zoroastrianism have been co-existing. However, some individuals/organisations with misplaced notions have been spreading mistrust among people and contributing towards disharmony among religions leading to communal and religious violence. Religions by and large advocate peaceful co-existence. Studies in depth and research on various religions would contribute towards better understanding and appreciation of each other's faiths and religions leading to harmony and peace.

International scenario regarding Peace and international relations is also not presenting a good picture either. Peaceful co-existence seems to be difficult. International relations seem to be devoid of humanitarian considerations. It is the right time to make serious and sincere efforts to build good relations among the nations for peaceful co-existence. 'Cross cultural and global dialogues,' Peace initiatives, formation of regional trade blocks and unions, regional cooperation, area studies are some of the contributing mechanisms towards building good international relations. Nuclear non-proliferation treaty, Nuclear disarmament, No war pacts, Restructuring and Strengthening the United Nations Organisation (UNO) are some of the instruments and actions that would contribute towards peaceful co-existence of nations. The present picture in the realm of peace, freedom and international understanding and relations is not that bright and encouraging. Continued studies, research and dialogues are needed to search for new ways, methods and instruments that would contribute to usher in a new era of peace, freedom and good international relations.

What is happening around us today? Violence, hatred, mistrust, growing divisive forces, narrow parochialism, separatist tendencies, considerable fall in moral, social, ethical land national values both in personal and public life. Materialistic outlook is manifest in almost every dimension of man's life style and day-to-day living. Materialism has become a major force influencing his conduct and behaviour. It is shaping his character and personality and even determining his life's goal. Human dignity and self-respect founded on good character and integrity are overtaken by arrogance, conceit, hypocrisy and artificial postures. The erosion of character is noticed in social and national life. Personal ethics and moral responsibility towards society have become meaningless where there is dominance of self-interest above everything. Man seems to have completely forgotten his true nature and spirit.

The Kothari Education Commission observed:

> "Modernisation did not mean—least of all in our national situation—a refusal to recognise the importance of or to inculcate necessary moral and spiritual values and self-discipline. While a combination of ignorance with goodness may be futile, that of knowledge with a lack of essential values may be dangerous".

DEVELOPMENT

India is poised to become a developed nation by 2020. The factors that would contribute towards making India a developed Nation are:

(a) Economic superiority propelled by 'Technology';
(b) Defence deterrent
(c) Strengthening the moral fabric of the country; (d) Synergising the Youth Power for development and National Reconstruction; (e) Maintaining Socio-economic-political-cultural and gender equity and (f) Bestowing due attention to maintaining balance between development process and environmental protection.

Development and Environmental Concerns need not be at logger heads. The development process should give consideration for environmental protection and to maintain ecological balance. At the same time "equity" factor should also be kept in view. As such the development should be based on eco-friendly, pro-poor and gender equity parameters.

There should be a strategic shift to clean and green technologies. Sustainable Industrial development is not a matter of mere high-tech but also of appropriate sci-tech. We have to phase out older and inappropriate technologies while simultaneously developing and disseminating a new generation of sophisticated and environmentally benign technologies. We have to encourage indigenous research effort to be directed at green technologies through a system of incentives and penalties.

ROLE OF NON-GOVERNMENTAL ORGANIZATIONS (NGOS)

The NGO's and other Civil Societies are known for their mass contact and therefore their role in contributing to peace, security and development is important.

The following Actions are suggested to play their role effectively:

1. **DEVELOPMENT PROGRAMMES:**
   a. Take up programmes on their own or supplement the programmes of the government relating to education, literacy, health, nutrition, housing, safe drinking water, sanitation, economic empowerment of the poor and women, children's welfare and development etc.
   b. Exhibit activism on Rehabilitation of displaced persons effected due to irrigation and other development projects and due to natural and manmade calamities.

2. **SOCIAL EMPOWERMENT:**
   a. Organise programmes of social empowerment of the weaker sections.
   b. Promotion of human values.

3. **PEACE AND HARMONY:**
   a. Organise communal harmony programmes.
   b. Organise religious harmony programmes.
   c. Organise cross-cultural and global dialogues for peace and harmony.

4. SECURITY :

    a. Organise awareness programmes on internal and external security concerns.

    b. Opening dialogues and counselling of the extremist and terrorist elements wherever possible.

5. Formation of Networking of NGOs to synergize their efforts and to share resources.

CONCLUSION

India, with all its complexities of different socio-economic, political, religious, linguistic, regional and cultural shades, should acquire strength to stand against forces disturbing peace and stability and strengthen its moral fabric upholding and promoting Indian ethos and human values. The sources of such strength are education, media, religious organisations, healthy politics, civil societies; NGO's and appropriate instruments of governance. The reinforcing thread in all these is the spirit of Indian freedom movement, which we have to recapture and utilise it for binding on every Indian to become an active partner in this whole process of peace, security and development. The Civil Societies and NGOs have to chalk out their own Charter of Action Path to make their contributions more visible in this regard.

SUPPLEMENTARY DETAILS OF THE SELECTED SPEECHES OF Dr. D. SWAMINADHAN

FIRST PART

HIGHER EDUCATION

1. Added Role For Indian Universities—Address Delivered At The National Conference Of Vice-Chancellors Organised By Association Of Indian Universities, October-November, 1992.

2. Address As Chief Guest At The Inaugural Session Of The10th Annual Management Convention Of The Bhubaneswar Management Forum Held At Bhubaneswar, 2nd April, 1993.

3. Convocation Address At The 15th Convocation Of The Institute Of Medical Sciences, Banaras Hindu University, Varanasi Held On 10th April, 1993.

4. Address At Ugc Special Meeting Of Vice-Chancellor's Held On Programme Of Action 92—New Delhi, 25th May, 1993.

5. Approach To Higher Education Development In India In Nineties—Key Note Address At The Silver Jubilee Celebrations Of Madurai Kamaraj University, Madurai, 14th July, 1993.

6. Role Of Sri Sathya Sai Education In 21st Century—Speech Delivered At The Sri Sathya Sai Institute Of Higher Learning, Prasanthi Nilayam, Puttaparthi – 20th November, 1993.

7. Changed Economic Scenario – Imperatives For Higher Education In India—Speech Delivered At The Mysore University, Mysore—25th November, 1993.

8. Address At The Inaugural Function Of The 68th Annual Meeting Of The Association Of Indian Universities Held On 18th December, 1993 At The University Of Delhi.

9. Convocation Address At The 12th Convocation Of The Dayalbagh Educational Institute, Agra Held On 28th January, 1994.

10. Inaugural Address At The Ii National Conference On "Increasing Access To Distance Education: An Agenda For Action" Organized By The Indian Distance Education Association (Idea) Held At Sri Venkateswara University, Tirupati – 13th May, 1994.

11. Challenges To Higher Education And Research In India– Lecture At Himachal Pradesh University,Shimla,11thoct,1994.

12. Address At The Inaugural Session Of The A.I.U. National Seminar On "Accountability In Higher Education" Held At University Of Poona, Pune On 12th November,1994.

13. Presentation At The Unesco Forum On "Strategies For University-Industry Cooperation In Engineering, Sciences And Technology In India" Organised By Unesco At New Delhi—19th January,1996

14. Speech On "Changing Times-Need For Universities Reorientation" At The University College Of Engineering, Osmania University. Hyderabad On 15th February, 1996.

15. Presentation On Rural Higher Education In India At The Workshop On Rural Higher Education Organised By The National Council Of Rural Institutes, Hyderabad—2nd March, 1996.

16. Convocation Address On The Occasion Of The Golden Jubilee Convocation Of The D.A.V. (Pg) College, Dehradun Held On 22nd April, 1996.

17. Higher Education And Research In India – Perspectives And Innovations (Note:This Invited Sree Sanakara Lecture As A Part Of Sree Sanakara Jayanthi Celebrations At Sree Sankaracharya University,Kaladi Could Not Be Delivered In Person But Text Preserved)

TECHNICAL EDUCATION

18. Technical Education In India – Problems And Prospects—Fourth Prof. Y. Nayudamma Memorial Lecture

19. Sri Rebala Lakshminarsa Reddy Endowment Lecture On 'Imperatives Of University-Industry—R&D Organisation Interaction For National Development Delivered At Sri Venkateswara University, Tirupati On 28th February,1992.

20. Inaugural Address At The Fourth Annual Management Education Convention Of The Association Of Indian Management Schools, Jamshedpur,—20th August ,1992

21. Inaugural Address At The National Seminar And I.S.T.E. Silver Jubilee Celebrations Held On 19th October, 1992.

22. Presentation On 'A Model For University-Industry—R & D Organisations Interaction'—October, 1992

23. Brain Storming Session On Polytechnics Held At Yojana Bhavan, New Delhi On 26th November, 1992.

24. 'Accreditation And Assessment Council—System And Modus Operandi' Address At The Conference Of Vice-Chancellors Held At University Of Poona—13th November, 1994.

25. Inaugural Address At The International Conference On "Engineering Education—An Indian Perspective" Organised By The College Of Engineering, Andhra University And Indian Society For Technical Education, Au Chapter, Visakhapatnam On 21st November,1994.

26. Key Note Address Delivered At The Seminar On "Industry-Management Institution Interface" Organised By The Department Of Commerce & Business Management, Punjab University, Chandigarh—27th November, 1994.

27. Inaugural Address At The Second International Conference On "Remote Sensing And Gis – 'Icorg – 94'" Organised By The Jntu, Hyderabad—3rd December, 1994.

28. Inaugural Address At The Seminar On "Technology For A Better Tomorrow" Delivered At The 9th Indian Engineering Congress Organised By The. Institution Of Engineers (India) At Calcutta On 18th December, 1994.

29. 'Technical Education And Research In India –Need For Reorientation'—Seventh A.N. Khosla Memorial Lecture At The Ninth Indian Engineering Congress Organized At Calcutta

30. Extra Mural Lecture At The Roorkee University, Roorkee—9th February, 1996.

31. "Technological Superiority—Pre-Requisite For Economic Survival In The Changed Economic Global Scenario" Foundation Day Lecture Delivered At Central Building Research Institute (Cbri), Roorkee—10th February,1996.

39. Inaugural Address At The Golden Jubilee Seminar On "Computer Aided Engineering Of Process Plants", Organised By Indian Institute Of Chemical Technology, Hyderabad—16th November, 1994.

ENVIRONMENT

40. Address Delivered As A Guest Of Honour On The Occasion Of World Environment Day Celebrations Organised By The World Institution Building Programme On 5th June, 1993

41. Address Delivered At The Inaugural Function Of 1993 World Environment Congress On Global Environmental Education – Visions Of 2001, Held On 22-24 December, 1993

42. Address Delivered As A Guest Of Honour At The Inaugural Function Of Ugc Sponsored National Symposium And Workshop On "Environmental Education In University Curricula" Organised By A.P. State Council For Higher Education In Collaboration With The Jawaharlal Nehru Technological University, Hyderabad On 21ˢᵗ March,1994.

SCIENCE

43. Address At The 58ᵗʰ Annual Conference Of The Indian Mathematical Society Held At Banaras Hindu University, Varanasi On 22ⁿᵈ March, 1993.

44. Address Delivered As Chief Guest On The Occasion Of Science Day Celebrations At The Avinashilingam Institute For Home Science And Higher Education For Women—26ᵗʰ March, 1993.

45. Resource Crunch And Science Education—6th January, 1994.

46. Address As The Chief Guest At The Valedictory Function Of The National Children's Science Congress On 31ˢᵗ December, 1994.

SECOND PART

DEVELOPMENT STUDIES

1. Address At The Expert Group Meeting To Deliberate On Implications Of Economic Reforms For The Urban Sector Held On 17th March, 1993.

2. Inaugural Address At The Policy Seminar On "Integrated Human Settlement Programme" Organised By Society For Development Studies (Sds)—8th December,1994

ECONOMY

3. Inaugural Address At The National Seminar On 'Dr. Babasaheb Ambedkar And His Ideas On Economic Growth With Justice' Organised By The Centre For Rayalaseema Development Studies, Department Of Economics Sri Krishnadevaraya University, Anantapur—29th January, 1992.

4. Speech At The Conference Of The International Friendship Society Of India, New Delhi On "Economic Growth And National Integration"—3rd February,1994

FINANCE

5. National Meet To Discuss Issues And Guidelines Pertaining To The State Finance Commissions Held In Vigyan Bhavan, New Delhi Held On 28th And 29th October, 1994.

GENERAL

6. Inaugural Address Delivered At The Rural Project Of Thakur Hari Prasad Institute Of Research And Rehabilitation For The Mentally Handicapped At Rajamundry On 11th October, 1991.

7. Presidential Address On "Life And Message Of Swami Vivekananda" Delivered At The Anniversary Day Public Meeting Organised By The Ramakrishna Mission, New Delhi On 6th February, 1994.

8. Speech As A Special Guest Of Honour Delivered At The 15th India—Nri World Convention—22nd December, 1994.

9. Speech At The Tyagaraja Aradhana Festival Organised By Sree Shanmukhananda Sangeetha Sabha, New Delhi—27th February, 1996.

10. Integration Of The Aged Into The Development Process In India.

PLANNING

11. Inaugural Address At The Seminar On 'Planning In Nineties And Beyond' Organised By The Prakasam Institute Of Development Studies, Hyderabad—14th December, 1991.

12. 'India's Planning In Nineties' Andhra Bank Endowment, Lecture, At Andhra University, Waltair, March, 1992.

RURAL DEVELOPMENT

URBAN DEVELOPMENT

22. Inaugural Address At The Conference On 'Problems & Prospects Of Industrial Development In The National Capital Region', Organised By The Federation Of Indian Chambers Of Commerce & Industry On 5th June, 1993 At Bhiwadi.

23. Inaugural Address On The Occasion Of The Training Programme On "Formulation And Financing Of Urban Water Supply Projects" Organised By Indian Institute Of Public Administration, New Delhi From 29th September To 12th October, 1993.

24. Inaugural Address At The High Level Policy Seminar On "Subsidy Issues In Urban Sector" Organised By The Society For Development Studies, New Delhi On 17th November, 1993.

25. India's Urbanisation

26. Speech At The Meeting Of State Urban Development Strategy And Housing Development Programmes Held On 15th July,1994 In Vigyan Bhavan, New Delhi.

27. Speech At The Two-Day Workshop On "Hyderabad Master Plan 2011" Sponsored By Hyderabad Urban Development Authority.—17th August,1994.

28. Address At The National Forum On Capacity Building For The Urban Environment Project On 31st January, 1996.

TRIBAL DEVELOPMENT

29. Tribal Development In India And Recognition Of Forest Rights Act—2006—Address At The National Workshop Of The Spokes Persons Of Pradesh Congress Committees Of States—23rd February,2008

NON-GOVERNMENTAL ORGANISATIONS (NGOS)

30. Inaugural Address At The National Seminar On "The Role Of Voluntary Agencies In Implementing The Cbr Approach For Mentally Handicapped And Mentally Ill"—23rd April,1994

31. Peace, Security And Development: Role Of N.G.Os—Address At Sri Ramanuja Mission Trust, Chennai, International Peace Day Celebrations, Trust Anniversary—21-22 September, 2012